Cognitive Psychology
for Teachers

JOHN A. GLOVER
BALL STATE UNIVERSITY

ROYCE R. RONNING
UNIVERSITY OF NEBRASKA, LINCOLN

ROGER H. BRUNING
UNIVERSITY OF NEBRASKA, LINCOLN

Cognitive Psychology for Teachers

MACMILLAN PUBLISHING COMPANY
NEW YORK

Editor: Robert Miller
Production Supervision: Till & Till, Inc.
Cover Design: Blake Logan
Illustrations: Jean S. Morley

This book was set in Baskerville by Huron Valley Graphics, Inc., printed and bound by
R. R. Donnelly. The cover was printed by Phoenix Color Corp.

Macmillan Publishing Company
866 Third Avenue, New York, New York, 10022
Collier Macmillan Canada, Inc.

LIBRARY OF CONGRESS CATALOGING-IN-PUBLICATION DATA

Glover, John A., 1949–
    Cognitive psychology for teachers / John Glover, Royce Ronning,
Roger Bruning.
        p. cm.
    Includes index.
    ISBN 0-02-344133-X
    1. Learning.   2. Cognitive psychology.   3. Cognitive learning.
I. Ronning, Royce R.   II. Bruning, Roger H.   III. Title.
LB1060.G56   1990   89-12311
370.15'2—dc20   CIP

Printing: 5 6 7   Year: 3 4 5 6

Preface

The seeds for this book were sown in the late 1970s as we struggled with the directions of our individual programs of research and as we together developed a graduate level course in "learning" for teachers. By 1978 we were convinced that a cognitive focus on student learning would lead to the most useful data. Similarly, our experimenting with the learning course convinced us that the most relevant learning content for teachers came out of research on cognition. Further, we observed experienced teachers almost inevitably had an intuitive "feel" for cognitive psychology and could see its applications in many areas of classroom life.

As our learning course took shape, it became clear an appropriate textbook for such a course would be very rare. For several years we employed excellent cognitive psychology texts and supplemented them with teaching applications taken from our own experiences. Still, it seemed the cognitive processes involved in many basic academic skills were not getting the coverage they deserved. The cognitive psychology we wanted to share with teachers had to focus on their issues and needs.

This volume represents our effort to give teachers a solid grounding in cognitive psychology, at the same time covering important information directly relevant to critical areas of classroom instruction. As you can see, the book is broken into two major parts. The first seven chapters are an introduction to cognitive psychology. Although our emphasis throughout is on the applications of cognitive psychology to teaching, these chapters could as well be employed in a psychology department's "cognition" course as in an educational psychology department's "learning" course.

Chapter 1, "An Introduction to Cognitive Psychology," introduces the text and traces the historical emergence of cognitive psychology. Chapter 2, "The Necessity of Knowledge," focuses on the importance of knowledge in each aspect of human cognition. It is here that the major theme of our text emerges and the stage is set for subsequent chapters. Chapter

3, "Perception and Attention," builds directly on issues related to the role of knowledge in how we sense and interpret information in our environments. Chapters 4, 5, and 6 deal with memory issues. "Memory: Structures and Models" is the title of Chapter 4. Here we present basic views of how memory is conceived and the ways in which contemporary cognitive psychologists understand the organization of information in memory. The processes involved in getting new information into memory are the topic of Chapter 5, "Encoding Processes." Calling previously learned information up from memory is the topic of Chapter 6, "Retrieval Processes." The first part of the volume then closes in Chapter 7 with a topic closely linked to the role of knowledge in cognition and to our goals as educators, "Problem Solving."

The second part of our volume may be considered a contemporary approach to the psychology of school subjects. Here we focus on issues critical to subject-matter instruction. Chapters 8, 9, 10, and 11 all are related to literacy issues. Chapter 8, "Language Development in the School Years," sets the stage for these chapters as we present basic information about the nature of language and how children acquire it. The most important of all academic skills—reading—is the topic of Chapter 9, "Learning to Read." Reading also is the topic of Chapter 10, "Reading to Learn," but here we shift our emphasis from the emergence of the skill to the use of reading to gain information about the world. Chapter 11, "Writing," is an integral part of any discussion of literacy, and in this chapter we explore the nature of writing and means of enhancing instruction in writing. Chapter 12, "Cognitive Approaches to Mathematics," provides a contemporary, cognitive approach to understanding this important academic skill. We also stress the application of principles of cognitive psychology to instruction in basic arithmetic and advanced mathematics. Chapter 13, "Problem Solving in Science," covers one of the most salient areas of instruction in American schools. Our emphasis in this chapter is on a cognitive analysis of science learning and applications of research in cognition to science teaching. Our volume closes with Chapter 14, "Social Science Problem Solving," which deals with a topic of increasing importance in today's complex world.

We do not argue cognitive psychology is the only perspective teachers can or should take on learning. Indeed, behavioral psychology is of direct relevance to the classroom—the skills of applied behavior analysis should be a part of every teacher's repertoire. Humanistic views of learning also offer much, especially in reminding us always to think of the whole student. Still, we believe cognitive psychology is especially relevant to today's teachers and that its applications can be seen in all facets of the educational process.

Many people were involved in the development of this volume—too many for us to list in this brief space. We must mention Chris Jennison, who gave us the impetus to put together a prospectus for the book. We also want to thank a very special group of scholars who reviewed this volume during its evolution: Peter Denner, Idaho State University; Robert C. Matthews, Louisiana State University; Elizabeth Ghatala, University of Houston; Steven Owen, University of Connecticut, Storrs; Donald Cunningham, Indiana University, Bloomington; and Richard Mueller, Northern Illinois University. Each of these persons helped us greatly in shaping the final form of the book. Our editors, Robert Miller and Diane Kraut, also deserve many thanks for seeing this project through. Finally, we very much want to thank our families, who put up with a great deal in the writing of this book.

J.A.G.
R.R.R.
R.H.B.

Contents

CHAPTER 3

Perception and Attention   29

CHAPTER 4

Memory: Structures and Models   61

PART **II**

Cognitive Skills in the Schools

CHAPTER 8

Language Development in the School Years   185

CHAPTER 9

Learning to Read   219

CHAPTER 10

Reading to Learn   241

CHAPTER 11

Writing

CHAPTER 12

Cognitive Approaches to Mathematics

CHAPTER 13

Problem Solving in Science 329

CHAPTER 14

Social Science Problem Solving 355

References   369

Index   411

An Introduction to Cognitive Psychology

This book is about cognitive psychology and its implications for education. Cognitive psychology is a theoretical perspective that focuses on the realms of human perception, thought, and memory. It portrays learners as processors of information—a metaphor borrowed from the computer world—and assigns critical roles to the knowledge and perspective students bring to their learning. What learners do, in the view of cognitive psychology, determines the level of understanding they ultimately achieve.

The cognitive psychology we describe is a major force, perhaps *the* major force in American psychology. The past 20 years have witnessed its rise from relative obscurity to today, where advertisements for new faculty members in "cognitive psychology" and "cognitive science" outnumber those for "human learning" and "educational psychology." A number of new concepts have arisen with cognitive psychology, each with considerable explanatory power in education—concepts such as **schemata,** the idea that there are mental frameworks for comprehension; **constructive memory,** the view that knowledge is created by learners as they confront new situations; and **levels of processing,** the notion that memory is a byproduct of the kind of processing that information receives. Description and elaboration of these and other concepts of cognitive psychology will be a major emphasis of this book.

A Brief History

The Associationist Era

Each of us has our own view of the world, a "world hypothesis" (Pepper, 1942/1961) that guides our observations, our actions, and our understanding of our experience. Any theoretical perspective in psychology similarly rests on a particular view of the world; it counts some things as evidence and not others, organizes that evidence, and makes hypotheses about what the evidence means and how it is interrelated. Cognitive psychology is one such theoretical perspective; it makes the claim that the purpose of scientific psychology is to observe behavior—the observable responses of individuals—in order to make inferences about unobservable, underlying factors that can explain the actions we see. In cognitive psychology, observations are used to generate inferences about such factors as thought, language, meaning, and imagery. Our everyday psychology is cognitive psychology (Baars, 1986).

From about 1920 to around 1970, however, the world of psychology in the United States was dominated by a theoretical perspective of an entirely different sort—**associationism** (Dellarosa, 1988). The general goal of associationism was the derivation of elementary laws of behavior and learning and their extension to more complex settings. Inferences about underlying processes were tied closely to observed behavior. Animals as well as humans were suitable objects of study; investigations of learning and memory in "lower organisms" were fueled by a faith that the laws of learning were universal and that work with animals in the laboratory could be extrapolated to humans. As Glover and Ronning (1987) have stated, associationism was *the* American psychology during this 50-year period; there was no real alternative in the United States.

Perhaps the clearest formulations of associationistic principles of learning were made by Clark Hull (1934, 1952) and his colleague Kenneth Spence (1936, 1956). Reasoning from the data of numerous experiments with laboratory animals, Hull and Spence derived equations based on hypothesized variables such as strength of habits, drive, and inhibition that enabled predictions to be made about behavior in laboratory settings. As Hull (1952) was able to demonstrate, the elementary laws of learning captured in equations such as these were able to account for many phenomena of simple trial-and-error learning and simple discrimination learning in animals.

The use of an associationistic theoretical framework was by no means limited to only those psychologists interested in simple learning phenomena in animals, however. Especially in the United States, the associationistic paradigm also dominated the study of memory, of thinking, and of problem solving (Dellarosa, 1988). The focus of study for the vast majority of research in memory during this period was so-called rote or nonmeaningful learning. Following a tradition begun by Hermann Ebbinghaus well before the turn of the century, researchers studied memory for individual items, most commonly nonsense syllables and individual words. The assumption underlying these investigations was that understanding complex learning and memory phenomena would follow from understanding simpler forms of learning and memory.

The preferred research methods were those of **serial list learning** (in which one item cues the next item in the list) and **paired associate learning** (in which a "response" must be linked to a "stimulus"). These were methods in which the development of associations most clearly could be predicted and studied. As this research was further refined, tables of norms were developed in which nonsense syllables and words were calibrated for their "meaningfulness." That is, they were related for the likelihood that they could "generate associates"—elicit responses from learners. Knowing these characteristics of words and syllables permitted researchers to manipulate "associative strength" of materials with precision (see Glaze, 1928; Noble, 1952; and Underwood & Schultz, 1960, for examples of these materials). Like the aims of Hull's and Spence's work with animals, the goal of this research was to develop a basic set of associationistic principles derived from the study of learning in its "pure" form that would apply to broader contexts, such as learning and recall of materials in school.

A fundamental difficulty, however, was that as experimental psychologists made finer and finer distinctions within the confines of their research on animal "trial-and-error" learning and their studies of rote memory, their findings seemed to become less and less relevant for education and, for that matter, for understanding all but very limited aspects of human functioning. As experimental methodologies for studying learning and memory were refined and experiments became more internally valid (Campbell & Stanley, 1963), they became less valid externally. As elucidated by experimental psychology in the United States, the "laws of learning" seemed more properly to be described as the "laws of animal learning," the "laws of animals learning to make choices in mazes," or the "laws of human rote memory" than the universal principles that the associationists sought.

Not all associationistic psychologies were leading to theoretical and applied dead-ends, however. The so-called radical behaviorists, led by scientist-philosopher B. F. Skinner, began to make a strong impact on both psychology and education near the end of this period. Skinner's views were strongly environmental, in the tradition of the early behaviorist John B. Watson. Like Watson, Skinner rejected the idea that the purpose of psychology was to study consciousness; the goal of psychology, he asserted, was to predict and control behavior. What organisms do, Skinner contended, largely is a function of the environmental context in which they are placed and their learning histories (Skinner, 1938, 1953). By controlling the antecedents and consequences for behavior, prediction and control can be achieved. Consequences for behavior are particularly critical, he argued. By providing positive consequences for behavior and by controlling the schedule by which these consequences were delivered, behavior could be shaped and controlled. In his research, Skinner demonstrated that his laboratory animals indeed are exquisitely sensitive to manipulations of both antecedents and consequences of their actions. Simple responses such as bar pressing or pecking were shown to have highly predictable characteristics linked to the patterns by which they resulted in consequences, such as food or drink (see Ferster & Skinner, 1957). Similarly, Skinner demonstrated that by working backward from consequences to the behaviors that preceded them, very complex sequences or chains of behaviors could be developed in even "simple" organisms such as rats and pigeons.

By the mid 1960s, behaviorism as guided by Skinner's views had become such a potent force in American psychology that, in many settings, consciousness was discredited as a respectable topic of research and theory (Baars, 1986). Part of the reason for the extraordinary influence wielded by the behaviorists is that Skinner and his students had recognized the potential utility of behavioral principles in human learning and had successfully applied them to the design of programs in a variety of applied settings. Initial applications were in residential treatment facilities for the mentally ill and mentally retarded; careful specification of behavioral goals and regularization of the environment were shown to be highly useful for treating a wide range of problems. Applications of behavioral principles to education soon followed, incorporated in such technologies as classroom management (e.g., Baer, Wolf, & Risley, 1968; Homme, Csanyi, Gonzales, & Rechs, 1968) and teaching machines (Holland & Skinner, 1961; Skinner, 1968). Teaching machines, Skinner contended, had particularly great potential for providing the key elements of learning—frequent responding, progess in small steps, shaping, and positive reinforcement. By the early 1970s, as the cognitive movement was just beginning to emerge in American psychology, a wide range of applications of behavioral principles already had been explored and were being used in education.

Much about our current educational system reflects the influence of behaviorism. For instance, one readily can recognize the behavioral perspective in such familiar features of our educational system as instructional objectives, task analyses, and the use of positive reinforcers for achieving learning goals. All can be linked to a behavioral philosophy of learning in which responses must be appropriately sequenced, made overtly, and rewarded. Many of these derivations from behavioral psychology, it can be argued, have helped make education more effective, more accountable, and more humane.

At the same time that Skinner's behaviorism was beginning to have its greatest impact on education, however, the American psychological community was growing more and more dissatisfied with the ability of associationistic and behavioral psychologies to provide an adequate account of human activity and thought. For instance, the behaviorists' preoccupation with observable activity was considered by many to be much too limiting, even by those who considered careful observation the *sine qua non* of any scientific enterprise. Others decried what they saw as behaviorism's mechanistic view of human beings as controlled by their environments and feared that behavioral principles would be misused. They saw the possibility of a highly effective technology that could be used in society by those with totalitarian goals.

At the same time, many psychologists who were interested in mental processes seemed to be engaging in a futile exercise as they attempted to use an associationist framework and behavioral concepts to describe the complexity of human thinking, memory, problem solving, decision making, and creativity. To call this vast array of mental processes "mediating responses" (see Goss, 1961) seemed neither to satisfy nor to contribute greatly to our understanding of the human being. As an explanatory system, associationism seemed to have reached its limits and to fail as a scientific, yet generalizable, psychology.

Adding to the growing perception of the narrowness of the prevailing associationism was a set of voices from outside psychology—the linguistic community—which were raised when some psychologists began to try to explain language development from a behavioral perspective. For instance, the publication of Skinner's *Verbal Behavior* in 1957 prompted strong reactions from linguists and set off a general debate about the adequacy of behavioral explanations of language development. In Skinner's view, language was acquired largely through processes of imitation, shaping, and reinforcement. These assertions were countered by linguists, however, who produced strong theoretical and empirical arguments against them. Rapid developments in linguistic theory (e.g., Chomsky, 1957, 1965) and research that showed qualitative differences in child and adult speech and less-than-theoretically-expected levels of imitation (see Brown, Cazden, & Bellugi, 1968; Ervin, 1964) did much to weaken behaviorism as a general theory of language development.

The Cognitive Era

Probably no single event, then, signaled an end to the associationistic era and the beginning of the "cognitive revolution" in American psychology. Early on, at least, the cognitive revolution was a quiet one. Certainly the "time was right," as American psychologists were becoming increasingly frustrated with the limitations of both their theory and their methods. As mentioned above, research by linguists on the nature of language development provided evidence against the radical environmentalist perspective offered by the behaviorists. Another prominent factor was the emergence of computers (Baars, 1986), which provided both a credible metaphor for human information processing and a significant tool for exploring human cognitive processes.

Beyond these general trends, the work of a number of individuals clearly was pivotal in leading to the cognitive revolution. For instance, some point to the publication of Ulrich Neisser's *Cognitive Psychology* in 1967, which provided early definition to the new area of cognitive psychology, or even earlier, to the work of Jerome Bruner (Bruner, Goodnow, & Austin, 1956) or David Ausubel (Ausubel, 1960; Ausbel & Youssef, 1963), which emphasized structural features of cognition. Others would nominate G. A. Miller's frequently cited 1956 article, "The Magical Number Seven, Plus-or-Minus Two: Some Limits on Our Capacity for Processing Information," or his founding, with Jerome Bruner, of the Center for Cognitive Studies at Harvard in 1960 (Baars, 1986). Many cite J. J. Jenkins's 1974 *American Psychologist* article, in which the fundamental differences between the mass of rote learning research he and others had done for a generation and their work within the new cognitive paradigm were contrasted. Still others would cite Marvin Minsky's "frames" paper (1975), which outlined the necessary features of a vision system that could recognize simple objects. This paper highlighted the critical role of mental structures in human thinking and decision making, a theme echoed by others in the related concepts of "scripts" (Schank & Abelson, 1977) and "schemata" (Rumelhart, 1975).

Today, cognitive psychology is mainstream American psychology and the cognitive perspective no longer is revolutionary. In education, however, except in isolated areas, the cognitive revolution is just beginning (DiVesta, 1987). Thus, our first goal in this text is to present the important concepts and points of view of cognitive psychology as clearly as we are able. Equally important to us, however, is our desire to build bridges between cognitive psychology and education.

Cognitive Psychology and Education

Our experience tells us that if we describe the concepts of cognitive psychology well, you will see their considerable power for education. They "fit" well with many of our beliefs as educators—our sense of students as whole human beings; our advocacy of active, not passive learning; and our valuing of individual differences. We believe you will find yourself drawn to this perspective and a "cognitive view" will begin to affect your thinking about your students and your beliefs about how they should be taught.

An Example

To get a more complete flavor of the directions a cognitive view might take, we would like you to think for a moment about one such student—Kari, a 15-year-old girl in her first year at Southeast High School. It's now midway through the fall semester and, all in all, Kari has made a reasonably good transition from junior to senior high school. Her grades are holding up fairly well—with one exception, a history class with the dreaded Mr. Bergstrom. But then, at this point, no one in the class has higher than a B anyway. Kari's immediate concern, however, is with an assignment for Ms. Lawrence's "Citizenship Issues" class. Printed on a half-sheet of ditto paper, here's how it reads:

> Produce a first draft of a two-page paper on the issue YOU consider to be the most critical issue facing American youth today. Please type your draft and double space it. As we have done in the past, you need to make 4 copies. As usual, plan to read it to your small group and to get written comments from each of them. This draft is due Friday, the 17th. Final drafts are due a week from Friday. P.S. Papers with typed lines shorter than 4 inches in length are NOT acceptable. This means you, Bobby!

We next see Kari the following Thursday in the school computer lab, where she has signed up for an hour's time before school. She pulls out the assignment from her notebook. "Hmmm. . . . A two-pager. . . . Problems facing youth. Let's see, what should I pick? Jobs? Stress and suicide? Drugs? AIDS? The threat of nuclear war?

"Jobs . . . much too dull," she thinks. "Stress and suicide? I've been reading about that, but writing about that would be so depressing. Drugs? Maybe. AIDS? But I could never write about intercourse and anyway, I'm not going to have sex until I'm 18. Nuclear war. Maybe, . . . there's those demonstrations going on over at the Bentex plant. I'd have something I could get out of the newspaper." She smiles at Ms. Lawrence's instructions to Bobby.

Twenty minutes later, Kari has yet to type a word, but by the half-hour, she is busily typing, occasionally looking into two books she has gotten from the school library. Ten minutes before the hour ends, we see success—the printer is clattering away and is well into the second page, and with 6-inch lines, no less.

In many ways, Kari's assignment is a straightforward one and not much different from those given hundreds of thousands of times every day by teachers in schools across the United States and around the world. In each of them, a directive to action stimulates the need to recall earlier events, to make decisions, to gather and use information, and to take action. Most are simple assignments, yet all are rich from a cognitive perspective. For Kari to be successful (and we are presuming that she will be), she needs to have engaged in cognitive operations as diverse as extracting meaning from written instructions, translating thoughts into plans of action, combining newly acquired and stored information into words and sentences, and, of course, just making the word processor and printer work! When all these dimensions are considered, the array of cognitive functions required seems almost so complex as to defy understanding.

In Kari's sequence of activities, however, we can see certain basic elements that must be present in her cognitive system in order for her to succeed. She needs to have a body of knowledge in memory to draw on. She must be able to direct her attention toward some things and away from others, to make sense out of the details she encounters, and to get information in and out of memory. She must use language to express this information and, in order for the assignment to be completed successfully, must make appropriate decisions about whether the emerging document "solves the problem"—that is, meets the criteria of the assignment.

We chose Kari as an example not because she is unique, but because the cognitive resources she must draw on and the actions she takes represent many of the features of cognitive psychology. Her actions, although thoroughly familiar, illustrate key elements of human cognitive functioning—perception, attention, short- and long-term memory, associative processes, and problem solving and decision making. At the same time, they raise a number of important questions about our information-processing capabilities—questions we address in the following chapters. These questions are:

1. What is knowledge, and what role does it play in the performance of complex cognitive acts?

2. How do learners focus their attention on certain elements in the world "out there" while ignoring others, and what are the limits of learners' capacities for "paying attention"?

3. How do learners acquire information, make sense of it, store it in memory, and retrieve it for use? Then, once information is stored, *how* is it stored and what makes it more or less available when the learner wishes to recall it? In other words, why do we remember and why do we sometimes forget?

4. How are learners' cognitive processes used to solve problems, and what is a "cognitive perspective" on problem solving?

In the chapters that follow in Part I, we examine these questions. Chapter 2, "The Necessity of Knowledge," focuses on the first. Basing our discussion on the large body of research relating cognitive processes to knowledge, we illustrate how our cognitive processing system is knowledge-based and show the key role of knowledge in all of cognition. In Chapter 3, "Perception and Attention," the critical cognitive operations of perception and attention are defined and related to processes of education. Chapter 4, "Memory: Structures and Models," is an introduction to a topic of concern to all educators—memory. In this chapter, we open with a discussion of the topic of memory by examining the research and theory on the nature and organization of memory. Chapter 5, "Encoding Processes," expands our discussion of memory. It describes how the nature of activities that take place during learning affects memory. Chapter 6, "Retrieval Processes," explores factors that direct and control recognition and recall as we retrieve information from memory. Finally, in the last chapter in this first section, Chapter 7, "Problem Solving," we examine a set of processes many educators would place highest among their goals for students—the ability to consider issues, to think clearly about them, and to reach toward effective resolutions of problems. These processes are those of problem solving.

By the time you have completed the first section of this text, then, you should have a clear sense of cognitive psychology's concepts and perspectives and some feeling for what it has to offer education. If you are interested in only an overview of cognitive psychology, this might be a reasonable stopping point. Those who are interested in specific applications of cognitive psychology in education, however, must read on. Part II, "Cognitive Skills in the Schools," explores the utility of the cognitive perspective in relation to the fundamental skills that run across all subject areas—language use, reading, and writing—and examines the growing number of applications of cognitive psychology to mathematics, science, and social sciences instruction.

Summary

For most of this century, associationism was *the* American psychology. Working within this tradition, American psychologists attempted to derive basic laws governing learning and memory by studying these phenomena in simplified, rigorously controlled experimental settings. As this research became more and more focused, however, it seemed to become less and less relevant. Nonetheless, one branch of associationistic psychology—radical behaviorism, with its stress on objective observation of responses and environmental design—had a powerful impact on education that continues today. Radical behaviorism eschewed the "life of the mind," and instead stressed the objective observation of responses and the effects of the environment.

In psychology itself, however, there was increasing dissatisfaction with associationistic theories, which increasingly were judged to be lacking explanatory power for understanding complex mental events. Memory researchers experienced greater and greater frustration as they attempted to use associationistic theory and experimental investigations of rote learning to explain human memory. The behavioral perspective was attacked by linguists, who questioned its account of language development, and by others who criticized the idea of behavioral control and feared a technology of behavior management.

Now, at the beginning of the 1990s, a cognitive revolution has occurred in American psychology. Cognitive psychology portrays humans as processors of information, a computer-based metaphor reflected in both the theorizing and methods of cognitive psychologists. It stresses the role of the learner's activities and mental structures in comprehension and the creation of meaning by the learner.

Although it is now well accepted in psychology, cognitive psychology has just begun to have a significant impact on education. Our goal, therefore, is to present the concepts, principles, and perspectives of current cognitive psychology in detail and to challenge you to explore their implications for educational practice.

I

Information Processing

CHAPTER 2

The Necessity of Knowledge

How much do you know? What do you know? This chapter addresses an issue not often found in traditional psychology textbooks—the significance of our base of past experience, our knowledge, for guiding our present activities. As cognitive psychologists examine complex human behavior, it has become increasingly apparent that the acquisition of a large and varied knowledge base is critical to the development of expertise in any area of human effort.

In the example given in Chapter 1, Kari faced a "problem"—the need to produce an assignment for a teacher. The quality of the completed assignment will give some indication of Kari's understanding of the topic. But what is the basis for the understanding? We believe that in very large measure, the basis is sheer knowledge. Although knowledge often has been neglected as a topic of inquiry, the evidence (e.g., Davis, 1986) is mounting for the central role it plays in all human cognition.

The neglect of knowledge is understandable. Compared to such topics as insight, intelligence, and creativity, the knowledge component of cognition does not seem very profound. Discussions of creativity, for instance, often place greater emphasis on inspiration than perspiration, the knowledge/work side of creativity.

Recent research, however, provides convincing support for the necessity of not one, but several kinds of knowledge in order to carry out complex tasks (Geary & Wideman, 1987). Thus, we have chosen to highlight it as the starting point in our discussion of cognition. Knowledge is at the core of human cognition. Knowledge creates our perceptions, focuses our attention, and is the "stuff" of our memories. Also, unless there is a strong knowledge base, problem solving is unlikely to occur.

We begin our discussion of the necessity of knowledge by distinguishing among three kinds of knowledge: domain-specific knowledge, general knowledge, and strategic knowledge. As we will see, each underlies the performance of complex cognitive activities.

Types of Knowledge

Domain-Specific Knowledge

Return for a moment to the example of Kari we presented in Chapter 1. You recall, no doubt, that she was faced with choosing a topic for a two-page paper. In order to write this paper, Kari had to have information about the specific topic she selected. Such specific knowledge about a topic is called **domain-specific** knowledge. For many tasks, the amount of domain-specific knowledge is very large indeed. For instance, try to visualize the amount of knowledge needed to make sense out of novels such as *The Color Purple* and *Moby Dick.*

In many cases, the extent of knowledge for a successful performance is not obvious. Consider, for example, the amount of domain-specific information needed to solve the following deceptively simple physics problems:

A river flows due north. Which side of the bank should be most worn?

Or consider this somewhat more conventional physics problem:

If 10 joules of work are done in moving 0.30 coulomb of positive charge from point A to point B, what is the difference in potential of the points A and B?

Solving the first problem requires some rather arcane knowledge such as seeing that the answer depends on the hemisphere in which the river flows. For the second problem it is easy to point out at least three units of domain-specific knowledge—joule, coulomb, and potential, for instance—one must know prior to solving it. To many people, the first problem seems difficult because the language is so simple and conventional, yet the question does not seem to make simple, conventional sense. In the second case, the knowledge required is apparent, but for most individuals, so is our lack of knowledge! Other, everyday examples of domain-specific knowledge can be seen all about us: the knowledge needed to make sense of a road map, the information required for filling out a job application, the knowledge a secretary needs about office equipment to duplicate a report, and the background required by a mechanic to diagnose a poorly running machine.

General Knowledge

Although domain-specific knowledge is vital for performing day-to-day activities, other kinds of knowledge also must be used. If you'll think back once again to our example of Kari and her paper, you'll see she needed information and skills beyond domain-specific knowledge in order to write her paper successfully. For instance, Kari needed a basic vocabulary, rules for punctuation and grammar, general knowledge about how reports are written, and skills such as how to operate the word processor. Such knowledge, not directly related to understanding the topic she chose to write about, is called **general knowledge.** General knowledge is essential in the completion of any academic task; it is not enough simply to have knowledge of a specific topic. Success depends on information qualitatively different from domain-specific knowledge—information that could apply to almost any academic task.

We can think of general knowledge as knowledge appropriate to a wide range of tasks but not tied to any one task. Vocabulary, knowledge of current affairs, information about history, mathematical skills, and understanding the rules of grammar are examples of general knowledge. Such knowledge is useful for an extremely broad array of activities. Indeed, there is an almost infinite amount of general knowledge necessary for a 15-year-old such as Kari to function on a day-to-day basis.

Strategic Knowledge

In addition to domain-specific and general knowledge, students must possess the strategic skills to combine those knowledges in such a way as to produce a product satisfactory to themselves and to other potential audiences (e.g., teachers, classmates, and perhaps parents). **Strategic knowledge** refers to these combinational skills—knowledge about the manner in which tasks are completed. Kari well might have written her paper differently if it were to be evaluated by an English teacher rather than by her peers and the history teacher.

Students' abilities to think about assignments, to organize their ideas into an appropriate sequence, to use language suitable to their audience, and to write in a way that reflects the perspective of the reader all are examples of strategic knowledge. As students become more mature, we expect they will develop an increasing number of strategic skills for communicating effectively with a wider range of audiences for a wider range of purposes.

Strategic skills play an important role in most school-related tasks, from completing assignments appropriately to reading effectively (e.g., Brown, Day, & Jones, 1983b). As children become aware of their own cognitive functioning and are better able to monitor and control their own thought processes, strategic skills come to play a more and more important role in their actions (see Chapter 5).

The Role of Knowledge in Cognition

The influence of knowledge is so pervasive we often lose sight of it. Consider, for example, the role of knowledge in reading. Typically, we think of differences in what students comprehend and remember about a reading passage as due to their basic abilities in reading, not to their knowledge levels.

When we begin to ask questions about the role of knowledge in reading comprehension, however, we seem to enter a circular loop. In general, good readers remember more of what they read (Ryan, 1981) and possess a much greater amount of general world knowledge than poor readers (see Taft & Leslie, 1985). Good readers not only remember more about what they read, but they read a great deal more than poor readers. This close relationship of reading ability and general knowledge has made research in the area difficult. However, a recent study by Recht and Leslie (1988) was designed in a way that allowed them to see what effect domain-specific knowledge had on students' memory for reading materials.

Recht and Leslie cast about for a topic that some good readers and some poor readers would know a great deal about, but also a topic that some good and some poor readers would know very little about. They settled on the topic of baseball. After identifying junior high students who were very good readers and junior high students who were poor readers, Recht and Leslie tested the students about their knowledge of baseball. This procedure allowed them to identify good readers who knew a great deal about baseball, good readers who knew very little about baseball, poor readers who knew a great deal about baseball, and poor readers who knew very little about baseball. Next the children were asked to read a passage of 625 words that described half of an inning of a baseball game between a local team and a visiting rival. Then the children were tested for their ability to remember the passage in several ways: (1) reenacting the inning with a model field and miniature wooden players while verbally describing what happened, (2) summarizing the passage, and (3) sorting 22 sentences taken from the passage on the basis of how important the sentences were to the happenings of the inning.

The results of Recht and Leslie's study were striking. On each of the measures of memory, poor readers who knew a great deal about baseball greatly outperformed good readers who knew little about baseball. In fact, they performed nearly as well as the good readers who knew much about baseball. Poor readers who knew little about baseball, however, remembered the least about the passage on all measures. Apparently, domain-specific knowledge has a very powerful influence on how much and what we remember about what we read. Further, as we will see in Chapter 10, "Reading to Learn," the role of domain-specific knowledge in reading has important implications for improving students' reading abilities.

The influence of students' knowledge on new learning is far broader than baseball. Remembering information about chess, the game of bridge (Charness, 1979), computer programming (Adelson, 1981), science (Burbules & Linn, 1988), and electronics (Egan & Schwartz, 1979) all have been shown to be related to previous knowledge. In general, as students know more about a specific topic, it is easier for them to learn and remember new information about that topic. Not surprisingly, knowledge also is related to problem-solving abilities. Beyond the obvious outcome that people who are expert in an area (e.g., physics, teaching, law) are better problem solvers within their domain of expertise than are novices, the research shows that experts approach problems differently than novices (see, for example, Hayes & Flower, 1986; Larkin, McDermott, Simon, & Simon, 1980; Schoenfeld, 1985). Using a procedure known as **protocol analysis,** in which research participants provide a verbal account of their thoughts as they solve problems (i.e., "talking their way through the situation"), studies show that experts begin by spending substantial time attempting to "understand" problems. That is, they think before they act. In many cases, this effort leads to categorizing the problem as a member of a general case. (For example, classifying a physics problem as an instance of one of the three categories of problems in classical mechanics is an unlikely event for novices.) In addition, experts are more likely than novices to make a visual sketch of the problem. Also, given the initial thoughtful attempt at understanding, experts work from the "givens" of a problem forward toward a solution.

In contrast to experts, novices appear to have little sense of how to organize the limited information they do have. Protocols show that novices' solution strategies typically consist of attempts to generate formulas or rules from memory, class notes, or other sources that somehow relate to the specific elements of the problem. Little time is spent in "understanding" the problem by relating it to an underlying class of problems (of which, of course, they may be unaware). Formulas or rules are used to work backward from the desired (but unknown) goal to where the novice is now.

These different strategies are based directly on knowledge. Domain-specific experts understand that problems in their field are most easily solved when they can be understood and classed with other, similar problems. Experts also understand the importance of sketches and dia-grams to problem understanding. Novices, in contrast, may work very hard—even harder than experts—but because of their limited knowl-edge and the much less efficient way they go about organizing new knowledge relevant to problems, their strategies are inefficient.

The influence of knowledge extends beyond memory and problem solving. As we will see in chapters devoted specifically to perception and language, knowledge of all three forms—domain-specific, general, and strategic—permeates every aspect of cognition. Indeed, it is impossible to consider any aspect of cognition without simultaneously thinking of the knowledge underlying it.

Knowledge Acquisition

Our discussion of knowledge thus far begs a significant question. How is it acquired? A substantial literature exists that has examined the condi-tions under which new information is most readily learned and remem-bered. As discussed in Chapter 1, however, much of this literature now seems curiously uninformative, because in literally thousands of studies virtually all the topics examined were simple tasks such as learning lists of nonsense syllables, isolated words, and the like. Rarely was the learn-ing of complex tasks studied directly, since prior to the 1970s the general research strategy was based on the assumption that the best way to study a psychological phenomenon was to reduce it to as simple a task as possible. A major part of the "cognitive revolution" was a rejection of this reductionistic strategy and associationist theory and the choice to study learning and memory in more realistic, ecologically valid contexts.

Recently, however, interest has been rekindled among cognitive psy-chologists in studying how basic knowledge and skills are built up. There is increasing emphasis on such topics as frequency and the distribution of practice (Newell & Rosenbloom, 1981) and how knowledge is com-piled (put together). We begin our discussion by briefly reviewing some of the "classic" findings in this area and then move to a more current view of knowledge acquisition, that presented by Neves and Anderson (1981).

Frequency Effects

All of us are familiar with the "practice makes perfect" maxim. Like most maxims, it is only partially correct in that it fails to specify the sort of practice, the degree of "perfection," and the amount of practice necessary. For example, sheer repetition leads to improvement on a learning task only if some sort of feedback (information on consequences) is presented to the learner after each or most efforts to learn. For instance, imagine yourself as a subject in one early study (Thorndike, 1932) being blindfolded and then asked to draw 2-, 4-, 6-, 8-, or 10-inch lines on a piece of paper with one quick sweep of a pencil. Imagine what your performance would be on 50 attempts if you never were given feedback on the adequacy of your performance. The odds are good that you would demonstrate little increase in skill in drawing lines of the proper lengths! As Thorndike found, only with feedback will you show gradual improvement over time.

When there is feedback, the frequency of an activity is a powerful determiner of the learning and the availability of basic knowledge. In the line-drawing task described above, for instance, the more attempts you make with feedback, the more accurate you will become. These same frequency effects have been demonstrated in a multitude of areas, ranging from perceptual skills (Snoddy, 1926) to memory for words (Underwood, 1957) to problem solving (Newell & Rosenbloom, 1981). With repetition and feedback, responses become more coordinated, more rapid, and more automatic. Frequency effects extend beyond simple skill building, however. The meaningfulness of words and even syllables correlates very highly with frequency of encounter (Underwood & Schulz, 1960).

Frequency and Interference Effects

Most of us have a vague idea that learning new material can **interfere** with our recall of "old" (already learned) material, especially if the new material is similar to the old and the material is not especially meaningful. Thus, learning the third list in a series of 20 lists of new Russian vocabulary words may begin to interfere with our recall of words on the first and second lists of words. On the other hand, if the three lists are quite different, say a list of Cyrillic letters, of Russian cities, and of the Russian words for colors, the effects of interference will be greatly diminished.

A large body of research (for a review, see Staddon, 1984) has explored questions related to interference. From this research has come a series of principles that seem to govern the interference of past events with present learning (called **proactive interference**) and interference of present learning activities with what already has been learned (called **retroactive interference**). In general, this research has shown that interference effects occur especially in the learning of materials that have **little inherent meaning** to the learner. Thus, interference would be greatest when new materials are being learned by novices or when they are being learned by "rote." Even with such "nonmeaningful" materials, however, interference diminishes as materials become better and better learned (and hence become more meaningful). Further, the more dissimilar materials are from one another, the less likely they are to interfere (Ceraso, 1967; Postman & Underwood, 1973).

Distribution of Practice

Another issue of interest in early research was the **distribution of practice** (McGeoch & Irion, 1952). This line of research examined the different forms practice could take as individuals learned simple lists of various lengths. In general, distributed practice (i.e., a number of list-learning trials, each of brief duration, separated by a rest period) proved superior to massed practice (i.e., the same number of trials performed immediately one after another). In spite of the simplicity of the learning tasks on which these results are based, these findings have proven to be quite hardy and the topic again has begun to enjoy attention in the literature (e.g, Dellarosa & Bourne, 1985; Glover & Corkill, in press).

Overall, in learning of a relatively simple nature, such as learning dates, locations, capitals of states, and so forth, distributing practice efforts does make a difference—spaced practice typically is more effective than massed practice (Madigan, 1969; Reynolds & Glaser, 1964). For more complex learning, however, these principles probably do not hold. For instance, it would appear logical that in attempting a set of mathematics word problems, one might benefit more from one 30- or 40-minute period of concentrated effort rather than several 5- or 10-minute periods spaced over a number of hours or days.

Neves and Anderson's Theory of Knowledge Compilation

Among contemporary researchers who have grown increasingly interested in the acquisition of knowledge are David Neves and John R. Anderson. They have proposed that knowledge is compiled in three steps: **encoding,** in which a set of facts is committed to memory; **proceduralization,** in which facts are turned into procedures; and **composition,** in which procedures are made faster with practice.

Encoding   In Neves and Anderson's (1981) view, all knowledge is **encoded** initially as a set of facts within a network. For instance, when a student first begins to learn to use a word processor, one might expect that she would learn such facts as "The ESCAPE key is used to get the Command Line" or " 'PrtSc' stands for 'Print Screen'." Each of these facts can be analyzed, considered along with other facts (e.g., "The 'Print' command is the usual way that documents are printed out"), and turned into actions. The difficulty with this kind of knowledge, called **declarative knowledge** (Winograd, 1975; also see Chapter 4), is that it takes time to interpret each fact and turn it into action. Thus, declarative knowledge can determine action, but actions based on declarative information are likely to be very slow paced. If a student must think about and decide the function of each key, then work with the word processor will be very slow. Of course, that is the way much of our learning begins.

Proceduralization   The second step in knowledge utilization is **proceduralization,** in which encoded, declarative facts are transformed into procedures. Declarative knowledge becomes procedural knowledge. Procedural knowledge can be directly executed—it needs no interpretation. Thus, as a student gains skill in using the word processor, her knowledge changes from a network of facts to a set of procedures. She now uses her knowledge of the ESCAPE command without thinking about it, and her performance improves dramatically. Memory load also is reduced, because she does not need to retrieve her knowledge from memory. It is implicit in what she does.

Composition   The third stage in the transformation and use of knowledge is **composition.** In composition, actions that occur in sequence are integrated and combined. Thus, learning continues well after proceduralization has occurred, as procedures are organized into integrated sequences. In her use of the word processor, even months after she first became fairly comfortable with it, our student likely still is gaining facility in its use.

Implications of the Neves and Anderson Model   In general, the Neves and Anderson model of learning implies that, in the beginning, performance on any cognitive activity will be awkward and slow, since knowledge is not yet proceduralized. If learning proceeds, however, knowledge of facts can become knowledge of how to use those facts. This proceduralized knowledge is much more readily and quickly available for use. If, finally, there is compilation as procedures are combined and recombined, efficiency in mental tasks increases over a very long period of time.

In fact, there is a startling consistency in the research findings on skill acquisition in a wide range of tasks. Although performance initially may be halting, it soon improves to a reasonable level of competence. In most areas where "expertise" has been investigated, performance continues to improve, even after hundreds and even thousands of hours of practice! Such findings have been shown in studies as diverse as Crossman's (1959) classic investigation of cigar rolling (in which performance continued to improve over almost 3 million trials and two years!), to the reading of inverted text after hundreds of pages (Kolers, 1975), to the continued learning of a card game after hundreds of hands (Neves & Anderson, 1981). Consider, for example, students' efforts to learn to ski, to ride a bicycle, or to develop mastery of a foreign language. Careful examination of their performance, even after many hours of practice, will reveal skill improvement.

One reason for continued improvement over long periods is that the amount of knowledge required for high-level performance in any field is immense. In chess, estimates of the amount of time spent learning by master chess players are on the order of 50,000 hours (Chase & Simon, 1973). From this tremendous investment of time (as much as many adults have spent reading in their entire lives), the chess master has acquired an enormous amount of knowledge about chess positions, organized into meaningful groupings that can be almost instantly recognized and acted on (Chase & Simon, 1973; DeGroot, 1965). Similarly, it seems reasonable to expect that to read well, to write well, to reason well, and to perform well in music, dance, or athletic competition, students need to acquire and be able to use large amounts of knowledge. Such abilities do not develop in a matter of hours, days, or even weeks—years of effort may be needed to acquire necessary knowledge and skills. Thus, our 15-year-old, Kari, is unlikely to be an expert either on the topic she has written about or in writing itself. Yet our discussion to this point suggests that she already has acquired large amounts of knowledge and that this information is organized in very complex and varied ways.

A substantial goal of education is to provide students with still greater amounts of knowledge aimed, ultimately, at the development of expertise in one or more domains. As mentioned previously, evidence suggests that "real" expertise in even a fairly narrow topic (e.g., physics, music, composition, mathematics, film making) may require on the order of 10 years of intensive and extensive knowledge collection and organization (see Hayes, 1981; Larkin et al., 1980). In acquiring such expertise, learners increasingly are able to fit seemingly disparate bits of information together as they attempt to perform routine actions, learn new information, and solve problems. Novice learners, on the other hand, are unable to recognize that even fairly closely related bits of information are, in fact, related. The next section of this chapter, contextualism, suggests a reason why this may be so. Viewed from a contextualist perspective, all learning is a function of one's context—one's perspective.

Knowledge in Context

All knowledge is acquired in a context—the context of a classroom, a home, a social setting, or a workplace. This crucial fact was largely overlooked in most of the early laboratory studies of learning. As learning researchers began to consider contextual matters, however, its relevance to present-day issues of schooling was enhanced.

What do we mean by context? What are the effects of context in using knowledge? Our dictionary defines context as "that part of a discourse in which a word or passage occurs and which helps to explain the meaning of the word or passage." More broadly, any event humans experience takes place in some setting—a context. The nature of the context gives meaning and structure to the event. Thus, when a student learns a mathematical relationship in a mathematics class, the fact that it is embedded in the context of mathematics instruction may make it difficult, if not impossible, for the student to use that relationship later when it is required to solve a problem in a physics course. Similarly, students in education courses who argue that the content of such courses is unrelated to "real" teaching simply may not have the proper cognitive structures to see the relationships. Alternatively, the fact that the content of the courses is learned in the context of the "student as student," not "student as teacher," may contribute to the inability of some students to see the relevance of the course content to the process of becoming a teacher.

The effects of context first were highlighted by a group of German psychologists who migrated to the United States in the 1930s. These psychologists, Karl Duncker, Max Wertheimer, Wolfgang Köhler, and George Katona, published a series of papers and books on what is now commonly called "Gestalt" psychology. Much of what they said anticipated modern cognitive psychology. They presented many demonstrations of the impact of context in determining the extent and sort of learning that occur in humans. Many of these demonstrations grew out of examinations of perceptual phenomena and, as Chapter 3 illustrates, contextual effects in perception are pronounced. It has become clear, however, that contextual effects extend far beyond simple perceptual phenomena.

Knowledge in human memory seems to be "stored" in a contextual fashion. As we will see in Chapter 4, at least some elements of information (knowledge) in memory are organized schematically or structurally (in frameworks or networks) rather than semantically (as if memory were organized like a dictionary). Clearly, one aspect of expertise is recognizing the value of knowledge in its widest possible set of contexts. Research evidence suggests that when faced with a problem, experts are more likely to use a wide array of knowledge because it is organized and contextually linked in a system of great breadth and depth.

One might reasonably speculate that the key to achieving expertise in teaching or in any other domain is to (1) acquire a substantial amount of information for use in many contexts and (2) actively seek means to link all elements of new knowledge to each other as well as to already stored "relevant" knowledge. In this view, both the teacher and the learner should strive to place new knowledge in a broad context. Thus it becomes apparent to the learner that the information will be useful in many different situations with which it is consistent. Teachers cannot, however, count on students' "seeing" these relationships; rather, the relationships often must be pointed out specifically. Indeed, evidence from a rather large number of "transfer of learning" studies suggests that the learner must experience the use of a bit of information in many different settings before that bit has contextual breadth (Duncker, 1945; Luchins, 1942). The less expert the learner, the greater the difficulty of forming appropriate contextual connections and the greater the probability of learning information as isolated bits.

Consider for a moment a fourth-grader of average reading ability who sets out to read aloud the following material written at the sixth- or seventh-grade level. How is the child to make sense of the material?

Box 2-1

A Fourth-Grade Child Reading Aloud a Sixth-Grade-Level Paragraph

(job)   (opened)
So it was a big task. I flipped open the dictionary and

(picked)   (thought)   (Ex_____)
selected a word I determined was important. "Exculpate," I

shouted. I decided to begin by learning the meaning of the

(Exco_____)
word. "Exculpate: to free from blame or guilt."

Words in parentheses above the lines indicate misreadings. In general, the misreadings are not random word choices, but fit, at least in part, the context of the passage.

As the sentence fragment suggests, some words are likely to be new to the reader. The child needs to understand the context of the entire sentence as a tool for understanding the meaning of the previously unknown words. The task of the reader is not simply to decode a string of letters (the new word), but to use prior knowledge about word sequence, word meaning, and prior sentences to make sense of it. A cursory examination of the errors indicates that the fourth-grader in our example is not making random guesses about the words; instead, the child is using prior knowledge to make informal hypotheses about their meaning. A more complete account of this extraordinarily complex process of understanding words in context is presented in Chapter 9.

Not only vocabulary learning is contextual, however. Any new bit of knowledge is acquired in a context—both cognitive and affective. In general, the probability of acquisition and retrieval (memory) grows out of the fit of the new item of knowledge with the prior information (context) held by the learner. Consider the following sentence from Auble, Franks, and Soraci (1979):

The haystack was important because the cloth ripped.

For even a reasonably skilled reader, each word is understandable in isolation, yet the sentence as a whole does not "make sense." If the word *parachute* is mentioned, however, the sentence immediately takes on meaning.

Context is a function of prior experience; a more complete description of the role of experience on context is presented in Chapter 6. If doubt exists that students have the context appropriate to a task, the teacher should seriously consider using pretask exercises to enhance context development, which in turn will help students make sense of what they read and learn.

Implications for Teaching

Beginning our treatment of cognition with a chapter such as this one runs several risks. Readers on the one hand may infer that "education" is only the accumulation of knowledge—hence teaching can be understood as involving the simple presentation of information to students. Or one might argue from a purely contextual perspective that learning occurs only when students learn in context. From this view, teaching students to teach, for example, is useless, or worse, unless such instruction takes place in the context of actual teaching. One might even argue for a view of cognitive development that says one must wait until students are sufficiently "mature" (e.g., have the appropriate context) before learning can proceed.

We take a more difficult middle course. Not all learning can or should take place in the full context of a task (i.e., on the job). Should surgeons initially learn surgery techniques by practicing on living patients? Should a 16-year-old first learn to drive on a busy freeway at rush hour? Obviously not. For most learners, specific knowledge acquired from reading, listening, or observing permits them to function effectively in a variety of settings. Observation gives credence to the idea that not all useful learning is acquired in a directly applied context. Following, then, are a number of significant implications about knowledge and its acquisition.

1. To acquire useful and well-integrated knowledge, children need to be helped to understand the value of domain-specific, general, and strategic knowledge. They need to learn that many tasks cannot be completed successfully without domain-specific information. At the same time, they need to understand that they have general knowledge that permits them to attack many problems. Finally, strategic understanding is required in order to use task-relevant information to solve a particular problem in its particular context. An understanding of the value of these different types of information will lead to greater appreciation of the need to acquire new knowledge.

2. Knowledge acquisition and retention can be enhanced by examining research from traditional areas of learning. Whereas early learning research in the associationistic framework was focused on very simple tasks such as list learning, a number of consistent findings have emerged that hold for many educational tasks.

- **Frequency.** Both acquisition and retention of new information are enhanced by multiple rehearsals with feedback on correctness of response.
- **Distributed practice.** Acquisition and retention are enhanced when the new information is rehearsed in trials separated by time.
- **Interference effects.** Interference is especially probable when it is difficult for learners to distinguish one task from another. Interference also is more likely to occur in novice learners. For novices, distinctions among the different aspects of a topic are much less clear than they are for teachers; hence, teachers must be particularly sensitive to possible student confusion.

3. Most skills children acquire in school require a much more substantial knowledge base than we typically realize or acknowledge. For instance, to succeed at reading, beginning readers not only must make letter discriminations, they also must have a reasonably extensive vocabulary. Vocabulary, of course, may be acquired in a great variety of ways— through being read to, by taking part in conversations, by reading, by listening to verbal interactions (TV, records, etc.), and through direct instruction. Further, knowledge about discourse structures is critical. For instance, availability of a "story schema," a sense of the nature of story development (see Chapter 9), may be crucial to reading comprehension. Similarly, elementary school subjects such as mathematics and science vividly demonstrate the need for specific vocabulary and concepts.

4. Sheer knowledge is not enough. Because students often are unable to use information learned in one setting (context) in another, instruction must provide the frameworks for establishing relationships among information. Keep in mind that interrelating knowledge is not valuable for only younger students. As students at junior and high school levels learn an increasingly varied set of roles, they actually may need increasing assistance with contextual aspects of learning.

5. Knowledge must be considered in the context of children's experience. New information is likely to be meaningful only when it can be related in some way to what they already know.

6. Demands to acquire knowledge may conflict with the requirement for understanding the context within which knowledge is to be used. At present, schoolteachers are faced with demands to give their students more information. At the same time, most schools are not prepared to provide the contexts for helping students effectively comprehend and store new information. Thus, a social studies student may "know" the Constitution and the Bill of Rights to the extent of passing an examination, yet fail to recognize "obvious" situations where individual rights are violated by a majority. At all educational levels, it is vital to relate knowledge to as many contexts as possible to help students recognize the value of organized, structured, and integrated information. Role playing, readings, television documentaries, and films all help give a broader context to learning. Nonetheless, even with excellent instruction, students often are far from achieving the sort of expertise possessed by the sophisticated and well-informed adult.

The only reasonable strategy for dealing with the issue of context is to create opportunities for students to acquire and store new information from the broadest array of contexts possible. Often this will limit the amount of information that can be taught. This is a serious dilemma, since expertise requires knowledge acquisition. To recognize that knowledge acquired out of context is not usable knowledge is to appreciate that demand for knowledge itself must be balanced against the need to present contexts within which knowledge may be used. Out of this recognition comes realization that the first dozen or so years of education should not be judged solely on a criterion of expertise. Instead, judgments should be formed on the soundness and connectedness of the knowledge base students acquire. It is this knowledge base that leads, finally, to expertise.

7. Teaching demands knowledge about children's cognitive processes. To understand how humans attend to information from their environments and how they interpret, store, and use that information has been a central focus of cognitive science for the past 30 years. It should be no surprise to the reader of this chapter that issues of attention and perception (making sense out of that to which one attends) heavily involve prior knowledge and context. We must realize, however, that cognitive processes work as a whole. Discussion in coming chapters of attention, perception, memory, and problem solving as separate topics should not obscure the fact that in the human they are continuous, ongoing, and interactive processes.

Summary

This chapter focused on the importance of knowledge to cognitive functioning. We consider three kinds of knowledge: domain-specific, general, and strategic. Domain-specific knowledge is knowledge specific to performance of a particular task. General knowledge refers to knowledge that is not domain-specific, but essential to utilization of domain-specific information. Strategic knowledge focuses on how domain-specific and general knowledge should be organized and sequenced for effective use.

Knowledge underlies all cognitive activities. For instance, domain-specific knowledge is closely linked to what students remember about reading materials. Knowledge also influences problem solving. The problem-solving behavior of experts and novices reveals that experts differ from novices in both the extent of their knowledge and its organization. Experts spend more time trying to understand difficult problems as well as devising methods that work forward to solution. In contrast, novices tend to begin problem solving before they thoroughly understand the task, and respond erratically, in many cases attempting to work backward from what they believe the solution will be.

In the traditional research on learning, three factors were shown to have particularly strong effects on knowledge acquisition: frequency, interference, and distribution of practice. Frequency refers to the effects of sheer repetition (with feedback) on learning new knowledge. Interference involves the effects of prior or subsequent learning on acquisition and recall. Distribution of practice refers to the effects of spacing rehearsal activity. For simple learning tasks, spaced practice seems more effective than massed practice. With complex tasks, the spacing effect is not so evident.

In general, cognitive psychologists view knowledge acquisition as a three-phase process. First, knowledge is encoded into memory as a set of elements called declarative knowledge. This knowledge then is transformed into sequences (procedural knowledge) that can be directly executed as units. Finally, a third process (composition) occurs when a sequence of procedures is integrated and combined in order to deal with the demands of a particular task.

Although the essential value of knowledge has been demonstrated, it is equally important to recognize that all knowledge is acquired in a context of prior and present learning. Context is strongly involved in our ability to recall and use knowledge in new situations.

CHAPTER 3

Perception and Attention

Understanding the value of knowledge and the context in which it is used is an important step in learning about human cognition. Nowhere are the roles of knowledge and context more clear than in human perception, the topic of this chapter. Consider the following phrases:

THE CAT

OPEN DOOR

Although the print was somewhat unusual, you no doubt had little trouble reading THE CAT, and OPEN DOOR. If you'll glance back at the phrases, though, you'll see that something fairly remarkable occurred. The same printed symbol H worked as an H in THE and as an A in CAT. Similarly, one printed symbol was a C in CAT and an O in OPEN and DOOR. Somehow, the context in which these symbols appear influenced how you interpreted them. The context, of course, was provided by you—your knowledge of three-letter words beginning with C and ending with T, for example, allowed the H symbol to be read as an A instead of an H or something else.

The process by which meaning is assigned to stimuli (such as the H in CAT above) is referred to as **perception.** Perception is critical to all aspects of cognition and is itself directly influenced by the student's knowledge and the context of events created by his or her knowledge. Closely related to perception is **attention,** the allocation of a person's cognitive abilities. As your read this page, you also may be listening to the radio or snacking on some popcorn. What you perceive at any given moment depends on how your attention is divided among various tasks. If most of it is devoted to a weather forecast on the radio, you may not correctly perceive the meaning of some of what you are reading. On the other hand, if you are immersed in this chapter, you may not hear your name when the radio announcer calls it and says that you have five minutes to phone to collect a $1,000 prize. This chapter deals with perception and attention and their implications for the classroom teacher. It begins with an overview of the process of perception and then examines different models of attention.

Perception

Let's think for a moment about what is required for perception—the assignment of meaning to incoming stimuli—to occur. First, some aspect of the environment—some stimulus—has to be picked up by the person (e.g., has to be seen). Next, that stimulus has to be transformed and held, somehow. A body of knowledge has to be available and brought to bear on the stimulus (e.g., *cat, cut,* and *cot* are the three-letter words beginning with *c* and ending with *t*). Finally, some decision has to be made—a meaning must be assigned. ("It's an *a*.")

The very common phenomenon of identifying the letter *a* seems far more complex when we consider what may happen during the process of perception. One important observation is the fact that perception takes time—identifying the **H** figure (or any other stimulus, for that matter) is not instantaneous. (Recall that the stimulus must be picked up and transformed, memory must be called up, the stimulus must be compared to what is in memory, and a decision must be made.) The fact that perception requires time leads to a problem of sorts. Because environments may change rapidly (as when watching a film or driving a car), a stimulus could stop being available before a meaning was assigned. (Imagine seeing **DCCR** projected by a slide projector for, say, one-tenth of a second.) Unless there is some way in which we can "hold" that stimulus for a while, our perceptual processes would have to stop in midstream (Fisher, Duffy, Young, & Pollatsek, 1988). The experience of watching a movie, for example, would be terribly frustrating if stimulus after stimulus disappeared before we could interpret their meaning. Our experience, however, tells us that such breakdowns in our perceptual processes occur infrequently. This is because our cognitive systems are equipped to register sensory information.

Sensory Registers

One of the capabilities of our cognitive system is that it can temporarily retain environmental information after it has disappeared (DiLollo & Dixon, 1988). Apparently, each of our senses has this ability, a **sensory register,** but research has focused almost entirely on vision and hearing. Here we discuss the visual and auditory sensory registers in turn, emphasizing evidence for their existence and research on their characteristics.

Visual Registers   The classic work on the visual registers was performed more than 30 years ago by George Sperling (1960). Sperling was engaged in basic perception research, attempting to identify the nature of the visual registers. As a part of his study, he showed subjects slides depicting arrays of letters such as the one shown in Figure 3-1.

Sperling noted that when subjects were shown such an array of letters for less than 500 milliseconds (msec), they could recall about 4 of the letters. This number didn't change regardless of whether Sperling altered the length of time subjects saw the array (from 15 msec to 500 msec) or whether he altered the number of letters they saw from 4 to 12. He developed three hypotheses that could account for his results. First, it was possible that only the 4 letters reported by subjects were registered. That is, subjects saw only 4 letters and couldn't recall any more because they had never registered. Second, it might have been that all 12 letters were registered, but that the letters were somehow lost before they could be reported. Third, it was possible that all 12 letters had been registered and were in memory, but that somehow only the 4 reported were accessible at the time of recall.

To test these hypotheses, Sperling developed what has come to be called the **partial report method.** He reasoned that if subjects had more information available than they could report, he could sample their knowledge. So, rather than asking subjects to report all they saw, he asked them to recall only *one* of the rows of letters in the matrices they were shown (see Figure 3-1).

Sperling's partial report procedure was extremely clever. Subjects were told that after the array of letters disappeared from the screen, they would hear a tone. If the tone was of high pitch, subjects were to recall the top row. If the tone was of middle-range pitch, they were to recall the middle row. If the tone was low, they were to report the bottom row. Since the subjects had no way of knowing which row they would be asked to recall until *after* the array disappeared from view, the number of letters they recalled could be used as an estimate of the total number of letters they actually had available when they began their recalls. By varying the delay between the disappearance of the array and the tone, Sperling was able to estimate how long such information was retained.

C   Z   K   L

D   P   M   B

R   L   X   N

FIGURE 3-1.   Stimulus array similar to that used by Sperling.

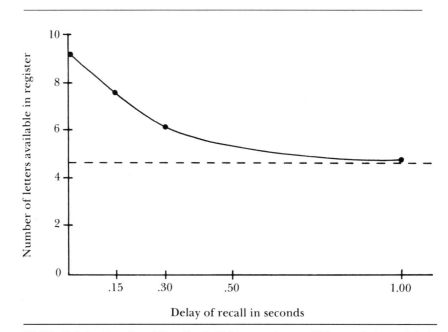

FIGURE 3-2. Results of Sperling's 1960 experiment. This graph is modeled after that presented by Sperling (1960). The dashed line represents recall without sampling.

The results of Sperling's study are summarized in Figure 3-2. As you can see, when the tone occurred immediately after the array was terminated, the subjects were able to remember about three of the four letters in the row for which they were cued. The value of 9 in Sperling's chart in Figure 3-2 is obtained by multiplying the average number of letters recalled in a row by the number of rows (3) in order to obtain an estimate of the total number of available letters. The longer the tone was delayed, however, the fewer letters were recalled. This decrease was very rapid. After only a half-second delay, subjects recalled an average of slightly more than one letter per row overall, indicating that about four letters were available.

The data thus supported Sperling's second hypothesis. That is, all or most of the letters in the arrays were registered, but most were lost before they could be reported. Apparently, Sperling's subjects were able to hold visual information for about half a second. After that time (just about the length of time it takes to recite the four letters they could report), it no longer was available.

The answer to Sperling's question was clear. People register a great deal of the information they see in brief presentations. After the information is removed from sight, however, it is available only briefly—about a half-second in Sperling's study. By the time Sperling's subjects could say the letters from one row (e.g., *c, z, k*), the rest of the information was gone.

Another question Sperling addressed in his 1960 paper was whether meaning had been assigned to information in the visual sensory register (or **icon,** as it has been called). To examine this question, Sperling (see also Sperling, 1983; von Wright, 1972) presented arrays such as the one in Figure 3-1 that contained both numbers and letters. Participants in the study then were given cues indicating that they were to recall either numbers or letters. Such cues would work only if meaning (number or letter) had been assigned to the information in the array. The results indicated that unlike the location cues we described earlier, number/ letter cues were ineffective. This outcome strongly suggests that the information in the icon is held with limited processing. Had the arrays been processed (in other words, if meaning had been assigned), then the number/letter cues would have made a difference.

Our purpose here is not to detail all that is known about the icon (for excellent reviews see Chase, 1987; Sperling & Dosher, 1986). Rather, it is to point out that people do possess capabilities permitting visual information to be held for a time after it is no longer physically available. We also want to show the rather severe limits of our ability to perceive visual information (see Mewhort, Butler, Feldman-Stewart, & Tramer, 1988). A similar capability limits our ability to perceive auditory information.

Auditory   Although a majority of research on sensory registers has centered on the
Registers   icon, considerable work also has been devoted to understanding the auditory register (the echo) (see Deutsch, 1987; Handel, 1988; Hawkins & Presson, 1987; Schwab & Nusbaum, 1986; Scharf & Buus, 1986; Scharf & Houtsma, 1986, for reviews). A particularly helpful study in the area is one by Darwin, Turvey, and Crowder (1972), using auditorially presented information, which replicated Sperling's work on the icon.

Darwin et al. presented the participants in their study with three brief lists containing numbers and letters. The lists were presented simultaneously over headphones so that it seemed that one list came from the right, a second list from the left, and the third list from behind. After hearing the lists, subjects were given position cues to remember one of the lists. Darwin et al. delayed these cues from 0 to 4 seconds after the lists were presented.

The results closely resembled those reported by Sperling for the icon. That is, as the cue delay increased, recall performance decreased, until at about 3 seconds after the presentation, subjects' recall with cues was no better than without cues. When Darwin et al. contrasted number/letter cues with position cues, they found the number/letter cues to be relatively ineffective. So, much like the icon, it appears that an echo exists that holds relatively unprocessed information while perceptual processing begins. For example, a sixth-grader's echo will hold the first part of the words *direct object* (i.e., the sound of *dir*) until the rest of the sound has appeared (*ect*) so that meaning may be assigned to the phrase.

Comparisons of the visual and auditory sensory stores indicate that there are some interesting differences (see Handel, 1988). The most obvious is the length of time information is stored in the registers: less than .5 second in the icon and slightly more than 3 seconds in the echo (see Chase, 1987; Hawkins & Presson, 1987). This greater ability of the echo to retain information seems to be related to the processing of language (see Schwab & Nusbaum, 1986).

One interesting phenomenon related to differences in the icon and the echo is the **modality effort** (Pisoni & Luce, 1986). This effect is seen when subjects are given lists of seven or eight items to remember. It turns out that subjects remember items better if they are presented auditorily rather than visually—the modality effect. Careful analyses of this phenomenon (see Crowder, 1976; Darwin & Baddeley, 1974; Grossberg, 1986) have shown that the difference in memory for visually and auditorily presented information can be traced to recall of the last few items. That is, people who are given auditory information (a list of seven to eight things) make fewer errors at the end of the list than people who receive the same information visually.

Early commentaries on the modality effect suggested that this ability to recall more of the items at the end of a list when information is presented auditorily was due to the fact that the echo is larger than the icon (Crowder, 1976). More recently, however, researchers have shown that the modality effect does not occur equally for vowels and consonants (Deutsch, 1987) and that vowels and consonants are processed differently (Jusczyk, 1987). These differences (see Schwab & Nusbaum, 1986, for a review) have suggested to many researchers that the echo has evolved as a component of our cognitive system specifically adopted for language processing. Certainly, work demonstrating that more information in spoken language is carried by vowels than consonants supports this notion (Scharf & Buus, 1986; Scharf & Houtsma, 1986). In any event, both the icon and the echo are critical to the process of perception, for it is here that the initial processing of information begins.

Implications of Research on the Sensory Registers

Our brief review of research on the icon and echo suggests some very direct implications for teaching. First, there are limits to the amount of information that can be perceived at any one time. The short duration of memory in the sensory registers should remind us of the need to carefully pace the delivery of information to students. Further, some work on developmental differences in cognition (e.g., Case, 1985) suggests that the size of the sensory registers increases with age. Children's sensory registers have more stringent constraints than those of adults. Especially with early elementary-age children, teachers must be aware of the need to manage the amount of information children are expected to perceive at any one time.

Second, there may be real benefits to presenting information both visually and auditorily. Given the limits of students' ability to hold information in their sensory registers, we would expect that information presented both visually and auditorily would have a higher likelihood of being perceived than information presented only in one format. Hence, the use of visual aids for auditory presentations and discussions accompanying visual materials seem to be reasonable approaches to increasing the likelihood that instructional materials will be perceived. It also is reasonable to assume that tactile, gustatory, and olfactory stimulation may enhance learning.

The sensory registers are crucial to perception, but becoming aware of the nature of the icon and echo explains only the initial stages of perceptual processing. This further processing—the assignment of meaning—is the topic of the next major section of the chapter.

The Assignment of Meaning

The assignment of meaning to incoming stimuli is such a common occurrence that we often take it for granted. Only when we face uncommon or unusual stimuli do we notice ourselves actively trying to assign meaning. However, most psychologists argue that the same processes occur in the nearly automatic assignment of meaning (reading the word *cheese,* for instance) and in our efforts to puzzle out obscure meanings (e.g., deciphering a scribbled note) (Roth & Frisby, 1986).

The assignment of meaning to incoming stimuli depends on two things: the nature of the stimuli and our background knowledge (Marr, 1982, 1985). Clearly, visual perception cannot occur if nothing is seen. Not as obvious, however, is the fact that perception—the assignment of meaning—also could not occur if there were no knowledge available. Consider, for example, the differences in the assignment of meaning to a large plant with a tall, central trunk. One student, who has lived all his life in the city, looks at the object and announces to us that he sees a tree. In contrast, a second person, who spent her childhood in the countryside and plans to go to college and major in forestry, indicates that she sees a hybrid American elm grafted onto a Chinese elm stock. Further, she states that it is an Ann Arbor variety and. . . . Although we left the second person before she could tell us all that she saw, it is clear that the relative levels of knowledge these two persons have about trees determine what they perceive.

Another important facet of the assignment of meaning is that various subprocesses must be involved (see Brown, McDonald, Brown, & Carr, 1988). A person's sense receptors must be oriented toward the source of the stimulation (the tree must be looked at), elements of the environmental stimulation have to be extracted, and these elements must be compared to what is in memory. Staying with the tree example, elements such as the texture of the bark; the shape of the crown; the shape, texture, and color of the leaves; and the overall shape of the tree must be noted and compared to existing knowledge in order to make a correct identification.

When elements match what is in memory ("Hmmm. Elms do have leaves with serrated edges."), recognition occurs. Recognition can occur on the basis of one cycle of information (orientation to the stimulus, feature extraction, comparison to memory, decision) or it can require considerable recycling as a person struggles to assign the correct meaning to an obscure stimulus.

In the remainder of the chapter we examine each part of the perception cycle. We begin by reviewing the process of feature extraction or, as it is usually called, pattern recognition.

Pattern Recognition

Pattern recognition refers to how stimuli in the environment are recognized as something stored in memory (Goldstein, 1988). Although there are different ways of conceiving of the pattern recognition process, each presumes that stimuli are picked up by the sense receptors and are held in the sensory registers while analyses of meaning are carried out. Incoming information is compared to knowledge stored in memory so that a decision can be made. ("It's a frebus!")

Although there has been little argument about the general nature of pattern recognition (however, see Gibson & Spelke, 1983), there has been considerable debate about exactly how the analyses in pattern recognition occur. In particular, disagreements center on how the knowledge necessary to recognize stimuli is represented in memory. In general, four positions on how knowledge is maintained for perception have been put forward by psychologists studying pattern recognition: (1) templates, (2) prototypes, (3) distinctive features, and (4) structural descriptions. In the following sections we examine each of these positions.

TEMPLATES. The simplest perspective on pattern recognition holds that templates or mental copies of environmental objects are held in memory (Bruce & Green, 1985). In this view, incoming patterns of stimuli are compared to a person's existing templates. If the incoming pattern fits a template (ℕ, the template for the letter N, for example), the person then categorizes the stimulus pattern as being a part of the class of things represented by the template. For example, when the pattern N is picked up, it is matched to a person's template (ℕ), and the pattern then is perceived as the letter N.

As Bruce and Green point out, however, this seemingly reasonable hypothesis starts to break down when we consider stimulus patterns that vary from the template. Consider the following: N Z Z ᴎ ⌣ ᴨ ⌣ ᴎ. Deciding whether all of these patterns are N's would seem to require a different template for each. In fact, there would have to be a template for every possible variation of N.

Templates could be made to work with letters if we presumed that they could be rotated to align with incoming stimuli (however, is ⇗ a Z or an N?), but they don't fit real-life objects well or the ways in which pattern matching can work on shapes that are almost totally hidden from view (see Shimojo & Richards, 1986). Still, templates can be modified (see Caelli & Moraglia, 1986; Posner & Keele, 1968, 1970) so that they are more general and less tied to specific patterns. This variation of the template is referred to as a prototype.

PROTOTYPES.   Prototypes differ from templates in that they are hypothesized to represent the key features of some *set* of objects rather than being representations of *specific* objects (Caelli & Moraglia, 1986). An example of a prototype will help clarify the idea. Think about playground swings. There are many kinds of swings, but if we ask you to draw a picture of a swing, you'd probably produce something like the object we show in Figure 3-3. Our swing isn't a special make or model; it's a *typical*, ordinary swing. It has the basic elements of a swing: large A-shaped ends joined by a solid bar across the top and pairs of chains hanging down with seats attached to them. This "average" playground

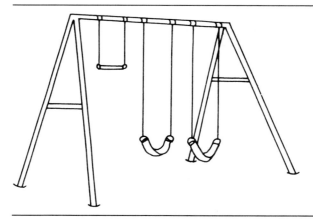

FIGURE 3-3.   A typical playground swing.

swing demonstrates the idea of prototype. It is a form representing the critical features of a set of objects we call swings. It isn't, though, a representation of any specific swing.

The prototype perspective on pattern recognition holds that pattern recognition amounts to deciding whether a stimulus pattern matches the basic form of a prototype. If it does, the stimulus pattern is identified. Returning to our playground swing example, if you see a large object in a schoolyard that matches your prototype of swing, then you call it a swing.

There is little doubt that people employ prototypes in many aspects of perception (see Roth & Frisby, 1986). Perception of faces (Reed, 1972) and problem types, for instance, seems consistent with the use of prototypes. Still, human perception is far more flexible than even prototypes would allow. For example, humans often are able to recognize brief, fragmentary glimpses of hidden objects (see Figure 3-4) and sometimes can recognize specific songs on the basis of very limited input (e.g., two or three notes). Perceptions based on such limited information would seem to indicate that prototypes alone could not be responsible for pattern recognition (Caelli & Moragalia, 1986; Shimojo & Richards, 1986). The ability to account for how people can recognize objects on the basis of very limited information is one of the strengths of the feature analysis model.

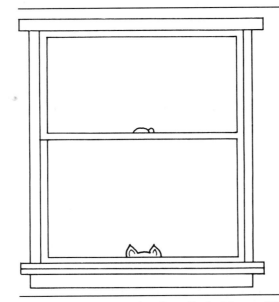

FIGURE 3-4.   Perception from limited input. What animal is outside the window?

FEATURE ANALYSIS.   Most of the people who see Figure 3-4 decide that a cat is outside the window. They make this decision because some critical **features** distinguish cats from other animals. In particular, cats have triangular ears on a rounded head. Similarly, other objects easily are identified if their critical features are picked up (e.g., a Mercedes can be recognized because of its distinctive hood ornament; oak trees have acorns and may be identified readily regardless of how unusual their bark or leaves may be).

Several different feature analysis models were developed in the 1950s and 1960s, the most famous being Selfridge's Pandemonium model. Feature analysis models continued to be popular because they seemed to be consistent with the neurophysiology of the visual cortex. That is, various cells in the cortex of the brain respond differently to different kinds of visual stimulation; roughly like certain aspects of Selfridge's model. More recent work, however, has suggested that the match to human neurophysiology is not as good as once thought (see Bruce & Green, 1985, for a detailed critique). Further, feature analysis models depend on sets of features in memory (the cat's ears, for example), which are themselves no more than miniature templates (Bruce & Green, 1985).

Some pattern recognition processes indeed are governed by the analysis of distinctive features (Kellas, Ferraro, & Simpson, 1988). Still, human perception is more flexible yet. If pattern recognition depended solely on distinctive features, however, we could not identify a lop-eared manx (a tailless cat) as a cat. That is, this animal does not possess the distinctive features normally associated with cats, but it is still a cat. Similarly, to return to the playground swing example we used earlier, many contemporary swing sets have almost no features in common with typical swings except that they can be used by children to swing suspended above the ground. A still more flexible approach is needed to describe human pattern recognition.

STRUCTURAL DESCRIPTIONS.   Based largely on the work of the late David Marr (e.g., 1982, 1985) is the idea of pattern recognition occurring as a result of structural descriptions. As Marr (1985) pointed out, the idea of structural descriptions offers a highly flexible way of thinking about the use of knowledge in perception. Rather than imagining that knowledge is stored as templates, prototypes, or the mini-templates of distinctive features, a structural description approach argues that knowledge is stored as a set of statements about a particular object or class of objects.

In the structural description view, people construct "models" of objects with a set of relevant statements. Incoming information is then matched against these models. The models focus on necessary features but are less particular about other details. To use the example offered by Bruce and Green (1985, p. 175), a model for the letter T would likely be described as a vertical line bisecting a horizontal line with the bisection occurring more than halfway up the vertical line and away from the ends of the horizontal line. This structural description, then, could identify ⊢, T, ⸀ , T , and 𝒯 as T's. The T's with slanted lines are allowed because the top lines do not diverge very far from horizontal. However, the following figures, ⊥ , ⌐ , ⊥,   and Ⅴ, would not be identified as T's on the basis of the structural description. Structural descriptions also allow for pattern recognition based on fragmentary evidence, as when only part of a *T* is seen (Caelli & Moraglia, 1986).

An example drawn from school would be the structural description of a "strait" in geography. A strait is described as a narrow body of water separating two land areas. This structural description allows a student to recognize the illustrations in Figure 3-5 as straits or bodies of water that

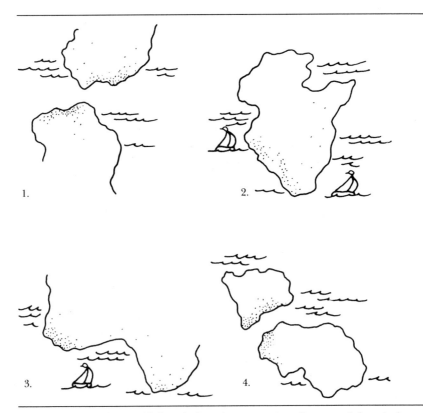

FIGURE 3-5.   Structural descriptions in perception. Structural descriptions such as that for a "strait" in geography allow for flexible recognition. Most students easily can identify drawings 1 and 4 above as depicting "straits."

are not straits. Similarly, structural descriptions readily are devised for other school-related concepts such as alliteration, literary style, form of historical event, and so on.

Thinking of a structural description basis for pattern recognition is helpful to teachers because it suggests that perception can be guided by teaching students the proper knowledge needed for an accurate structural description. The structural description of a strait, for example, can be readily taught. Students quickly master the ability to identify straits given practice with feedback in tasks such as the one shown in Figure 3-5. Similar instructional processes can be used to teach students to recognize specific problem types in mathematics, science, and social studies, as well as in industrial arts, business, and home economics. It is important to keep in mind, though, that instruction designed to teach concepts also should include the presentation of prototypes (e.g., "One of the things that sets democracies apart from other forms of government is . . .") in addition to structural descriptions (see Chapter 4).

The Role of Knowledge in Perception
Knowledge directly influences perception. Knowing what we see (or hear) and even how to look (or listen) depends on the knowledge we have (see McCann, Besner, & Davelaar, 1988). An expert chessplayer, for example, perceives midgame chess boards very differently than a person who has never played the game. The expert sees that a king is in check, that a certain style of defense is being played, and so on, whereas a nonplayer merely perceives pieces he or she may not even be able to name on a checkerboard playing surface.

Knowledge also influences how we look for things to perceive. For example, an accomplished baseball fan knows the need to watch the shortstop's behavior in order to find out whether the pitcher is going to throw a fastball, curveball, or slider. A nonfan may have no inkling why the shortstop takes steps right or left as soon as the pitcher releases the ball. Similarly, an accomplished debater understands what to look for in evaluating other debaters, much as an expert welder knows what to examine in judging another person's work.

It is clear, then, that knowledge permits perception to occur and guides our perception of new information (see Mandler, 1984). As we will see in Chapter 4, one compelling way to envision our knowledge is via **schemata** (singular, schema). Schemata are hypothesized knowledge structures in permanent memory that contain elements of related information and provide plans for gathering additional information (R. C. Anderson, 1984; Mandler, 1984; Rumelhart, 1980a). Schemata incorporate the prototypes, distinctive features, and structural descriptions we described earlier. For example, a person's schema for "tree" will contain not only its structural description, but also information about the nature of trees (they take in carbon dioxide and give off oxygen), where trees are found (not above certain elevations or in areas that are too dry or cold), and the care of trees (they must be pruned and watered).

Schemata are complex representations of knowledge. For example, a student may have a schema for "average speed" problems (e.g., Mr. Smith drives 200 miles to Louisville and then 425 miles to Obion. If his trip took 7 hours and 15 minutes, what was his average speed?). Beyond the minimal structural description necessary to recognize the type of problem (a distance is given, a time is given, and the questioner wants to know an average speed), the student's schema may include procedures for solving some kinds of "average speed" problems (add up the total distance; convert driving time to minutes; etc.) and a rough idea of what a reasonable answer would look like. For complex problems like these, well-developed schemata are necessary to *guide* the student's perception in looking for additional information relevant to solving the problem (R. C. Anderson, 1984; Sternberg & Detterman, 1986). A more detailed discussion of schemata appears in Chapter 4.

KNOWLEDGE AND PERCEPTION: IMPLICATIONS FOR TEACHING.   As we've seen in this section, perception depends on knowledge. Instruction in, say, long division is hardly likely to be accurately perceived if the students have not yet mastered the necessary prerequisites that make a lesson meaningful. Teachers therefore need to carefully match their instruction to students' levels of knowledge. In those cases where sophisticated perceptions are the goal (e.g., noting different textures in chemicals, hearing when a clarinet is slightly "out of tune," recognizing a certain defense being used by opponents in a basketball game), an extensive knowledge base is critical (see Chapter 2).

Of course, students' perceptions of any event will differ depending on their background knowledge. Their reactions to a poem, their unraveling of an author's meaning in a short story, and their interpretations of an historical event all will be unique in some ways. Although there may be some agreed-upon understanding of things among critics, historians, and political scientists, each person perceives events depending on his or her own experiential background. Teachers need to be aware that the ability to state facts (e.g., "Robert Frost was born in 1875") and the perceptions of subtler meanings (e.g., "Is *Stopping by the Woods on a Snowy Evening* about death, or is it a lyrical celebration of winter?") are not the same.

PERCEPTION AND CONTEXT.   In some situations, appropriate schemata seem to be activated because of the results of pattern recognition processes. For example, if you are sitting quietly in your office and smell smoke from a fire, schemata for reacting to that situation are activated by the data—from bottom up. The activation of the schemata results pri-

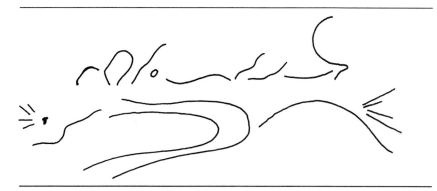

FIGURE 3-6.   Simple line drawings.

marily from the analysis of an environmental event. In such instances, schemata allow us to make sense of what we encounter and prepare us for continued analyses of the environment. Because schemata are activated by the data in the environment in such situations, this type of processing has been referred to as **data-driven** or "bottom-up" processing.

In contrast to data-driven processing is **conceptually driven** processing (see Norman, 1976; Norman & Bobrow, 1976; Roth & Frisby, 1986; Solso, 1988). In conceptually driven or top-down processing, schemata are activated by instructions ("First, look for the main idea.") or related schemata (e.g., thinking about how early memories are stored may activate your schemata for the first memories you have). Here, the schemata are *not* primarily activated by some item being perceived. Instead, schema activation results from the context in which an item is encountered (as, say, making an A+ on your first cognitive psychology test causes you to interpret much of what your instructor says as "brilliant").

As intuitively appealing as the distinction between conceptually driven and data-driven perception has been, this view has become increasingly difficult to support. Simply, the line between conceptually and data-driven processes is too fuzzy to be of much help. Rather than being concerned with whether the context of perception is top-down or bottom-up, we have chosen to emphasize the **quality** of context for learning.

As we saw in Chapter 2, context is created by both knowledge and surroundings. Without knowledge, surroundings have no meaning. Without surroundings, there is nothing to analyze for context. Although there have been several studies of the influence of context on perception, the clearest way to demonstrate the phenomenon is with some simple exercises. Look at Figure 3-6, where several line drawings are presented and take a moment to identify each. When you have finished, look at Figure 3-7 and locate the line drawings. Now label them once again.

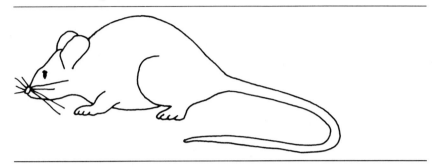

FIGURE 3-7.   Simple lines in context.

Most people have difficulty labeling the drawings shown in Figure 3-6. Few people, however, have any trouble identifying these fragments when they are presented in Figure 3-7. The mouse's ear, nose, back, stomach, and tail readily are perceived *if* they are seen in the proper context.

Examples of context are not limited to line drawings. Consider the following sentences:

*The man walked into the quiet **wood**.*

*The man threw the **wood** into the fire.*

*The man got good **wood** on the ball.*

In each instance, the word *wood* is perceived differently because of the sentence context. Of course, these contexts only work if the reader possesses appropriate schemata for a grove of trees, firewood, and a baseball bat.

Now consider, if you will, the game of baseball. Sparkling diamonds, the old horsehide, the good lumber, the hit and run, stealing. Ah, springtime! Stop thinking about baseball now and think instead of, say, crimes: the hit and run, stealing, sparkling diamonds. Okay, now think about home building and the good lumber. When you've finished that, think about the worn jacket your friend wears made from horsehide.

If everything worked as we intended, we should have been able to invoke your baseball schema with the sentence asking you to consider baseball. In this context, the *hit and run* refers to the batter hitting the ball while the base runner sprints from first base. A very different meaning for *hit and run* is constructed when your "crime" schema is activated. Finally, the schemata of "home building" and "worn jackets" also shape your perceptions.

The setting of context for perception is a critical element of effective teaching. Given an improper, confusing, or poorly organized context, students may never really understand what teachers are trying to get across. Given a clear context, perception and learning are far more likely.

As we've seen, context depends both on the students' knowledge and on the external environment. The ways in which teachers structure their classrooms and choose materials are important components in setting a context for learning. Teachers can help set an appropriate context by giving instructions ("Remember, you will be looking for bodies of water that *separate* areas of land.") or activating students' schemata ("Recall that we heard how people in southern China have developed an agriculture based on the climate. When we think about northern China, what kind of crops do you suppose are grown?"). Context also can be created by the materials teachers employ (filmstrips, slides, bulletin boards, reading materials, etc.). Beyond the importance of context, though, there are a set of important "laws of perceptual organization" that seem to govern why some perceptions are more likely to occur than others. We will examine these "laws" in the next section.

THE GESTALT LAWS.   Gestalt psychology was an important school of thought on which much of contemporary cognitive psychology is based. The school was founded by Max Wertheimer, Kurt Koffka, and Wolfgang Köhler in 1912. Their primary focus was the study of perception; as a part of their research, they formulated a set of principles or laws that seemed to govern how people assign meanings to visual stimuli. These laws are helpful to teachers in understanding why students respond to information as they do and in predicting the ways in which students will react to novel information.

The law of **continuity** holds that perceptual organization tends to preserve smooth continuities rather than abrupt changes. For example, the zigzag line in the top part of Figure 3-8 usually is perceived as a continuous line rather than as separate lines making up the sides of triangles. Similarly, the bottom part of Figure 3-8 typically is seen as two smooth lines crossing at A rather than as a pair of "V-like" shapes touching at A.

The law of **closure** states that incomplete figures tend to be seen as complete. Consider, for instance, the two drawings in Figure 3-9. Both figures are incomplete, but most people see them as a rectangle and a circle, respectively. Another example of the law of closure happens when we look up at a crescent moon and "see" the rest of the moon's disk finishing out the circle. The unlit part of the moon is, in fact, invisible and the dark part of the circle we "see" is finished by our perception.

The law of **proximity** holds that things close together are grouped together in perception. Figure 3-10 shows two rows of eight vertical lines each. In the top row, most people see the lines as four pairs of vertical lines because of the proximity of the lines in each pair. In contrast, the vertical lines in the bottom row tend to be seen as three pairs (each pair

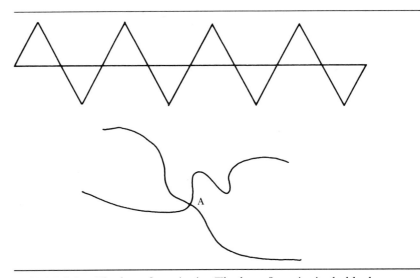

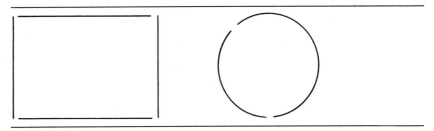

FIGURE 3-8.   The law of continuity. The law of continuity holds that perceptual organization tends to preserve smooth continuities rather than abrupt
changes.

FIGURE 3-9.   The law of closure. Incomplete figures tend to be seen as
complete.

surrounds a building), with an extra at each end of the row. Similarly, the
dots in Figure 3-11a are seen as columns because they are closer together
vertically than horizontally. Meanwhile, in Figure 3-11b, the dots are
seen as rows.

The law of **similarity** refers to the phenomenon of similar objects
tending to be perceived as related. Figure 3-12 demonstrates the law of
similarity with a set of letters. In this case, the horizontal and vertical
distances among the letters are the same, but most people perceive rows
rather than columns because the same letter is repeated in rows.

The Gestalt laws appeared in several works by Gestalt psychologists
from the mid 1910s into the 1930s. By 1933, Koffka (1933) described the
Law of Pragnanz as an overarching principle of perception from which

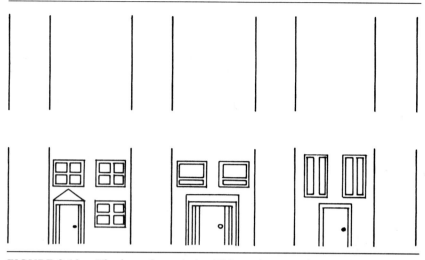

FIGURE 3-10. The law of proximity. Things close together are grouped together in perception.

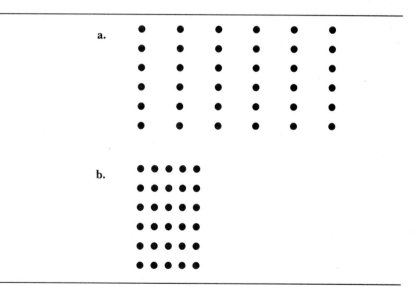

FIGURE 3-11. Columns and rows by proximity.

each of the separate laws of perception stemmed. In short, the Law of Pragnanz holds that of all the possible organizations that could be perceived in a stimulus array, the one that actually will occur will be the one that possesses the best, simplest, and most stable form. In these terms,

```
A  A  A  A  A
C  C  C  C  C
F  F  F  F  F
G  G  G  G  G
Z  Z  Z  Z  Z

A  C  F  G  Z
A  C  F  G  Z
A  C  F  G  Z
A  C  F  G  Z
A  C  F  G  Z
```

FIGURE 3-12.   The law of similarity. Similar objects tend to be perceived as related.

Koffka would have argued that the rows of letters in Figure 3-12, the three pairs of columns in Figure 3-11a, and so on are perceived rather than their alternatives because they are the "best" forms.

The logic behind the Law of Pragnanz (as well as its subordinate laws) has been disputed (see Roth & Frisby, 1986), but the general validity of these perceptual laws remains unaltered. More recent views of organization in perception, however, allow us to speculate more directly about why these Gestalt laws are valid. In the next section we examine some of these views, but first it is appropriate to briefly describe work done on the Gestalt principles by Jean Piaget.

PIAGET AND PERCEPTION.   As a byproduct of his work on cognitive development, Piaget also focused on perceptual development (Piaget, 1969; see also Daehler & Bukatko, 1985). He did not argue that there is a one-to-one correspondence between cognitive and perceptual development, but he did propose that the two were closely linked. One of his primary examples of this linkage was the way in which children's perceptions tend to become less **centered** as they develop.

For Piaget, **cognitive centration** referred to the tendency to focus attention and thinking on a single dimension of a problem or situation. Cognitive centration is seen clearly in Piaget's conservation tasks such as the one pictured in Figure 3-13. Here, children under about the age of 6 or so are asked if there are more wrapped candies (row A) than lemon drops (row B). Typically, children of this age state that there are the same number of the two types of candies. However, when we ask these children whether there are more wrapped candies in the first row or lemon drops in the third row (row C), most respond that there are more lemon

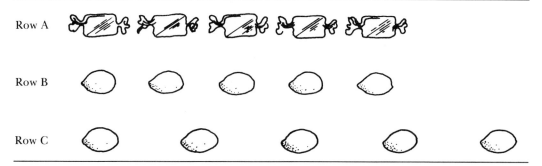

Row A

Row B

Row C

FIGURE 3-13.   Cognitive centration.

drops. From Piaget's perspective, these children are focusing only on a single dimension of the problem—the length of the rows. Because they are centered on length, they cannot coordinate two sources of information, length and number of items.

Similar to cognitive centration, **perceptual centration** is the tendency to focus on only one aspect of a stimulus array. Piaget postulated that children who showed cognitive centration would be more likely than other people to show perceptual centration, especially that described by the Gestalt rules. Indeed, Piaget's research demonstrated that young children are especially susceptible to the laws of continuity, closure, proximity, and similarity. Children find it difficult to see the zigzag lines in Figure 3-8a as a series of triangles, even when they are guided to this by adults. Similarly, children seem more prone than adults to see incomplete figures as complete. Further, they have great difficulty not centering on the kinds of proximity shown in Figures 3-10 and 3-11.

Children's perceptual centration is important to teachers, especially those who work with early elementary school children. Besides setting a context for learning, teachers also must be aware of the Gestalt rules and how centration is likely to occur. Simply, young children tend to center on single aspects of their perceptions and need guidance in developing perceptual flexibility.

RECENT CONCEPTIONS OF ORGANIZATION IN PERCEPTION.   As helpful as the Gestalt laws are for describing perceptual phenomena, they have had limited value in explaining *why* they work (Roth & Frisby, 1986). The Gestalt approach cannot, for example, explain why the shape in Figure 3-14a is seen as a circle in Figure 3-14b. Recent research, as might be expected, has examined such problems with an emphasis on the role of context in perception (e.g., Pomerantz, 1985; Roth & Frisby, 1986). The oval shape in Figure 3-14a is seen as a circle in Figure 3-14b because observers' bicycle schemata contain information telling them

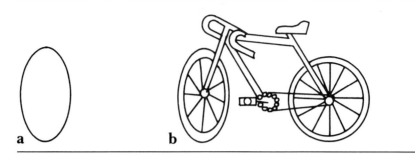

FIGURE 3-14.   A figure in two contexts.

that bicycles have two round wheels. When the bicycle is identified, the front wheel (the shape from Figure 3-14a) is perceived as being turned at an angle, and so a different perspective of the circle is seen.

Roth and Frisby (1986) argue that the Gestalt laws operate on the basis of context. For example, the law of closure allows us to see the middle shape in the left side of Figure 3-15 as a B. However, the law of closure does not seem to operate on this same shape in the right side of Figure 3-15. In this context, most people see the shape as the number 13 rather than the letter B. These differences in perception clearly are due to context effects. The shape is embedded in familiar contexts (the reader's schema for either letters or numbers is activated) and the law of closure operates in the A–B–C row, but it does not operate in the equally familiar 12–13–14 row. In this schema theory perspective, then, the Gestalt laws are seen as manifestations of the impact of context on perception.

IMPLICATIONS OF RESEARCH ON ORGANIZATION IN PERCEPTION. There are important age-related changes in perception, which were highlighted in our discussion of the Gestalt laws of perception and how they described perceptual phenomena. In particular, we saw that young children have trouble decentering on perceptual input. Instead, they tend to focus on just one aspect of environmental information. These age-related differences also are reflective of knowledge-based differences. That is, older, better-versed students are more likely to be able to attend to multiple aspects of environmental information than less-knowledgeable students. For example, third-year students in high school

A BC   12 B 14

FIGURE 3-15.   Context effects in perception.

French are far better able to attend to pronunciation, dialect, grammar, and proper usage in critiquing a speech than students in beginning French.

Especially with beginning or less-knowledgeable students, teachers must carefully guide students' perceptions to critical information (Brown et al., 1988). For example, if a language teacher is working on dialogue with students, the teacher will need to guide students' attention to relevant aspects of the discourse being taught, including inflections and intonation. Without such guidance, the appropriate perceptions will not take place.

Attention

Interwoven with perception is attention, a person's allocation of cognitive resources to the tasks at hand. In general, the research on attention shows that human beings are severely limited in the number of things they can pay attention to simultaneously (e.g., Friedman, Polson, & DaFoe, 1988; Halpain, Glover, & Harvey, 1985). Although there *are* individual differences in this regard—some people can do more things at the same time than others (see Friedman et al., 1988)—even the most able person can perform only a limited number of tasks simultaneously. This limitation makes what students attend to a significant part of instructional effectiveness. Simply, that which is not attended to will not be perceived (see Fisher et al., 1988, for a discussion).

In most school settings, children can select only a few of the things going on around them for thorough analysis. A sixth-grader might begin to pay careful attention to her teacher's explanation of an arithmetic problem, but then start listening to her friend's description of a recently purchased sweater. Her attention might then wander to the aroma drifting into the room from the cafeteria and later to the snow falling outside. Hence, the explanation for how to work the new set of problems may not be remembered. At any given moment, of course, a great deal of other environmental information is *not* being selected, such as the papers posted on the bulletin boards, the materials at a "reading center," and the comments of two boys behind her concerning a recent football game.

How does attention operate? Does the selection of what to attend to happen very early, before much processing of information has occurred, or does it happen later, after a great deal of information has been obtained? To help answer this question, we will review three models of attention, examine the kinds of tasks students are asked to perform, describe cognitive skills that reduce the demands on students' attention, and then review the implications of research on attention for teachers.

Research on this question sheds considerable light on how students allocate attention.

Broadbent's Early Selection Model

The first theories of attention proposed that selection occurred very early in the analysis of information (Cohen, in press; Nusbaum & Schwab, 1986). Characteristic of early selection models was Broadbent's (1958). Broadbent proposed that only a very limited processing capacity was available for dealing with information in the sensory registers. Because little capacity was available, he reasoned that selective attention was caused by the limited available resources being used on some small component of environmental information. He further argued that any information not attended to would go unprocessed and be totally lost.

Broadbent speculated that predetermined physical characteristics of environmental stimuli are the basis for the selection process. In this view, students might process sounds from a specific voice (the teacher's) or attend to certain aspects of material on the blackboard, but not both. Figure 3-16 shows a simple schematic of Broadbent's model.

Although contemporary research has shown early selection models to be somewhat simplistic, Broadbent's model generated a great deal of work in the 1950s and 1960s. Most of this research employed what are referred to as **dichotic listening tasks.** These tasks still are important in attention research and mirror many classroom situations.

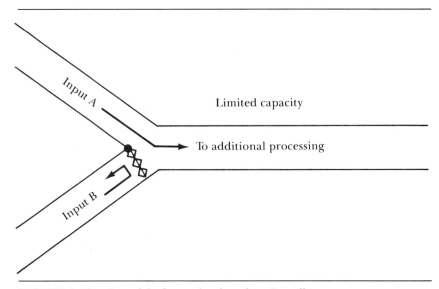

FIGURE 3-16.   A model of attention based on Broadbent.

Dichotic listening tasks take advantage of multiple channel-recording possibilities. A tape is prepared so that it carries two messages, one to be delivered through each channel. Then, experimental subjects listen to the tape through headphones. One message comes to one ear, the second to the other ear. Typically, subjects are asked to shadow (repeat) the message being presented to one of the two ears. This shadowing is used to ensure that the subjects indeed are attending to one of the messages and not the other.

Dichotic listening tasks are roughly comparable to what happens in a classroom when, say, a student listens to what a classmate has to say and not the teacher's explanation. Studies employing dichotic listening tasks almost uniformly have found that subjects are able to remember very little of the information presented to their unshadowed ear except for some very basic properties of the unshadowed signal, such as whether the voice was male or female, the general pitch of the voice, and so on (Nusbaum & Schwab, 1986). Attention seems highly focused.

When people encounter too much information to process with their limited resources, Broadbent postulated, their processing is directed to parts of the environmental input. Unprocessed information, from this perspective, is lost. Broadbent also argued that people possess a "switching mechanism" that allows them to switch quickly from one source of environmental input to another and thereby seem to be able to process two sources of information at the same time. "Switching ability" is limited, however, and becomes less functional as the information in any channel becomes more complex. In other words, switching might explain how people seem to be able to listen to the radio and work a crossword puzzle at the same time, but if the complexity of one of these tasks is increased (a lecture on perception rather than music from a radio), switching back and forth would be far more difficult and ultimately break down altogether.

Despite the general relevance of Broadbent's ideas, our everyday experiences and recent research both suggest that early selection models present an incomplete picture of attention. Consider, for example, the well-known "cocktail party" phenomenon. In this instance, a person may have all of her attention focused on an intense conversation with someone—cognitively shadowing the other person's arguments, as it were—but still look around when she hears her name mentioned across the room. Similarly, think about the undergraduate immersed in his studies on the third floor of a house who hears the word *pizza* spoken by another person on the ground floor.

Anne Triesman performed a study in 1964 in which she employed the traditional dichotic listening task. Her study differed from previous work, however, in that she switched messages from ear to ear in midexperiment. Subjects were asked to shadow their right ears. Rather than presenting a consistent message, though, she switched messages on the subjects so that the message into the left ear now was appearing in the right ear and vice versa. The subjects were not informed that this would happen and instead merely were instructed to shadow one ear.

If Broadbent's model were correct, not much should have happened. That is, subjects who shadowed their right ears should simply have continued to repeat what they heard without missing a beat. In fact, Triesman found that subjects occasionally switched the ear they shadowed when the message shifted. That is, they followed the *meaning* of the material rather than its source. The inescapable conclusion from this outcome is that the subjects had to be processing at least a little bit of the meaning of the message coming to the unshadowed ear. Because they could do this, Broadbent's model could not be wholly correct. Not surprisingly, one of the two major alternatives to Broadbent's model has been offered by Triesman.

Triesman's Attenuated Processing Model

Anne Triesman and her colleagues (Triesman, 1964, 1969; Triesman & Geffen, 1967; Triesman & Gelade, 1980; Triesman & Riley, 1969; Triesman & Schmidt, 1982; Triesman, Squire, & Green, 1974) created a model of attention selection that has come to be known as an **attenuated processing model.** Similar to Broadbent, Triesman argued that there is a limited capacity for processing incoming information. However, she hypothesized that different channels of information may use this capacity simultaneously. Because capacity is limited, though, some channels receive fairly complete processing, and others get only reduced or attenuated processing. This attenuated processing is enough to account for the cocktail party phenomenon and for the results of dichotic listening studies in which messages are shifted from ear to ear. (A depiction of Triesman's model appears in Figure 3-17.)

To test her model, Triesman (Triesman & Geffen, 1967; Triesman et

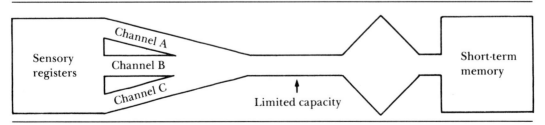

FIGURE 3-17.   A model of attention based on Triesman.

al., 1974) performed a clever set of experiments. In one, subjects performed a dichotic listening task in which they shadowed one ear and signaled when they heard certain key words in *either* ear. If the subjects could recognize none of the key words in the unshadowed ear, the results would support Broadbent's model. If subjects did equally well in identifying the key words in both ears, however, a full processing model (see below) would be supported. To confirm the attenuated processing model, subjects would have to identify most of the key words in the shadowed ear and a smaller portion of them in the unshadowed ear.

The results strongly supported the attenuated processing model. Nearly 90 percent of the key words in the shadowed ear were identified and almost 10 percent of the key words in the unshadowed ear were identified. More recent work (see Nusbaum & Schwab, 1986) also indicates that the pattern observed by Triesman and her associates is reliable. These data ruled out the early selection model and seemed to dismiss the full processing model. However, a closer examination of research on the full processing model revealed some unresolved issues.

Shiffrin's Full Processing Model

R. M. Shiffrin, working from the base provided by Atkinson and Shiffrin's model of human information processing (Atkinson & Schiffrin, 1968), has developed what may be referred to as the **full processing model of attention** (Shiffrin, 1976; Shiffrin & Schneider, 1977). In this model, the selection of which stimulus to attend does not occur until *after* the pattern recognition processes have been completed. Further, Shiffrin presumed that pattern recognition processes occur automatically and without conscious attention (unless, of course, the person is trying to puzzle through an ambiguous stimulus array). These processes go to completion when either the pattern is recognized or no recognition is possible. The results of pattern recognition then are passed on to working memory. (*Consciousness* is a close approximation of the meaning of working memory in the current context.) When pattern recognition is complete, selection of what to attend to occurs in the working memory.

In the full processing model, the limitation on attention occurs in **memory,** not in the perceptual processes. It is the inability to retain all the perceptual analyses we perform that limits our attention.

Interestingly, the full processing model is supported by research results that seem just as compelling as those that support the attenuated processing model (see Nusbaum & Schwab, 1986). For example, Shiffrin, Pisoni, and Casteneda-Mendez (1974) presented their subjects with white noise (white noise is random background noise) over their headphones. Embedded in the white noise were consonants (K, D, etc.) that the subjects were asked to recognize. As one element of the study, conditions in the experiment were varied so that subjects either (1) knew which ear the consonants would be heard in or (2) did not know. If subjects' performance in recognizing the consonants was poorer when they did not know which ear the consonants were coming to, the results would support the attenuation model. That is, the attenuation model would predict that knowing which ear the consonants were coming to would allow subjects to focus their attention on the relevant ear and thereby improve their performance. In contrast, if there was no difference between the two conditions (that is, if knowing which ear the consonants were coming to made no difference), the results would support the full processing model.

The results of the Shiffrin et al. study supported the full processing model: The rate at which subjects could detect consonants was independent of the amount of information (one channel or two) they were monitoring. Other studies have confirmed these results (see Posner & Boies, 1971; Shiffrin & Gardner, 1972; Shiffrin & Schneider 1977; Sorkin & Pohlmann, 1973; Wickens, 1980). The fact that strong evidence seems to support both the attenuated and the full processing models is a problem. Can both theories be correct? Are both wrong in some way? It turns out that this problem is resolved by examining the kinds of tasks people perform in studies of attention.

Cognitive Tasks: Resource-Limited and Data-Limited

The problem of different studies supporting the attenuated processing and full processing models of attention can be resolved if we make a distinction in the kinds of cognitive tasks people perform (Fisher et al., 1988). We may refer to some tasks as data-limited and others as resource-limited (see Norman & Bobrow, 1976; Nusbaum & Schwab, 1986). In this perspective, a learner's **cognitive resources** are those things that may be used to complete a task: memory capacity, number of channels of input, cognitive effort, and so on. As we have seen, our cognitive resources are limited—only so much effort and memory capacity are available at any given gime. When all a person's cognitive resources are being devoted to one task (e.g., filling out federal income tax forms), there may be no resources left for other tasks (hearing a daughter's question about her schoolwork).

In this context, then, **resource-limited** tasks are those in which performance will improve if more resources are shifted to them. To return to the example in the previous paragraph, a parent's performance in listening to a child's question will improve if the parent shifts resources to that task. Similarly, performance in reading this chapter will be poor if most cognitive resources are devoted to watching television, worrying about other classes, or thinking about lunch. If these resources are reallocated to reading, however, reading comprehension will improve.

Data-limited tasks, on the other hand, are those in which performance is limited by the quality of data available in the task. Above some minimal amount of resources needed to perform the task in the first place, allocating more resources to a data-limited task will not improve performance. Trying to make sense of a poor-quality tape recording is an example of a data-limited task. If the tape is bad, after a certain amount of resources have been assigned to the task, no amount of additional effort will help. For many students, following complicated instructions or "analyzing" Shakespearean sonnets may fit into the category of data-limited tasks—no matter how many resources they assign to the job, performance will not improve.

Besides helping us think about instructional events, the distinction between resource-limited and data-limited tasks also helps us make sense of the conflicting results of studies on the allocation of attention. Indeed, the results of various studies in the area have depended less on their theoretical assumptions than on the type of tasks they employed (Nusbaum & Schwab, 1986). Triesman and Geffen (1967), for example, employed a resource-limited task, whereas Shiffrin et al. (1974) used a data-limited task.

As you recall, in Triesman and Geffen's study, subjects shadowed the message coming to one ear (a task requiring a great many resources) and simultaneously listened for target words in one ear or the other (a task that also requires a great many resources). Basically, Triesman and Geffen's results were due to the fact that most of their subjects' resources were devoted to the shadowing task. Very few resources remained available for the monitoring task, and so performance was poor. If more resources could have been devoted to monitoring key words (by, say, eliminating the need to shadow the message), subjects' performance would have improved. Overall, then, we may conclude that Triesman and Geffen found support for the attenuated processing model because they used a resource-limited task in their study.

In contrast, Shiffrin et al. employed a data-limited task. Recall that Shiffrin et al. had subjects listen for consonants against a background of white noise. Since the subjects in this study only had to identify the sound of consonants rather than deal with meaning (as was the case in Triesman and Geffen's study), relatively few resources were necessary. When subjects had to listen in both ears for the consonants rather than in just one ear, they still had considerable resources left. Assigning more resources could not improve performance. So, Shiffrin et al.'s results support the full processing model because of the type of task they used— a data-limited task.

From the perspective of resource- and data-limited tasks, we see that students have limited resources to allocate to tasks (Fisher et al., 1988). As long as the tasks leave some unused resources, students can take on additional tasks. If students are engaged in a resource-limited task, their performance may improve by shifting more resources to it. Thus, when students perform tasks that do not use all their resources (e.g., listening to a teacher read the correct answers on a quiz, doodling on a note pad, and monitoring a nearby conversation in case baseball comes up), they appear to be able to completely possess all the available information before selection decisions are required. In contrast, when we involve students in tasks that require more resources than they have available (e.g., when they are trying to remember a complicated explanation for how to complete an assignment), performance will suffer as students must reach the limits of their cognitive resources.

Automatic Processes

Listen as a capable fifth-grader talks through the solution of a division problem (963/7). "Okay. Seven into nine goes once, seven under nine. That's two, bring down the six. It'll go three times, that's twenty-one, leaves five. That's fifty-three. OK. That's seven remainder, uh, four! How'd I do?"

One of the interesting aspects of this student's performance is how much of it was **automatic**—that is, how much did not require conscious attention. If you'll look back over her protocol, you can see that she didn't seem to have to think about how to start solving the problem. There was some thought about where to place the seven, but then subtraction took place without thinking about it. Throughout the solution of the problem, many steps were performed without appearing to require any conscious effort. Automatic cognitive processes require few resources. (See the discussion of Neves and Anderson in Chapter 2.)

The notion of automatic processes, or **automaticity,** was first conceived of by Neisser (1967) and has been elaborated by LaBerge and Samuels (1974), Shiffrin and Schneider (1977), Neves and Anderson (1981), and Nusbaum and Schwab (1986). Although there are differences of opinion concerning the specifics of automatic processes, it is generally agreed that they (1) require little or no attention for their execution and (2) are acquired only through extended practice.

The existence of automatic processes helps us explain why people are able to perform different tasks simultaneously. Examples of automatic processes are decoding by good readers, shifting gears by accomplished drivers, punctuation of sentences by skilled writers, and finger movements by expert typists. Each of these processes appears to require few cognitive resources (e.g., being able to downshift into second while also talking to your passenger, watching traffic, and making a turn) and no conscious attention (how often have you thought about the process of shifting gears while doing it?).

Since automatic processes are a part of so many cognitive skills (reading, mathematics, etc.), we do not spend more time on them here but defer to later discussions of automaticity in specific chapters dealing with these skill areas. Still, we can see how automatic processes are determinants of how students allocate their attention to tasks. For example, if the student in our example could not perform most of the processes of division automatically, resources could not be devoted to making estimates and evaluating. Similarly, good readers can devote their attention to reading for meaning because decoding the words no longer requires much in the way of cognitive resources. Poor readers, in contrast, may have trouble with meaning because so many of their resources have to be used for decoding words (LeBerge & Samuels, 1974; Samuels, 1988).

Implications of Attention Research for Teaching

Teachers need to remember that students have limited attentional resources. This limitation makes teachers' choice of tasks for children and the management of their attention critical. Many school-related tasks demand all of a student's attention. Students cannot listen to the stereo, watch television, talk on the telephone, eat a piece of chocolate cake, and do their homework simultaneously without the homework suffering as a result. Similarly, students cannot talk among themselves in class, doodle, and read the history text in order to answer study questions without hurting their performance. The challenge is to structure the classroom environment so that students' attention is focused on important tasks. Teachers also must help students learn to manage their studying behaviors.

Automatic processes allow students to use fewer cognitive resources in completing the same task. Teachers need to remember that cognitive processes become automatic only after extensive practice. For example, true automatic decoding in reading requires hundreds of hours of practice. Of course, to keep students on task during the extensive practice needed to make any process automatic, the exercises must be kept reasonably enjoyable. If not, students will lose the motivation necessary to keep them going until they have attained mastery.

Summary

In this chapter we reviewed the processes of perception and attention. Perception is the assignment of meaning to incoming stimuli; attention refers to the allocation of cognitive resources to the tasks at hand.

Perception begins with the sense receptors. Each of our senses apparently has a sensory register. However, the majority of research has focused on the visual sensory register (icon) and the auditory sensory register (echo). The sensory registers are brief repositories of unprocessed information. They allow analyses of incoming stimuli to occur at the outset of the perception process.

Perception involves pattern recognition processes in which a person's knowledge is used to make decisions about the meaning of the stimuli. The exact mechanisms of pattern recognition are not clear, but many aspects of perception conform to the use of prototypes, distinctive features, and structural descriptions.

What is certain is that knowledge plays a powerful role in perception. Expectations and context affect perception. In addition, our perceptions seem to be governed by a set of laws first derived by the Gestalt psychologists.

There are several views of how attention is directed. The frame of reference of data-limited and resource-limited tasks lets us see that both the attenuated processing and the full processing models have explanatory strengths, depending on the kinds of tasks students are required to perform.

Accurate perception, however, is not our ultimate goal as teachers. A next step is helping students *remember* what is perceived and to build more complex understandings. In the next chapter, we focus on the structure of human memory.

CHAPTER 4

Memory: Structures and Models

Depending on the moment, our memory—the register of our experiences—can be a source of frustration, of pain, of delight, or of wonder. When we want to access it, often we cannot. Sometimes, when we wish memories would fade, they will not. At unaccountable moments, sweet dreams may find their way into our consciousness. Now and then, our sure recall of figure or fact may allow us to act with uncommon confidence and authority.

For as long as we have thought about "human nature," that aspect called "memory" has intrigued us. The scientific study of memory is a recent matter, however, tracing back only a little more than a century to the beginnings of psychology as a systematic, experimental science. Most remarkable among the early studies of memory were those of Hermann Ebbinghaus (1850–1909), the first of which was published in 1885. Ebbinghaus's genius was to reduce the study of memory to its most elementary forms. What Ebbinghaus studied was rote memory. The materials on which he tested retention were the simplest of all possible units—lists of nonmeaningful syllables, so-called nonsense syllables (e.g., FOH, TAF). "Savings" in relearning was the measure of memory; the fewer the number of repetitions of a list needed to achieve errorless recall, the greater the level of memory inferred. Of particular interest to Ebbinghaus was how memory decreased over time. To explore this variable, Ebbinghaus attempted relearning after intervals ranging from 20 minutes to a month.

The tradition of memory research first begun by Ebbinghaus dominated the study of memory for nearly a century (see Chapters 1 and 2; also see MacLeod, 1988). In general, this tradition was based on the following assumptions (Jenkins, 1974): (1) that words were the primary mental units of language, (2) that when units were used together they became linked and were chained into larger units, (3) that complex behaviors and patterns of thought were assembled from simple units, and (4) that the mechanisms that produced learning and memory largely were automatic.

Today, however, our conception of what constitutes the valid study of memory has been broadened considerably. Memory theories based on rote memorization and extrapolation of basic principles from simple to complex behavior largely have been supplanted by those that have attempted to describe complex, meaningful cognitive processes more directly (Baars, 1986). In the past two decades, especially, memory theorists have made immense strides in describing the nature of knowledge and in developing theories that permit predictions about the nature of learning, memory, and utilization of meaningful information.

In this chapter, we introduce you to current conceptualizations of memory and to key concepts and principles of a cognitive view of memory processes. We begin with a discussion of several fundamental distinctions theorists have proposed concerning the overall nature of knowledge and its storage in memory. We then move to a description of the variety of units cognitive theorists have proposed as "building blocks of cognition." Then, in the concluding section of this chapter, we present several recent models of memory organization, each of which has been devised by memory theorists in an attempt to best capture the overall functioning of human memory.

Fundamental Distinctions in the Study of Memory

As cognitive theorists began more and more to grapple with issues in the learning and recall of **meaningful** materials, they quickly faced questions about the nature of knowledge and how it is stored in memory. Are there basic differences, for instance, between "knowing" something and "knowing how to do" something? Does personal experience lead to different storage and retrieval than the more abstracted general knowledge of, say, subject areas such as history and chemistry? Is memory for language different than memory for images? Are there differences between memory for events just experienced and those experienced some time in the past? Questions such as these have led to a number of distinctions. Among the most useful and enduring have been those between episodic and semantic memory, between declarative and procedural knowledge, between language-based and imagery-based systems in memory, and between short-term and long-term memory.

Episodic versus Semantic Memory

In proposing a distinction between episodic and semantic memory, Tulving (1972) argued for the utility of distinguishing between the traces of personal experience, on one hand, and general knowledge, on the other. Specifically, **episodic memory** refers to storage and retrieval of personally dated, autobiographical experiences (Tulving, 1983, 1985). Recall of childhood experiences, recollection of the details of a conversation with a friend, and remembering what you had for breakfast all would fall within the realm of episodic memory. The critical feature of episodic memory is the existence of a "personal tag," and the basis for retrieval is an association with a particular time or place. Obviously, a great deal of what we must recall in order to function effectively in our daily lives is of an episodic nature.

Semantic memory, in contrast, refers to memory of general concepts and principles and their associations. Unlike episodic memory, semantic memory is not linked to a particular time and place. In our semantic memory is such information as the fact that lemons are yellow and that computers contain chips. Semantic memory contains the **organized** knowledge we have about words and concepts and how they are associated. For instance, a subject area such as English literature or American history represents a vast body of semantic information that we (as we become more expert in the area) encode, organize, and have available for retrieval. Recalling word meanings, geographic locations, and chemical formulas similarly requires searches of semantic memory.

Although the psychological validity of the episodic–semantic distinction has been criticized (e.g., McKoon & Ratcliff, 1986), it continues to be useful in helping us think about the different types of information we and our students must remember. On one hand, the episodic aspect of our memories must function well enough for us to locate ourselves in time and space and have a reasonably accurate record of our experiences. At the same time, we have to have available a general knowledge base in order to think and reason effectively (see Chapter 2). Of course, the episodic–semantic distinction does not presuppose two physically separate systems in the brain, but rather is a conceptual distinction useful to researchers and practitioners.

Tulving (1972; see also Tulving, 1985) pointed out that the vast majority of early laboratory studies of memory involving recall of words and syllables, which might superficially appear to be classed as studies of semantic memory, in fact are studies of episodic memory. When a research subject is asked to recognize whether the word *book* has been presented earlier as part of a list in an experiment, that person is not being asked to reveal semantic knowledge about the word *book* (e.g., its definition or use), but to remember if it has been presented at a particular time and place within the experiment. Although considerable research interest has continued on the topic of episodic memory (e.g, Neisser, 1982; Rabinowitz & Craik, 1986), there has been a growing emphasis in cognitive psychology on topics of semantic memory—how fields of semantic knowledge are organized and searched, and specific information retrieved.

Declarative versus Procedural Knowledge

A second important distinction in the study of memory is between declarative and procedural knowledge (J. R. Anderson, 1976, 1983, 1987; Woltz, 1988). As mentioned in Chapter 2, **declarative knowledge** is knowledge about facts and things, knowledge that *something is the case*. In contrast, **procedural knowledge** is knowledge about *how to perform* certain cognitive activities, such as reasoning, decision making, and problem solving.

One important use for the declarative–procedural distinction is to describe the kinds of learning students may achieve. A novice student in a teacher education program, for instance, may memorize principles of classroom management (e.g, "Allow students to make value judgments.") as declarative knowledge, but he may have little or no notion of how these principles actually would be used in effective teaching (procedural knowledge).

Although it has not been described with the terms *declarative knowledge* and *procedural knowledge,* the declarative–procedural distinction has been implicit in the work of a number of learning theorists—for instance, in Robert Gagne's hierarchical analysis of learning (1977) and, earlier, in the work of Benjamin Bloom and his associates (Bloom, Englehart, Furst, Hill, & Krathwohl, 1956). In Bloom's analysis, for instance, a contrast was drawn between lower levels of learning (i.e., knowledge, comprehension), in which facts, concepts, and rules are learned and understood, and "higher-order" learning (i.e., application, analysis, synthesis, and evaluation), in which knowledge is used as part of higher-level cognitive processes.

Of course, not all procedural knowledge is "higher-order" knowledge based on more fundamental declarative knowledge. Procedural knowledge can be quite simple and only implicitly linked with declarative knowledge. A young child, for instance, who remembers how to unlatch the door, turn off a faucet, brush her teeth, and open a book is showing her recall of procedural knowledge.

Also, procedural knowledge often is "automatized"—we often begin "doing" without any apparent conscious attention to what we are doing or why we are doing it. In a lecture class at a university, for example, most students will enter the class, find a seat, take out a notebook, and begin taking notes with little or no conscious attention to the task. Similarly, as we read, decoding words and comprehending the meaning of what we are reading ordinarily occurs quite automatically (see Chapter 3). Sometimes, however, our searches of declarative knowledge come at least partially under conscious control. ("Who IS the author of *The Polar Express?* Let's see, wasn't that book a Caldecott Medal winner? That guy also wrote *Jumanji.* Just give me a minute; I'll think of his name!")

In most learning, of course, there is an interplay between declarative and procedural knowledge. A concert pianist learning a new song by Domenico Scarlatti, for instance, may search her memory for declarative knowledge about that composer's preferred method of executing certain embellishments such as the appoggiatura, mordent, and trill—declarative knowledge that will be utilized in the development of procedural knowledge. Conversely, procedural knowledge has undeniable impact on declarative knowledge. Like most experts, our pianist has procedural knowledge about how she best recalls information about composers and their works and will search her declarative knowledge accordingly. Yet another cluster of procedural knowledge—her skills in performing—enhances and gives substance to the declarative knowledge she possesses (e.g., "Scarlatti intended for the mordents to be played according to the basic tempo of the passage. That would mean that they should be thirty-second notes here").

In most school learning, similarly, there will be goals for the acquisition of both declarative and procedural knowledge. As we have argued in Chapter 2, one important goal of education is the development of relatively large, stable, and interrelated sets of declarative knowledge. As educators, we expect students will be "knowledgeable." At the same time, however, we place a considerable premium on knowing "how to." For the practitioner, usable knowledge is critical. Especially in applied programs such as journalism, architecture, teaching, business, and medicine, procedural knowledge is an important outcome of the educational process.

Verbal and Imaginal Representation in Memory

"A picture is worth a thousand words." Although the validity of this aphorism may be debatable, there is little doubt that we humans have extraordinary capabilities for remembering information about visual events. For example, Standing, Conezio, and Haber (1970), in an early study of visual recognition memory, showed subjects 2,500 slides for 10 seconds each. Recognition, estimated from a test on a subset of these slides, was over 90 percent! In another study by Standing (1973), participants viewed an even larger number of pictures—10,000—over a five-day period and then were given a recognition memory test that sampled these and other pictures. Based on their performance on the test, Standing estimated subjects' memory at 6,600 pictures, remembered in at least enough detail to distinguish these pictures from ones they had not seen before. Given evidence such as this, there is little doubt that pictorial information can be represented in our memories quite well. Certainly, our subjective experiences would tell us so. Most of us easily can conjure up an image of a book, a soaring bird, a train wreck, or a walk in the woods.

One of the main contributions of cognitive psychology has been a revitalization of interest in the study of mental imagery. Once largely banished from experimental psychology as subjective, mentalistic, and therefore unscientific (Watson, 1924), imagery has become a significant feature of the work of a number of cognitive psychologists.

One such psychologist, Alan Paivio (1971, 1986b), has proposed that information can be represented in two fundamentally distinct systems, one suited to verbal information and the other to images. The **verbal coding system** is adapted for linguistically based information and emphasizes verbal associations. According to Paivio, words, sentences, the content of conversations, and stories are coded within this system. In contrast, nonverbal information is stored within the **imaginal coding system.** Pictures, sensations, and sounds are coded here (Paivio, Clark, & Lambert, 1988).

Paivio's theory has been called a **dual coding theory,** in that incoming information can be coded within one or both of the systems. Although the systems are separate, they are strongly interconnected in their impact on the recallability of information. To the extent that information can be coded into both systems, memory will be enhanced, whereas information coded only in the verbal system or imaginal system will be less well recalled. In Paivio's view, the verbal and nonverbal codes basically are functionally independent and "contribute additively to memory performance" (1986b, p. 226). Paivio also hypothesizes that nonverbal components of memory traces generally are stronger than verbal memories.

Much of Paivio's early work was devoted to demonstrating the effects of the abstractness of materials on its memorability and relating these results to dual coding theory. For instance, some words (bird, star, ball, desk) have **concrete** referents and presumably are highly imaginable. Thus, when presented with such words, both the verbal (e.g., the linguistic representation of the word *bird,* its pronunciation, its meaning) and the imaginal (an image of a bird soaring) representations are activated simultaneously. Other words, however, are more **abstract** and far less readily imaginable (e.g., *aspect, value, unable*). These words, although they activate the verbal coding system, are hypothesized to activate the nonverbal system only minimally. In Paivio's view, memory for abstract materials should be poorer since such materials are represented only within a single system. Pictures, since they tend to be automatically labeled, should be more memorable than words (Paivio, 1986a) because, although pictures are automatically labeled (and hence dual-coded), words, even concrete ones, are not necessarily automatically imaged (see also Svengas & Johnson, 1988).

In a large number of studies, Paivio and his associates (e.g., Paivio, Yuille, & Madigan, 1968; Paivio, 1971; Paivio & Csapo, 1975) have demonstrated the beneficial effects of imagery on learning and memory, consistent with his predictions. Words rated high in imagery have been shown to be better remembered in free recall, in serial learning (where a series of words must be recalled in order), and in paired-associate learning (in which the "associate" of a word must be recalled when the word is presented). Similarly, instructions to subjects to "form images" also have been shown to enhance memory.

Mental Rotation   An intriguing set of studies carried out by Roger Shepard and his associates has provided additional information about the nature of mental images, their distinctiveness from verbal information, and the role they play in cognition (see Shepard, in press). In an early study, Shepard (1966) had subjects think about such questions as the number of windows in their house. He noted that the time required to produce an answer increased with the number of windows counted, consistent with the idea that individuals actually were mentally manipulating some sort of image. Further, subjects described themselves as taking a "mental tour" of their house in order to respond to this question. At least subjectively, there was a strong impression of mentally picturing—"looking at" or scanning—images (Kosslyn, 1981).

In a later series of studies, Shepard and his co-workers (Shepard, 1975; Shepard & Chipman, 1970; Shepard & Metzler, 1971) showed that mental images generated by subjects underlie a number of cognitive operations. In one set of studies (Shepard & Metzler, 1971), for example, subjects were asked to judge whether three-dimensional objects presented in different orientations were identical (see Figure 4-1). The fascinating result was that the time required to make the judgments increased linearly with the extent of rotation required. That is, it appeared that subjects were mentally rotating the objects (see also Cooper & Shepard, 1973) in order to make the comparison; the greater the rotation, the longer it took to make a judgment.

More recently, Stephen Kosslyn and his colleagues (see Kosslyn, 1980, 1981, 1987) have demonstrated other interesting effects. For example, in one study, subjects were asked to memorize a map of an island on which such objects as a tree, rock, or hut were depicted at varying locations (see

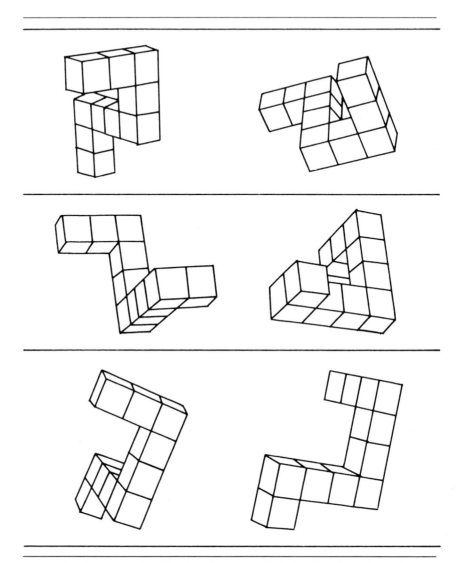

FIGURE 4-1. Examples of pairs of patterns differing in orientation. These pairs of figures are similar to those used by Shepard and Metzler (1971) in their study of the mental rotation of three-dimensional objects.

Figure 4-2). After the map was committed to memory, they were asked to focus on a named object on the map. They then were given the name of a second object and told to locate it by imagining a black speck moving in a straight line from the first object to the second. Objects were, of course, varying distances from one another on the map. If the mental image is being scanned, as Kosslyn hypothesized, then time required to move

FIGURE 4-2.   An island map.

from one object to the next should vary directly with the distance on the image. In fact, this was what Kosslyn and his associates found. "Distant" objects took longer to reach than "near" objects, demonstrating that images, like pictures, contain information about the spatial relations among objects.

Using subjects' ability to form images of different sizes (e.g., a large rabbit versus a very tiny rabbit) and at different locations (e.g, nearby versus far away), Kosslyn also has shown that when subjects are asked to verify certain features of mental images (e.g., "Do rabbits have whiskers?"), details of "small" images (e.g., a small rabbit) take longer to verify than those of "large" images (a large rabbit). According to Kosslyn, such evidence points to the conclusion that images have a "grain" or resolution (Kosslyn, 1981). Thus, portions of images visualized as subjectively smaller actually make details harder to discern.

One of the most widespread uses of imagery in real-life learning and memory tasks has been in mnemonics, in which to-be-learned materials are actively imaged or linked to other images in order to improve their memorability. Such techniques are discussed in detail in Chapter 5. Beyond a large body of research on uses of imagery in mnemonics, however, others (e.g., Denis, 1986; Mastropieri & Scruggs, in press; Mc-

Cormick & Levin, 1984; Peters, Levin, McGivern, & Pressley, 1985; Scruggs, Mastropieri, McLoone, Levin, & Morrison, 1987) have shown the benefit of imagery in learning reading material. Denis (1986), for example, found that students who reported having vivid imagery took significantly longer to read highly imaginable materials than students who reported lower levels of imagery. In addition, students with higher imagery scored significantly better on a recognition test over the material. Interestingly, under specific instructions to use imagery, low imagers especially increased their reading times (40 percent increase) compared to high imagers (19 percent increase); under these conditions, both groups had the same levels of test performance.

The Nature of Imagery

Considerable argument has raged over the nature and function of imagery. On one hand, individuals such as Kosslyn have claimed that images are a special kind of mental representation that have certain properties (e.g., images are analogical, they retain spatial characteristics) and not others (e.g., they are not language-based symbolic representations that bear only an arbitrary correspondence to the thing being represented). Others (e.g., Pylyshyn, 1973, 1981), however, have argued that other mental factors—such as an individual's world and linguistic knowledge, beliefs, and goals—inevitably affect imagery and its use.

In Pylyshyn's view, imagery does not have the intrinsic autonomy claimed for it by some (e.g., Kosslyn, 1981, 1987). For one thing, imagery is easily "penetrable" (influenced) by other knowledge, often without the individual's awareness. Taking an example supplied by Pylyshyn (1981), imagine first turning a heavy flywheel and then applying the same torque to a small aluminum pulley. In your image, which will complete one revolution first? Or imagine a tub of water, filled to the brim, to which a large stone is added. In your image, what happens? In Pylyshyn's view, the way our images unfold invariably is affected by our knowledge of the physical world, our beliefs, and our values. In the examples above, for instance, our knowledge of the concepts of inertia (or having watched contestants on "Wheel of Fortune"!) and of displacement govern our images. What might seem at first blush to be purely an automatic process of imagery is in fact strongly under the control of intellectual factors. These factors include such things as individuals' knowledge of concepts and principles and ways of making inferences. Rather than an autonomous, independent system, imagery is a process in which knowledge is indispensable.

Irrespective of the debate about the mechanisms by which imagery functions, there is an abundance of evidence that shows that imagery plays an important role in cognition. The distinction between verbal and imaginal information also reminds us that, as educators, we often are biased toward verbal instruction and rely heavily, even excessively, on verbal communication. Spoken and written words dominate our class-rooms, whereas the potential roles of visual, auditory, and kinesthetic images often seem to be neglected. A large body of evidence shows that materials high in imagery are more memorable and that learners instructed to create images will enhance their learning.

Short-Term versus Long-Term Memory

Beginning in the late 1950s and increasing rapidly thereafter, the research journals in learning and memory began to be flooded with research on a new topic. What was being studied and reported on was not a new phenomenon, but a new dimension of the already well studied area of human memory. The new dimension being investigated was the nature of memory over very short intervals—seconds or minutes. The name given to this phenomenon was short-term memory, or simply STM (Broadbent, 1958; Brown, 1958; Melton, 1963; Peterson & Peterson, 1959).

Memory theorists long had proposed that there may not be one, but two, mechanisms for memory storage (e.g., Hebb, 1949; James, 1890). What they suggested was that one type of storage mechanism is available for events recently experienced. This mechanism is the realm of STM. Another type of storage system seems to exist, however, for traces of experiences developed over longer periods through repetition, habit, and study. This aspect of memory is called long-term memory, or LTM.

Several differences between STM and LTM were hypothesized (Melton, 1963). First, it was contended that STM involves "activity" traces in contrast to LTM's "structural" traces. That is, STM is dependent on ongoing electrochemical brain activity; in contrast, LTM is based on relatively permanent changes in brain cell structure. Another, related contention was that STM decays autonomously, whenever attention is diverted from what is to be remembered. LTM, however, is based on irreversible, nondecaying traces. Third, obvious differences in capacity between STM and LTM were noted. Whereas STM has relatively fixed limits, LTM was judged to have apparently unlimited capacity.

These distinctions match well with our own introspective assessment of our memory capabilities. For instance, when we encounter new information, we generally need to continue to pay attention to it and rehearse it in order to "keep it in mind." Remembering a phone number we have just looked up or the names of several new acquaintances, for most of us, requires some attention and repetition. Especially on first encounter, our memory for such information can be exceedingly fragile—even a brief interruption or distraction may cause us to "lose" the thought entirely.

Once information has been well learned and committed to memory, however, rehearsal and repetition seem much less critical. We easily can state our uncles' names, recall the names of two large cities on the East Coast, or give three examples of large hairy animals without having to rehearse any of this information—despite the fact that we may not have thought of these topics for months or even years!

The distinctions between STM and LTM also have been well supported by research. For instance, in a ground-breaking early study, Peterson and Peterson (1959) demonstrated just how dependent STM was on rehearsal and repetition. In their study, they presented subjects with three-letter syllables (e.g., XJM) and tested their recall over intervals ranging from 3 to 18 seconds. On its face, this would seem to be an almost ridiculously simple task. In the interval between presentation of the syllable and the signal to recall, however, the subjects were presented with a three-digit number. To prevent them from rehearsing the to-be-remembered syllable, they were required to count backward from this number by threes immediately after having been given the syllable. Thus, the sequence on each trial was this: Subjects were given a syllable, then given a three-digit number, and then required to count backward by threes from the number until they were signaled to attempt recall. Under these conditions, recall deteriorated rapidly to the extent that after 18 seconds, recall was only around 10 percent. Later research verified these findings and found that both number of repetitions (Melton, 1963) and number of "chunks" of information (Murdock, 1961) are critical variables in what will be retained.

The concept of a separate STM and LTM was a critical component of many early models of memory (e.g., Atkinson & Shiffrin, 1968; Waugh & Norman, 1965), with rehearsal posited as the key to keeping items "circulating" in STM and as the critical variable in determining whether information would be transferred from STM to LTM. Because these models proposed separate storage for STM and LTM, they have come to be referred to as **duplex models of memory.** One such model, based on that of Atkinson and Shiffrin (1968), is presented in Figure 4-3.

In more recent models of memory, however, the importance of the STM–LTM distinction has diminished. Although memory theorists have continued to pay attention to the differences between STM and LTM (Trieman & Danis, 1988), most models of memory have shifted from a "storage" to a "processing" emphasis (e.g., J. R. Anderson, 1976, 1983a; Collins & Loftus, 1975; Craik & Lockhart, 1972; Jenkins, 1974). This processing emphasis is retained in most current models. Rather than being conceived of as a "place" where information is held for brief periods, the concept of STM has been broadened so that it reflects the many different ways in which we deal with information. The STM now more and more reflects the concept of "working memory"—that part of our cognitive systems we would refer to as our consciousness. For example, J.

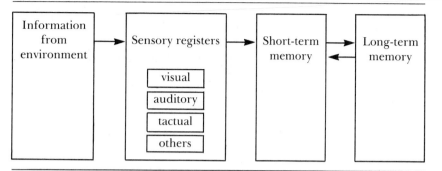

FIGURE 4-3.   An information processing model of memory.

R. Anderson's ACT* model, discussed later in this chapter, incorporates a "working memory" and a "long-term memory." These two are not emphasized as "separate places," however, but rather as being closely interrelated. The current contents of consciousness set up a pattern of activation in LTM; this activation of LTM, in turn, may "reverberate" (Anderson, 1983b, p. 265) back into working memory.

The Building Blocks of Cognition

A fundamental challenge for a science of cognition is to find a meaningful "unit" to use to describe cognitive operations. In the following section, we describe five concepts proposed by theorists as "building blocks of cognition." These concepts share many features in common, but each represents a somewhat different view of memory and how best to conceptualize it. The five concepts are **chunks, concepts, propositions, productions,** and **schemata.** Each has occupied and continues to occupy an important role in memory theory.

Chunks

"If you throw a handful of marbles on the floor," wrote the Scottish metaphysician Sir William Hamilton, "you will find it difficult to view at once more than six, or seven at most without confusion." With this pronouncement, according to George A. Miller (1956a), Hamilton became the first person to propose an experimental test of how much can be mentally grasped at a given time. Later experimental work did, in fact, confirm Hamilton's conjecture—the limit on the number of units we are able to perceive accurately without counting is about six. Beyond this number, errors begin to occur.

A related and probably better measure of mental capacity, however, is the ability to remember symbols *in sequence*. An experiment to test this ability first was performed with digits by the English scientist Joseph Jacobs. His findings, too, were confirmed by later, more-controlled experimentation. In general, when presented with a sequence of numbers one at a time, the maximum number of digits a normal adult can recall is about seven or eight. This number, called the **digit span,** has been of considerable interest to psychologists because of its relationship to intelligence (an unusually short span often is associated with low intelligence) and because this span increases with development (Dempster, 1981; Hung, 1987; Miller, 1956a).

An individual who can recall eight numbers usually can manage about seven letters or six words. However, six randomly chosen words contain far more information than seven letters or eight digits. How is it that we can recall so much more information in word form than in numerical form? Miller (1956a) responded to this question by proposing an analogy. In terms of what we can "keep in mind," we seem to be in a position analogous to carrying a purse that will hold no more than seven coins— whether they are pennies or dollars. Obviously, we can carry far more in our memory if we stock it with information-rich "dollars" than with "pennies," such as single letters or digits. The more information that can be combined or unitized, the greater the amount of information we can hold in memory, even though the number of units remains invariant.

In a landmark paper published in 1956 (Miller, 1956b) titled "The Magical Number Seven, Plus-or-Minus Two: Some Limits on Our Capacity for Processing Information," Miller not only presented considerable evidence regarding the limits of our active memory, but also introduced a unit against which this limit could be calibrated—the chunk. A *chunk* is any stimulus (e.g., letter, number, word, phrase) that has become unitized through previous experience (Simon, 1986). Thus, the sequence of letters *X–J–M* consists of three chunks of information, as does the word sequence *cat–dog–fin* or the number sequence *7–1–9*. With learning, however, comes recoding and an increase in the amount of information included in a chunk. For most people, the units *IBM, 911,* and *a fat cat* each are a single chunk. Thus, the immediate memory limits of "7 plus or minus 2" should be measured in chunks, not the absolute amount of information being encoded.

A striking demonstration of an individual's ability to recode information into ever-larger chunks has been presented by Ericsson, Chase, and Faloon (1980). Their study had but a single subject, a college undergraduate. This person had a simple task to perform: After being read a sequence of random digits at the rate of one per second, he was to recall that sequence. If he succeeded, the length of the sequence was increased by one. If he failed, it was reduced by one. Practice on the task continued an hour a day, 3 to 5 days a week, for over a year and a half! At the end of each practice session, he recalled as many digits as he could.

The remarkable result of this study was that the subject's digit span improved from 7 (recall this number?) to nearly 80 digits (see Figure 4-4)!

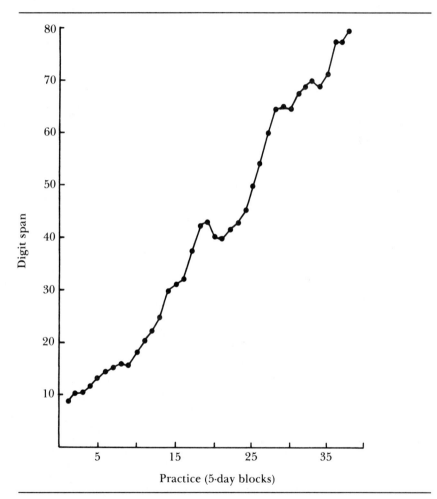

FIGURE 4-4.   Results of Ericsson, Chase, and Faloon's (1980) study. This graph shows the change in average digit span for the person who participated in the Ericsson et al. study. Each day represents about an hour's practice. As you can see, the person's digit span increased enormously. [Reprinted by permission from Ericsson, K. A., Chase, W. G., & Faloon, S. (1980). Acquisition of a memory skill. *Science, 208,* 1181–1182.]

His ability to recall digits after the session also improved dramatically, from virtually no recall to more than 80 percent after 20 months of practice. His recognition scores were even higher.

As Ericsson et al. point out, this extraordinary performance was not a feat based on an individual's exceptional innate ability. Instead, it was achieved through his learning through an extended practice period to recode and recategorize information into meaningful chunks. Thus, the four-digit sequence *3–4–9–2* became "3 minutes 49 point 2 seconds, near world-record mile time." (The subject was a good long-distance runner.) But this recoding was only the beginning. Soon he adopted the strategy of recoding the first six digits as two running times, while rehearsing the most recently presented digits. When he reached the limits of this strategy and his performance plateaued (at about 18 digits), he began to segment his groups into subgroups: He used two four-digit groups followed by two three-digit groups and the rehearsal group. When he reached yet another plateau, he introduced another level of organization, ending up with a retrieval organization consisting of three levels in a hierarchy that enabled him to store an average of nearly 80 digits. By imposing increasingly sophisticated hierarchical structures on what he was learning and practicing them extensively, he was able to chunk more and more information.

The special significance of the concept of chunk is that it emphasizes the importance of prior knowledge in facilitating memory. The difficulty of recalling the letter string OSNIWTOTPODN certainly is different from remembering the sequence SON WIT TOP NOD. The primary determiner of whether the limits of immediate memory are reached is how easily and rapidly information can be coded—that is, immediately perceived as meaningful. As we have seen in Chapters 2 and 3, this ability to code rapidly depends on the extent of prior experience and learning. The more expert the individual, the more easily this coding will occur (DeGroot, 1965; Chase & Simon, 1973; Simon, 1986)—a factor critical in cognitive processes ranging from simple pattern recognition to high-level problem solving.

Concepts

One of the major ways in which we deal with the bewildering array of information in the world is to form categories. Our language mirrors these categories—the words *grandfather, data, bird, psychology, red, dog,* and *hair* each represent a category meaningful to most of us. **Concepts** are the mental structures by which we represent these categories. Particular objects or events are grouped together based on perceived similarites; those that "fit" the category are **examples** or instances of the concept;

those that do not are **nonexamples.** The similar features across examples of a concept (e.g., all oceans *contain water* and are *large*) are called **attributes;** features essential to defining the concept are called **defining attributes.** Learning concepts involves discovering the defining attributes along with discovering the rule or rules that relate the attributes to one another.

Rule-Governed Theories of Conceptual Structure

There is a rich tradition of psychological research on how we identify and acquire concepts. One such tradition, exemplified by the early work of Bruner et al. (1956), focused on **concept identification.** Bruner et al. presented students with an array of simple stimuli such as triangles and squares for which there were only four defining features—number, size, color, and form. The subjects' task was to discover the unknown concept. The experimenters determined the rules defining the concepts, which could be either relatively simple (e.g., "All green objects are examples.") or quite complex (e.g., "Either green patterns or large patterns are examples.") A single stimulus (e.g., a green triangle) within the array was specified to the subject as a positive instance of the unknown concept to be discovered. On the basis of that example, the subjects were asked to formulate their best guess—their hypothesis—about the unknown concept. They then were allowed to pick another stimulus from the array and to ask whether it was a positive or negative example of the concept, to which the experimenter responded truthfully. The procedure continued until subjects were confident in their ability to identify the concept.

Bruner et al.'s work showed quite clearly that most individuals quickly formulate hypotheses about relevant attributes and choose their stimuli accordingly. To test their hypotheses, a sizable number of individuals adopt what is called a **conservative focusing strategy** (Bruner et al., 1956) Their first hypothesis is quite global. A protocol follows:

This is a single large, green triangle. I can't rule any of these things out. But what I can rule out are examples with two and three objects, small and medium sized objects, red and blue objects, and circles and squares. Now, I'll pick a new example that differs in one and only one attribute from the first; that way, I'm guaranteed to get new information.

Other individuals, Bruner et al. found, adopt a strategy called **focus gambling,** in which they vary more than one attribute of a stimulus at once. In this strategy, subjects may shortcut the methodical steps of conservative focusing, but also run the risk of getting no information at all by their selection. Still others use **scanning** strategies in which they attempt to test several hypotheses at once, a technique that puts some strain on subjects' ability to remember and process information.

The work of Bruner et al. (1956) and others (e.g., Haygood & Bourne, 1965; Levine, 1966; Neisser & Weene, 1962) has shown that individuals typically solve concept identification problems by trying to discover the rules relating the concept attributes. In general, concepts that have more difficult rules are more difficult to learn. The simplest rules involve **affirmation** (e.g., any green object) and **negation** (e.g., any object that is not green), which apply if there is only one attribute being considered. Most concepts, however, involve more than one relevant attribute and hence more complex rules. Among the most common are **conjunctive rules,** in which two or more attributes must be present (e.g., any triangle that is green), and **disjunctive rules,** in which an object is an example of a concept if it has one or the other attribute (e.g., either a triangle OR a green object).

In recent years, Bourne's work (Bourne, 1970, 1982) has represented the clearest statement of rule-governed conceptual structure. In his view, concepts are differentiated from one another on the basis of rules such as the above. These rules provide the means for classifying new instances as either linked to a concept or not. According to Bourne, membership in a conceptual class (e.g., grandfathers, data, birds) is determined by applying a set of rules. These rules can be learned either through instruction or through experience with instances that either are members of the class (positive instances) or are not (negative instances). Thus, one learns to classify a set of animals as birds or nonbirds on the basis of instruction or experience that leads to acquiring rules for combining characteristic attributes of birds (e.g., wings, bills, feathers). Instruction, according to Bourne, should involve presentation of both positive and negative instances (e.g., for birds, pigeons versus bats) so that critical attributes clearly can be linked to the concept. Presumably, use of these rules unambiguously classifies a new instance as either a bird or nonbird. Note, however, that this classification is a very simple one—a new instance either is a bird or is something else, a nonbird!

Although a rule-based conceptual system works to organize information for many concepts, it is inadequate for others. Most natural or "real-world" concepts are more "fuzzy" and differ qualitatively from those studied in the laboratory. For instance, consider the concept *furniture*. Our past experience would let all of us quickly agree that *furniture* includes tables, chairs, sofas, and floor lamps. Furthermore, we can describe many rules that differentiate articles of furniture from other objects. But some of our attempts at rule formation quickly run into trouble. Presence of legs? But what about some floor lamps? A seating surface? But what about tables or a desk? Is a rug furniture? Some would say that it is, but would wish to include a qualifying statement or "hedge"—it is like furniture, but not **exactly** like it. What is the set of rules that unambiguously determine which objects are members of the concept class *furniture*? Logical efforts to determine such sets of rules mostly have been unsuccessful, especially with ambiguous examples such as *rug*. Rosch and Mervis (1975), dissatisfied both with the artificiality of laboratory work on concept formation and with the difficulties of classifying concepts with rule-governed approaches, proposed an alternative view based on "degree of family resemblance" to a highly typical instance of the concept, a **prototype.**

Prototype Theories of Conceptual Structure

Prototype theories of concepts, in contrast to rule-governed theories, do not assume an either–or, member–nonmember process of concept identification. Instead, prototype theorists (Rosch, 1978; Rosch & Mervis, 1975) have argued that conceptual class membership is determined by the degree to which an example is similar to a known instance in memory—a particular instance that seems to exemplify the concept best. As you recall from Chapter 3, this line of reasoning is similar to that employed by perception theorists in accounting for pattern recognition in perception. Wattenmaker, Dewey, Murphy, and Medin (1986) suggest that the majority of "natural" or real-world concepts are structured in terms of sets of typical features. Particular instances of concepts in the real world do not have all of the defining features, but rather a family resemblance. Thus, for North Americans, robins or bluejays often are prototypes of birds. We also might classify animals such as emus or penguins as "birds," but with less assurance. With instances like the latter ones, we frequently **hedge;** that is, we qualify our judgments with a statement such as "Well, they are birds, but not the best examples of birds." The hedge is necessary because the emu and penguin do not exhibit a particularly strong family resemblance to robins or bluejays, yet they do have some resemblance. Table 4-1 gives examples of the typicality of members of certain superordinate categories, that is, how closely each instance corresponds to most individuals' prototypes for that concept class. Rosch (1978), Anglin (1977), and others have provided evidence that young children learn category memberships for prototypical and near-prototypical instances before they learn the less typical ones.

Both rule-governed and prototype conceptual theories correctly classify many simple, naturally occurring phenomena. Both systems, however, have difficulty developing clear categorizations for abstract concepts such as "wisdom," "justice," and "equality." What are the rules for defining a particular act as "wise" or "just"? Most of us find making such distinctions quite difficult, since in most cases we can only categorize whether an act fits these categories if we understand the **context** in which the act occurred. As a result, a number of theorists have begun to suggest that both rule-governed and prototype theories of concepts are inadequate. In their place, they propose a probabilistic view in which a sufficient number of attributes of either an abstract or concrete concept must be present to reach a "critical mass"—the number sufficient to make a category judgment. This view incorporates some of the charac-

TABLE 4-1.   Typicality of Members in Six Superordinate Categories.

			Category			
Item	Furniture	Vehicle	Fruit	Weapons	Vegetable	Clothing
1	Chair	Car	Orange	Gun	Peas	Pants
2	Sofa	Truck	Apple	Knife	Carrots	Shirt
3	Table	Bus	Banana	Sword	String beans	Dress
4	Dresser	Motorcycle	Peach	Bomb	Spinach	Skirt
5	Desk	Train	Pear	Hand grenade	Broccoli	Jacket
6	Bed	Trolley car	Apricot	Spear	Asparagus	Coat
7	Bookcase	Bicycle	Plum	Cannon	Corn	Sweater
8	Footstool	Airplane	Grapes	Bow and arrow	Cauliflower	Underpants
9	Lamp	Boat	Strawberry	Club	Brussel sprouts	Socks
10	Piano	Tractor	Grapefruit	Tank	Lettuce	Pajamas
11	Cushion	Cart	Pineapple	Teargas	Beets	Bathing suit
12	Mirror	Wheelchair	Blueberry	Whip	Tomato	Shoes
13	Rug	Tank	Lemon	Icepick	Lima beans	Vest
14	Radio	Raft	Watermelon	Fists	Eggplant	Tie
15	Stove	Sled	Honeydew	Rocket	Onion	Mittens
16	Clock	Horse	Pomegranate	Poison	Potato	Hat
17	Picture	Blimp	Date	Scissors	Yam	Apron
18	Closet	Skates	Coconut	Words	Mushroom	Purse
19	Vase	Wheelbarrow	Tomato	Foot	Pumpkin	Wristwatch
20	Telephone	Elevator	Olive	Screwdriver	Rice	Necklace

From "Family Resemblance: Studies in the Internal Structure of Categories," by E. Rosch and C. B. Mervis, 1975, *Cognitive Psychology*, 7, pp. 573–605. Copyright 1975 by Academic Press, Inc. Reprinted by permission.

teristics of rule-governed approaches, but retains the "naturalness" of prototype views.

Probabilistic Theories of Concept Structure

Wattenmaker et al. (1986) suggest that concept learning involves weighing probabilities. When faced with a new instance, the learner searches it for characteristic, but not necessarily defining attributes (e.g., flying and singing in an animal that looks like a bird). Categorization as a bird, however, is determined by the summing of evidence for category membership against a criterion stored in memory. If a particular instance reaches a critical sum of properties consistent with category membership, it is classed as an example of that concept. Thus, the emu, although it does not fly nor sing melodiously, *does* lay and hatch eggs, feed its young in "birdlike" ways, and, in general, looks like most birds. Thus it exhibits enough characteristics to be classified as a bird.

In general, the greater the sum beyond the critical value, the quicker the classification. Robins and bluejays are quickly identified as birds and not mammals because they have many characteristics of birds and relatively few of mammals. On the other hand, emus and penguins have comparatively fewer bird characteristics (compared, say, to robins) and consequently are less likely to be quickly identified as birds. These expectations are similar to those of prototype theory. Note that the "critical sum" approach also has some characteristics of rule-governed conceptual behavior, however, since the learner must have a "rule" for determining when a set of features reaches the critical value.

We should emphasize that the greater difficulty of categorizing emus and penguins as birds is probably at least in part because of our lack of familiarity with these animals. Nevertheless, probabilistic models emphasize that those exotic birds exhibit sufficient attributes common to birds that they are so classified. In the same way, a rug, although not exactly like a "piece of furniture," often is classified as furniture by virtue of its being used as furniture, its presence in homes, and so on.

Summary of Concepts

Whether concepts are conceived of in terms of rules, prototypes, or probabilistic judgments, each of the theories of concept learning suggests that different cultures may define concepts in different ways, depending on the set of properties the culture uses to characterize the concept. For instance, Schwaneflugel and Rey (1986) compared Spanish- and English-speaking individuals on prototype tasks similar to those Rosch had used and found clear cultural differences, even in such simple tasks as determining prototypical birds. One would expect even greater difference in classifying abstract concepts, in which the relevant attributes are much less obvious. Thus, classifications of abstract concepts such as "just" (or "unjust") or "wise" (or "unwise") could be expected to strongly reflect the cultural context in which they are used. Although meanings may vary across cultures, however, they nonetheless should have, in the words of Murphy and Medin (1985), **conceptual coherence** for individuals in a particular culture.

Medin, Wattenmaker, and Hampson (1987) suggest that simple rule-governed or prototype conceptual sortings are common and are widely used when conceptual categorizations are easy to make. When objects contain attributes from multiple categories, however, or are heavily influenced by the context within which they occur (for example, "ethical behavior"), people make categorizations probabilistically. It should be clear from the above that no unambiguous evidence exists supporting a single view of the nature of concepts. Some consensus, however, appears to be emerging concerning a probabilistic view.

Propositions

Suppose you read the following sentence:

The trainer of the Kentucky Derby winner, Alysheba, was Jack Van Berg, who always wore a brown suit.

How can its meaning be represented? In general, the most common way cognitive psychologists have used to represent declarative knowledge, especially linguistic information, is by propositions (J. R. Anderson, 1976; Fredericksen, 1975; Kintsch, 1974; Rumelhart & Norman, 1978). A **proposition** is the smallest unit of knowledge that can stand as a separate assertion, that is, the smallest unit about which it makes sense to make the judgment true or false (J. R. Anderson, 1985).

Compared to concepts, propositions are somewhat more complex representations of information. Where concepts are the relatively elemental categories into which events, objects, and experiences can be classified, propositions can be thought of as the mental equivalent of statements or assertions about observed experience and about the relationships among concepts. Propositions can be judged to be true or false.

Propositional analysis has been used extensively in analyzing semantic units such as sentences or paragraphs. When we analyze the sentence above, for instance, we can see that it can be broken into the following simpler sentences or "idea units":

1. *Jack Van Berg was the trainer of Alysheba.*
2. *Alysheba won the Kentucky Derby.*
3. *Jack Van Berg always wore a brown suit.*

These simple sentences are closely related to the three propositions underlying the complex sentence above. Each represents a unit of meaning about which a judgment of truth or falsity can be made. If any of these units of meaning is false, then of course the complex sentence is false. Propositions, of course, are not the sentences themselves; they are the meanings of the sentences. What we represent in our memories is the **meaning** of information, not its exact form.

Now examine the following two sentences without looking back. Have you seen either of them before?

1. *The Kentucky Derby was won by Alysheba.*
2. *Jack Van Berg always wore a blue suit.*

Most individuals readily will reject having seen sentence 2; after all, we have just read that Jack Van Berg always wore a brown, not a blue, suit. Many will "recognize" having seen sentence 1, however, even though they have not. We remember the "sense" of oral and written statements; the meaning of propositions is what is preserved. In contrast, the surface structure of the information (e.g., whether the first sentence above read *Alysheba won the Kentucky Derby.* or *The Kentucky Derby was won by Alysheba.*) ordinarily is quickly lost unless we are making a special effort to attend to it.

Propositions usually do not stand alone; they are connected to one another and may be embedded within one another. Kintsch (1974, 1986, 1988) has argued that texts can be viewed as ordered lists of propositions, in which the elements are word concepts; he has analyzed propositions as sets of formal relations. In Kintsch's system of analysis, each proposition consists of a **predicator** and one or more **arguments.** Several examples are written below, using Kintsch's notation, in which predicators always are written first and propositions are enclosed by parentheses.

1. *John sleeps.*	(SLEEP, JOHN)
2. *A bird has feathers.*	(HAVE, BIRD, FEATHERS)
3. *If Mary trusts John, she is a fool.*	IF, (TRUST, MARY, JOHN)(FOOL, MARY).

Kintsch and others have done propositional analyses of many texts, transforming them into *text bases,* which are ordered lists of propositions. Using such propositional analyses, Kintsch has shown that the rate of reading paragraphs is directly related to the number of propositions in the text. Moreover, Kintsch and others (e.g., Meyer, 1975; Meyer & Rice, 1984; Kintsch, 1988) also have been able to demonstrate experimentally that free recall patterns reflect the hierarchical propositional structure of the text.

As discussed below, theorists such as J. R. Anderson have hypothesized that propositions sharing one or more elements are linked to one another in **propositional networks.** As we will see, the notion that ideas are linked in large networks is a useful one for thinking about the way information is stored in memory and about how it can be retrieved. Students' ability to relate information appropriately and to use it effectively in other cognitive operations such as problem solving hinges on the quality of the networks of information they are able to create.

Productions

Whereas propositions can be seen as the basic units of declarative knowledge, **productions** are a way of representing procedural knowledge. Productions can be thought of as condition–action rules—IF/THEN rules that state an action to be performed and the conditions under which that action should be taken (J. R. Anderson, 1983a; Just & Carpenter, 1987). The idea of productions can be illustrated by the following set of instructions and actions for unlocking one's car:

Production A: *If car is locked, then insert key in lock.*

Production B: *If key is inserted in lock, then turn key.*

Production C: *If door unlocks, then return the key to vertical.*

Production D: *If key is vertical, then withdraw key.*

In general, productions are seen as having the capability of "firing" automatically—if the conditions specified exist, then the action will occur. Conscious thought typically is not involved, especially when proceduralization has occurred (see Chapter 2). Also, the outcome of a production often may supply the conditions, as in the example above, to "fire" other productions in a sequence of cognitive processes and actions.

The idea of productions has several useful characteristics. First, the concept of production systems not only captures the automatic nature of much of cognition, but also lends itself to modeling many cognitive processes on the computer. Productions can be formally specified as instructions in computer programs that operate on a set of data and simulate cognitive processes. In reading, for example, Just and Carpenter incorporated the idea of production systems in an elaborate computer model (READER) they have used to simulate and study various aspects of reading. In this model are productions such as the following:

If the word the *occurs, assume a noun phrase is starting.*

Thus, if READER encounters the word *the* in a text it is analyzing, this production will fire (an instruction is triggered in READER), leading

READER to "infer" that it currently is processing a noun phrase (Just & Carpenter, 1987).

Like propositions, productions are seen as organized in networks (J. R. Anderson, 1985; Just & Carpenter, 1987), called **production systems.** In production systems, multiple productions may be active at a given time. The outcomes of these productions constantly are tested against current knowledge. The outcomes of the productions modify memory and activate new knowledge, which in turn may activate new productions and new knowledge. Cognition moves ahead from state to state until its ultimate goal is accomplished.

Production systems enable us to represent the dynamic, changing aspects of cognitive processes. In reading, for instance, Just and Carpenter point out that one of the strengths of conceptualizing certain cognitive processes as production systems is that they nicely capture the "automatic side" of reading. In reading, as in many of our cognitive functions, we do not necessarily "think" about what we are doing—we simply do it. Similarly, J. R. Anderson (1983b, 1987) has used the concept of production systems in modeling the many automatic processes of problem solving (see Chapter 7). In his view, the critical productions of problem solving are those that recognize general goals and conditions and translate them into a series of subgoals.

Schemata

The concepts of "chunks" and "concepts" have been of particular utility to memory theorists studying questions about how specific units of knowledge are stored and retrieved from memory. Theorists who have utilized such concepts as "propositions" and "productions," on the other hand, typically have been interested in the larger-scale organization of memory and how knowledge is used to **interpret** experience. In this latter group of theorists are those individuals who could be called "schema theorists." These individuals have proposed that knowledge is organized into complex representations called **schemata,** which control the encoding of new information, the storage of information in memory, and the retrieval of stored information (Kolodner, 1985; Rumelhart, 1980a, 1984; Seifert, McKoon, Abelson, & Ratcliff, 1986).

According to Rumelhart (1981) schemata are the fundamental elements on which all information processing depends, hypothesized data structures within which the knowledge stored in memory is represented. Schemata are presumed to serve as "ideational scaffolding" (Ausubel, 1960; Anderson, Spiro, & Anderson, 1978; Rumelhart, 1981) for organizing experience. Schemata contain "slots," which hold the contents of memory as a range of slot values. In other words, knowledge is perceived, encoded, stored, and retrieved according to the slots in which it is placed. Some schemata represent our knowledge about objects and others about events, sequences of events, actions, and sequences of actions (Rumelhart, 1981).

Whenever a particular configuration of values is linked to the representation of variables of a schema, the schema is said to be **instantiated** (Rumelhart, 1981). Much like a play is enacted whenever actors, speaking their lines, perform at a particular time and place, so schemata are instantiated by specific instances of concepts and events. Thus, one's schema for TEACHING may be instantiated by viewing a particular situation in which enough of the requisite values to activate the schema are present—presence of a teacher, some students, and evidence for transactions between them. Once they are instantiated, traces of the schemata serve as a basis of our recollections (Rumelhart, 1981).

Schemata have been likened to **scripts** (in which the actors may change but the essence of the play remains), to **theories** (in which events are interpreted within a certain framework), and to **computer programs** (in which the function of the "program" is to carry out a set of procedures to determine whether the program "fits" a pattern of observations). Schemata represent knowledge at all levels of abstraction—from knowledge about our culture to knowledge about sentences, words, letters, and numbers. In the view of schema theorists, all of our generic knowledge is embedded in schemata.

Before 1970, the notion of schemata was an obscure one in psychology, appearing in historical perspective in the early work of Bartlett (1932) and in the work of the eighteenth-century philosopher Immanuel Kant, who referred to the "rules of the imagination" through which experience was interpreted. By the mid 1970s, however, the concept of schemata had become so central to the study of memory and cognition that it and related concepts were the focus of many leading theorists and researchers (e.g., Bobrow & Norman, 1975; Minsky, 1975; Rumelhart, 1975; Rumelhart & Ortony, 1977; Schank & Abelson, 1977; Winograd, 1975). Why did this concept assume such importance? In our judgment, the reason "schema theory" came to the fore so rapidly had to do with its extraordinary explanatory power in accounting for memory and other cognitive phenomena.

To get a better feel for the idea of schemata, consider the following paragraph. Read it carefully a time or two.

Death of Piggo

The girl sat looking at her piggybank. "Old friend," she thought, "this hurts me." A tear rolled down her cheek. She hesitated, then picked up her tap shoe by the toe and raised her arm. Crash! Pieces of Piggo—that was its name—rained in all directions. She closed her eyes for a moment to block out the sight. Then she began to do what she had to do.

Think now about some of the things you need to know in order to comprehend this passage—a passage with fairly simple sentence construction, no rare words, and dealing with a topic familiar to most—piggybanks. Let's start with piggybanks. What do we know about them? A short list follows. Piggybanks:

1. are representations of pigs
2. hold money
3. the money is usually coins
4. have a slot to put the money in
5. are hard to retrieve money from
6. have fat bodies
7. are not alive
8. usually are made of brittle material
9. can be shattered by dropping or a blow
10. look friendly
11. usually are smaller than real pigs
12. once broken, usually stay that way
13. etc.

Of course, this list of "piggybank facts" could be continued indefinitely. Note that the list does not **define** the concept of piggybank (i.e., a piggybank is . . ."), but rather is a partial description of our overall conception of piggybanks—how they look, how they work, how large they are, how they are valued, and so on. Our overall mental representation of even a single concept like "piggybanks," we discover, is an immensely complex array of information and its interrelationships. Within and related to this global representation, too, are embedded many other schemata—for instance, schemata for "tap shoe," for "striking something with a hard object," for "saving money," and so on.

As you turn again to "Death of Piggo" and examine it closely, you quickly see the vital role your schemata for piggybanks and for many other objects and events play in your ability to comprehend this paragraph. The notions that piggybanks hold money, that they can be shattered, that shattering is necessary to retrieve their contents, that they are friendly looking—none of this information actually is stated in the passage. Yet, all this had to have been activated automatically as we read or we could not have comprehended. We somehow "filled in" the information based on our world knowledge. In Rumelhart's terms, the slots in our schemata had expected or **default values** assigned to them when they were activated. Although specific information actually was not presented on, say, the piggybank containing money or its brittleness, we assumed these to be true based on our general knowledge of piggybanks. Of course, the list of schemata needed to understand even this single paragraph can be extended almost indefintely to include schemata for (to name only a few possibilities) human beings, tap dancing shoes, gravity, rain, and Newton's Laws of Motion.

Even the simplest event or message has an infinite number of features that *could* be attended to. As we saw in Chapter 3, however, only a few of these actually become a part of memory. One critical function of schemata is to guide this selection process (Alba & Hasher, 1983; Watt, 1988). An interesting early demonstration of this selection function was provided by Pichert and Anderson (1977), who presented two groups of individuals with a passage describing two boys playing hooky and the house belonging to one of them. One group was instructed to read the passage from the perspective of a potential home buyer, the second from the perspective of a burglar. The results of Pichert and Anderson's study showed that the information recalled from the passage was strongly influenced by the perspective taken. Those reading from the perspective of a home buyer tended to recall more information relevant to that perspective, such as number of bedrooms, the presence of stone siding, newly painted rooms, and a nursery. Those taking the "burglar" perspective, however, showed significantly better recall for such details as the presence of 10-speed bicycles in the garage, a valuable painting, jewels, and a color TV. Pichert and Anderson commented on their findings as follows:

> The striking effect of perspective on which elements of a passage were learned is easily explained in terms of schema theory. A schema is an abstract description of a thing or event. It characterizes the typical relations among its components and contains a slot or placeholder for each component that can be instantiated with particular cases. Interpreting a message is a matter of matching the information in the message to the slots in a schema. The information entered into the slots is said to be subsumed by the schema. (1977, p. 314)

Since "home buying" and "burglary" each represents a strong but quite different schema, information likely to instantiate important variables in one was less likely to instantiate the other. What individuals paid attention to and subsequently recalled was information most consistent with their currently activated schema. Thus, depending on which schemata are activated, the information selected for recall will vary (Rowe & Rayford, 1987).

Besides the role of schemata in selecting information to be processed, schemata play several other critical roles. One such function is **interpreta-**

tion. For example, given sentence 1 below, most people later will recall sentence 2.

1. *The paratrooper leaped out the door.*
2. *The paratrooper jumped out of the plane.*

Or, to take a second example, the first sentence below also is likely to be recalled as the second.

1. *The student spoke to the department chair about her instructor's sexist comments.*
2. *The student complained to the department chair about her instructor's sexist comments.*

Much of our recall is transformed, often subtly, by our schemata. Especially if information is general or vague, instantiation transforms it into familiar form. The importance of instantiation is demonstrated by the following passage, used in early research by Bransford and Johnson (1972, 1973) and Dooling and Lachman (1971).

> *The procedure is actually quite simple. First you arrange items into different groups. Of course one pile may be sufficient depending on how much there is to do. If you have to go somewhere else due to lack of facilities that is the next step; otherwise, you are pretty well set. It is important not to overdo things. That is, it is better to do too few things at once than too many. In the short run this may not seem important but complications can easily arise. A mistake can be expensive as well. At first, the whole procedure will seem complicated. Soon, however, it will become just another facet of life. It is difficult to foresee any end to the necessity for this task in the immediate future, but then, one never can tell. After the procedure is completed one arranges the materials into different groups again. Then they can be put into their appropriate places. Eventually they will be used once more and the whole cycle will then have to be repeated. However, that is part of life.*

For most individuals asked to read and recall Bransford and Johnson's passage, comprehension and subsequent recall is poor. However, simply adding a title, "Washing Clothes," will improve both significantly. The presence of an appropriate context for information is critical. However, when schemata are not or cannot be activated during learning, new knowledge will not be meaningful and cannot be assimilated easily.

Schema theory provides an explanation for a number of memory phenomena. Because the contents of memory are likely to consist of abstractions of knowledge rather than exact copies of it, encoding will vary according to the schema or schemata activated at the time of encoding. Thus, schema theory provides an explanation for the effect of context in memory storage. Recall is seen as a reconstructive process (Goldman & Varnhagen, 1986; Spiro, 1980) in which schemata provide frameworks that direct the recall process. Recall is not simply remembering stored information, but rather **recreating** information and events on the basis of stored schemata. Memory, in this view, is not so much a reproductive process as a **constructive** one (see Chapter 6).

Schema theory has been tremendously appealing to both cognitive theorists and educators because it emphasizes the application of what individuals already know. It also helps us understand that many recall and recognition "errors" are not so much errors as they are constructions logically consistent with the mental structures learners employ. In general, schema theory portrays the learner in a dynamic, interactive way. Although schema theory has been criticized for its generality and vagueness (Alba & Hasher, 1983), current cognitive research more reflects schema-based than conceptually based approaches. Although initially developed to explain perceptual and memory phenomena, the concept of schemata recently has become a key element in theories of problem solving (e.g., Gick & Holyoak, 1983; Holyoak, 1985; Rumelhart, 1984). As you will see in Chapter 7, individuals faced with the need to solve a problem initially must represent the task in terms of schemata and search a "problem space" consisting of schemata in memory. Successful problem solving requires not only creating the appropriate frameworks for understanding problems, but activating them in the right contexts.

Models of Memory

Through the 1960s and well into the 1970s, the prominent models of memory were "stage" models, such as those of Waugh and Norman (1965) and Atkinson and Shiffrin (1968). These models portrayed human cognition by means of a computer-like, information-processing metaphor. Such models emphasized sequential steps in processing (see Figure 4-2), as information moved from the sense receptors and sensory registers into short-term or working memory and, depending on the rehearsal that took place, into long-term memory.

By the late 1960s, however, the wisdom of separating memory into discrete short-term and long-term components was questioned. Cognition, it seemed, was not as neatly separable into components or steps as the models implied. Nor could "meaning" be excluded or easily controlled. Perception, for instance, was shown to be strongly influenced by semantic knowledge from the "later" stage of long-term memory, a "backward" effect not easily accommodated by existing computer models.

Also, many cognitive activities seemed to be automatic, driven by the information coming in, and to depend only minimally on "central processing." These models seemed static, unable to capture very much of the active, dynamic nature of cognition and its ability to interpret and restructure new information to make it conform to prior knowledge. So-called network models of memory, it seemed, had features that allowed them to better capture and portray the nature of human learning and memory.

Network Models

In *network models of memory*, knowledge is represented by a web or network; memory processes are defined within that network (J. R. Anderson, 1983b). In most such models, the networks are hypothesized to consist of **nodes,** which consist of cognitive units (usually either concepts or schemata), and **links,** which represent relations between these cognitive units.

The Collins and Quillian (1969) and Collins and Loftus (1975) Models

Quillian (1962, 1967, 1968) and Collins and Quillian (1969) proposed an early network model, called the *Teachable Language Comprehender* (TLC), as a model for semantic memory. Devised as a computer program, the TLC was based on the assumption that memory could be represented by a semantic network arranged into a hierarchical structure. In this hierarchy, the nodes were concepts arranged in superordinate–subordinate relationships. Properties of each concept are labeled relational links or **pointers** going from the node to other concept nodes. An example of such a network is presented in Figure 4-5.

Links were of various types. Quillian proposed five different kinds: (1) superordinate (ISA) and subordinate links, (2) modifier (M) links, (3) disjunctive sets of links, (4) conjunctive sets of links, and (5) a residual class of links. These links can be embedded in one another. In Figure 4-5, the links from *are fast, are agile,* and *are gentle* to *quarterhorses* are modifier links, whereas the links between *quarterhorses* and *horses* and between *horses* and *mammals* are ISA links. In general, properties particular to a concept were assumed to be stored along with the concept (e.g., *are gentle* is stored with *quarterhorses*). Those not unique to that concept (e.g., *have manes, have hooves*), however, are assumed to be stored with more general concepts higher in the hierarchy.

When memory is searched, activation moves along the links from the node that has been stimulated (say, by reading the word *horse*). This **spreading activation** constantly expands, first to all the nodes directly linked to the concept (in our simple model, from *horses* to the superordinate concept *mammal* and to the subordinate concepts *Arabians,*

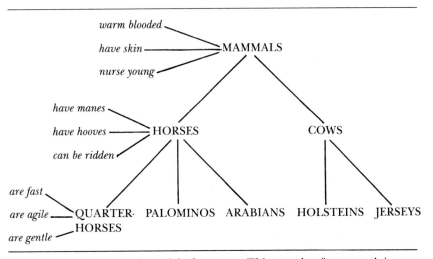

FIGURE 4-5.   A network model of memory. This sample of a network is modeled after those developed by Collins and Quillian (1969).

palominos, and *quarterhorses*) and then to the nodes linked to these nodes, and so on (Collins & Loftus, 1975). As activation moves forward through the nodes, an activation tag is left at each. When a tag from another starting node is encountered, an **intersection** has been found. By tracing the tags backward from the intersection to their sources, the path linking the starting nodes can be reconstructed. Thus, a question, *Are quarterhorses mammals?* would trace a path in the network from the starting nodes *quarterhorses* and *mammals* through the node for *horses*.

According to this model, language comprehension consists of path evaluation to see if it is consistent with the constraints imposed by language. For instance, the starting point in comprehending the question above, *Are quarterhorses mammals?* is activation of the path from quarterhorses to horses and from horses to mammals. The memory search is presumed to begin at the concepts included in the input question (*quarterhorses, mammals*). Beginning with the concept *quarterhorses*, this search would arrive in one step (link) at the properties *are fast, are agile,* and *are gentle* and at the superordinate concept, *horses*. A second step takes the search to *mammals*. If the relationship between the two nodes is permitted by the syntax and context of the question, the question can be comprehended.

One assumption of the original Collins and Quillian (1969) model was that traversing these links takes a fixed amount of time. Thus, if memory search traversed only a single link, that search should take less time than a search traversing additional links. Collins and Quillian set out to verify the prediction that time required for retrieval from memory structure will depend on the number of links traversed in memory search. To test this hypothesis, they presented subjects with sentences representing relationships in simple two- or three-level hierarchies. Some of these sentences described modifying (M) relations; other stated superordinate (ISA) relations (as in Figure 4-5). Sentences represented the presumed number of steps in the hierarchy that would need to be traversed in order to verify the truth or nontruth of the sentence. The following are samples of the kinds of sentences Collins and Quillian used.

Number of Links	Sentences	Type of Relation
0	*An oak has acorns.*	M
	A maple is a maple.	ISA
1	*A spruce has branches.*	M
	A cedar is a tree.	ISA
2	*A birch has seeds.*	M
	An elm is a plant.	ISA

Subjects were given both true and false sentences. The measure taken was reaction time to make a decision about the truth of the sentence. In general, their predictions were verified for both M and ISA sentences, as average reaction time increased for decisions about sentences that represented a greater number of links. For instance, average reaction times for the set of M (property) sentences was just over 1,300 msec for *A canary can sing* (0 links), close to 1,400 msec for *A canary can fly* (1 link), and nearly 1,475 msec for *A canary has skin* (2 links).

Like all models, however, the Collins and Quillian model had trouble accounting for some results. Although the prediction that time required to judge sentences true or false as a function of "semantic distance" usually has been borne out, there are frequency effects. For instance, it is easier to agree that a palomino is a horse than to agree that a tarpan is a horse, simply because most of us are more familiar with the former than the latter.

To deal with such findings as well as their own accumulating data from research relating to the model, Collins and Loftus (1975) extended the model. Several assumptions were included to make the model less "computer-like" and more "human." (Quillian's original theory was developed as a program for the computer, which imposed constraints on his theory that he himself felt were unrealistic.) Spreading activation remained a key assumption, but with activation decreasing over time. In addition, Collins and Loftus also proposed the existence of a separate **lexical network,** in which **names** of concepts were stored. Links in this lexical network could serve as an alternative source of entry into memory (e.g., words that "sound like" *horse*).

As Collins and Loftus were able to show, their revised network model now was able to account for results from a variety of studies and to deal with many criticisms of the original model. Their model continues to be influential in cognitive psychology, and key concepts from it, especially the conceptualization of memory as organized into networks of nodes and links and the idea of spreading activation, still dominate our views of how memory is organized and accessed.

The ACT* Model   Perhaps the most comprehensive model of memory and cognition is J. R. Anderson's ACT* model (1976, 1983a, 1983b). Based on the earlier Human Associative Memory (HAM) model, which he and Gordon Bower had developed (Anderson & Bower, 1973), ACT* is a broader model than that of Collins and Quillian (1969) and Collins and Loftus (1975). In formuating ACT*, Anderson's ambitious intention was to provide a single theoretical framework for all aspects of thinking. It includes principles of initial encoding of information, information storage, and information retrieval (Anderson, 1983) and encompasses both declarative and procedural knowledge.

Unlike the Collins and Quillian model, the basic building blocks of ACT* are propositions, not concepts. Anderson proposes a basic cognitive unit, consisting of a **unit node** (a proposition) and a **set of elements** (the relation and arguments of the proposition). Cognitive units are not limited to propositions, however. Images and word strings also may be cognitive units. The size of the cognitive unit may vary, but generally the upper limit of number of elements that can be encoded with any cognitive unit is five or fewer (J. R. Anderson, 1983a). Thus, a paragraph or 24-item word list could not be encoded as a single unit, but a simple sentence or pair of words to be associated could. A key assumption is that all elements of a unit are encoded together. For instance, when a proposition consisting of three elements is encoded (e.g., *Freddy proposed a toast*), all the elements (subject, predicate, object) are encoded in the unit, not just one or two.

As in most network models, the concept of spreading activation is a key feature in ACT* and is seen as determining the level of activity in long-term memory. Of course, activation must begin somewhere; the points where activation begins are called **focus units.** Once focus units are activated—either externally from perception (e.g., by reading a sentence) or from the current contents of working memory (e.g., thinking about what has been read)—activation spreads to associated elements. Thus, when the word *hot* is read, elements for *cold, warm, water,* and other related items also will be activated automatically. Attention determines the continued activation of the network; when the source of activation for the focus unit drops from attention, activation decays.

Since the contents of working memory and long-term memory overlap extensively, activation can spread from working memory to associated elements in long-term memory. As Anderson points out, activation can "reverberate back" to nodes in the network. If node 1 activates node 2, then activation from node 2 can spread to node 1. Retrieval occurs when focus units are reactivated. Activation is cumulative: The more units activated, the more likely it is that an item will be retrieved. Thus, although a student may not be able to recall a fact when first questioned about it, rephrasing the question or supplying "hints" may activate additional pathways that will stimulate recall.

The amount of activation sent into the network also can vary for other reasons. As portrayed in the model, well-learned concepts to which one has frequent exposure will produce more activation and hence be more easily retrieved than less well learned concepts. Well-learned information has many associations and wide-ranging activation that permit its access through multiple routes. Also, the model implies that more activation is captured by the paths leading to stronger nodes. Thus, Anderson would predict that students who are helped to relate new information to existing, well-learned knowledge will have superior recall.

Like the Collins and Loftus (1975) and Collins and Quillian (1968, 1969) models, the ACT* model has generated a great deal of research. Because of its breadth, ACT* has been adapted not only to the study of memory but to the study of other cognitive processes such as problem solving and decision making. Because it accounts for a wide variety of data (J. R. Anderson, 1983b) and addresses many important aspects of cognition, this model is likely to play an important role in directing cognitive research into the forseeable future.

Parallel Distributed Processing: A Connectionist Perspective

Throughout most of its short history, cognitive psychology has been dominated by a computer metaphor of information processing. Human cognition, cognitive scientists have argued, can be conceived of as computer-like; information is taken in, processed in a single central processor of working memory, and stored in and retrieved from long-term memory. The computer metaphor has generated models of memory (e.g., Atkinson & Shiffrin, 1968), knowledge representation (e.g., Kintsch, 1986, 1988), and problem solving (e.g., Newell & Simon, 1972). Beyond providing a metaphor for cognition, computers have provided a mechanism for simulating cognition and for testing theories about human cognitive processes.

The architecture of the computers of the past two decades and of most computers today is one that requires sequential or **serial** processing; programs written for them typically consist of a series of instructions that the computer executes very rapidly one after the other. In modeling cognition, however, a serious difficulty that arises is that this kind of serial information processing is not very "brain-like." Where digital computers are quick and precise, executing thousands and even millions of operations in sequence per second (the Cray-2 Supercomputer can execute one operation each 4.5 billionths of a second), human information processing is far slower. However, it also is far more powerful than computers for many kinds of "messy" everyday cognitive tasks, such as recognizing objects in natural scenes, understanding language, searching memory when given only fragmentary information, making plans, and learning from experience.

Also, in contrast to most computer programs, our cognitive systems are capable of operating under **multiple constraints.** Although some cognitive processes are serial, many occur simultaneously. For instance, in the famous example from Selfridge (1955) that appears in the previous chapter, the interpretation of the middle letter in the words THE and CAT is determined by the context in which it appears. Similarly, we have little trouble identifying the words in Figure 4-6, even though parts of key letters are obscured. Our perceptual system somehow is capable of exploring a number of possibilities **simultaneously** without committing itself to one "interpretation" until all constraints are taken into account. Paradoxically, the identity of each letter is constrained by all the others. Many if not most cognitive tasks involve resolving multiple constraints: physical performances (e.g., hitting a ball, typing, playing a piano), orallanguage comprehension, reading, and understanding stories.

Given the characteristics of the brain and its cognitive capabilities, one group of cognitive theorists (McClelland, Rumelhart, & Hinton, 1986)

Figure 4-6.   Examples of information processing with multiple constraints.

has proposed replacing the "computer metaphor" with a "brain metaphor," a model called **parallel distributed processing** or, simply, PDP. The reason human beings are better at such tasks than conventional computers, they contend, is that the brain has an "architecture" that better fits natural information-processing tasks. What humans do so exceedingly well, far better than any computer, is to simultaneously consider many pieces of information. Processing occurs *in parallel,* along many dimensions at the same time. Although any single bit of information may be imprecise or ambiguous, the parallel processing capabilities of the system make it possible to make judgments and decisions with a high level of confidence.

According to McClelland (1988), the major difference between PDP models and other cognitive models is that in most models, knowledge is stored as a static copy of a pattern. When access is needed, the pattern is found in long-term memory and copied into working memory. In PDP, however, the units themselves are not stored. What is stored are the **connection strengths** among simple processing units. These connection strengths allow the patterns to be recreated when the system is activated.

As just indicated, one key concept in PDP models is that processing is parallel. That is, processing proceeds simultaneously along many different dimensions. In reading, for instance, the cognitive processes of reading are not portrayed as moving through steps from "lower levels," such as decoding, to "higher levels," such as comprehension processes. Instead, processing moves ahead on many different levels at once; as we read, we simultaneously depend on feature extraction processes (such as recognizing lines, curves, and angles in letters), on letter and word recognition processes, on syntactic assignment processes, and on activation of multiple schemata. These processes simultaneously trigger and inhibit one another as processing moves forward. Top-down, bottom-up, and interactive (a combination of top-down and bottom-up) processing all can occur within such a system (McClelland & Rumelhart, 1981; Rumelhart & McClelland, 1986). As you will see in Chapter 9, this conception of reading seems to fit well with the data.

Another key concept in PDP models in that of **distributed representation.** In PDP models, as we have indicated, knowledge is stored in the strengths of connections between processing units, not in the units themselves. Thus, knowledge of any specific pattern (e.g., a letter of the alphabet, a face) does not reside in a special processing unit reserved just for that pattern, but instead is **distributed** over the connections among a very large number of simple processing units. Thus, our comprehension of the word *toast* in the sentence *Freddy proposed a toast* arises through activation of connections among a host of processing units, including those for letter perception, word meanings, and syntactic roles, and those relating to the pragmatic context in which the sentence was uttered. Thus, we comprehend automatically that the "toast" Freddy proposed is something other than the whole wheat variety.

In the PDP model, processing units are roughly analogous to neurons or assemblies of neurons, and the connections by which units are linked are seen as roughly analogous to synapses. When stimulated by the environment, input units cause other units to be activated via their connections. Thus, there is the familiar spreading activation dimension to PDP models, in common with that of the Collins and Quillian and ACT* models.

Eventually, activation spreads to those units associated with responses. In typing the word *proposed,* for example, the decision to type the word causes activation of a unit (schema) for the word. That unit, in turn, activates units corresponding to the letters in the word. The unit for the first letter inhibits the units for the other letters; the second unit inhibits the first and other letters, and so on. The patterns of activation and inhibition among the units and the responses as they are carried out activate each letter in turn. When a response begins (e.g., typing the letter *p*), a strong inhibitory signal is sent to units associated with it. Thus, it is inhibited as subsequent units (e.g., *r, o*) are activated.

As Hinton, McClelland, and Rumelhart (1986) point out, it is a mistake to view distributed representations such as PDP as an **alternative** to representations such as semantic networks and production systems. Instead, they better may be seen as ways of understanding how these more-abstract entities are implemented and interact with one another. PDP may represent **primitives** of information processing; the more abstract models may usefully describe regularities at higher levels.

"Brainlike" models of information processing now also are appearing more frequently in computer hardware. In the computer world, there long has been a recognition that the conventional, von Neumann single central processor design has significant limitations. When instructions must be operated on serially, a bottleneck eventually will occur in the central processor, no matter how fast the computer. As a consequence, a number of new machines are being designed with multiple processors.

In such machines, each of the many processors can operate independently and simultaneously. No single processor has great processing power—each may be roughly equivalent to a microchip in a videogame—but each is associated with particular data points. That is, each is "dedicated" to a relatively simple task. The critical challenge is communication. Each processor communicates with all others by having access to its own and the memories of all other processors. Processors work in parallel; processing moves ahead as each processor sends and receives data. Whereas conventional computers are better at straightforward processing tasks, parallel processors appear to be notably superior in tasks like image analysis and language recognition—tasks that are extremely difficult for serial processing computers.

Whether computers based on parallel distributed processing and connectionist models of cognition such as PDP are the "wave of the future" is unknown. It is clear, however, that the connectionist models have some intriguing qualities. Although a fair amount of work has been done applying the PDP model in a wide variety of areas (see McClelland, 1988; also the volumes by Rumelhart, McClelland, & PDP Research Group, 1986), connectionist models of cognition still are in their infancy. Because of their higher degree of correspondence to the characteristics of the brain and their ability to more closely match certain aspects of human cognition, however, such models are attracting a great deal of attention among both computer specialists and cognitive psychologists (Holyoak, 1987; McClelland, 1988). As these are refined, they seem likely to make a major contribution to cognitive psychology and to our understanding of human learning and memory.

Summary

Memory is one of the central concerns of cognitive psychologists. Memory first was studied scientifically a little more than a century ago by Ebbinghaus. Following the Ebbinghaus tradition, early studies of memory focused on experimental investigations of rote learning phenomena. In the past quarter-century, however, our conception of what constitutes valid study of memory has been broadened considerably, and memory theorists have made immense strides in describing the nature of learning, memory, and the utilization of meaningful information.

Several fundamental distinctions useful to educators have been made by cognitive theorists as they have shifted from the study of "rote" to "meaningful" learning. Among them have been the distinctions between episodic and semantic memory, declarative and procedural knowledge, verbal and imaginal representation in memory, and short-term and long-term memory. Each of these is useful not only for a theoretical understanding of memory processes but in thinking about the nature of learning and the educational process.

In their quest to adequately describe memory, psychologists have proposed a number of cognitive units. Among the most useful have been **chunks, concepts, propositions, productions,** and **schemata.** These units, in turn, have served as building blocks for more global models of memory, such as the duplex model of Atkinson and Shiffrin (1968) and the network models of Collins, Quillian, and Loftus (Quillian, 1968;

Collins and Quillian, 1969; Collins & Loftus, 1975). A particularly comprehensive network model, ACT*, has been developed by John Anderson. More recently, a connectionist model, PDP, which emphasizes parallel processing, has been proposed by Rumelhart and McClelland and their associates. As these models are further refined, our understanding of the nature of human memory should expand greatly, along with our ability to enhance our students' abilities to comprehend, recall, and use the information they learn.

CHAPTER 5

Encoding Processes

In Chapter 2, we saw how central knowledge is to human performance. In Chapter 3, we reviewed perception and attention and noted how both were powerfully affected by people's knowledge of the world. In Chapter 4, we introduced the topic of memory and how it is stored. The topic of this chapter is the processes involved in placing knowledge into memory. Let's begin our discussion of how information is encoded—placed into memory—by examining how some students prepare for a test.

It is the night before Mrs. Thompson's American history test at Junction High School. She has informed the students that the major emphasis of her test will be on the politicians she has discussed and their major beliefs. The students in her third-period class all are studying but, as you might imagine, they are doing different things.

Nathan sits at his kitchen table, history book open to page 112. He has just finished reading about the politicians the test will cover and has glanced over his notes. Nathan figures he's done enough. He closes his book and turns his stereo on, the night's work completed.

Across the street, Robert has decided to go over the politicians one more time. He closes his eyes and envisions John Calhoun sitting at the head of his parents' table. On Calhoun's right, Robert pictures Henry Clay. Daniel Webster sits next to Clay, eating a piece of devil's food cake. After Robert completes his "rounds" of the imaginary table, he goes back around and has each politician summarize his beliefs as though they were arguing with one another. Daniel Webster throws his cake at John Calhoun.

Down the block from Robert lives Karen. She, too, is working on remembering the politicians. She first draws up a list of politicians with each man's position noted alongside his name. Next, Karen covers the page and tries to recite it all from memory. She continues this process for the next hour until her recall is perfect. Satisfied, she visits the kitchen and snatches some oatmeal cookies and ice cream.

On the basis of our brief visits with three of Mrs. Thompson's students, it is very difficult to make a judgment about which of them will do well on tomorrow's exam. However, we did see three very different approaches to **encoding** (placing into memory) the information. Although many factors influence how students will remember information (e.g., amount to be learned, difficulty, novelty, how long they study), the way in which they encode the information makes a profound difference. In this section of the chapter we examine encoding processes and see how we may enhance student's memory. We begin by reviewing how students think about their memory.

Thinking about Memory: The Role of Metacognition

Even though the three students we visited all did different things as they tried to remember the politicians, some common factors can be seen: All three knew they had to remember the information, all three were thinking about what they were trying to remember, and at some point all three estimated they had done enough to allow for successful recall on the test. Not surprisingly, these three factors are related to the knowledge people possess about how they remember.

Metacognition refers to knowledge people have about their own thought processes; **metamemory** refers to knowledge people have about their own memory (Brown, Bransford, Ferrara, & Campione, 1983). An example of metamemory can be seen in the teacher who knows she does not remember names well and who has her students wear nametags for several days. Another example can be seen in the student who listens to a teacher's explanation of how to solve a problem and who takes notes only on those points she expects will be difficult. Still another example is students' asking a teacher whether an upcoming test will be essay or multiple choice.

The kinds of knowledge about one's memory exemplified above seem second nature to adults. We all know a great deal about our strengths and weaknesses and understand that difficult memory tasks require different methods of study (e.g., studying for a test versus remembering a good joke). Metamemory, however, develops only gradually in children.

There are three related skills involved in metamemory (Kail, 1984): awareness, diagnosis, and monitoring. Following we examine the development of each of these skills in more detail.

Awareness

Being aware of the need to remember is a critical prerequisite to effective memory (Armbruster, in press). For example, if your professor announces that you will be tested on this chapter, you no doubt understand you are being asked to remember the chapter's content. Knowing that you need to remember the material in the chapter affects how you read it. Because of this awareness, you may reread the chapter several times, underline some parts of it, take notes about specific points, or ask yourself questions as you read.

The rudiments of awareness appear as early as the age of two (see Deloache, Cassidy, & Brown, 1985) and demonstrable awareness of the need to remember shows up in preschoolers, even though their awareness is limited. For example, Acredolo, Pick, and Olson (1975) studied the development of awareness by taking preschoolers and older children on short walks through various hallways. As the experimenter walked along with each child, she dropped her keys and picked them up at a given point along the route. Later, when the preschoolers were asked where the keys had been dropped, they were able to locate the spot at reasonable levels of accuracy. However, when the children were taken to a particular spot during their walks and *asked* to remember it, their level of accuracy in relocating the same place was considerably better than it had been for remembering where the keys had been dropped. Because the children's performance was better when they were asked to remember as opposed to when they were not asked, Acredolo et al. inferred that preschool children have some awareness of their own memories and how to improve them. Without such an awareness, of course, memory performance should have been the same in the two conditions.

Recognizing the need to remember develops slowly throughout childhood (Johnson & Wellman, 1980; Kail, 1984). Whereas preschoolers may need to be instructed to remember things, older children have learned that certain information is likely to be important to remember (e.g., concepts in a unit on China, directions for how to solve a problem, assignments for the next day). By the time students are the age of Mrs. Thompson's, most know a great deal about what should be remembered and are very selective about what they will and won't try to remember.

Diagnosis

Beyond awareness of the need to remember some information is an understanding of what it will take to remember it. In metamemory, **diagnosis** refers to two related subskills: **assessing the difficulty** of the memory task and **determining the retrieval demands** of the task (see Baker, in press; Brainerd & Pressley, 1985; Kail, 1984). We examine each of these subskills more closely in the following subsections.

Understanding that some memory tasks are more difficult than others is integral to metamemory. As adults, we understand that the sheer amount of material to be remembered makes a difference. For instance, we know learning 1 phone number is considerably less demanding than committing 10 new phone numbers to memory. Similarly, we know learning, say, 5 new psychological terms will take less effort than memorizing 30 terms.

Beyond the amount to be learned, we also understand that the familiarity of information makes a difference. For example, the student who already knows a good deal about, say, Daniel Webster will find it far easier to remember a new anecdote about Webster's actions in Congress than would another student who had never heard of him.

Other factors influencing our assessments of task difficulty include the speed at which the information is given and how it is organized. As an example, it is easy to be overwhelmed by a lecturer who covers an enormous amount of material in a very brief time. Likewise, remembering the material in a poorly organized text can be a daunting task.

In contrast to adults and older children, small children have only a rudimentary knowledge of the factors influencing task difficulty. Their diagnostic skills are immature and will develop only slowly (Brainerd & Pressley, 1985; Flavell, Freidrichs, & Hoyt, 1970; Kail, 1984; Yussen & Levy, 1975). Still, teachers can make an important difference in children's diagnostic skills by providing instruction in how to make estimates of task difficulty, prompting children to make such estimates, and providing practice in making diagnoses.

The second subskill involved in diagnosis is determining a memory task's retrieval demands. For example, we usually prepare differently for a multiple-choice test than, say, for an open-book essay test or an oral examination, knowing the retrieval demands of these situations are different. Similarly, if you knew you would have to stand in front of your class and give examples of the two subskills involved in diagnosis, you no doubt would prepare differently than if you merely expected to review this content during the next class period.

Children's retrieval demands, of course, also vary. For instance, children may need only to recognize the information in a story or they could be asked to retell the story in their own words. Preschoolers have little understanding of retrieval demands (Brainerd & Pressley, 1985; Kreutzer, Leonard, & Flavell, 1975), but early elementary school-age children begin to see that the purpose for remembering makes a difference (Brainerd & Pressley, 1985). It is not until the age of about nine, however, that children are able to state reasons why different kinds of retrieval demands require different kinds of encoding. Even then, upper elementary-age children often are able to say why some retrieval demands are more difficult than others, but they still do not study differently (Brainerd & Pressley, 1985). For example, it is not surprising to have a sixth-grader announce that she must study hard because she has a fill-in-the-blank test coming up. As you talk to her, it is clear that she believes such a test will be more difficult than a recognition test. However, the odds are good that she isn't sure how she should study differently.

Ultimately, of course, successful students develop sophisticated patterns of study designed to match retrieval demands. (Consider how Robert used imagery to help him sort out the various politicians.) In fact, it can be argued that successful recall depends on the formation of excellent strategies for dealing with the material (Cross & Paris, 1988). These patterns of study usually develop slowly. As we will see later in the chapter, however, teachers can facilitate the process by providing students with instruction focused on *how* to study.

Monitoring

The third major skill involved in metamemory is monitoring. **Monitoring** refers to keeping track of one's progress as materials are committed to memory. It is, in essence, the continual asking and answering of the question, "How well do I know this material?" Not surprisingly, skilled learners constantly monitor their own progress. As they study, they ascertain what has been adequately learned, what is near mastery, and what will require further effort (Kail, 1984).

As with other aspects of metamemory, monitoring develops gradually. You have, no doubt, determined how well you have learned this chapter's content and perhaps have made notes to yourself about what you will reread and what you will merely skim as you go back over the material. In contrast, a seventh-grader of our acquaintance had just finished studying for an upcoming health test. When asked how ready he was for the test, he responded that he thought he'd do well. (He almost always did.) On further questioning, he decided that he might not know some parts of the content as well as the rest, but he saw no way to approach the task except to study it all again.

An example of research on monitoring was reported by Goodman and Gardiner (1981; see also Bisanz, Vesonder, & Voss, 1978; Masur, McIntyre, & Flavell, 1973). In their study, Goodman and Gardiner gave children of different ages lists to memorize and tested their memory after several lists had been studied. When the testing was completed, the children were shown each of the words from the list one at a time and were asked to judge whether they had remembered the words on the test. Even the youngest children in the study, six-year-olds, were able to make fairly accurate judgments about which words they had learned. However, the judgments were more accurate among older children.

Memory monitoring is important to memory performance because it allows students to shift their efforts away from things that have been learned to content needing additional effort (Weinert & Kluwe, 1987). The fourth-grader who tests her memory for spelling words and then spends her time studying the words she missed is more likely to perform well than a classmate who cannot make such judgments.

A Framework for Encoding Processes

Although students' metamemories are important to their ability to remember new information, so too are the ways we ask them to encode it. Intuitively, it would seem that some activities should lead to better memory for content than others. For example, most of us would agree that marking the places where an author used alliteration would do very little to enhance students' memories for the main ideas in a story. Conversely, most of us would probably agree that some other activities such as highlighting key points or answering thought-provoking questions might better help students.

One important framework for thinking about how different kinds of encoding activities influence memory was developed by Craik and Lockhart (1972). Reacting to the mechanistic nature of computer models of human memory, Craik and Lockhart argued that memory depends on what learners do as they encode new information (see also Jenkins, 1974).

In the "levels" perspective, memory for new information is seen as a byproduct of the learner's perceptual and cognitive analyses performed on incoming information. If the semantic base or meaning of the new information is the focus of processing, then the information will be stored in a semantic memory code and be well remembered. On the other hand, if only superficial or surface aspects of the new information are analyzed, the information will be less well remembered. In Craik and Lockhart's terms, memory depends on **depth of processing.** Deep processing is seen as that processing centered on meaning. Shallow processing refers to keying on superficial aspects of new material.

Two different levels of processing may be seen in two common classroom assignments. In the first, students are asked to underline a set of vocabulary words in a brief essay. In the second, students are asked to read the same essay and be prepared to tell the class about it in their own words. If the students follow directions, the first assignment is a clear example of shallow processing—all they have to do is recognize the words and underline them. To perform this task, students do not have to deal with the **meaning** of the paragraph and perhaps not even with the meaning of the words. Nor surprisingly, if we tested our hypothetical students for their memory of the paragraph contents, the odds are they would remember relatively little.

In contrast, if the students who were asked to explain the essay to their classmates followed instructions, we would likely see a very different outcome. In order to put an essay into one's own words, it is necessary to deal with the **meaning** of the content. In so doing, the students would be carefully analyzing the material. If we were to surprise these students with a test of the material, they almost certainly would remember far more about the contents than could the group who underlined vocabulary words.

It can be argued that the two assignments described above were given for different instructional purposes. In fact, the vocabulary word group might remember a larger number of vocabulary words (but probably not their meanings) than the group asked to read and explain the materials. In this instance, students' recall would be appropriate to the type of processing in which they engaged (see Moeser, 1983), a topic we examine in more detail a bit later. In any event, students in the underlining group engaged in an activity poorly suited for learning vocabulary words and one almost guaranteed not to result in memory for the essay.

Another example of levels of processing can be seen in an incidental learning paradigm (one in which subjects are not directed to learn material but in which their memory for that material is unexpectedly tested). Let us suppose that one group of students is asked to count the number of i's in a list of words, and another group is asked to rate the pleasantness of the same words on a 1-to-5 scale. If, after both groups finish their tasks, we give them a surprise test and ask them to recall as many words on the list as possible, the probability is very high that the group that rated the pleasantness of the words will recall far more than the group that counted the number of i's. The reason for this difference in performance is quite simple: Rating the pleasantness of words requires students to deal with their meanings. In contrast, counting the number of i's merely requires a superficial analysis (see Hyde & Jenkins, 1969).

The levels-of-processing framework is intuitively appealing and has led to a great deal of research emphasizing educationally relevant applications (see Andre, 1987a, for an extensive review). The "levels" position, however, has been extensively criticized. Essentially, these criticisms center on the absence of an independent measure of "depth" and the apparent circularity of the "depth" formulation (Baddeley, 1978; Loftus, Greene, & Smith, 1980; Nelson, 1977; Postman, Thompkins, & Gray, 1978). That is, saying that something is well remembered because it was deeply processed does not tell us *how* we may ensure deep processing in students.

In response to these criticisms, Craik and his associates developed two variants of their original "levels" perspective: distinctiveness of encoding (Jacoby & Craik, 1979; Jacoby, Craik, & Begg, 1979) and elaboration of encoding (e.g., Craik & Tulving, 1975). By the late 1980s, the elaboration position clearly was dominant (see Walker, 1986, for a critical discussion) but both are useful in considering the applications of the "levels" framework. We examine each of these positions next and then one proposed by Bransford and his associates.

Distinctiveness of Encoding

The **distinctiveness of encoding** position suggests that the memorability of information is determined, at least in part, by its distinctiveness (Jacoby & Craik, 1979; Jacoby et al., 1979). In a series of experiments in which distinctiveness was defined by the difficulty of decisions required of students during various learning episodes (more-difficult decisions were equated with more-distinctive encoding), Jacoby et al. (1979) found that materials requiring more-difficult decisions at the time of encoding were better recalled than materials requiring less-difficult decisions.

The experiments conducted by Jacoby et al. led to a series of studies focusing on distinctiveness of encoding in reading and mastering various learning tasks (Benton, Glover, Monkowski, & Shaughnessy, 1983b; Glover, Bruning, & Plake, 1982a; Glover, Plake, & Zimmer, 1982b). These studies were designed to determine how student decision making during reading affected recall and to examine the possibility that an independent means of specifying "depth" of processing (or, in this case, distinctiveness) could be developed. In general, requiring students to make decisions about what they read leads to greater recall than when no decisions are required. In addition, when the Bloom et al. (1956) taxonomy was employed as a means of calibrating different levels of difficulty (and, hence, distinctiveness), the results showed increasing recall as students moved from decisions at the lower end of the taxonomy to the upper end.

In other words, as students make more-complex, more-difficult decisions during encoding, they remember the content better. In terms of the Bloom et al. taxonomy, materials requiring processing at the synthesis and analysis levels are recalled far better than materials processed at the knowledge or comprehension level. If we want to enhance students' recall, one important approach is to require students to make decisions during encoding. Further, recall will be greater if they are required to make decisions at the analysis and synthesis levels rather than at lower levels of the taxonomy.

Elaboration of Processing

The **elaboration of processing** perspective was first outlined by Craik and Tulving (1975) and has been further specified by J. R. Anderson and Reder (1979), J. R. Anderson (1983a), and Walker (1986). This position was most clearly articulated by Anderson and Reder (p. 388), who stated:

> The basic idea is that a memory episode is encoded as a set of propositions. This set can vary in its richness and redundancy. At the time of recall, only a subset of these propositions will be activated. The richer the original set, the richer will be the subset. Memory for any particular proposition will depend on the subjects' ability to reconstruct it from those propositions that are active. This ability will in turn depend on the richness of the original set and hence the amount of elaboration made at study.

Considerable research on the acquisition of educationally relevant material has been performed (McDaniel, Einstein, Dunay, & Cobb, 1986; Palmere, Benton, Glover, & Ronning, 1983; Phifer, McNickle, Ronning & Glover, 1983). The results of this research generally have shown that as the elaborateness of students' encoding of information increases, so too does their memory for the content (see McDaniel & Einstein, in press, for a review). Elaborate processing is not merely reprocessing the same information. Rather, it is encoding the same content in different but related ways. For example, in an explanation of how to solve a specific type of problem, students are far more likely to remember the explanation if different examples are given rather than if the same example is merely restated (Glover & Corkill, in press). Similarly, when students read about a famous person, their ability to recall information about that person is strongly related to the number of different details provided (Dinnel & Glover, 1985; Palmere et al., 1983).

Transfer-Appropriate Processing

Morris, Bransford, and Franks (1977) reacted to the original "levels" perspective by offering an alternative. In their view, differences in memory are the result of what is contained in various semantic memory codes (see Glover, Rankin, Langer, Todero, & Dinnel, 1985; Moeser,

1983, for extended contrasts of the original levels position with transfer-appropriate processing). From a transfer-appropriate processing perspective, "shallow" processing leads not to the encoding of, say, the image of the letter *i* if people are seeking the number of *i*'s in a passage. Instead, a semantic memory is produced (e.g., "There were 43 *i*'s in the passage."), but one that does not contain information about the meaning of the content. In Morris et al.'s view, "deep" processing differs from "shallow" processing primarily because the semantic memories formed in deep processing contain the meaning of the content students encounter (e.g., the main idea in a paragraph).

Transfer-appropriate processing is an interesting alternative to the original levels perspective, and it does seem clear that students' memories for to-be-learned information almost inevitably are semantic (see Bransford et al., 1982). For instance, in the example we first used to show the difference between deep and shallow processing, one group of students read to find key words and another group read in order to be able to explain the contents of the material. In the original levels perspective, differences in memory performance between these two groups are due to different kinds of memory codes brought about by different levels of analysis. In contrast, transfer-appropriate processing holds that both groups of children form semantic memory codes. The differences in memory are due to the contents of those memories—the vocabulary group's codes likely would contain very little more than some of the words, whereas the "explanation" group's codes would contain information about the topic of the reading passage. Finally, a recent development in this area has been the concept of material-appropriate elaboration (see McDaniel & Einstein, in press). From this point of view, deep or elaborate processing activities depend on what learners do and on the type of material they encounter. In McDaniel and Einstein's view, for example, prose requires different activities for elaborate, deep processing than does poetry.

Summary of Levels of Processing

The levels perspective and its more recently developing variations all portray memory as determined by what students do with to-be-learned information at the time of encoding. To the extent that students are required to deal with the **meaning** of content, their memory improves. Tasks focusing on superficial or surface aspects of to-be-learned materials result in poor memory for content.

The levels-of-processing framework points to several useful encoding strategies. In particular, encoding activities at the analysis, synthesis, and evaluation levels of the Bloom et al. taxonomy will lead to greater levels of recall than encoding activities at the knowledge or comprehension level. Similarly, elaborate encodings lead to far better memory than sparse or redundant encoding activities. That is, multiple examples, varied details, and alternative explanations of content will lead to the best recall. Sophisticated levels of processing are not restricted to older students or students of greater-than-average ability. Average students as young as eight years of age have performed analysis, synthesis, and evaluation encoding activities after being given practice and feedback by their teachers (Glover, 1979b; Glover & Corkill, in press). When these students were contrasted with those encoding at the comprehension level, the students who were required to analyze, synthesize, and evaluate remembered significantly more content with no more study time. In sum, encoding strategies that focus students on the meaning of content lead to better memory.

The levels-of-processing framework emphasizes the criticalness of what students *do* while encoding information. Because encoding is so important to memory, we examine several different encoding activities later in the chapter. However, keep in mind that the material students encounter interacts with what they do. In the next section, we examine how the organization of material influences memory.

Organization

As we saw in Chapter 2, organization of knowledge is critical in cognition. Early research on the role of organization involved studies of subjects' free recall of word lists. In this approach, subjects were given a set of words to learn and then were asked to recall these words in any order they preferred (free recall). Because subjects could remember the materials in any order they wanted, analyses of the order in which words were recalled (i.e., how they were "clustered") shed light on how subjects organized the words in memory. The goal of such research was to examine the "natural" organization of information in memory.

In general, two methods have been used to study the organization of words in recall. The first involves giving subjects word lists in which some organization is apparent in the materials. For instance, subjects could be given a list to memorize that contained, say, the names of tools or drinks, brands of automobiles, and types of fabrics. Researchers then examine the free recalls of subjects to determine whether subjects used the categories to organize their recalls. Of course, this material-induced approach assumes subjects have knowledge of the categories, so the focus is on the interaction of subject knowledge with organization of the material.

The second method differs from the first because the word lists contain no inherent structure. Here, the method is designed to determine if subjects impose some organization of their own on the material. The assumption is that if an organization emerges, it is due to the subjects' knowledge and manipulation of the material.

Material-Induced Organization

Two classic studies were conducted in the 1950s that focused on the effects of material-induced organization on free recall. In the first, Jenkins and Russell (1952) gave their subjects 48 words to learn. These 48 words were 24 pairs of highly associated words (e.g., *man–woman, black–white*). However, the words were presented in random order such that members of the pairs did not occur together. Even so, at the time of recall Jenkins and Russell's subjects tended to recall the words in a very organized way. In general, the subjects recalled the pairs of words together (*man–woman*), regardless of where they appeared on the original list. Apparently, subjects' prior knowledge was influencing recall. Rather than recapitulating the random order in which the words appeared on the list they studied, the subjects followed their own organization based on their knowledge of the relationships between the word pairs.

The second important study that focused on material-induced organization was performed by Bousfield (1953). In his study, Bousfield gave subjects a list of 60 words to learn. This list consisted of four categories of 15 words each (animals, occupations, men's names, vegetables). As in the Jenkins and Russell study, the words were given in a completely random order. In examining students' recall, Bousfield found they did not remember the words in the order in which they were given. Instead, students tended to cluster the words they recalled on the basis of the four categories. That is, names tended to be remembered together, animals tended to be remembered together, and so forth.

The two studies we described above formed the base for a whole series of studies examining the effects of material-induced organization on people's recall. Although some studies have reported results inconsistent with those of Jenkins and Russell and Bousfield (see Cofer, Bruce, & Reicher, 1966; Puff, 1970), the evidence generally seems to support the fact that the way in which material is organized strongly influences the amount of material students recall and the way in which they recall it. The evidence is especially strong in studies that have focused on the structure of reading materials and their effects on recall (e.g., Chen, 1986; Rayner & Duffy, 1986; Kintsch, 1986).

In general, when reading or lecture materials are well organized, students recall more of the information than when organization is poor (Glover & Corkill, in press). In addition, when clear organizational structures are employed in developing lectures and reading materials (e.g., outlines, section headings, chronological orderings), students tend to use these structures in their memory for the content (Davison & Green, 1987). At this point it seems that an important factor in students' recall of to-be-learned information is the way it is organized. Teachers need to focus on organization, especially of novel or difficult materials. As the organization of material better matches learners' understanding, we can expect improved memory.

Subject-Imposed Organization

The second approach to examining organization in recall has focused on how subjects impose organization in the absence of readily apparent organizers provided in the materials. The best-known work in this area has been done by Tulving (1962). In his study, subjects were presented a list of 16 unrelated words and then tested for free recall. After the recall test, he presented the list to the subjects again, but this time the words were in a different order. After another free-recall test, Tulving again presented the list with the words in a new order. He kept this process up through 16 presentations of the list. Finally, Tulving analyzed the 16 free-recall tests to determine whether people tended to group words together across the 16 trials. Since the words always were given in a different random order, Tulving reasoned that any consistency in subjects' recalls would be indicative of an organization they imposed on the materials.

Tulving's results were striking. Even in the face of random presentations, subjects tended to adopt an organization for their recalls and use it consistently across trials. In addition, there was a distinct relationship between the amount of organization and the amount of material recalled. Apparently, even in the absence of any readily discerned organization, people impose an organization on to-be-learned materials—they do not simply attempt to overwhelm new material by committing it to rote memory. Of course, some ways of organizing materials during encoding are more effective than others. In the remainder of the chapter, we examine strategies that impose organization on material.

Encoding Strategies

Types of Rehearsal

How we process to-be-remembered information makes a difference in how well we remember it. In particular, the way in which we rehearse information influences the quality of our memory.

As a means of examining rehearsal more closely, let's take a look at two sixth-graders studying for a spelling test. For our purposes, we'll assume the two children are of equal ability save for how they rehearse the spelling words. Susan starts at the top of the list, reads the first word, and spells it to herself over and over (*"familiar—f, a, m, i . . ."*). She does this six times for each of the 25 words on the list and then sets it aside. Sheila also starts by reading the first word on the list, but she rehearses the information differently by breaking the words into smaller words and syllables she already knows how to spell (*"familiar—fam, i, liar.* That's *'fam—f, a, m; 'i'—i;* and *'liar'—l, i, a, r"*). Sheila also cycles through her list six times for each word.

If we give Susan and Sheila a test of the spelling words after they finish studying, the odds are extremely good that Sheila will obtain a higher score than Susan. The reason for this difference is obvious to us, if not to the sixth-graders—the way in which the information was rehearsed influenced its memorability.

Typically, the kind of rehearsal Susan engaged in is called **maintenance rehearsal** (Craik, 1979; Klatzky, 1984). Maintenance rehearsal refers to the direct recycling of information in order to keep it active in short-term memory. It is the sort of rehearsal we perform when we look up a phone number and want to retain it just long enough to dial the number (e.g., repeating 472-2225 over and over until the number is dialed). The results of such maintenance rehearsal seldom are long-term (McKeown & Curtis, 1987). How often, for example, have you repeated a phone number to yourself until you dialed it, obtained a busy signal, and then had to look up the number two minutes later to try to call again?

Several studies have examined maintenance rehearsal (e.g., Bjork, 1975; Schweickert & Boruff, 1986). In general, it seems that maintenance rehearsal is highly efficient for retaining information for a short time without taxing a person's cognitive resources. For example, you can cycle 472-2225 over and over while looking for a pencil and a pad of paper, picking up the phone, and thinking about what you're going to say once you reach the person at 472-2225. Maintenance rehearsal also can enhance long-term memory (Glenberg, Smith, & Green, 1977), but it is very effortful and inefficient.

In contrast to maintenance rehearsal is elaborative rehearsal. **Elaborative rehearsal** is any form of rehearsal in which the to-be-remembered information is related to other information (Craik & Lockhart, 1986). In terms of the levels-of-processing framework, elaborative rehearsal amounts to deep or elaborate encoding activities, whereas maintenance rehearsal can be seen as shallow encoding.

Sheila's rehearsal of the spelling words is a clear example of elaborative rehearsal. Rather than merely recycling the spelling words over and over, she broke them into components and elaborated (related) the to-be-remembered information to what she already knew. In contrast to Susan, Sheila's encoding activities are much more likely to lead to high levels of recall.

Another example of elaborative rehearsal in the learning of spelling words can be seen in how the fourth-grade daughter of one of the authors learned to spell *respectfully*. While getting ready to study her spelling, she heard an old rock song in which the word *respect* is spelled out in the lyrics to a very strong beat. Later, when her father walked by, the fourth-grader had her spelling list turned out of sight and was mimicking the singer's lyric line—*r,e,s,p,e,c,t, fully*.

Research suggests that elaborative rehearsal is far superior to maintenance rehearsal for long-term recall but that it tends to use considerably more of a person's cognitive resources than maintenance rehearsal (Bjork, 1975; Craik, 1979; Elmes & Bjork, 1975). It also suggests that maintenance and elaborative rehearsal need to be thought of as representing opposite ends on a continuum of rehearsal (Craik, 1979). At one extreme of the continuum would be the minimal processing needed to repeat a term over and over, and at the other end would be processing activities in which the to-be-learned information was linked to several bits of information already in memory.

Different methods of rehearsal can be taught (Palmere et al., 1983; Phifer et al., 1983). One implication to be drawn from our review of rehearsal is that different types of rehearsal are appropriate for different tasks. When long-term memory is desired (such as when a student will be tested over content or when the information will be important for later understandings), some form of elaborative rehearsal should be employed. As you might suspect, there are many encoding strategies employing elaborative rehearsal, and we review several of them in the next few pages.

Mediation

One of the simplest encoding strategies is mediation. **Mediation** refers to tying difficult-to-remember items to something more meaningful. The original research on mediation in memory was based on the learning of paired nonsense syllables (Montague, Adams, & Kiess, 1966). Although we hope none of what we teach is at the level of nonsense syllables (e.g., ZOB, BUH), the strategy has some implications for instruction.

In early research on mediation (Montague et al., 1966), it became apparent that subjects who used mediators in committing pairs of nonsense syllables to memory outperformed subjects who used no mediators. That is, when subjects could devise a mediator such as *race car* when faced with a pair of nonsense syllables (e.g., *ris-kir*), they were able to tie their memory for the meaningless information to something meaningful and greatly ease their memory task.

Although mediation is a very simple and easily learned technique to enhance memory for a limited range of information, it is congruent with the theme of this chapter. That is, what people *do* with to-be-learned information determines how it will be remembered. Mediation results in deeper, more-elaborate encodings than simple repetition of new content.

Imagery

Our emphasis up to this point has been on the encoding of verbal information. One powerful adjunct to verbal encoding is the use of imagery. (See Chapter 4 for a discussion of imagery and Paivio's dual-coding theory.) Recall in the example at the outset of this chapter that one of the students used images of John C. Calhoun and Daniel Webster as he prepared for an examination. Although this student also was encoding verbal information, he was clearly using imagery. Consider also the fourth-grader who conjures up an image of an emperor (complete with rich robes, a crown, and a jewel-encrusted scepter) when trying to learn the meaning of the word *czar*. Finally, think about the chemistry student who shuts her eyes and visualizes a three-dimensional picture of the bromination of benzene as she studies for a quiz. In each of these examples, imagery is an important part of the encoding of information.

As we saw in Chapter 4, imagery usually leads to better memory performance (Bower, 1970; Kraft & Glover, 1981). There *are* some provisos, however, to consider when we discuss the facilitative effects of imagery. One is the imagery value of various to-be-learned materials. For example, the word *car* much more easily leads to an image than does, say, the word *truth*. Similarly, the word *turban* leads easily to a clear picture, whereas the word *freedom* does not.

Easily imaged words tend to be remembered more readily than hard-to-image words, even in the absence of instructions to use imagery (Paivio, 1975). When subjects are instructed to use imagery, the difference is even more pronounced. Even subjects' memory for meaningless nonsense syllables is enhanced when they use imagery in learning (Kraft & Glover, 1981).

Imagery value should not be thought of as being restricted to individual words (Paivio, 1975). The idea can be extended to the imagery value of concepts (e.g., compare internal combustion to entropy), people (e.g., compare Theodore Roosevelt to Calvin Coolidge), and whole segments of information (e.g., compare *Macbeth* to 99 percent of the situation comedies ever produced). Simply, some sets of information are easier to image than others.

A second issue to be considered when we discuss imagery is the possibility of individual differences among students in their ability to image information (Ahsen, 1987; Kraft & Glover, 1981; Scruggs et al., 1987). Even though very little research has been conducted on this question, the results suggest that some students are better able to employ imagery than others. These differences seem to lead to differences in memory performance. Unfortunately, no evidence exists pointing to whether an ability to image is learned or whether it can be improved with practice. Still, even students who score very low on measures of ability to image do show improved memory performance when they employ imagery (Scruggs et al., 1987).

A third factor associated with imagery has to do with the nature of the images people conjure up. Many memory experts have argued that the best images are bizarre, colorful, and strange. For example, if you wanted to remember that one of J. P. Morgan's characteristics was greed, you could image J. P. Morgan as a hog wearing a business suit with a watch fob and a large black cigar fighting with other industrialists for a share of the spoils. Similarly, if you want to remember that the word *peduncle* refers to the stem bearing a flower, you could imagine a garish flower being carried by its stalk with the word *peduncle* pictured on each side of the stalk.

Research on the value of bizarre imagery, however, has been inconclusive. Early work (e.g., Collyer, Jonides, & Bevan, 1972; Wollen, Weber, & Lowery, 1972) sometimes found no advantage for bizarre imagery as opposed to mundane imagery (e.g., trying to remember *peduncle* by picturing a daisy) and sometimes found it to be valuable (Furst, 1954). More recently, two studies reported in the same issue of the *Journal of Experimental Psychology: Learning, Memory, and Cognition* continued the tradition of conflicting results.

In the first, Kroll, Schelper, and Angin (1986) reported on two experiments in which subjects were exposed to 48 pairs of high-imagery nouns (e.g., *ant–comb*). Each pair of nouns was embedded in five kinds of sentences, with each subject seeing all of the 48 pairs of nouns but only one kind of sentence for each pair. The sentences varied, among other things, on their rated imagery value (e.g., *An ant goes around a comb.* versus *A large black ant carefully fixes its hair with a plastic comb.*). Subjects were told the experiment was about visual imagery and were not told there would be a memory test. Subjects further were asked to conjure up the most vivid image possible for each word pair based on the sentence they saw. Then, subjects were asked to rate the image in terms of its bizarreness, vividness, and how much the two words in the pair interacted in the image. The results of the unanticipated recall test indicated that bizarre imagery did not contribute to either short- (5 minutes after task completion) or long-term (1 week later) recall of the nouns.

In direct contrast to Kroll et al. (1986), McDaniel and Einstein (1986) reported on five experiments in which bizarre imagery did facilitate subjects' recall of words. In McDaniel and Einstein's experiments, subjects also were placed in an incidental-learning situation (they were told that the study was designed to examine ability differences in imagery) and they also used bizarre imagery with some words but not others. McDaniel and Einstein consistently found that when subjects employed both bizarre (e.g., *The dog rode the bicycle down the street.*) and mundane images (e.g., *The dog chased the bicycle down the street.*) on different items in the same list, bizarre imagery facilitated recall. However, when subjects employed only bizarre imagery (when all the words on the list required bizarre imagery), no facilitation appeared. Apparently, bizarre imagery was helpful only when it made some of the items distinct.

Who is correct, Kroll et al. or McDaniel and Einstein? The answer is that both probably are correct. Enough differences exist in the two sets of experiments that direct comparisons are hard to draw. Their results may well have been due to differences in methods and materials. So, recent research on the utility of bizarre imagery falls in the same category as most of previous work in this area—inconclusive (see Cox & Wollen, 1981; Hauck, Walsh, & Kroll, 1976; Merry, 1980; Wollen & Cox, 1981). Our best analysis of this issue is that bizarre imagery probably does not hurt recall (but see Emmerich & Ackerman, 1979), although it does not have a clear advantage over mundane imagery.

As we will see below, imagery is an important component of many mnemonic encoding strategies. By itself, imagery has considerable value in enhancing memory. In conjunction with some of the mnemonic techniques described below, it can be a powerful tool for improving memory performance.

Mnemonics

Mnemonics are very precise memory strategies that help people remember information. Typically, mnemonics operate by pairing to-be-learned information with well-learned information in order to make the new information more memorable. In other words, mnemonics are techniques for elaborately encoding new information.

Mnemonic techniques can include the use of rhymes (*i before e except after c*), sayings (*thirty days hath September, April, June, and November . . .*), gestures (the "right-hand rule" in physics is a mnemonic for determining the flow of a magnetic field around an electrical current—merely put the thumb of the right hand in the direction of the current and the curl of the fingers around the conductor will show the direction of the magnetic field), and imagery. Teachers often use mnemonics as a part of their instruction (Boltwood & Blick, 1978; Higbee & Kunihara, 1985). For example, music teachers may instruct students in the use of "**E**very **G**ood **B**oy **D**oes **F**ine" to help them remember the lines of the treble clef and FACE to remember the spaces. Students report that they often use mnemonics without being instructed to do so (Morris & Cook, 1978; Kilpatrick, 1985; Nickerson, Perkins, & Smith, 1986).

As might be expected, some mnemonics are more effective than others (Levin, 1986), and different mnemonics seem especially suited to specific forms of learning. In the remainder of this section we examine several mnemonic techniques and see how they may be implemented in instruction.

The Peg Method   In the **peg or hook method,** students memorize a series of "pegs" on which to-be-learned information can be "hung," one item at a time. The pegs can be any well-learned set of items, but the most popular approach involves the use of a very simple rhyme.

> One is a bun.
>
> Two is a shoe.
>
> Three is a tree.
>
> Four is a door.
>
> Five is a hive.
>
> Six is sticks.
>
> Seven is heaven.
>
> Eight is a gate.
>
> Nine is a pine.
>
> Ten is a hen.

Students who have mastered this rhyme can use it to learn lists of items such as the names of authors, politicians, or terms in a social studies course. The technique is simple and effective. Its use can be seen, for example, in the learning of the following grocery list: pickles, bread, milk, oranges, and lightbulbs.

If you actually were to use the rhyme, the first step is to construct a visual image of the first thing on the to-be-learned list **interacting** with the object named in the first line of the rhyme. For instance, to remember pickles, we could imagine a very large pickle stuffed into the center of a bun. Next a loaf of bread could be imagined shoved into a shoe as it sits in the closet. The third item, milk, could be visualized as a milk tree— a large tree with glass quart bottles of milk hanging from it rather than fruit. Oranges could be remembered by picturing the knob of the door to be an orange and, when the door is opened, it opens into a closet full of oranges that then fall out all over the person opening the door and roll across the floor. Finally, lightbulbs readily could be seen as interacting with a beehive such as picturing a beehive with a flashing lightbulb on its top with additional bulbs lighting a doorway to the hive.

After each item on the list has been carefully imagined interacting with the corresponding item in the rhyme, the learner is finished until time for recall. At recall, the learner simply recites the rhyme. Each image is retrieved as the recitation proceeds, and so recall of the list follows.

When it is well learned, the peg system has been shown to be effective with word lists of various sorts (Bugelski, Kidd, & Segmen, 1968; Miller, Galanter, & Pribram, 1960). Interestingly, the peg system can be used over and over without losing its effectiveness. It isn't clear why, but previous uses of the peg system (e.g., the grocery list we gave) do not seem to diminish the effectiveness of the system when it is reused.

Beyond its use for committing various lists to memory, the peg system has been shown to be an effective means of learning written directions (Glover, Harvey, & Corkill, 1986), of learning oral directions (Glover, Timme, Deyloff, Rogers, & Dinnel, 1987b), and in the learning of the steps in complex procedures (Glover, Timme, Deyloff, & Rogers, 1987a). For example, Glover et al. (1987b) contrasted several encoding procedures with the pegword mnemonic in terms of students' ability to remember the steps to follow in assembling office equipment. The results indicated that the pegword mnemonic was more effective than other techniques in facilitating students' recall. Indeed, an analysis of many of the procedures students learn indicated that the steps in these procedures essentially are lists to be learned and that list-learning techniques such as the peg system facilitate their memorability.

The Method of Loci

One of the best-known mnemonic procedures dates all the way back to the ancient Greeks. According to Bower (1970) and Yates (1966), the **method of loci** got its name when the poet Simonides was attending a banquet and was called outside. While Simonides was outside, the roof of the banquet hall collapsed, killing everyone left inside. The disaster was especially cruel because the bodies were so badly mangled that not even the victims' loved ones could identify them. Simonides, however, was able to remember each person on the basis of where the person sat at the banquet table. Hence, the name "method of loci" came from Simonides' use of location to recall information.

Despite its longevity, the method of loci has received relatively little research attention (Glover & Corkill, in press). However, the method still is widely used, especially by memory experts (Neisser, 1982). To use the method of loci to learn new information, a very imaginable location such as one's home or the path one walks to school must be learned flawlessly. The location is then practiced so that the person can easily imagine various "drops" in the location such as the sofa, coffee table, window, television, and armchair in a living room. These drops must be learned such that they are recalled in exactly the same order each time.

Once the location and its drops have been overlearned, the system is ready for use as a mnemonic. Let us suppose a student must recall five famous confederate generals: Lee, Jackson, Stuart, Forrest, and Johnston. We could imagine Lee sitting on the sofa; Jackson with his boots propped up on the coffee table, his campaign hat tilted back on his head; Stuart looking out the window; Forrest tuning the television; and Johnston sitting in the armchair. If our list were longer, we could continue to place people in locations until we completed the list.

At the time of recall, we would take our mental "stroll" back through the location and each drop would lead to the image of the to-be-remembered person. As with the peg system, the method of loci can be used over and over without losing its effectiveness. In addition, it can be employed to help students remember a wide variety of information.

In comparing the method of loci with the peg system, there are many similarities. First, rhyme or location must be learned to perfection. Effective use of either of these mnemonics requires that their "base" be flawless. Second, each item in the to-be-learned list must be clearly pictured interacting with its appropriate "partner" in either the rhyme or the location. Third, recall depends on reciting the original rhyme or location and retrieving the appropriate image. For certain kinds of information, both methods work well indeed—they are excellent means of enhancing memory and reducing the effort required to commit new information to memory. In addition, both methods can be used over and over with a wide variety of to-be-learned materials. Both methods, however, exact a price. The price, simply, is the effort required to learn the original "base" on which the mnemonic depends. Students sometimes balk at giving the effort needed to develop one of these mmemonics, but they almost always report that the effort was well worth it after they begin using the mnemonics (Kilpatrick, 1985).

The Link Method Very little research has been done on the link method (Bellezza, 1981; Glover & Corkill, in press). Memory experts, however, report using it (Neisser, 1982), and it has the advantage over the method of loci and the peg system of not needing an external system or previously learned set of materials.

The **link method** is best suited for learning lists of things. In this method, a student forms an image for each item in a list of things to be learned. Each image is pictured as interacting with the next item on the list so that all the items are linked in imagination. For example, if a student needed to remember to bring her homework, lab notebook, chemistry text, goggles, lab apron, and pencil to class tomorrow, she could imagine a scene in which the homework papers were tucked inside the lab notebook. The lab notebook then could be placed into the text-book with her goggles stretched around it. Next, the total package could be wrapped up in the lab apron with the ties of the apron wrapped around a pencil in order to make a nice bow. The next morning, when she attempts to recall what she must take to school, she would recall the image and gradually unwrap it. The interactive image makes it probable that recall of any item on the list will cue recall of the others.

Stories   Another simple mnemonic is the use of **stories** constructed from the words to be remembered in a list (Bellezza, 1981; Bower & Clark, 1969). To use this method, the to-be-learned words in a list are put together in a story such that the to-be-learned words are highlighted. Then, at recall, the story is remembered and the to-be-remembered words are plucked from the story.

For example, let's suppose a student is expected to be able to remember to bring a pair of scissors, a ruler, a compass, a protractor, and a sharp pencil to school. Our student could construct the following story to help remember these items: "The king drew a *pencil* line with his *ruler* before he cut the line with *scissors*. Then he measured an angle with a *protractor* and marked the point with a *compass*."

The story method seems so simple it is hard to believe its effectiveness. However, an early study shows its power. Bower and Clark (1969) gave subjects in two conditions 12 lists of 10 words each. The subjects in one condition merely were asked to learn the words in each list, as they would be tested over the words at a later point. Subjects in the other condition, however, were asked to construct stories around each list of 10 words. Holding study time equal in the two conditions, Bower and Clark tested for recall after each list was presented and found no difference in recall between the two conditions. However, when they tested subjects for recall of all 120 words on completion of the entire experiment, subjects in the story condition recalled 93 percent of the words, whereas subjects in the control condition recalled only 13 percent. The story mnemonic was extremely facilitative in subjects' recall of content.

First-Letter   Among all mnemonics, the one students most often report using is the
Mnemonics   **first-letter mnemonic** (Boltwood & Blick, 1978; Glover & Corkill, in press). This method is similar to the story mnemonic except that it in-volves using the first letters of to-be-learned words to construct acro-nyms or words. These acronyms or words then function as the mnemon-ics. At recall, students recall the acronym and then, using its letters, recall the items on the list.

For example, let us suppose a high school student is trying to remember that borax is made of boron, oxygen, and sodium. The student could take the first letter of each component and construct a word, *bos,* as a mnemonic. Then, when she attempts to recall the constituents of borax on a test, she would remember the word *bos* and generate the constituents from the first letters. Similarly, if we asked you to remember a grocery list consisting of cheese, ham, eggs, radishes, razor blades, and yogurt, the word *cherry* could be constructed from the first letter of each item on the list. Then, when you visit the store, if you remember the mnemonic *cherry,* you should be able to use the letters in the word to reconstruct the items in your list.

As straightforward as their appeal might be, the results of research on first-letter mnemonics have been mixed (Bellezza, 1981; Boltwood & Blick, 1978; Carlson, Zimmer & Glover, 1981). Students already familiar with its use do seem to benefit from the strategy. On the other hand, students who have not previously used first-letter mnemonics on their own receive little benefit from using the procedure (Carlson et al., 1981). To this point, however, it is difficult to draw conclusions about first-letter mnemonics because of the sparsity of research on the technique. It would seem that students who use the procedure should be encouraged to continue, but there is no compelling evidence for teaching the method.

The Keyword Method Of all the mnemonic techniques, probably the most flexible and powerful is the **keyword method.** This method originally was developed to facilitate vocabulary acquisition but, as we'll see, it has many other uses. As in the link method, the method of loci, and the peg method, imagery is critical to the effectiveness of the keyword method. However, the use of imagery in the keyword method varies considerably from how imagery is used in the other techniques.

There are two separate stages in the keyword mnemonic: an acoustic link and an imagery link. In vocabulary learning, for example, the first stage requires the identification of a "keyword." The keyword sounds like a part of the to-be-learned vocabulary word and furnishes the acoustic link necessary to the method (Levin, 1981, 1986). The second stage, the imagery link, requires the learner to imagine a visual image of the keyword **interacting** with the **meaning** of the to-be-learned vocabulary word. Finally, at the time of recall, the original vocabulary word on a test should evoke the interactive image in memory, which will allow for recall of the word's meaning.

An example will clarify these stages. Let's suppose a sixth-grader has the assignment of learning 10 vocabulary words in a language arts unit. Among these words is *captivate.* Although our sixth-grader has a fine vocabulary, *captivate* isn't in it. So, he decides to use the keyword method to help him remember this word. First, he searches for a keyword within the to-be-learned word and settles on *cap,* which he can readily picture in imagination. He then links his keyword to an image, in this case his Uncle Bill, who always wears a cap and, whenever he visits, holds everyone's attention with outrageous stories. So, the student's image linked to the word's meaning is of his Uncle Bill captivating him with a story. If all goes well, when he has his test and sees the word *captivate,* he will remember his keyword, *cap,* and remember his image of Uncle Bill and the word's meaning.

The keyword method does not depend on a perfect match of the keyword to the vocabulary word. For example, the word *exiguous* does not contain an easily located keyword. However, with a little Kentucky windage worked in, the keyword *exit* (rather than *exig*) can be selected. Then, if you will imagine an extremely tiny exit (ours is in a darkened movie theater with red neon letters spelling out "exit" on a mouse-sized sign above it), you should have a workable interactive image. Next time you see *exiguous,* find the "exig" or "exit" and recall the image of the miniature exit. This should be all you need to remember that exiguous means "small."

Although it is an effective means of enhancing the learning of English-language vocabulary, the keyword method actually was originally developed for the acquisition of foreign-language vocabulary (Atkinson, 1975). Consider, for example, the Spanish word *caballo,* which means "horse." The keyword *ball* easily can be picked out, and an image of a horse balancing on a ball readily comes to mind. Alternatively, the keyword *cab* could be chosen, and the interactive image could be of a horse driving a cab on Chicago's Wabash Avenue.

The keyword method is not, by any stretch of the imagination, limited to vocabulary items. For example, let us suppose some history teacher out there has suggested it is important to remember that N. B. Forrest was the only cavalry commander ever to win a naval engagement. The keyword *rest* could be chosen from Forrest's name and an image of cavalrymen lounging on gunboats easily could be conjured up to serve as the interactive image. In the future, when Forrest's name is seen, it should evoke the image of cavalrymen lounging on gunboats and help you remember that Forrest once won a naval engagement. (He did so by having his cavalry ride their horses off the bluffs of the Tennessee River onto the decks of Union gunboats.)

Since 1975, an enormous amount of research has been done on the keyword method. In general, the results have been positive among students of all ages (Levin, 1986; Pressley, Levin, & Delaney, 1982) across several languages (e.g., Atkinson & Raugh, 1975; Pressley, 1977) and has been exceptionally effective in improving the learning of mildly retarded and learning-disabled students (Mastropieri & Scruggs, in press). The method also has been an effective means of enhancing memory for facts other than vocabulary (Levin, 1986) and has been useful in increasing learning from text (Mastropieri & Scruggs, in press; McCormick & Levin, 1984).

Even though study after study since 1975 has shown the benefits of the keyword method, recommendations for its use have not yet made their way into most teaching-method textbooks. The method is easy to teach, it is readily learned by even the youngest children, and students enjoy using it. Since students generate their own keyword and image, very little work is required of the teacher except in actually teaching students how to use the keyword method and reminding them to use it. (Keywords and images, however, can be generated by teachers, an approach somewhat less effective than when students perform the method on their own. Levin, 1986; Pressley et al., 1982.)

Yodai Mnemonics   **Yodai mnemonics** were developed in the 1920s by a Japanese educator, Masachika Nakane, but only recently came to the attention of Western psychologists (Higbee & Kunihira, 1985; Levin, 1985; Pressley, 1985). Actual research on the method is scant (Pressley, 1985), especially in Western settings. However, the method has achieved such widespread use in Japan that a brief review seems warranted.

The term *yodai* means "the essence of structure" (Higbee & Kunihira, 1985) and the yodai mnemonics were so named because they are designed as verbal mediators that attempt to spell out the essence of rules for solving problems. An example taken from Higbee and Kunihira (1985, pp. 58–59) will help describe the nature of yodai mnemonics.

> To teach kindergarten children mathematical operations with fractions, the mnemonics use familiar metaphors expressed in familiar words. Thus, a fraction is called a *bug* with a *head* and a *wing* (Japanese children like to play with bugs). The head is the numerator and the wing is the denominator (words such as *fraction, numerator,* and *denominator* are not used). To add fractions with equal denominators, for example, the child is instructed to "count the heads when the wings are the same." Multiplying involves putting the heads together and putting the wings together. The multiplication sign (×) represents the bug's crossed *horns* or feelers. Dividing fractions requires turning one of the bugs upside down and then multiplying.

As you can see, a fairly complex set of skills can be taught through yodai procedures by putting the operations involved in the skills into concrete terms with which the students are familiar. Higbee and Kunihira report that such methods show a high rate of success, leading to better overall skill acquisition than traditional methods of teaching. Presumably, other mnemonics with similar levels of success could be devised for children who do not like to play with bugs.

The major criticism of yodai techniques (the fractions example being representative) has been that, used in isolation, the techniques can lead to the phenomenon of children's being able to perform skills without understanding what they are doing (see Kilpatrick, 1985). An analysis of the method indeed does suggest this is possible. Kindergartners may be able to add, subtract, multiply, and divide fractions, for instance, without any sense of what they are doing or why it is being done—after all, the children are counting heads and wings, not "adding," "subtracting," "multiplying," or "dividing" in any real sense. This criticism, of course, is very similar to that leveled against the Suzuki method of teaching music, a method that also relies on yodai mnemonics (Higbee & Kunihira, 1985).

On balance, it seems to us there is little point in teaching skills without understanding. On the other hand, though, it also seems clear that yodai mnemonics can be used in conjunction with other methods of instruction. That is, mnemonics such as the bug counting used in teaching fractions could be employed as an adjunct to more-traditional approaches. Certainly, fractions are difficult enough for fourth-, fifth-, and sixth-graders, so providing a mnemonic aid seems highly reasonable. Still, as promising as yodai mnemonics seem, more research is required to demonstrate their value in diverse cultural settings when used in conjunction with other teaching methods.

Summary of Mnemonics

Mnemonics are rhymes, sayings, and other procedures designed to make new material more memorable. From the perspective of levels of processing, mnemonics allow for more-elaborate encodings of new materials and stronger memory traces. The peg method and the method of loci both depend on a well-learned base to which to-be-learned information is related. The link and story methods put to-be-learned items together in a list and rely on the recall of the overall image or story to facilitate recall. Similar to the use of stories, the first-letter mnemonic chains to-be-learned items together by forming a word or acronym out of the first letters of the words in a to-be-learned list. The most-powerful and flexible mnemonic is the keyword method, which employs interactive imagery to form an acoustic and a visual link. Finally, yodai mnemonics use images and terms familiar to students to describe the actions to be followed in performing skills.

Although mnemonics may be helpful used in isolation—such as employing the peg system to memorize a list of items or employing the keyword mnemonic to learn new vocabulary words—these techniques are best seen as adjuncts to instruction. In this context, it seems to us that teachers ought to teach the use of mnemonics to students and encourage their use whenever appropriate. Any time memory demands on students can be lessened, more time is available to focus on higher-order instructional goals.

Encoding Complex Materials

Even though mnemonics have a relatively broad range of applications, they generally are limited to lists of facts, sets of vocabulary items, groups of ideas, or steps in a skill. A good deal of instruction, of course, is much broader in scope, such as when students learn about John Steinbeck's portrayal of human nature, Newton's laws of physics, or American foreign diplomacy in the 1920s. Cognitive psychologists have given a great deal of thought to how students' encoding of such complex materials can be facilitated, and a general consensus has been emerging over the past several years.

Most of the research on improving students' acquisition of complex materials has focused on reading (Andre, 1987b). In Chapter 10, "Reading to Learn," we examine in depth several strategies designed to facilitate students' encoding of reading materials. Here, we briefly review two general approaches for improving students' encoding of complex materials: advance organizers and schema activation.

Advance Organizers

Advance organizers are general overviews of new information provided to learners before they actually are exposed to the new information. For example, prior to a discussion of President Roosevelt's social legislation after taking office in 1932, a high school class could be given an overview of contemporary social services available through the federal government. Ausubel (1960, 1968), who originally devised advance organizers for use with reading materials, argued that new information is most easily learned when it can be linked to stable cognitive structures already possessed by learners. In the example we gave earlier, even the least-knowledgeable student will have *some* knowledge of various social programs, if only through exposure to television. From Ausubel's perspective, advance organizers provide learners with a kind of "scaffolding" to which more detailed material can be related. Returning to our example, a discussion of Roosevelt's actions after being elected should be better encoded and remembered *if* students are able to relate this information to knowledge they already possess.

As we will see when we examine advance organizers in Chapter 10, the concept frequently has been criticized (e.g., Anderson, Spiro, & Anderson, 1978), primarily in terms of the theoretical basis for advance organizers (Derry, 1984) and the difficulty of exactly specifying advance organizers. Recently, however, schema theorists (e.g., Derry, 1984; Mayer, 1984) have avoided many of the problems inherent in Ausubel's (1960, 1968) early views by suggesting that advance organizers function by (1) activating relevant schemata for to-be-learned material and (2) correcting the activated schemata so that new material is assimilated to them. In this view, the interaction of students' prior knowledge and the new information form a richer, broader schema that contains both the original information (e.g., what a student knew about social services provided by the government in contemporary times) and the new information (e.g., the changes brought about by Franklin Roosevelt).

Recent work also has indicated that the problem of specifying the nature of advance organizers can be resolved. In general, organizers employing examples, especially concrete examples of things akin to what students will encounter later, are more effective than abstract organizers. Further, the organizers should be both familiar to learners and well learned by them (see Dinnel & Glover, 1985; Corkill, Glover, Bruning, & Krug, 1988b). Other than the dimensions of containing an example and being concrete, familiar, and well learned, advance organizers could take many different forms—discussions, brief segments of text, schematic diagrams, drawings, and so forth.

Schema Activation

Another approach that emphasizes relating new information to students' prior knowledge as a means of enhancing learning is schema activation (Pearson, 1984). **Schema activation** refers to various methods designed to activate relevant schemata prior to a learning activity. For instance, prior to a lesson on internal combustion, seventh-grade students can be asked to describe the characteristics of their parents' cars or lawn mowers, their own model cars or airplanes, and city buses in order to activate relevant schemata. Similarly, high school students preparing for a lesson on the holocaust can be asked to talk about their knowledge of dictatorships, racism, and "scapegoating" in order to activate relevant schemata. Fourth-grade students, as another example, can be led in a discussion of various neighborhood mammals prior to a lesson on the characteristics of mammals.

The idea underlying schema activation is that students at any age will have *some* relevant knowledge to which new information can be related. A class of fourth-graders we know, for example, began to learn about heat conductance and the relationship of a substance's density to its heat conductivity by first thinking of examples of objects that carried heat or cold (the handle of a metal frying pan, the wall of a room facing outside on a cold day, the end of a burning match), and then doing a simple but carefully supervised experiment in which several rods of the same length and cross section were put into a flame (e.g., iron, glass, wood). They then discussed why some of the rods became warm rapidly, whereas others seemed to remain cool, and related the results of the experiment to their own experiences. (One girl camped out frequently and knew that a metal frying pan would become too hot to touch very quickly, whereas even a burning stick would remain comfortable to the touch at the nonburning end. A boy noted how his metal cup would burn his lips when it was filled with hot chocolate but that the same hot chocolate in a porcelain cup did not make it too hot.)

With their schemata for heat conduction presumably activated, the students weighed the various rods on a balance scale and recorded the weights, noting next to each whether it had become hot rapidly or slowly. Then, the students were asked to make guesses as to why some of the rods conducted heat more readily than others. Finally, the teacher gave a brief lesson about density, heat conduction, and the relationship of the two.

The relationship of density to heat conduction is, of course, a fairly sophisticated concept many adults do not clearly understand. By carefully activating her students' relevant schemata, however, the teacher in our example was able to help her students learn and remember a difficult concept.

Schema activation is a general procedure for enhancing students' encoding of new information. It can involve having students describe examples from their experiences, perform an experiment, review previous learning, or use the context in which new material is presented (Pearson, 1984). Overall, any teaching procedure that helps students form conceptual bridges between what they already know and what they are to learn can be considered a form of schema activation.

Summary

This chapter focused on encoding processes. In the first major section of the chapter, we examined metamemory. Metamemory consists of three types of knowledge about memory: awareness, diagnosis, and monitoring. Awareness refers to understanding that certain things need to be remembered, a facet of metamemory that develops gradually as children mature. Diagnosis refers to two related subskills: assessing the difficulty of the memory task and determining the retrieval demands of the task. Memory performance depends on students' ability to determine what they need to do at encoding and what to expect at the time of retrieval. Monitoring refers to keeping track of one's progress as materials are committed to memory. Metamemory can be facilitated when teachers focus their instruction on having students practice awareness, diagnosis, and monitoring with feedback.

The general framework we provided for thinking about encoding was based on the levels of processing. This framework holds that what students do while encoding determines the quality of their memories. In this view, activities that focus students on the meaning of to-be-learned information result in better memory performance than activities centering on superficial aspects of to-be-learned materials.

However, as critical as what students do while encoding is to memory, the nature of the materials students encounter also influence memory performance. In particular, well-organized materials tend to be better remembered than poorly organized materials. In addition, students are likely to employ the organization given to materials in their encoding. Finally, in the absence of organization, students impose their own organization on to-be-remembered information.

Several strategies that result in more-elaborate encodings are available to students. We can begin to think about encoding strategies in terms of the way students temporarily cycle or rehearse information in memory. We can conceive of a continuum of rehearsal strategies running from maintenance rehearsal at one extreme to elaborative rehearsal at the other. Maintenance rehearsal refers to the recycling of information for brief periods of time to keep it ready for use, such as when a person repeats a phone number over and over while getting ready to dial the phone. Elaborative rehearsal, on the other hand, is the recycling of information in ways that relate it to other, previously learned knowledge. In general, elaborative rehearsal results in superior memory performance, but both types of rehearsal have distinct uses.

One form of elaborative rehearsal involves mediation, in which difficult-to-remember items are converted into something more meaningful and easily remembered. Other strategies for elaborative rehearsal can be derived by working from the levels-of-processing framework.

Another approach to encoding involves the use of imagery. Generally speaking, when students construct images associated with to-be-learned information, their memory performance is enhanced. Imagery is a common component of mnemonic techniques.

Mnemonics are memory aids designed to help people remember information. They include the peg method, the method of loci, the link method, the use of stories, first-letter mnemonics, the keyword method, and yodai mnemonics. The various mnemonics differ, but all share the use of familiar information to facilitate remembering unfamiliar information. Students enjoy using mnemonics and they generally are easy to teach. In our view, mnemonics are best seen as adjuncts to regular classroom methods.

More-complex learning materials are better encoded when procedures designed to tie new information into what students already know are employed. Two general approaches for facilitating the encoding of complex information are the use of advance organizers and schema activation.

CHAPTER 6

Retrieval Processes

In Chapters 4 and 5 we examined the nature of memory, its structure, and the processes involved in encoding. Our description of human memory is not complete, however, until we describe the processes involved in retrieving information from memory. Our focus in this chapter is on **retrieval,** the process involved in accessing and placing into consciousness information from long-term memory. We'll begin our discussion of retrieval by examining some common retrieval phenomena.

Mrs. Thompson has just finished passing out her American history test. Most of the students begin writing immediately, but Ronald reads the first question and feels a cold shiver run up his spine. Not only can he not remember the answer, he can't even remember that the topic was ever talked about. He gulps and proceeds to the next question.

Laura, in contrast, reads the first question and smiles to herself, remembering a joke Mrs. Thompson told on the day she covered the material. Laura starts to write her answer and finds that the words come easily. For Laura, the question is a perfect cue for remembering.

Barbara, meanwhile, writes part of the answer and then stops. She knows she knows the rest of the answer but somehow the words won't come to her. She raises her hand and Mrs. Thompson drifts over to Barbara's desk. Mrs. Thompson briefly clarifies the question. After hearing just a sentence from her teacher, Barbara has a powerful "ah ha" feeling and she returns to her writing, confident that she can answer Mrs. Thompson's question.

Across the room, Bobby is having trouble remembering the answers to the test. Finally, he flips the test over and scratches out the outline he used to organize his studying the night before. Then he uses his outline to help him remember what to say. Mrs. Thompson watches Bobby, bemused because he so often seems to provide his own cues for her tests.

The experiences of the four students in Mrs. Thompson's history class were varied, but the probability is high that we've all shared similar experiences. Sometimes our retrieval processes seem very ineffective and, like Ronald, we draw a blank. Other times, we marvel at our own abilities to retrieve information in great detail. Still other times, we do retrieve the information we need, but not without a struggle.

Research on human memory primarily has focused on understanding encoding and storage. Still, many important issues related to retrieval have come to light in recent years. We begin our discussion of retrieval processes by examining a phenomenon that has come to be known as encoding specificity.

Encoding Specificity

In our discussion of encoding, we pointed out that the organization of material has considerable influence on how well the material is remembered. For several years, psychologists have wondered whether this organization was important only at the time of encoding, only at the time of retrieval, or at both times. In an important early study, Tulving and Osler (1968) addressed this question.

In their study, Tulving and Osler divided their subjects into two conditions. In one condition, the subjects merely were presented a 24-item word list to learn. In the second condition, the subjects received the same word list but in this instance, each of the 24 to-be-learned words was paired with a weak associate (e.g., boy–child). Then, when the subjects were tested for their ability to remember the words, the two conditions were further divided. Half of the subjects in both of the original conditions simply were asked for free recall of the 24 words. The remainder also were asked to recall the 24 words, but these subjects were given the 24 weak associates that originally were given only to the subjects in the weak-associates condition. In this way, Tulving and Osler constructed four groups: (1) word list to learn *without* associates, test *without* associates; (2) word list to learn *without* associates, test *with* associates; (3) word list to learn *with* associates, test *without* associates; and (4) word list to learn *with* associates, test *with* associates.

The results of the study indicated that the weak associates or cue words facilitated memory performance only when they were available to the subjects *both* at encoding *and* at retrieval. Having cues present at encoding only or at retrieval only did not enhance memory performance. The conclusion is that cues indeed make a difference in memory performance, but only when cues present at encoding are reinstated at the time of retrieval. The phenomenon Tulving and Osler observed in their experiment is known as **encoding specificity,** and it has become a basic principle of memory performance.

Many examples of the principle of encoding specificity have been reported in the literature (see R. C. Anderson & Ortony, 1975; Tulving, 1983, 1985; Tulving & Thompson, 1973). Recently, for instance, Rabinowitz and Craik (1986) reexamined some aspects of the "generation" effect and found another instance of encoding specificity.

The **generation effect** refers to the finding that verbal material self-generated at the time of encoding is better remembered than material students merely read at encoding. In Rabinowitz and Craik's Experiment 1, they presented subjects with 56 words to learn. Each word in the list was paired with an associated item. Half of the to-be-learned or target words merely were read by the subjects. The remaining target words had letters deleted from them that were replaced with blanks. As the subjects encoded these words, they had to generate the missing letters from memory. At the time of the test, half of the target words that subjects read were cued by the original associates, and the other half were cued with different words that rhymed with the target words. The target words students had to generate also were split at the time of test so that half received the original cue and half got a rhyming cue.

The results were striking. As Rabinowitz and Craik had predicted from the generation-effect literature (see Jacoby, 1978; Slamecka & Graf, 1978; Slamecka & Katsaiti, 1987; McElroy & Slamecka, 1982), a large generation effect was observed. That is, students remembered far more of the words for which they had to generate missing letters than words they merely read. The generation effect only worked, however, when the cues present at encoding also were present at recall. Apparently, even one of the most durable phenomena known to memory researchers, the generation effect, is governed by the principle of encoding specificity.

Another recent instance of research on encoding specificity can be seen in a study by Corkill, Bruning, and Glover (1988a) which focused on some of the factors that make for an effective advance organizer. Advance organizers are prefatory materials given students prior to reading designed to tie the to-be-learned material in an upcoming passage into what students already know. In their Experiment 3, Corkill et al. divided students into conditions on the basis of whether or not they read an advance organizer prior to reading a chapter on astronomy. Then at recall, Corkill et al. examined the effects of presenting advance organizers as cues for retrieval. In contrast to no cue conditions and other conditions (in which other types of cues were furnished students at the time of retrieval), giving readers the advance organizer as a retrieval cue led to significantly greater levels of recall of the passage content. However, presenting the advance organizer as a retrieval cue only worked if the students had read the advance organizer prior to reading the chapter on astronomy. Students who merely read the chapter on astronomy without an advance organizer obtained no benefit from having the advance organizer presented to them at the time of retrieval. Apparently, even the recall of long reading passages can be facilitated when students are given cues at retrieval that were present when they first activated schemata for reading the material.

The type of cues used in studies of encoding specificity seem to make little difference, as long as the cues are present both at encoding and at retrieval. Tulving (see 1983; or Sloman, Hayman, Ohta, Law, & Tulving, 1988), for example, has set out a distinction between semantic and episodic elements of memory (contrast with J. R. Anderson's declarative and procedural aspects of memory discussed in Chapter 5). In Tulving's view, semantic information refers to general knowledge (e.g., that canaries are yellow or that Greenland has an ice cap) not tied to a specific occurrence in a person's lifetime. (For example, to remember that Pluto's moon is named Charon, it is unlikely that we remember any personal experience related to this knowledge, at least until well after we have retrieved the information.) In contrast, episodic memory refers to our memories for specific events in our lives (e.g., yesterday, one of the authors' daughters caught a two-pound bass; this morning one of the authors had a poached egg and toast for breakfast). Apparently both semantic and episodic information may be used as effective retrieval cues. For example, a teacher could construct an item that used episodic information as a cue (e.g., "As you recall from our class demonstration in which Kerry bent the glass tubes . . .") or an item that used semantic information ("As you recall, many historians have urged that Hoover actually laid the groundwork for recovery from the Depression. What were the . . ."). Either of these retrieval cues could facilitate retrieval as long as they were present at encoding.

The results of studies focusing on encoding specificity are important for educators because they underscore the importance of context in memory. In these studies, the context of retrieval situations is varied by the presence or absence of cues available to students at encoding. However, the effects of context on retrieval go beyond the presence or absence of study cues. Smith (e.g., 1986, 1985, 1979; Smith, Vela, & Williamson, 1988), for example, has shown that even the general environmental context in which encoding and retrieval occur influences memory. It turns out that students' memory for information depends not only on study cues but also on the classroom in which students study. That is, when students are tested in the same room in which they study, their memory performance is better than if they are tested in a room different from the one in which they studied.

Studies of the influence of context on retrieval and the principle of encoding specificity have become integral to our understanding of memory. Encoding specificity helps explain why some test items seem to facilitate our recall and others do not. In short, test items (whether multiple-choice, true–false, or essay) that reinstate cues that were present at the time of encoding facilitate students' retrieval of the content. Test questions that do not provide cues from encoding are less able to enhance recall.

Encoding specificity also helps us explain everyday memory experiences. For example, all of us have had the experience of hearing an old song on the radio and then remembering things we haven't thought of in years. Similarly, most of us have experienced a rush of memories we thought were forgotten when we met an old college roommate or a friend from our high school days. In these examples, the music or the sight of the old friend reinstates cues present when we encoded information. Without the cues, retrieval may be very difficult. With the cues, retrieval becomes much easier.

Last, encoding specificity once again emphasizes the importance of knowledge and context in cognition. Students' memories do not function like tape recorders or videotape machines—they cannot simply replay events at their choosing. Instead, retrieval depends on the cues they have available to call forth memory. Further, the context of a remembering event determines what will be remembered. A rich context providing multiple cues for retrieval will lead to good memory performance. A poor context with few or no retrieval cues is apt to give us a poor indication of what students really do have in memory.

One of the ways in which context at retrieval may be varied is by the demands we place on students at the time of testing. On the one hand, we could provide students with some information and ask them whether they recognize it, such as when a simple multiple-choice or true–false item is used. On the other hand, we could ask that students supply information from memory, such as when we ask them to discuss the reasons for the Treaty of Ghent, the causes of the War of the Roses, or the major characteristics of Hemingway's protagonists. In these situations we are asking students to recall information. A good deal of attention has focused on how recognition and recall operate. We briefly review each of these approaches to retrieving information from long-term memory in the following section.

Recognition and Recall

Imagine that you are preparing to take your midterm examination for this course. The professor has announced that the test will be multiple-choice (recognition), and so you work hard readying yourself to recognize pertinent ideas on the test and to discriminate important facts from other material. You finally finish studying at four in the morning—

exhausted, but joyful in the knowledge that you have mastered the content. Unfortunately, your joy lasts only until you walk into the testing room and see that the instructor has had a change of heart—the test won't be multiple-choice, but instead will be essay.

The events described above are not especially uncommon in education (even though they represent poor pedagogical practice). Even so, studies find switching the type of test students are to take from one form to another to be upsetting (whether from multiple-choice to essay or vice versa). The reactions students have to changing the type of test they expect would lead us to believe there are significant differences between recall and recognition.

Further evidence for a difference between recall and recognition comes from research on how students prepare themselves for tests. In laboratory settings, students who expect recall tests tend to focus on the organization of material, whereas subjects who anticipate recognition tend to emphasize discriminating items from each other so that they will be able to pick out the relevant items from the distractors on the test (Kintsch, 1977, 1986). These different methods of preparation lead to test taking performances shaped to the type of test expected. Students who are tested in a manner consistent with their expectations for testing far outperform students who receive a type of test they did not expect (Carey & Lockhart, 1973; Glover & Corkill, 1987).

Students' actual study habits bear out the laboratory work. Typically, students prepare differently for essay tests than they do for recognition tests. They report that when they study for an essay examination, they emphasize organizing content, relating important ideas to each other, and practicing the recall of information. In contrast, when students prepare for a recognition test, they report focusing on becoming familiar with the material and discriminating the to-be-learned information from other materials. They also recall studying harder for essay tests than for recognition tests. This latter difference makes especially good sense given that laboratory studies indicate that recognition is easier than recall. In almost all situations, students' performance is better on recognition tests than on recall tests (J. R. Anderson, 1985; Mitchell & Brown, 1988).

Despite the overwhelming array of circumstantial evidence indicating that there almost certainly must be important process differences in recall and recognition, the nature of these differences has been very elusive (see Nilsson, Law, & Tulving, 1988). An early hypothesis offered to account for differences in recall and recognition was put forward by McDougall in 1904. This "threshold" hypothesis held that both recognition and recall performance depend on the strength of information in memory. Further, the hypothesis held that a bit of information must have a specific strength before it can be recognized, the so-called **recognition**

threshold. The threshold hypothesis also held that a greater amount of strength is necessary in order for information to be recalled, the **recall threshold.**

The implications of the threshold hypothesis were very clear and seemed to account for most of the data from studies that contrasted recognition and recall. This hypothesis predicted that some bits of very well learned information would be both recognized and recalled as the strength of that information in memory would be above both the recognition threshold and recall threshold. However, when information was poorly learned, it would be neither recalled nor recognized—its strength in memory being below the recall and recognition thresholds. The threshold hypothesis also predicted that some information would be recognizable but not recallable—due to its strength being above the recognition threshold but below the recall threshold.

As appealing as the threshold hypothesis was for more than a half-century, it is not longer accepted by cognitive psychologists. There are two reasons for abandoning the threshold hypothesis. First, it is quite possible for some items in memory to be recalled but not recognized (Kintsch, 1970; Nilsson et al., 1988). The hypothesis, of course, would hold that this was not possible. Second, the threshold hypothesis never offered an explanation of *how* recall or recognition operated. Instead, it was a hypothesis to account for why recall seemed more difficult than recognition.

The threshold hypothesis has been replaced by two contemporary perspectives. The first, typified by Tulving and his colleagues (e.g., Tulving, 1983, 1985; Flexser & Tulving, 1978; Nilsson et al, 1988), argues that differences in recall and recognition are a part of larger contextual phenomena in memory akin to encoding specificity. That is, Tulving argues that it is the match of the encoding and retrieval operations that determines performance. Tulving's argument, of course, is less of an attempt to examine the processes involved in recall and recognition than it is an attempt to account for performance differences in recall and recognition. The second contemporary perspective on recall and recognition is referred to as a **dual process** model. This view holds that recall and recognition essentially are the same save that a much more extensive memory search is required in recall than in recognition (e.g., J. R. Anderson, 1983b, 1985; Rabinowitz, Mandler, & Patterson, 1977).

To understand how recall and recognition searches differ (see Chapter 5 for a detailed discussion of memory searches), we will employ J. R. Anderson's (1985) model. Consider, for example, the following two questions, modeled on similar questions posed by Anderson:

1. *Who was president after Madison?*
2. *Was Monroe the president after Madison?*

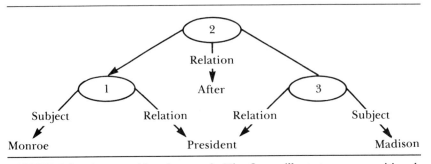

FIGURE 6-1.   A propositional network. The figure illustrates a propositional
network of the information that Monroe followed Madison as President of the
United States. [This figure is based on a similar figure in J. R. Anderson
(1985). *Cognitive psychology and its implications* (2nd ed.) (p. 158). New York:
Freeman.]

The first question (*Who was . . .*) is a recall question, and the second (*Was
Monroe . . .*) is a recognition question. Figure 6-1 pictures the kind of
propositional network Anderson (1983, 1985) believes is involved in representing the information that Monroe was president after Madison.

The recall question gives students *Madison* as a point of access from
which to begin a memory search. From Anderson's perspective, such a
question requires that readers enter memory at *Madison* and search to
Monroe. In order to accomplish this, a student would first activate the
Madison node and have activation spread until it reached *Monroe*. If,
however, the link between the second and third proposition was weak or
if it could not be sufficiently activated, then recall would fail.

In contrast to the recall question, the recognition question provides
two points of access in memory from which activation could spread—
*Madison **and** Monroe*. Presumably, if students cannot activate the appropriate link from *Madison,* they might do so from *Monroe*. In Anderson's
opinion, recognition questions typically are easier than recall questions
because they offer more ways to search memory. Otherwise, however,
recognition and recall essentially are the same process.

Most contemporary psychologists take a position midway between Anderson's and the context-dependent position exemplified by Tulving.
Craik (1979; Craik & Lockhart, 1986), for example, argues that similar
processes probably do operate in recall and recognition but that the
requirements of retrieval differ. That is, Craik holds that in recognition
an item is presented, but that information related to the item must be
retrieved to allow for discrimination of the item from distractor items.
For example, *Did Smith perform research on (a) context dependent retrieval, (b)
the generation effect, or (c) keyword mnemonics?* The item is given: On what
did Smith perform research? To answer the question, you must retrieve

information about Smith so that you can distinguish among the three alternatives. In this case, the answer is context-dependent retrieval. The demands of recall, in Craik's view, differ from those of recognition in that a to-be-recalled item is presented (e.g., *Who won the American League batting championship in 1968?*) and the person must retrieve the item (Carl Yastrzemski).

A full theoretical analysis of potential differences between recall and recognition is beyond the scope of our text. Our brief discussion of recognition and recall may tend to imply that retrieval, provided students are given the proper cues, is a matter of searching for the appropriate memory, finding it, and then just reading it off. Thus, when you sit down to take a test over this content, it might seem that all you have to do is find where you stored your memories and then merely read them off. This view of memory would be incorrect, however. It presumes that the entire content of a memory event (for example, the results of studying this chapter) is stored and that it is stored in the same spot. Further, it assumes that all that must be done is to locate the memory event and read it off. If memory indeed were stored in this fashion, each of us would need a barn to hold our memories. We simply encounter far too much information during a lifetime to allow for such massive storage.

Reconstruction

If retrieval doesn't just consist of the straightforward reading out of memory, what is it? Considerable evidence suggests that retrieval is **reconstructive** (e.g., Mandler, 1984; Spiro, 1977, 1980). In other words, rather than remembering the entirety of a memory event, only key elements of an episode are stored, guided by schemata (see Chapter 4). At retrieval, we bring up these key elements and put them together with general knowledge (both domain-specific and general—see Chapter 2) to reconstruct what we encountered.

For example, suppose you witness an automobile accident this afternoon. Later, when a police officer asks you to tell what happened, you probably will retrieve some key elements of the event and reconstruct the rest. For instance, you clearly can recall that the pickup truck broadsided the Mercedes in the intersection. You also recall that you were waiting for the "walk" sign to come on. But you may not actually have been in a position to see the traffic lights. So, to describe which vehicle ran the red light, you work from what you know to conclude that the pickup *must* have ignored a red light. For all you know, though, the traffic lights could have been stuck so that both vehicles had a green light.

A similar example can be seen in trying to remember how a baseball team scored its runs during a rally. You may remember that the cleanup batter put one in the bleachers and that the weak-hitting pitcher led off the inning with an unexpected double off the wall. You may then remember that the lead-off batter singled when, in fact, he reached first on a sacrifice that the third baseman muffed.

Mistakes such as which vehicle ran a light and how a batter reached base are common when we retrieve events from memory. Students make similar errors in their recall of text and lecture information. They may write about George Washington having been elected the first president of the United States and note that John Adams ran with him as vice-president. In fact, Adams finished second in the race for president and so became vice-president. The election laws that set up our current system of "running mates" for president and vice-president were not formulated until well after Washington's time. In this instance, students remember who was president and who was vice-president but reconstruct how the vice-president came to office. A similar phenomenon often occurs when psychology students describe John B. Watson's famous study of Little Albert. As you know, Watson conditioned a fear response in the child Albert by pairing a loud noise with white objects until the white objects themselves elicited the fear response. However, we have seen several students who went on to state that Watson then "unconditioned" Little Albert and removed the fear response. In fact, no such thing happened. Students use their knowledge of contemporary approaches to psychology research to reconstruct a plausible ending for the story.

As can be seen from the examples we've given, a reconstructive memory system should be far less demanding of memory "space" than a "readout" system. Only key elements need to be remembered about a memory event when general knowledge can be used to reconstruct events. Of course, a reconstructive system also will be open to far more errors that give evidence of improper reconstruction. In fact, it is errors of just this type that have convinced many psychologists of the reconstructive nature of memory (Mandler, 1984; Spiro, 1980).

Two classic studies performed in the 1930s have been central to arguments for the reconstructive nature of human memory. Each has been replicated several times and the results remain consistent (see Klatzky, 1984). The best known of the studies was reported in Bartlett's excellent book, *Remembering* (1932). Bartlett, an English psychologist, had subjects read a very brief story titled, "The War of the Ghosts." This particular story was an abstraction of a North American Native legend that was firmly grounded in their culture. Bartlett's subjects, however, were British and had no cultural background for the story.

After the subjects read the story, Bartlett assessed their recall at differing time intervals. Bartlett noted that recall for the passage was poor even at short intervals. More importantly, Bartlett observed that subjects seemed to recall only the gist or theme of the story. From this gist, they constructed a reasonable story that made a kind of sense out of the information recalled. Not surprisingly, the reconstructed stories often contained errors and distortions—mistakes that made the story fit the general cultural knowledge possessed by the British subjects (see Box 6-1).

In the same year that Bartlett's book was published, Carmichael, Hogan, and Walter (1932) reported convincing evidence for reconstructive processes in subjects' memory for drawings. In their experiment, all of Carmichael et al.'s subjects were shown the same set of line drawings similar to those pictured in Figure 6–2. The subjects were split into three conditions on the basis of the labels they received with the drawings. The subjects in the control condition received no labels. They merely were shown the drawings. The subjects in one experimental condition received the labels shown in List A in Figure 6-2, and the subjects in the second experimental condition were provided the labels pictured in List B in Figure 6-2. For example, the subjects in one experimental condition saw the two circles connected by a straight line labeled as "dumbbells," whereas the subjects in the other condition saw this drawing labeled as "eyeglasses."

When the subjects in Carmichael et al.'s study were asked to draw the figures from memory, some interesting differences among the conditions appeared. The subjects in the control condition most accurately depicted the drawings as originally shown. The experimental group given the labels in List A tended to systematically bias their drawings so that they fit the labels. In a classroom exercise in which we repeated the Carmichael et al. experiment, one student drew nosepieces and bands on the "glasses." Similarly, the subjects in the condition shown the labels in List B also biased their reproductions to fit the labels they saw. In our use of these materials, we've seen students who drew a cowboy hat for "hat" and another who put grips on the handle of the "trowel."

Although the results of Bartlett's and Carmichael et al.'s studies clearly demonstrated that memory is reconstructive, their explanations for how reconstruction operated were vague and not well accepted. It really was not until the early 1970s with the increasing acceptance of schema theory that more-refined theoretical accounts of reconstructive memory began to appear. In general, the view of reconstructive processes in memory emphasizes students' assimilating new information into existing memory structures. Rather than remembering all the details in an episode, students remember the gist of an event (e.g., Washington and Adams were the first president and vice-president) and then use their general knowledge about similar events (e.g., students' schemata for presidential elections) to reconstruct the information at the time of test. The rarity with which we see reconstructive memory in recitations of information committed to rote memory (e.g., the Pledge of Alle-

Box 6-1

Bartlett's Story, "The War of the Ghosts"; and One Student's Protocol

The War of the Ghosts

One night two young men from Egulac went down to the river to hunt seals, and while they were there it became foggy and calm. Then they heard war cries, and they thought: "Maybe this is a war party." They escaped to the shore, and hid behind a log. Now canoes came up, and they heard the noise of paddles, and saw one canoe coming up to them. There were five men in the canoe, and they said:

"What do you think? We wish to take you along. We are going up the river to make war on the people."

One of the young men said: "I have no arrows."

"Arrows are in the canoe," they said.

"I will not go along. I might be killed. My relatives do not know where I have gone. But you," he said, turning to the other, "may go with them."

So one of the young men went, but the other returned home.

And the warriors went on up the river to a town on the other side of Kalama. The people came down to the water, and they began to fight, and many were killed. But presently the young man heard one of the warriors say: "Quick, let us go home: that Indian has been hit." Now he thought, "Oh, they are ghosts." He did not feel sick, but they said he had been shot.

So the canoes went back to Egulac, and the young man went ashore to his house, and made a fire. And he told everybody and said: "Behold, I accompanied the ghosts, and we went to fight. Many of our fellows were killed, and many of those who attacked us were killed. They said I was hit, and I did not feel sick."

He told it all, and then he became quiet. When the sun rose he fell down. Something black came out of his mouth. His face became contorted. The people jumped up and cried. He was dead.

Student's Protocol

Two youths were standing by a river about to start seal-catching, when a boat appeared with five men in it. They were all armed for war.

The youths were at first frightened, but they were asked by the men to come and help them fight some enemies on the other bank. One youth said he could not come as his relations would be anxious about him; the other said he would go, and entered the boat.

In the evening he returned to his hut, and told his friends that he had been in a battle. A great many had been slain, and he had been wounded by an arrow; he had not felt any pain, he said. They told him that he must have been fighting in a battle of ghosts. Then he remembered that it had been queer and he became very excited.

In the morning, however, he became ill, and his friends gathered round; he fell down and his face became very pale. Then he writhed and shrieked and his friends were filled with terror. At last he became calm. Something hard and black came out of his mouth, and he lay contorted and dead.

From *Remembering: A Study in Experimental and Social Psychology* by F. C. Bartlett, F. C., 1932, Cambridge: Cambridge University Press. Pp. 23–26.

LIST A	LIST B	
Bottle	Stirrup	
Beehive	Hat	
Eyeglasses	Dumbbell	
Ship's wheel	Sun	
Pine tree	Trowel	

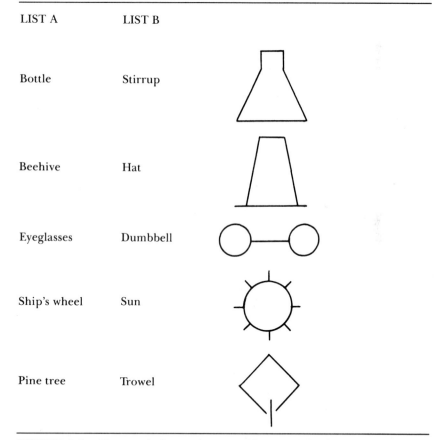

FIGURE 6-2.   Figures similar to those used by Carmichael, Hogan, and Walter (1932). [The drawings are based on those used by Carmichael, L., Hogan, H. P., & Walter, A. A. (1932). An experimental study of the effect of language on the reproduction of visually perceived form. *Journal of Experimental Psychology, 15,* 73–86.]

giance, Hamlet's soliloquy) also suggests that reconstructive memory is most likely when students learn meaningful information—information for which knowledge structures readily are available.

Relearning

There are times when information we once knew fairly well seems forgotten forever. One of the authors, for example, had two years of high school French and twenty-some years later could not remember anything but "Je ne parle pas Français." Apparently, two years of study had disappeared somewhere as recognition and recall of the French language seemed impossible. When the author recently visited Montreal, however, he found himself relearning basic French very rapidly—at least to the point that he was able to shop, ask directions, and even obtain the gist of the day's report on the Montreal Expos baseball team. Apparently, the knowledge of French only seemed to be forgotten since the relearning was far easier than the original learning had been.

The most sensitive measure of memory is not recall, recognition, or the ability to reconstruct events. Instead, it is the memory savings people experience when relearning information (MacLeod, 1988). The relearning approach was Ebbinghaus's (1885) favorite. In Ebbinghaus's use of the approach, he first practiced a list of nonsense syllables until he obtained one error-free recitation. Then, after varying delays, Ebbinghaus would relearn the materials to the same criterion. Ebbinghaus determined the level of memory savings by comparing the number of trials he needed in the first and second learning sessions. The existence of any savings (i.e., if fewer trials were required on the second than on the first session), even when recognition or recall were not possible, indicated that some parts of the information had been remembered between the first and second learning sessions.

Even though psychologists are aware that the memory-savings approach is the most sensitive measure of memory, the method is seldom used. A major reason is that the method often does not seem to be appropriate for complex stimulus materials. Further, a criterion of one error-free verbatim recall might seem reasonable for a list of nonsense syllables, but it hardly seems workable for the contents of a chapter on American history, a lecture on basic genetics, or a discussion of *The Grapes of Wrath*. In addition, after-the-fact attempts to measure savings in learning appear extraordinarily difficult and seldom have been attempted. Indeed, even though the author in our example above believed he experienced a savings in learning, no precise measures were possible even if he hadn't made straight C's in high school French and failed to meet Ebbinghaus's criterion.

Recently, Nelson (e.g., 1985) and MacLeod (e.g., 1988) have developed variations on Ebbinghaus' classic procedure. In this method, subjects learn a list of paired associates with nouns paired to numbers. Initially, subjects work until they can attain one error-free pass through the list in which they elicit the nouns paired to the provided numbers. After a lengthy delay (weeks or months in Nelson's work), a second session is conducted. There are two phases in this second session. The first is a test of recall in which subjects are given the numerical cues and attempt to remember as many nouns as they can. Then, in the second phase, subjects are asked to relearn the unrecalled items and an equivalent number of previously unseen items on a single trial. Differences then seen in the immediate recall of previously studied and new items are taken as indications of memory savings.

Glover (in press) has developed a variation of the approach used by Nelson and MacLeod in which readers are asked to read and study a passage until they can successfully complete a recognition test over the material at a 90 percent criterion level. Then, at the time of the second session, readers are tested via free recall. Subsequent to this testing, readers are given the original passage (containing both what was recalled and what was not recalled) as well as a new passage of equivalent difficulty and length. Readers then are given equal study times for the two passages (old and new) and are tested over their ability to recall passage content. If more of the old than the new passage is recalled at this final testing, this difference is taken as the readers' savings in learning. The results of the free-recall test given at the outset of the second learning session merely are used to obtain an indication of how much, if anything, is recalled of the old passage prior to relearning.

Although relearning procedures seem to hold promise for future research (see MacLeod for a discussion), the results to this point are sketchy. What is clear is that we remember far more than we are able to recall, recognize, or even reconstruct. The form of these memories and how, exactly, relearning differs from original learning are topics of future research.

Applications: Enhancing Memory Retrieval

There are some important guidelines teachers may follow to help students maximize memory retrieval. First, teachers should consider the context of remembering. We've seen that students' memory performance will be better when there is a match between cues present at encoding and cues present at retrieval. For example, we would expect better memory performance when a test furnishes cues that were present at the time of encoding. In general, it would seem that the facilitation of memory retrieval demands that teachers carefully construct tests that present rich contexts for retrieval.

Beyond the match of encoding cues to test cues is the issue of providing a match between encoding activities and retrieval activities (Rabinowitz & Craik, 1986). Students prepare differently for different types of tests, and their retrieval performance is best when the type of test is "as advertised." That is, students expecting a multiple-choice test will perform best on a multiple-choice test; students who have prepared for a true–false test will perform best on a true–false test; and so forth. Facilitation of retrieval also means alerting students to the type of test to be given.

As we've seen, the context of encoding also includes the situation in which learning occurs. Not surprisingly, students can improve their retrieval by reinstating as much of their encoding context as they can. When students are "stumped," it often is helpful for them to imagine the situation they were in when learning occurred (Glover & Corkill, 1987). Envisioning the study room or classroom in which information was first learned often can provide the cue for retrieving information. Other aspects of the context of remembering (e.g., remembering a song that was playing on the radio during studying, envisioning the people who sat nearby during a class period) also may provide retrieval cues. In fact, even a person's moods seem to provide retrieval contexts (Bower, Monteiro, & Gilligan, 1978). In general, as teacher and student both match the context of encoding during retrieval, retrieval performance improves.

Of course, teachers hope that the information acquired in their classes carries well beyond test performance. The knowledge imparted to students should be useful in their future educational experiences and throughout their lives. Such knowledge must be retrievable from cues in new contexts. As we have seen, the probability of retrieval hinges on whether such cues originally were encoded with the information. Consequently, teachers who seek to make their information "usable" will ensure that it is encoded in many ways and with the widest possible range of cues.

A second general guideline teachers should keep in mind is that memory is reconstructive. Memory is not the simple reading out of an event similar to playing back a tape recorder or video recorder. Our best description of recall suggests that students retrieve key elements and then use these key elements and their general knowledge to construct a reasonable response. Overall, it seems that as the richness and quantity of cues at retrieval increase, the reliance on reconstruction decreases. Regardless of how well a retrieval context is provided, however, recalls will vary from student to student based on their world knowledge. Two students with the "same" amount of learning may write very different essays—not because one knows more than another, but because of differences in knowledge available for reconstruction.

Summary

The context of retrieval has a powerful influence on memory performance. Generally speaking, for cues to be effective at retrieval, they must have been present at the time of encoding. This principle of encoding specificity has direct implications for teaching in terms of structuring tests providing contexts for retrieval, and teaching for transfer! One critical aspect of the context of retrieval is the type of test—recall or recognition—given at the time of retrieval. In general, students perform best on recognition tests, but it should be kept in mind that performance is better when there is a match between the type of test actually given and how students expected to be tested. A more important goal, however, is to make information available in a wide range of contexts by helping students encode it in many ways with a broad range of cues.

Much of recall is reconstructive. Students use their general world knowledge in conjunction with key elements of memory events to reconstruct information. Of course, world knowledge also is critical to other important aspects of cognition—especially problem solving, the topic of our next chapter.

CHAPTER 7

Problem Solving

This chapter represents a dividing point. In the past four chapters, we examined human information processing in an analytic manner. In large measure, we were concerned with separate aspects of cognition—attention, perception, encoding, storage, and retrieval. However, these elements do not operate separately. New situations require us to synthesize knowledge held in memory to produce new knowledge—problem solutions. Problem solving begins with the base of our acquired, encoded experience.

What Is a Problem?

It is Thursday night, and three students in Mr. McCoy's fourth-grade language arts class are busy with homework. Sam is writing the last line of a poem he was asked to compose. No matter how hard he tries, though, he can't find a word that rhymes with *orange*. Frustrated, he puts the work aside and turns on the television.

Next door, Jane isn't working on her language arts assignment at all. In fact, she has not begun the assignment. Jane doesn't want to go to school tomorrow and get into trouble with Mr. McCoy about not doing her work. So, Jane is trying to think of a really good reason to stay home so she can do the work over the weekend.

Vic, meanwhile, is trying to finish his report on mythology. He has told what myths are and how they developed among ancient people, but he is having real difficulty coming up with a modern example of a myth. In spite of all his reading, Vic is not quite sure what is and what is not a myth, and he doesn't know how to find out.

Although the challenges are quite different, each of Mr. McCoy's students is faced with a **problem.** In common terms, a problem exists when an obstacle separates our present state from some desired state. In our examples, Sam wants a good poem, Jane wants to stay home, and Vic wants to know what a myth really is. Each student is engaged in **problem solving.** Problem solving is finding a path (a solution) that overcomes the obstacle, permitting us to reach the desired goal state.

From an information-processing view, problem solving is a search for the best of a set of paths that may surmount the obstacle and lead to the goal state (Newell & Simon, 1972). Vic, for example, has several paths he could take in attempting to finish his report. He could continue to read about myths, ask his parents or older brother, visit the library and seek the librarian's help, or, as a last resort, ask his teacher!

The maze depicted in Figure 7-1 gives a visual representation of problem solving as a search process. In a complex maze, as in many complex

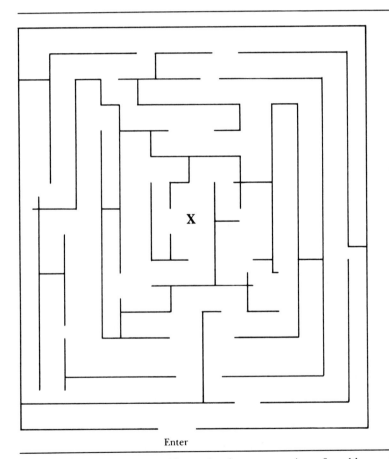

Enter

FIGURE 7-1.   A maze provides a visual representation of problem solving as a search process.

problems, a relatively large number of attractive alternatives are available, but only one is correct. This is true of many problems we face in our own lives. Consider a traditional algebra problem—solving a set of simultaneous equations for two unknowns. The choice of correct order of operations often is a crucial one. That is, the correct order is a path to be discovered.

Or consider an even more difficult problem—choosing a satisfying career. Not only are many careers possible, but the problem solver often is not entirely sure of the nature of the goal state. That is to say, will a choice of a particular vocation—welder, teacher, accountant, nurse, sociologist—result in happiness and satisfaction—an acceptable goal state? The career-choice problem clearly differs from the maze problem. We all know when we have solved a maze, but we seldom are sure we have made the best career choice. Some problems are well defined, and others much less so.

The preceding illustrations represent a variety of problems. As we indicated, the problems differ. Problem-solving theory frequently divides problems into two sometimes overlapping classes: well-defined and ill-defined problems. Vic's concern about the definition of a myth represents a well-defined problem, one for which somewhere (in a dictionary, an encyclopedia, etc.) there *is* an appropriate definition. Similarly, the maze in Figure 7-1 also is a well-defined problem. One correct path through the maze does exist. The "problem" is finding that single, correct path. On the other hand, Sam's attempt to find a last line for his poem represents an ill-defined problem. Although they may differ in quality, there are many possible last lines to his poem. Similarly, a choice of career is an ill-defined problem.

Types of Problems

Well-Defined
Problems
Well-defined problems are those problems for which a clear-cut solution (goal state) is readily available. In addition to the maze in Figure 7-1, many arithmetic, mathematics, and science problems are well-defined problems with one clearly correct goal state. Much of our "conventional" knowledge is made up of solutions to well-defined problems. We "know" how to start our cars, to order lunch at a restaurant, and to compute interest given the principal and the interest rate. Although such problems may seem mundane and uninteresting, we must remember that our daily life is made simple by use of production systems we have stored in memory to already solved, well-defined problems.

Ill-Defined
Problems
Ill-defined problems are those we cannot solve without taking some action to further define them (Hayes, 1981). Thus, Sam's struggle to complete his poem is an ill-defined problem because he has to take action

to create a last line he finds satisfying and that also meets his constraints. In fact, the entire act of writing a poem is an ill-defined problem. Writing requires the writer to represent a goal state—a sense of what the poem should be like—before serious attempts to complete the poem begin. The task of representing the goal state itself is difficult for many problems. In the career-choice problem we described, one must define (represent) for oneself a satisfying career before the problem can be systematically attacked.

Representations of well-defined problems are simple to generate and understand—for example, "Find a value of X that makes this equation true."; this simply is not the case for many tasks, however. Much of human creative behavior may be conceived of as representing problems in new, unusual, and useful ways. Studies of the creative process suggest that creativity is most common in situations where the problem solver makes a substantial contribution to the representation of the task (see Hayes, in press). Thus a sculptor, given a block of stone and appropriate tools, must develop a representation of the object to be produced from the block. However, ill-defined problems are not simply the domain of the arts. On the frontiers of every discipline are issues where a substantial task for the most-able members of the field is representing a problem appropriately. The invention by Einstein of his famous equation, $E = mc^2$, is a well-known example. Although Einstein did not invent the separate parts of the equation—energy, mass, and the speed of light—his creative contribution was to combine those bits of knowledge in a manner that revolutionized the field of physics. In 1913, Poincare, a famous French mathematician, stated that "to create consists of making new combinations of associative elements that are useful." Implied in this statement is the requirement for a large body of knowledge from which the possibility of "new combinations" arises.

In the fine arts, a substantial amount of the curriculum centers around tasks in which problem definition (representation) is a major task. What *is* a significant work of art? What is a "pleasing" arrangement of materials for a still life? In writing, what is a "creative" novel, short story, or poem? In all of these, the problem is ill defined.

In an interesting study of problem definition, Getzels and Csikszentmihalyi (1976) examined the processes advanced art students used in preparing to draw a picture. All the art students had a substantial base of knowledge growing out of, in most cases, four or more years of the formal study of art. Getzels and Csikszentmihalyi asked these advanced students to select and arrange a number of objects, and then to draw a still life. The processes they used to prepare the materials were recorded. Seven years later, students were rated on reasonably objective criteria of creativity (number of "showings," quality of art galleries where works were hung, etc). The more-creative students had handled the objects more often, examined them more closely, delayed starting the drawing longer, and made more restarts than the less-creative. These findings suggest the significance of both knowledge and task representation for successful solution of ill-defined problems. In general, all creative problem solving requires that old ideas or elements are combined in new ways (Martindale, in press).

For the most part, educators have not yet found ways to teach students how to search their memories for information helpful to represent ill-defined problems. Neither is it an easy task to convince students of the need to acquire large amounts of knowledge prior to attempting ill-defined or creative problems. In part, this is because early research on problem solving focused almost entirely on well-defined problems. However, these early studies provided the base from which contemporary views of problem solving emerged.

Studies of General Problem Solving

In 1972, Allen Newell and Herbert Simon described their attempts during the previous 15 years to develop an all-purpose model of problem solving, called the General Problem Solver or simply GPS. In their research, Newell and Simon asked subjects (usually adults) to verbalize their thought processes while solving problems. Because of the decision to study general strategies independently, as far as possible, of prior experience, Newell and Simon used artificial, game-like tasks such as the Tower of Hanoi and a variety of cryptarithmetic tasks (see Figures 7-2 and 7-3).

In both the Tower of Hanoi and the cryptarithmetic problems, little domain-specific information is required. Close examination, however, reveals that considerable general knowledge is necessary. For these problems, skill in reading, following instructions, and making simple mathe-

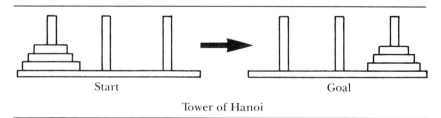

Start   Goal

Tower of Hanoi

FIGURE 7-2.   An example of problems used by Newell and Simon. Pictured is the three-disk version of the Tower of Hanoi problem. Only one disk at a time may be moved and a larger disk may never be placed on a smaller disk.

$$
\begin{array}{r}
D\ O\ N\ A\ L\ D \\
+\ G\ E\ R\ A\ L\ D \\
\hline
R\ O\ B\ E\ R\ T \quad D = 5
\end{array}
$$

FIGURE 7-3.   A cryptarithmetic problem. The task is to assign the values 0, 1, 2, and so on through 9 to each letter so that when the letters are replaced by the numbers, the sum is correct.

matical inferences all are areas of knowledge presumed to be available to most adults. In each problem, the problem solver reaches the goal state by making a sequence of steps or moves. Even preliminary attempts to solve such problems, however, suggest that some moves are better than others. Examination of protocols (typescripts of oral accounts by research participants) of the processes used in solving these puzzles revealed a number of strategies that seemed to enhance solution probability and speed. Among the strategies frequently encountered and replicated in other research (see Greeno, 1974; Jeffries, Polson, Razran, & Atwood, 1977, for examples) were hill climbing, means–ends analysis, and fractionation. We will consider each of these in turn.

Hill Climbing

Hill climbing is a simple technique for solving problems that works on the assumption that in problem solving any "move" that gets the problem solver one step closer to the goal is worth taking. The strategy works by first contrasting the problem solver's present condition (initial state) to the goal state, and then taking any step that moves closer to the goal. Thus in the DONALD + GERALD = ROBERT problem, use of the information that D = 5 leads to recognition that T must equal 0. That step takes the problem solver closer to solution; however, that step alone does not provide much help in terms of what to do next.

Hill climbing, then, consists of continuing to search for a next step that moves the problem solver closer to the goal. Since hill climbing focuses on moving the problem solver one step closer to solution, it commonly is called a "proximity" strategy. Unfortunately, in many problems (such as in the Tower of Hanoi), solutions require one or more moves away from the goal before movement toward solution is possible. For such problems, hill climbing is an unsuccessful strategy. The possibility that the solution to a problem may require a temporary move away from a solution often is unrecognized by problem solvers. Because hill climbing appears to be useful and easy, problem solvers may persist in the strategy when it is unproductive.

Simple examples that reveal both the advantages and disadvantages of hill climbing are paper-and-pencil mazes like those we described earlier in the chapter. These well-defined problems are found in many intelligence tests, as well as in a variety of children's games (see Figure 7-4). Note the advantage of a hill-climbing strategy in helping to choose a "move" that takes the solver closer to the goal. In the first maze in Figure 7-4, hill climbing works since virtually every move possible gets the solver closer to the goal. On the other hand, most relatively difficult mazes, such as the second shown in Figure 7-4, contain blind alleys into which hill climbing will lead the solver, since the blind alleys often seem to lead the solver closer to the goal state.

Means–Ends Analysis

Means–ends analysis is a second problem-solving strategy identified by Newell and Simon. It also is a proximity technique, but it is more powerful than hill climbing. Means–ends analysis is designed to handle more-complex problems, in which moves away from the goal state may be necessary. More importantly, means–ends analysis seeks to develop a sequence of steps (subgoals) that help the solver move toward a solution. Thus, in the DONALD + GERALD problem, one might use the information that D = 5 to recognize not only that T must equal zero (5 + 5 = **10**)

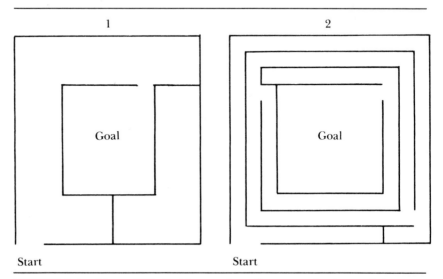

FIGURE 7-4.   Mazes. Hill climbing works well on maze 1, whereas it is unsuccessful in maze 2.

but also that there is a "carry" to the next column (L + L) and therefore that R must be one of the odd numbers 1, 3, 7, or 9. (Figure that out!) The use of general knowledge and the connection of one step to another is the beginning of a more-sophisticated solution strategy. Means–ends analysis attempts to link steps toward the goal state in a logical, purposive fashion. In many cases means–ends analysis strategies work well for parts of a complex problem, yet do not meet the solution requirements for the entire problem. In the Tower of Hanoi task, even with only three disks, a cycle of moves away from (or toward) the solution peg is the first means–ends sequence problem solvers employ. However, many problem solvers do not recognize that the choice of peg for the first move is critical. If the wrong choice is made, the solver inevitably engages in a series of moves that are more than the minimum number necessary to get all the disks on the solution peg in the correct order. Consideration of another subgoal, choice of peg for the first move, and then execution of the appropriate cycle of moves is required in order to reach solution. For many problem solvers, the need to consider several subgoals, and how they are sequenced or related, is not at all obvious. Since means–ends analysis may focus all attention on achieving one subgoal, other subgoals may be ignored.

It should be obvious that use of means–ends analysis techniques in maze solution would eliminate many of the blind alley mistakes resulting from simple hill-climbing techniques. Means–ends analysis requires the solver to look at many dimensions of difference between the present state and the goal state, often leading to the establishment of a set of subgoals in a sequence that will accomplish the next step and finally the goal state. In the following algebra example, it is easy to see a series of steps in solving for X that follow the means–ends strategy moving from the problem statement (1) to the goal state (5).

$$
\begin{aligned}
(1) \quad & 6X + 7 & = \; & 4X - 21 \\
(2) \quad & 6X & = \; & 4X - 21 - 7 \\
(3) \quad & 6X - 4X & = \; & -21 - 7 \\
(4) \quad & 2X & = \; & -28 \\
(5) \quad & X & = \; & -14
\end{aligned}
$$

Step (2) has the goal of moving the "knowns" to the right side of the equation, and step (3) moves the "unknowns" to the left side. Step (4) combines "similar terms," and step (5) reduces the unknown to its lowest terms by dividing the equation by 2. Note the amount of general knowledge such as simple addition, subtraction, and division necessary to solve the problem, and consider the issue of strategic knowledge with respect to how the order of operations facilitates solution of this task.

Fractionation

A still more powerful general strategy identified by Newell and Simon is that of dividing a problem into subproblems, or **fractionation.** A five-disk Tower of Hanoi problem is much more difficult to solve than a three-disk problem (31 minimum moves versus 7 minimum moves). One way to approach the five-disk problem is to divide it—to begin with the simpler three-disk problem—then to use those moves (and strategy developed to solve that subproblem) to solve the five-disk problem. In general, for any task in which the problem can be divided readily into coherent subproblems, fractionation is a useful approach.

For instance, suppose you were given the job of establishing 10 parent–teacher committees in your school. You are informed that each four-person committee must have at least one teacher, one parent, and two males and two females. You soon see that breaking the task into parts simplifies it. Thus you solve the first subproblem by choosing 10 teachers, assigning one to each group. This is easily achieved. Then you assign a mother and a father to each group—also easily achieved. Finally, after examining the composition of the three-person committees, you add either a teacher or a parent of the appropriate sex to make sure that each group has two males and two females. Note that not all groups will have the same composition of parents and teachers, but all will meet the criteria listed in the second sentence of the paragraph. Fractionation into subproblems has made the task simple.

Evaluation of GPS Methods

GPS methods work reasonably well. However, their weakness is revealed by the following problem: "If 15 joules are required to move .056 columbs of positive charge from point A to point B, what is the difference in potential of the two points?" What is a step toward solution? If we hadn't primed you back in Chapter 2, would you know it was an "electricity" problem? Clearly, solving problems like this requires domain-specific knowledge. No matter how familiar one is with general problem-solving strategies, many problems cannot be solved without domain-specific information. As a result of research with many real-life tasks, it has become clear that few problems exist that do not demand specific knowledge. Consequently, the search for a single general problem-solving strategy largely has been abandoned. Of course, GPS methods such as fractionation, means–ends analysis, and the like are useful techniques for many problems. However, they simply are not sufficient to solve most "real" problems. At best, they may aid in the more-effective use of domain-specific knowledge typically necessary for successful problem solving.

More effective approaches to understanding problem solving have come from recent studies that have focused on issues of problem definition—the creation of a problem space.

The Problem Space

One of the major aims of information-processing studies of problem solving has been to try to comprehend how individuals develop an understanding of problems. The understanding an individual has of a particular problem is referred to as a problem representation or **problem space.** The problem space includes a problem statement, the goal state, and potential paths from the problem statement to the goal state. An individual faced with a problem typically first searches memory for concepts or schemata related to the problem. If at all skillful, the problem solver uses existing knowledge about the task to define and understand the problem, thus constraining the memory search (Newell & Simon, 1972; J. R. Anderson, 1985).

Newell and Simon have provided a formal definition of the problem space as consisting of five specific components:

1. A **set of elements,** each representing a bit of knowledge about the problem task in general.
2. A **set of operators,** procedures for using combinations of bits of knowledge to produce new knowledge from the existing knowledge.
3. An **initial state of knowledge** about the specific problem—the total knowledge the problem solver has about the problem at the beginning of solving the specific problem.
4. The **problem itself,** consisting of a set of final, desired goal states to be reached by applying operators (procedures).
5. The **total knowledge available** to the problem solver. This includes knowledge not only about the specific problem, but also about how problems are solved, how to evaluate potential solutions, how analogous tasks have been dealt with, and so on.

Let's return to the example of Sam and the poetry assignment. Since Sam had finished all but the last line of the poem, we can infer that his problem space for poem writing included each of the components listed above. For instance, his prior work on the poem indicates that he understands the purpose of assignments and how to attempt them. Also, since he has produced all but the last line of the poem, clearly he has operators (procedures) for generating poem lines. Further, the lines already generated indicate a specific knowledge about the content of the current poem. Sam also has achieved a sense of the final goal state, since he is searching (now fruitlessly, unfortunately) for a last line that ends with a word rhyming with *orange*. Finally, Sam has available to him a wide range of general knowledge (see Chapter 2) that permits him to think about forms poems may take, places to search for rhyming words (e.g., a rhyming dictionary), and criteria for judging poems. He also has, of course, his writing or typing skills.

Another example of the problem space can be seen in arithmetic word problems. The initial state is the statement of the problem to be solved, and the final state is the "correct" solution. Evidence from studies of word problems (Kintsch & Greeno, 1985; Kintsch & van Dijk, 1978) suggests that most children's knowledge about arithmetic is represented in propositions (see Chapter 4) that consist of elements of knowledge that the solver combines to form a problem model. The problem model is a schema (see Chapter 4) for solving a particular sort of arithmetic problem (rate problems, time problems, etc.). Operators for solving the problem (reaching the goal state) are a part of the schema. The solver generates a problem schema—how rules for a particular problem type work, the order by which operators should be applied, criteria for evaluating progress toward solution, as well as the quality of the solution itself—to find a path to the goal state. Note that in trying to solve a word problem, three sorts of knowledge are involved. First, there is general knowledge about arithmetic, gained by experience with the subject up to the time of problem presentation. Second, the student must have knowledge about the specific type of problem to be solved. And third, the student must have a variety of other information related to the task. The latter type of information includes the context that permits the problem solver to devise ingenious, unusual, but appropriate solution paths. However, contextual information does not always lead to creativity. Sometimes students may apply operators that work well for straightforward problems, but leave the solver at a loss when new problems, somewhat different from those originally learned, are presented.

Newell and Simon's components of problem space outlined above emphasize the role of knowledge in problem solving. Using the classification scheme developed in Chapter 2, components 1, 3, and 4 of the problem spaces consist of domain-specific knowledge. Component 2, however, consists of strategic knowledge, and component 5 is a mixture of domain-specific and general knowledge. As noted above, however, **combining** that information appropriately is the essential task of the problem solver.

Do you recall the method of extracting square roots? Without the use of your pocket calculator, extract the square root of 7,225. Attempt the task before you examine Box 7-1.

Box 7-1

Problem Statement: Find the Square Root of 7,225

Steps		*Algorithm*	
1.		$\sqrt{7225.}$	
2.		$\sqrt{72.25}$	Mark off in units of two from the decimal point.
3.	8×8	$\overset{8}{\sqrt{72.25}}$ 64 825	Find the largest perfect square in the two numbers to the left of the decimal. Subtract from 72 and "bring down" the next two numbers.
4.	160	$\overset{8}{\sqrt{72.25}}$ 64 825	Double the 8 and add a zero. Use the number (160) as a trial divisor: 825 divided by 160 = 5 plus a remainder.
5.	165×5	$\overset{8\ 5}{\sqrt{72.25}}$ 64 825 825	Substitute the 5 for the zero and multiply (165 × 5). Product equals 825. Solution achieved.

In the age of the electronic and desk calculators, many readers may no longer have available a "square-root schema"—the specific knowledge of how to extract square roots. Although the operators are within the grasp of most of us, knowing exactly what operators apply and their order of application may be quite difficult. Were you asked to multiply 85 by 85, the problem would be simple—the routine running off a set of well-rehearsed operators in a sequence—$(85 \times 85) = (85 \times 5) + (85 \times 8 \times 10)$. However, for the less well known task of extracting a square root, lack of a well-remembered routine (schema) makes extracting square roots without a calculator or table of square roots difficult. Unless there is requisite knowledge, representing the square-root problem so that the correct operators will be applied is impossible.

Representing a problem as a problem space is the critical first step of the problem-solving process. Once the space is established, the solver must apply appropriate operators and evaluate the solution. J. R. Hayes and Simon (1974) provide a diagram (Figure 7-5) that suggests the nature of such problem-solving attempts.

As you can see, this diagram shows a solver's attempt first to understand a task and then to attempt to solve the problem based on that

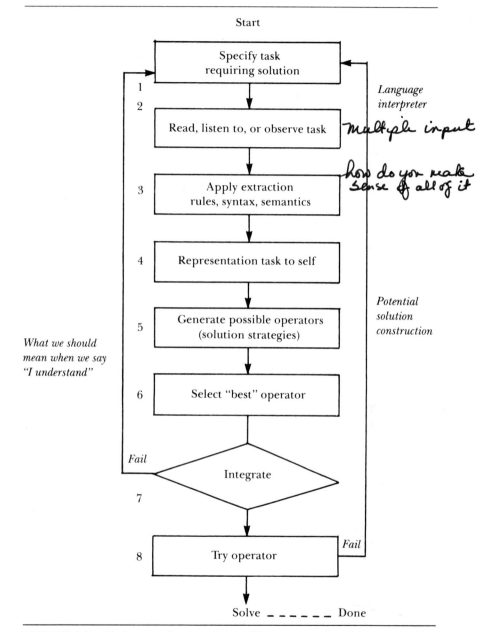

FIGURE 7-5. Trying to solve a problem: The concept of problem space. [Redrawn by permission from Hayes, J. R., & Simon, H. (1974). Understanding written problem instructions. In L. W. Gregg (Ed.), *Knowledge and cognition.* Hillsdale, NJ: Erlbaum.]

understanding. The first three steps in the diagram involve the use of general knowledge skills that permit the solver to make sense out of a problem statement. Thus the statement "Extract the square root of 7,225 " requires a set of reading and vocabulary schemata (see Chapter 4) we apply quite effortlessly. "Thinking" about the problem may generate a description such as "That means I must find a number that taken times itself equals 7,225 " (the problem representation and the goal state). Following this representation, the solver must construct a sequence of operators that, integrated into the correct sequence, will provide the "right" answer, the goal state. Note that the diagram assumes the course of problem solving will not always go smoothly. Thus, at the point of "integrating" the operators, the solver may recognize that the operators are inconsistent or impossible to apply, and that a return to the problem statement must occur to attempt to re-represent the problem. Alternatively, a number of operators may be generated, sequenced, and applied (a solution attempt), but result in an incorrect outcome, one that does not meet the criterion for solution. The problem solver then is directed to return to the problem statement to see if re-representation of the task is necessary in order to develop a different set or sequence of operators.

There is a schema-like quality of this process. Operator sequences appear to represent information (knowledge) stored in a set of associated nodes, but in addition, the information is to be used in a particular order, suggesting a schema form for knowledge storage. Experts seem to have very well developed schemata for examining problem statements and generating clear and meaningful problem representations, as well as a large repertoire of appropriate operators (Larkin et al., 1980; Voss, Greene, Post & Penner, 1983a).

The Importance of Problem Representation

A large body of problem-solving research has illustrated the importance of "appropriate" problem representation (Larkin, 1985). Emphasis on choice of operator, analogy, and other solution techniques obscure the importance of correctly representing the problem. If problems are inappropriately represented, the solution, no matter how successful, will not meet solution requirements (the goal state). The Maier (1931) two-string problem (see Figure 7-6) suggests one difficulty of problem representation called **functional fixedness.**

In the two-string problem, the problem solver's task is to find a means of tying the two strings together. This seems simple enough. There is a problem, however, because the strings are so far apart that both cannot be grasped at the same time. The problem is difficult—only 39 percent of college subjects solved it in 10 minutes. In the room, among several other items, is a pliers. The correct solution is to tie the pliers to one string and

FIGURE 7-6.   A depiction of Maier's two-string problem. The drawing is based on Maier's (1931) description.

set it in motion like a pendulum. Once it is swinging, the other string then is grasped, and the solver moves to the center of the room and waits for the weighted string to approach. The difficulty of the problem appears to grow out of students' inability to perceive the pliers as a pendulum bob (weight). Its function as a tool is fixed in their minds, and they find it difficult to conceptualize it in a different way. Unless the problem somehow is represented to include a pendulum using the pliers, solution is impossible, given the constraint of materials available in the room.

The nature of representation is equally important in other ways. Consider the ill-defined problem of establishing and maintaining an appropriate upper limit for automobile speed on the nation's highways. Although many representations of this problem are possible, two broad categories include (1) representing speed control as a "law enforcement" problem and (2) representing speed control as an energy-saving problem. Clearly the two representations result in vastly different solution strategies (choices of operators). The law-enforcement representation generates operators involving highway patrol personnel, "speed traps," radar, fines, penalties, and so forth. On the other hand, representing the problem as a solution to an energy crisis is more likely to invoke operators that include education, financial payoff (in the form of savings on costs of fuel as a result of lower speeds), pollution reduction, improvement in quality of life, and the like. Although neither of these representations is necessarily correct, the nature of each is likely to lead to vastly different "solutions."

As we have seen in the previous chapters, context is a significant determiner of how knowledge is stored. Context is equally important in representing problems. Thus, based on the knowledge they have accumulated and stored, a highway patrol officer might be likely to take the view (representation) of speed control as a law-enforcement problem, whereas an environmentalist would be much more likely to take the "energy" view. Furthermore, each may be largely unaware of the possibility of other representations.

A particularly demanding task for educators is that of helping students acquire problem-solving skills—some general, but most rather specific. Specific knowledge is crucial to problem-solving success—from the initial task of determining the problem space and the goal state to the task of choosing and utilizing the operators. The context within which knowledge is acquired also appears to be critical. Teachers must be especially aware of the problem representations their students choose. For instance, a teacher may feel that a particular presentation provides the context that will help lead to future student behaviors of societal importance. A student, however, may put the presentation in the context of "I need to remember this for the test," and, as a consequence, fail entirely to encode it with respect to the societally valued context (see Chapter 6). Such encoding may result in successful examination performance, but inability to see school learning as helpful in meeting "real-life" demands. Students not only need to learn new information, they also need to store that information in the memory contexts that enable it to be used appropriately.

Problem-Solving Expertise

Expert versus Naive Problem Solvers

If students hope to become successful problem solvers in mathematics, music, reading, social studies, or even football, they need a knowledge base specific to the domain in which success is sought. This realization led to the development of a research strategy to identify the nature of the knowledge base required to become a proficient problem solver within a domain. This strategy, to which we referred in Chapter 2, is **protocol analysis.** It consists of asking an individual to solve a difficult problem while verbalizing all his or her thoughts during solution. Transcriptions of people's thought during the problem-solving process, called **protocols,** are then analyzed for the domain-specific, general knowledge, and strategy requirements for each problem.

In the protocol analysis approach, researchers first identify specific knowledge domains (in early studies, mathematics and physics) and then, within these domains, identify individuals who are either "experts" or "novices" in that area. Both experts and novices then are asked to solve a set of difficult and challenging problems. During problem solving, subjects are asked to provide the experimenter with a verbal account (e.g., "Tell me what you are thinking.") of their thoughts as they attempt to solve the problem. Comments often include affective responses ("Wow! This is tough!") as well as more cognitive, task-relevant responses (e.g., "This is a Newton's Second Law problem.") Box 7-2 presents a portion of a typical protocol drawn from mathematics. The protocol presents verbal reports that accompany the steps the learner wrote while solving the problem. This student initiated the task with a series of comments that reflect time necessary to read the problem and search for an initial step toward solution.

Box 7-2

Protocol for a Student Solving the Equation $12X - 6 = 3(3X - 9)$

1. Uh-Huh. Solve for X.
2. OK, what to do?
3. Let's see, collect the X's to the left. I wonder why the left.
4. [Writes: $12X + 6 - 3(3X - 9) = 0$.]

Examiner: How did you do that?

5. I subtracted $3(3X - 9)$ from both sides of the equals sign.
6. Now I need to get rid of the numbers from the left side—but have to get rid of the parentheses first.
7. So multiply it out. Then get $-9X = 27$.
8. Collect like terms. Let's get this right. (I hate this stuff!)
9. [*Writes:* $12X + 6 - 9X + 27 = 0$.]
10. Collect terms, so [*Writes:* $3X + 33 = 0$].
11. Get the number on the right side by subtraction.
12. [*Writes:* $3X = -33$.]
13. Divide both sides by 3, $X = -11$. Done!

A finding that has been replicated over and over in protocol analysis research is that experts differ most markedly from novices in the amount and extent of their domain-specific knowledge. In other words, experts have many more "facts" related to the knowledge domain at their disposal. Although the differences in sheer amount of knowledge are striking, even more significant is the way in which these "facts" are organized and available to the expert for use in problem solving. As you saw in Chapter 2, expert–novice studies (e.g., Larkin et al., 1980; Schoenfeld, 1985; Hayes & Flower, 1986) also have shown that experts begin by spending substantial effort attempting to "understand" a problem, and they work from the givens of a problem forward to a solution.

In contrast to experts, novices appear to have little sense of how to organize the limited information they do have. For many novices, solution strategies consist of attempts to generate formulas or rules from memory, class notes, or other sources that they believe in some way relate to the specific elements of the problem. Little time is spent in "understanding" the problem by relating it to an underlying class of problems. The formulas or rules are used to attempt to determine the goal state and some associated formula(s); then the novice often tries to backtrack toward the givens of the problem in order to find a path from goal to the initial state. In many cases, the path appears to be a search for a chain of formulas or rules containing terms that trace backward, finally, to the givens in the problem.

Becoming an Expert

How does one become an expert problem solver? In many ways, the response to this question is quite clear: (1) acquire a large store of relevant information and (2) use that information to correctly represent problems so that they may be solved. This begs the question, however. Exactly how do we use the vast amount of information we accumulate over time? How do we organize bits of information into schemata that permit us not only to solve problems similar to those we have solved before, but also to solve novel problems?

Quite clearly, some problem-solving schemata are learned through direct instruction. In many school subjects, for instance, teachers instruct students in solution strategies. Mathematics and the sciences have many instances of this direct instruction. Similarly, many rules in areas such as writing, oral debate presentation, and music also are acquired through direct instruction; the goal is acquisition of particular sets of schemata.

A major concern for educators, however, is instruction that permits students to solve **novel** problems. How many algebra teachers have worked long and hard to teach schemata for solving equations only to find that a "new" (to the student) problem (a word problem, for example) fails to elicit appropriate, already learned schemata? Common sense suggests that direct instruction does not permit teaching all of the schemata students will need for solving the problems in even a single course, much less schemata for dealing with larger issues and problems. A high school composition course, for instance, cannot teach students all possible composition forms. Yet the course should be taught in such a way that helps students develop schemata for creating meaningful written communication in all the aspects of their lives.

Development of Schemata

Rumelhart and Norman (1978, 1981) and Rumelhart (1984) have suggested that most learning results in the formation of schemata. They propose that schemata are modified by one of three processes: accretion, tuning, or restructuring. Modifications in schemata are, of course, critical to problem solving.

Accretion Perhaps the simplest way to acquire additional problem-solving capability is **accretion,** adding new information to preexisting schemata (Rumelhart, 1984). The new information will give the schema system greater flexibility, thus permitting the schema to be used in situations where formerly it did not work. Thus, for the square-root problem we mentioned earlier, adding one or two bits of information to arithmetic schemata already in existence may permit one to extract square roots. Similarly, knowing more about community agencies and services may permit a teacher or school counselor to be a much more effective problem solver when faced with instances of students' drug or alcohol abuse. Accretion is a common sort of learning that is a large part of instruction in schools. No new schemata are acquired; however, existing schemata are given greater flexibility.

Tuning As one uses schemata, feedback about their value leads to consistent modification and refinement. With time and experience, a schema conforms more and more adequately to the kinds of situations to which it is directed. The general name given to this process is **tuning** (Rumelhart & Norman, 1981). Expertise develops from the continued evolution of schemata as a result of use and feedback. As schemata are used again and again, they are modified by the addition of new information that change them so they operate more effectively. For example, the schemata for shifting gears in an automobile are tuned by frequent practice and feedback so that eventually they become automatic—procedures that operate as a single unit (see Chapter 4). Practice and feedback create the generality and precision we commonly associate with expertise.

Restructuring Finally, Rumelhart and Norman (1981) posit a third mechanism, **restructuring,** that involves the creation of new schemata. When schemata are
modified by accretion and tuning, their basic nature does not change. In
restructuring, however, new frameworks—new schemata—are created
for understanding problems. The restructuring mechanism is significant
because it deals with a perennial human problem: How do we account
for the creation of new (novel) behavior?

Rumelhart and Norman (1981) and Rumelhart (1984) argue that
analogies are the major mechanism for restructuring. That is, new schemata are created by developing analogies to existing schemata (see also
O'Looney, Glynn, & Britton, in press). For instance, consider the acquisition of skills in using a word-processing program. For learners with prior
typing experience, an appropriate place to begin is with the recognition
that a word processor is analogous to a typewriter. Obviously, a word
processor does have some similarity to a typewriter: a keyboard, the
equivalent of paper (screen), and a connection (typing) between the keyboard and the screen. Consequently, many purchasers of microcomputers learn "word-processing" skills by very direct analogy to the typewriter. Yet the word processor is very different (e.g., the delete key,
"wraparound," a buffer, external storage) from the typewriter. Thus, the
analogy is not perfect—indeed, word-processing programs on microcomputers demand skills substantially different from those used with type-
writers, but the analogy is close enough to permit the beginnings of new
schema formation. Unless the schemata for using the word processor
finally are clearly differentiated from the typewriter schemata, however,
the full capabilities of the new technology will not be exploited. Nonetheless, the typewriter schema provides a very useful initial analogy for
word processor schema development.

Use of Analogies Gick and Holyoak (1983) conceived of analogical thinking as a "transfer
in Problem of knowledge from one situation to another by a process of mapping—
Solving finding a set of one-to-one correspondences (often incomplete) between
aspects of one body of information and aspects of another" (p. 2). They
suggest, for example, that learning how the heart functions might begin
with the analogy of the heart to a water pump. One begins with knowledge of how a water pump works. Then the learner either notes (or is
told to note) correspondences between the water pump and parts of the
heart (chambers, valves, etc). In general, Gick and Holyoak found that
the use of *two* or more analogies particularly facilitated the development
of new schemata. Similarly, Stein, Way, Benningfield, and Hedgecough
(1986) report that the understanding of new information in problem
solving ("spontaneous" transfer) is enhanced if learners are convinced
that the information already in their possession will be useful in terms of
solving the new problem. However, Stein et al. also discovered that for

most learners the "cue" to the existence of relevant information in memory needed to be quite direct before it was used to solve new problems. Thus, to effectively use the water pump analogy suggested above, learners often must be directly reminded of their existing information about water pumps and its value for understanding how the heart operates.

Holyoak (1985) has provided a description of how analogies help to develop new schemata for problem solving. Analogies may be used when direct solution attempts fail to solve a problem. However, even college students seldom spontaneously use analogies without direct instruction. A new, difficult problem must cue a similar (analogical) experience from memory. Exactly how this occurs is unclear, although instructions to search for analogies appear to be useful. Holyoak concludes that learners will understand the value of analogy in problem solving only when analogy is studied in the context of other aspects of cognitive functioning such as allocation of attention, memory retrieval issues, or perception.

The inability of most people to generate useful analogies without clues or other assistance presents a challenge for educators. Still, several approaches would seem promising. Teaching students to search for the critical aspects of a problem, for instance, should result in more-appropriate representations. The presentation of numerous opportunities to develop and use analogies in problem solving also seems a logical educational step. Clearly, the analogies selected for practice must share important features of the problem representation if they are to serve as models of analogy use.

Production Systems and Problem Solving

The view of problem solving and problem-solving expertise we have presented thus far points to the importance of memory, the significance of the problem space and problem representation, and the use of analogies to acquire new solution strategies. How do these parts work together to provide a picture of the problem-solving process? John R. Anderson's 1983 book, *The Architecture of Cognition,* has presented a model of cognition that includes memory, problem solving, and other cognitive processes as "different manifestations of the same underlying system" (p. 1). In his view, this "underlying system" is a vast network of production systems (see Chapter 4). He argues that a full understanding of cognitive processes occurs only when *all* aspects of cognition are put together in one unified model.

Production systems are not a new part of the information-processing movement. Their roots lie in the works of Newell and Simon (1972) and of J. R. Anderson (1976), and in research on "artificial" intelligence. As you recall from Chapter 4, a production-system approach proposes that the cognitions that drive problem solving are best represented by a set of condition–action pairs called productions. These productions, in Anderson's view, are organized into integrated units, **production systems.** Production systems form an especially valuable structure for describing the process of problem solving.

As outlined in Chapter 4, Anderson's ACT* model proposed two memory structures: a declarative memory organized in a network fashion similar to that described by Collins and Loftus (1975), and a procedural memory consisting of a set of rules for carrying out tasks. Anderson (1983a) emphasized the role of a third aspect of memory, **working memory,** that serves to combine information from declarative and procedural memory to deal with the particular task at hand. Figure 7-7 presents a framework for ACT* production systems as Anderson conceives of them. Working memory can be thought of as a "cognitive workbench" (Britton, Glynn, & Smith, 1985), whose function is to deal with the interaction of declarative and procedural memories as the individual meets external task demands.

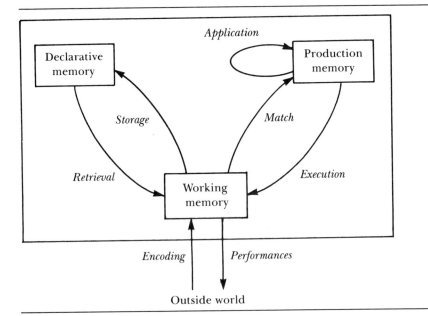

FIGURE 7-7.   A depiction of Anderson's ACT* production system. This figure presents a general framework for Anderson's ACT* production system. In it are identified the major structural components and their interlinking processes. [Redrawn by permission from J. R. Anderson (1983) *The architecture of cognition.* Cambridge, MA: Harvard University Press.]

In ACT*, declarative memory is made up of cognitive units that combine in larger units called tangled hierarchies. A **tangled hierarchy** is a complex piecing together of cognitive elements that may be of three types: temporal strings (one, two, three), spatial images (a rectangle in a circle), and abstract propositions (love, beauty). As we argue in the following paragraphs, tangled hierarchies seem to have many of the qualities of schemata.

Knowledge stored in the tangled hierarchies is the basis for the development of production systems for controlling performances stored in procedural memory. The square-root problem we discussed early in the chapter is an example of such a production system, as are most mathematics and science problem-solving methods. For the square-root problem, declarative memory holds elements of knowledge (the meaning of arithmetic terms such as addition, division, square root, etc.) as tangled hierarchies (the beginnings of schemata). As suggested in Figure 7-7, this information is combined in working memory with the specific problem (finding the square root of 7,225) being encoded into memory. Learning to extract square roots requires developing a procedure (a schema), which then is stored in memory as a production. Signing one's name is another example of an elaborate production system, but one so well rehearsed for most of us as to seem trivial. Observation of a 7- or 8-year-old child acquiring cursive writing productions reveals how difficult *that* production system once was for us. By the time we are adults, however, we have signed our names so many times, a request for a signature directly evokes the signature production system rather than a declarative search for the sequence of letters in our name.

As noted in Chapter 4, working memory is that aspect of our memory that contains our "consciousness" of our particular present-moment situation. As the diagram in Figure 7-7 suggests, working memory serves to encode external information for storage or retrieval from declarative memory. At the same time, if performance is required as a result of encoding, working memory searches production memory for appropriate rules of operation. The discussion in Chapter 5 of "schema activation" provides evidence for this interaction of external events with memory. If rules for a situation (e.g., signing one's name, opening a door) exist in production memory, they are executed. If no effective production system is located in memory, however, then a problem exists and a search schema is activated for a new solution (a new production system).

As we noted earlier, there is a close similarity between production systems and schemata. J. R. Anderson (1983a) recognizes this similarity and addresses it by declaring that ". . . ACT* can simulate the operation of any schema by the operation of some production set" (p. 38). He criticizes schema theory for blurring the procedural–declarative distinction and for its lack of precision—a criticism we already have discussed in

Chapter 4. In our view, however, production systems and schemata have many more commonalities than they do differences. Consequently, we treat them as functionally equivalent. Our assumption is that production systems are schemata in action.

Problem-Solving Procedures Using Productions

The acquisition of procedural responses is slow and the skill represented by a well-learned production appears to be gained only gradually. Fitts and Posner (1967) suggest a three-stage process for skill acquisition that illustrates why many procedures are not acquired easily. According to Fitts and Posner, in the first or **cognitive stage,** the learner encodes the declarative knowledge (cognitive units) appropriate to the particular skill. In stage 2, the **associative stage,** the declarative knowledge is organized and sequenced, errors are detected and eliminated, and a preliminary procedure is developed. In the final stage, the **autonomous stage,** the procedure becomes more and more automatic. With repetition, procedures (schemata) are run off as single units.

In advanced skills, the procedures are so well rehearsed and autonomous that even describing the sequence of steps in the skill is extremely difficult. Information that once was isolated now is stored as a schematic unit—a production system. However, the **acquisition** of that system is likely to have followed the steps outlined by Fitts and Posner. For example, many children face the task of memorizing a piano piece for a recital. Initially, the piece is played note by laborious note until eventually it is played through more or less without error. Once the piece is well memorized, though, it becomes difficult to stop in the middle and then resume. Now, the piece is recalled as a unit from beginning to end and run off as a single production system.

Learning to use a word processor to compose a paper likewise illustrates the complexity of acquiring productions. In this case, the problem is to acquire the skills for composing a paper on a word processor. Solution involves finding a path that permits a writer to enter text in a word processor, to control the quality of that text, to edit it, and to save or print the final product.

Let's look more closely at this process, using the Fitts and Posner model. In the **cognitive** stage of learning, knowledge that permits preliminary representation of the problem (e.g., the vocabulary of microcomputers and their operation—"formatting a disk," "wraparound," "buffer," "display," "files," "saving to memory") must be acquired. Use of an operator's manual and preliminary attempts (practice) help encode these terms in declarative memory. At the same time, a series of operations (formatting the disk, deleting, printing, saving, etc.) slowly begin to be encoded as productions. After preliminary trials in which the declarative and procedural information is used in isolation, this information begins to be associated as the writer attempts to compose a full paper on the word processor. Haltingly, with many errors and considerable frustration, the writer begins to activate productions that use the tangled hierarchies of declarative and procedural knowledge in memory. Once a draft of the paper has been produced, editing skills (more productions) permit the "polishing" of the draft to a final product, the problem solution. At that point, other subproblems of saving or printing the output are solved, using additional newly learned productions.

Following the first few complete cycles through the composing process, rehearsal with additional assignments leads to the development of an array of productions (the **associative** stage) that "run" from memory, without need to consult manuals and with few or no errors. Considerable effort, however, still must be spent in the process of entering text (using the word processor) as opposed to consideration of the nature and quality of what the writer is writing.

Nonetheless, with sufficient repetition of the productions, an **autonomous** stage of word processing is reached. At this point the condition–action units (the production system) for dealing with the word processor are run off so automatically that little or no time or memory is devoted to the procedures for entering material, permitting virtually full allocation of attention to the text being entered into the word processor. Clearly, the interplay of composition skills, paper topic knowledge, and word processor knowledge makes this a difficult problem—difficult even to describe!

Problem Solving and Instruction

Given its complexity, can we improve problem-solving skills? Our belief is that we can. As we have seen, problem solving is an active process that depends on knowledge. Knowledge is the basis, in turn, for the development of a problem representation and an associated problem space. Solution to the problem can be thought of as a search for productions (operators, in terms of Hayes & Simon, 1974) that move from the problem state to the goal state. Assuming that a particular set of productions "solves" the problem, the productions are stored in memory as a unit, ready for use in the event a similar problem occurs in the future. If available productions fail to solve a problem, however, then the problem must be "re-represented" by the solver, using both existing memory and new knowledge gained from reading, observation, asking questions, and the like. Thus, programs designed to teach problem solving can be evaluated with each of these factors—knowledge, problem representation and the problem space, and problem re-representation—in mind.

Building Knowledge

For problem solving to occur, declarative knowledge must be organized into schemata or production systems. A critical task for teachers and others who teach problem solving is specifying not only the knowledge needed for solving a problem, but helping students organize that knowledge schematically. Our belief is that helping learners acquire information that gives them flexibility in problem-solving skill is a challenge that educators have not fully met. For instance, a major problem for novice learners is their inability to "see" how knowledge they already have fits a particular problem (Gick & Holyoak, 1983). The way information has been encoded appears to make it unavailable for use in developing procedures that move the solver toward solution. For example, a child asked to write a "thank you" note may not recognize that he has composition skills learned in an English class that might make the task easy. Linkages between the immediate problem of writing the "thank you" note and composition procedures already acquired may not exist.

For educators, the challenge of building adequate knowledge bases is an organizational problem of great magnitude. How do we teach students to encode knowledge so that it is readily available for solving different problems? No matter how adequate the knowledge a learner possesses, however, its extent and organization is the basis for the next step in problem solving—problem representation.

Problem Representation and the Problem Space

In problem representation, problem solvers use whatever procedures they have available (including GPS-like activities) to "frame" (define) the problem and develop a problem space. In many cases, problem framing proceeds by an individual's seeing a new situation as similar or analogous to an already known one. As just noted, however, learners often cannot see such similarities without prompting from a teacher.

Oftentimes, using past experience to direct present behavior is exactly correct. We need to be aware, however, that the context of past experience may result in the construction of a problem space inappropriate to the present demands of a task. Past experience can psychologically blind us to the need to develop a new representation of the task in a different problem space. A common practical outcome of inappropriate use of past experience is the repeated "running off" of a production system that does not yield an acceptable answer. (Remember what you did the last time your car failed to start?) Many learners lack skill in re-

representing cognitive tasks, perhaps simply from never having done so. Since some problem space definitions are likely to be incorrect, re-representation of problems is necessary.

Re-representation

Failure of a production system to provide an acceptable solution to a problem should lead first to a check to see that the condition–action sequence of operators has been run off appropriately. If the production system simply doesn't work, then **re-representation** of the problem is required so that new, more appropriate productions may be developed. Earlier in this chapter we provided an argument that a rich source of information and an effective technique for re-representing tasks is analogies. We believe that one of the central challenges for developing expertise as a teacher is finding excellent instructive analogies. Of course, experience with a wide variety of problems will aid students in re-representing tasks (see Gick & Holyoak, 1983; Holyoak, 1985).

The production system approach provides a clear conception of how problem solving appears to occur and protocol analysis (see Chapter 2) of expert and novice problem solver behavior is consistent with production systems conceived of as schemata. Although many psychologists have focused on providing excellent models of the problem-solving process, relatively few have concerned themselves with the issue of **teaching** problem-solving skills. Instead, most researchers in problem solving study the problem-solving processes of individuals of varying levels of expertise, attempting to understand how different levels of expertise affect information processing. Nonetheless, because of the increasing demand for individuals with well-developed problem-solving skills, a number of instructional packages have been developed to teach problem solving in the schools. As is described below, most of these packages are designed to teach students general problem-solving methods. Whether these methods can be adapted to teaching domain-specific problem solving remains unanswered.

Methods for Teaching Problem Solving

According to Polson and Jeffries (1985), there is "general agreement that the educational system as currently constituted does not successfully teach general problem solving skills to a majority of its graduates" (p. 417). They claim that many secondary school graduates cannot solve simple problems of installment buying or income tax preparation that require elementary computational skills. Further, they argue that even advanced students find it difficult to apply theoretical material learned in school to out-of-school problems. Thus, the engineering graduate has difficulty applying information learned in school to the problems faced in engineering practice. The gap between theory and practice exists, observers claim, because students are not taught general problem-solving skills.

In the past two decades, a number of programs designed to teach such skills have appeared. Among them are the following: *The Productive Thinking Program* (Covington, Crutchfield, Davies, & Olton, 1974); *The IDEAL Problem Solver* (Bransford & Stein, 1984); the *CoRT Thinking Materials* (de Bono 1973); and the *Feuerstein Instrumental Enrichment* (FIE) program (Feuerstein, Rand, Hoffman, & Miller, 1980).

The Productive Thinking Program

This commerically available program is a set of 15 lessons designed to teach general problem-solving skills to upper-level elementary school children. Each lesson (see Covington et al., 1974, for more complete description) consists of a booklet describing a basic lesson accompanied by supplementary problems. The lessons describe two children who face a number of "mystery" situations requiring detective-like activities. Under the guidance of an uncle, the children attempt to solve the mystery (the problem). Presented in a game-like way, the lessons are grounded in a model of problem solving. Lessons deal with problem definition, getting the "facts" (knowledge), checking facts, making plans, and re-representing problems. The lessons are designed to be completed over a one-semester period. Evaluation reveals that students of a variety of levels of intelligence completing the program all show rather striking improvement on measures of problem-solving skill compared to comparable control groups (see Olton & Crutchfield, 1969; Mansfield, Busse, & Krepelka, 1978).

The IDEAL Problem Solver

The **IDEAL Problem Solver** (Bransford & Stein, 1984) is representative of a number of methods that have grown out of a model developed by Hayes and Simon (1974). After instructing potential problem solvers to face problems, rather than to avoid them, Bransford and Stein present what they call (p. 11) a "simple but powerful" approach to problem-solving methods under the mnemonic IDEAL. Similar to the work of John Hayes (*The Complete Problem Solver,* 1988), Bransford and Stein describe five stages consistent with the mnemonic. The first, *Identifying*

Problems (I), asks the solver to actively seek problems requiring solution. Bransford and Stein argue that problem identification is rarely taught—instead, most instruction in problem solving emphasizes finding solutions to teacher-provided problems. The second step, *Defining Problems* (D), focuses on problem representation. Emphasis is placed on obtaining a clear picture of the problem prior to any solution attempts. The third step, *Exploring Alternatives* (E), involves generation and analysis of alternatives (operators) that might deal with the problem. The GPS strategies discussed earlier (fractionation, for example) provide tools for analysis. The fourth step, *Acting on a Plan* (A), is closely linked to step 5, *Looking at the Effects* (L). In these steps an operator is selected and executed, coupled almost immediately with an evaluation of the value of the operator in meeting the demands of the problem.

Because it is a general model, IDEAL can be adapted to a wide range of age and ability groups. It also can be adapted to teaching problem solving in a large number of subject domains such as physics, history, composition, and the like. However, Bransford and Stein thus far have provided no research directly testing the effectiveness of the model; instead, its effectiveness is argued from its consistency with theoretical descriptions of the problem-solving process, which in turn grow out of empirical studies of (usually) individual problem solvers.

The CoRT Thinking Materials

CoRT (Cognitive Research Trust) materials consist of a two-year course for improving thinking skills (de Bono, 1973). The lessons include not only problem-solving skills, but the development of interpersonal skills and creative thinking. The lessons are presumed to be appropriate to children of a wide age range. The six units of materials include topics such as planning, generating alternatives, analyzing, comparing, selecting, evaluating, and the like. A unit designed for a 10-week period consists of a series of leaflets, each discussing a single topic. Also included are examples, practice items, and ideas for further practice on the topic. The leaflets easily can be used in group settings. A number of games, called Think Links, are designed to facilitate practice with the topics. In the Gestalt tradition (see Chapter 3), de Bono stresses the perceptual (pattern) aspect of problem solving and tries to teach students effective techniques for breaking loose from ineffective patterns. He also believes that problem solving is learned by practice; thus, following a brief description of each principle in a leaflet, the bulk of instructional time is spent practicing the principle. Although de Bono cites informal research he and his colleagues have done illustrating the effectiveness of the programs, little formal research exists to support claims for its effectiveness.

Feuerstein's Instrumental Enrichment

Feuerstein's **instrumental enrichment** (FIE) **system** centers on what he calls mediated-learning experiences (MLE). Mediated-learning experiences provide activities that teach learners to interpret their experience. MLEs are deliberate interventions by teachers, parents, or others designed to help learners interpret and organize events. The basic task of the MLE is to teach the child to play an active role in problem solving and, ultimately, to solve problems independently. For example, imagine a parent helping a student with a homework assignment. One parent simply may monitor the child's behavior, reminding her when necessary to stay "on task," with little concern for what the student does. Another parent may interact with the child about the assignment, helping her decide the most important cues in the assignment so that the child knows where to begin problem solving. Such an involved parent teaches the child the value of planning. Furthermore, the parent might point out the potential value of the homework assignment for other activities, thus broadening the student's sense of the usefulness of the task.

Instructionally, FIE provides a series of exercises (called "instruments" by Feuerstein) that provide the context for learning. At present, 14 or 15 instruments, arranged in order of increasing complexity, are available for 10- to 18-year-old students. The program is designed to be taught three to five times per week for 2–3 years. The exercises are paper-and-pencil activities designed to help the student identify problem-solving procedures and permit the teacher to "bridge" from the activities (problems) to subject matter of interest to student and teacher. Most FIE lessons provide "practice" exercises carried out under teacher supervision to provide feedback to students in their attempts to identify and evaluate the strategies used in solution attempts. FIE also provides a language of problem solving—teaching problem-solving concepts such as planning, strategy choice, evaluation, and the like. Each instrument is designed to have wide generality. A special feature of this program is the deliberate focus on instruction of special populations. Thus, it has been used with educable mentally retarded, learning-disabled, behavior-disordered, and hearing-impaired youngsters.

Bransford, Arbitman-Smith, Stein, and Vye (1985) and Savalle, Twohig, and Rachford (1986) summarize efforts to evaluate the effectiveness of FIE. Based on a wide range of evaluation studies conducted in Israel, Venezuela, the United States, and Canada, students exposed to the FIE program performed better than control groups on tests such as the Ravens Progressive Matrices and some achievement subtests such as mathematics. The effects were found with a wide variety of student types. However, there also have been a number of studies showing no significant difference as a result of FIE training. In general, the features present in "successful" studies were the presence of well-trained FIE teachers and student instruction that lasted 80 hours or more.

Evaluation of Methods for Teaching Problem Solving

The four programs just described are only a sample of those available. Unfortunately, two of the programs report little or no data on program effectiveness. For the other two, the productive thinking program and FIE, the outcome data are not conclusive. Given the changes that have occurred in the past decade in our conception of problem solving, the lack of success these programs have experienced is not surprising. How well do these programs deal with issues of knowledge, problem representation, problem space development, and problem re-representation in domain-specific areas? Since each of the programs is an attempt to teach general problem-solving skills, perhaps it is unfair to evaluate them in domain areas. We already have noted that most significant problems we face demand substantial amounts of domain-specific declarative and procedural knowledge.

On the other hand, each of the problem-solving programs teaches general problem-solving procedures that provide a basis for organizing the encoding of new domain-specific declarative information so that it ultimately may be encoded into productions appropriate to the knowledge domain. J. R. Anderson (1987) describes problem solving in new domains as the process of using GPS procedures on existing declarative knowledge. From these general problem-solving procedures, production rules may be developed that are more and more domain-specific. New information is incorporated into existing declarative knowledge. If programs such as IDEAL or FIE provide novice problem solvers with basic skills that permit them to analyze new information, encode it with existing declarative knowledge, and generate domain-specific productions, then such programs may be valuable. Also, the FIE program is noteworthy in its attempt to provide problem-solving skills to populations that might not have well-developed general problem-solving skills. All of the programs described attempt to provide instruction in problem representation and re-representation; however, this instruction takes place in general rather than domain-specific problem-solving settings.

In sum, existing instructional packages for teaching problem solving emphasize general, not domain-specific, problem-solving skills. Carefully used, and with sufficient opportunity for practice, they may help develop general problem-solving skills. There is at least suggestive evidence (J. R. Anderson, 1987) that these GPS skills are the basis for domain-specific problem solving. Intuitively, it seems that teachers using such programs must carefully show their students how skills learned from the programs can be used to help acquire new domain-specific information. The problem-solving skills must be encoded as productions dealing with specific content. Of course, confidence that these programs will enhance problem solving in domain-specific areas of problem solving awaits further research.

Implications for Instruction

What can educators do to improve the problem-solving capabilities of their students? One purpose of this chapter is to suggest that problem solving is not a mysterious process, but one we understand reasonably well. The following assertions are well grounded in research:

1. **Problem solving is knowledge based.** From the outset, a major goal of education should be the accumulation of organized knowledge (see Chapter 2). Although sheer amount of knowledge does not ensure problem-solving skill, problem solving is impossible without a sufficient knowledge base. Thus instruction with the intent of providing knowledge can never start too early. Of course, one begins with knowledge adapted to the understanding appropriate to the age of the learner.

2. **Formal instruction should provide learners with organizational schemata that permit easy encoding and retrieval of knowledge.** Conceiving of memory as storage of a large set of schemata suggests the importance of providing an organizational focus to learning. Teachers need to use models that demonstrate the relatedness of bits of information and avoid presenting information without a framework for encoding and storage. In most cases, this requires that teachers have a good sense of the knowledge their students have at the time of learning. This permits the teacher to tie problem solving to information already known and understood by students.

3. **Great care should be taken with issues of problem representation—developing an appropriate problem space.** Student failure to understand a problem may come from instructor failure to help students represent it meaningfully. Part of this challenge is making sure students have the appropriate knowledge. Beyond this, however, much instruction should take the form of asking the *students*, rather than teachers, to try to represent tasks in new ways. Emphasis needs to be given to careful, thoughtful analysis of tasks—identification of constraints, choice of operators, and criteria for evaluating solutions—all completed by the problem solver before problem solving actually begins.

4. **Existing programs designed to teach problem solving focus primarily on development of general problem-solving skills.** Although

these skills are valuable, most problem solving takes place within subject domains. Thus, teachers must take steps to ensure that general skills are used in conjunction with specific domain areas so that students learn the value of GPS skills in the early phases of understanding a "new" domain of information. GPS skills cannot substitute for problem-solving skills in specific knowledge domains.

5. **Instructors need to identify and develop analogies that take advantage of knowledge students already possess.** Analogies help students use knowledge they already possess. Since analogies are not identical to the subject being taught, however, teachers need to ensure that the analogies they choose are apt and that the limitations of analogies are carefully pointed out.

6. **Problem representation and re-representation should take a significant portion of teaching time.** Learners need time to represent and re-represent problems. Not only must materials be selected carefully, students must be given substantial opportunity, under low-threat conditions, to re-represent tasks for which an earlier representation has been unsatisfactory. The all-too-common practice of scoring examinations without giving students specific training and opportunity to "re-represent" their answers to "missed" problems is a case in point.

7. **Most significant real-world problems are ill-defined.** Teachers and schools need to provide many opportunities for students to try to represent and re-represent ill-defined problems. Students should be allowed, on their own, to verify the adequacy of representations. This requires well-prepared teachers, of course, who are confident of their own skills in dealing with ill-defined problems.

8. **The processes of problem solving are most adequately represented by production systems—condition–action pairs.** Declarative knowledge needs to be transformed into procedures. The development and use of the set of productions implied by a particular representation of a problem and its goal state may need to be modeled for students; furthermore, students should be taught to monitor their own production systems to search for knowledge errors as well as for flaws in the logic of the production sequence.

Summary

In this chapter, the elements of the information-processing system are combined as they describe human problem-solving performance. Problem solving is a search for the best of a set of paths that surmount an obstacle and reach a satisfying goal state (solution). Well-defined problems have a clear goal state and lead to a solution for which there is consensus. Ill-defined problems require actions by the solver to define the goal state. Early research was characterized by an emphasis on a general problem-solving model. More recently, the focus has been on the development of domain-specific problem spaces. Problem solving proceeds by first establishing a problem space, the understanding a solver has of a particular problem. The nature of the problem space is significantly shaped by the extent and kind of knowledge the problem solver brings to the problem.

Substantial differences exist in how novices and experts represent problems—not only in the amount of knowledge they bring to bear, but also in how they organize their knowledge. If a problem is inappropriately represented, it will not lead to a satisfying solution and must be re-represented if successful problem solving is to occur.

In problem solving, schemata are activated from memory. Individuals appear to gain in problem-solving skill through changes in the schemata used for problem solving. Such changes may result from accretion (adding to existing schemata), tuning (refining existing schemata), or restructuring (creating new schemata in memory). New schemata appear to be learned by seeing analogies with existing schemata.

In general, we view the process of problem solving as a production system. A production system is a series of condition–action units (productions) that represent the search through the space of possible problems for the best solution. Well-rehearsed condition–action sets called procedures are stored in memory for use as individual units.

Several instructional programs for teaching general problem solving exist. We briefly examined four: the Productive Thinking Program, the IDEAL Problem Solver, the CoRT Thinking Materials, and the Feuerstein Instrumental Enrichment System. Although research support for the effectiveness of these programs to teach problem solving is limited, they do appear to improve some aspects of thinking and lay the groundwork for the development of domain-specific problem-solving skills.

II

Cognitive Skills
in the Schools

CHAPTER 8

Language Development in the School Years

For a quarter-century now, language development has been one of the most exciting and fertile areas of investigation in child development. Researchers have recorded the tremendously rapid changes that take place as infants and preschoolers acquire language and have developed models to account for such aspects of child language as mother–infant communication and early acquisition of word meanings, morphology, syntax, and intentionality in language use (Anisfeld, 1984). Research testing these models has been richly rewarding; we now have a much more complete description of language acquisition than ever before. We also now can see in children's language many previously unrecognized precursors for later language and cognitive development.

The intense interest in early language now is being complemented by a growing body of research on language development in school-age children. Although many basic features of language are in place by age three or four, development is by no means finished. Language development continues along many critical dimensions through high school (Durkin, 1986), and linguists, psychologists, and educators have begun to examine the role of language in education more closely (Wells, 1985). We increasingly are realizing the prominent role language plays in classroom processes and school success. Language development in the school years and its interaction with educational processes are the topic of this chapter.

Language Use in Classrooms

Competent language use underlies a student's success in the classroom. A child who does not speak, read, or write well is unlikely to succeed. Four language-based processes are particularly critical to academic achievement. These are reading, writing, vocabulary development, and oral discourse.

Reading

Perhaps the most conspicuous language-based skill of schooling is **reading.** During the early school years, learning to read is one of the major developmental tasks to be mastered. As the educational process continues, reading becomes more and more important in students' ability to acquire information and learn independently. Even later, it is instrumental for successful entry into the workplace and for adapting to the requirements of society at large.

Teaching all students to read and helping students acquire the skills necessary to learn from reading are fundamental responsibilities of the school. The fact that at present many American students completing school cannot read well or even read at all is of great concern (R.C. Anderson, Hiebert, Scott, & Wilkinson, 1985). Because of the centrality of reading to cognitive development and education, we have devoted two chapters to this topic. Chapter 9, "Learning to Read," describes the language and cognitive processes of early reading and reading instruction in the primary grades. Chapter 10, "Reading to Learn," continues the examination of reading beyond the point at which basic skills have been acquired; it explores the development of reading strategies and skills in the middle grades and beyond.

Writing

Writing also is closely linked to language knowledge. Successful writing depends on language knowledge and is an expression of language. In recent years there has been increasing recognition of the potential of the writing process itself as an occasion for learning, motivation, self-expression, and cognitive development (see Jenkinson, 1988). Unfortunately, however, students still do not write much in American schools, especially the kind of writing that extends beyond a word or two (see Applebee, 1983, 1988). More common is a kind of truncated "writing" in which students supply a word or phrase in response to questions. We believe that extended writing can provide an excellent vehicle for achieving many aims of education. In Chapter 11, "Writing," we examine writing both as an important activity related to cognitive and language development and as a functional means of communication. There we take the position that having students express themselves in writing can add important dimensions to both their language and their cognitive development.

Verbal Reference: Acquiring Vocabulary

Vocabulary knowledge is fundamental to teaching and learning at all levels. The kindergartener, for instance, needs to learn labels for common objects, activities, and relationships. By middle school, children need to add to an already-extensive and increasingly technical vocabulary for describing their physical and social worlds. Words such as *divisor* (math), *tyrant* (social studies), *peninsula* (geography), and *parchment* (history) are the currency of their books and classroom discussions. By high school, the vocabulary of instruction has become more sophisticated and demanding. Because vocabulary knowledge is a key both to language use and to instruction, most educators see some form of direct vocabulary instruction as highly desirable. Later in this chapter we discuss vocabulary acquisition in detail and highlight the debate about the utility of direct instruction in vocabulary development.

Oral Discourse: The Language of Instruction

Most people's prototypical images of the classroom are those of lectures, teacher questions and student answers, and classroom discussions. In almost every classroom, spoken language is the medium by which concepts are presented and clarified and through which student knowledge typically is expressed and judged.

In a typical classroom there is great variability in language backgrounds and oral-language skills. Not only do students show wide differences in competence and rapid developmental changes in oral-language use, there also are great disparities in the way children of different social and cultural backgrounds express themselves. Oral language especially seems to show the imprint of patterns of language use in a student's home, community, and culture. Variations from "standard" English are only part of the difficulty many schools face in providing competent instruction to all children, however. Languages other than English increasingly are children's primary or only language.

Because oral-language use in the classroom and variations in it are vital concerns, we also devote a major portion of this chapter to the topic of classroom discourse. We examine how language is used in classrooms and explore the impact that contextual, social, and cultural factors have on language use, perceptions of competence, and actual classroom performance.

Before we discuss the topics of vocabulary and classroom discourse, however, it may be useful to consider the phenomenon of language itself more closely. What is human language? What are its components? How do these language components change during the years students are in school? The major dimensions of language are the topic of the next section.

The Dimensions of Language

Technically, a **language** is a system of conventions for linking symbols with meanings. The primary symbols in virtually all human languages are speech sounds; organized patterns of sounds represent meanings. In the sections that follow we discuss the nature of speech sounds and their perception and the three levels at which language is organized: (1) the assembly of sounds into words; (2) the combining of words into phrases, clauses, and sentences; and (3) the linking of sentences into coherent, higher-level units. We begin with the building blocks of language, speech sounds.

Language Sounds

Humans can vocalize a tremendous range of sounds, ranging from clicks to chirps, to babbling, cooing, and speaking. These vocalizations, called **phones,** are the raw material from which language is created. As theory and technology have advanced, great strides have been made in analyzing and understanding how the speech sounds are created, articulated, and formed into human oral language and comprehended by listeners (see Miller, 1981).

Among the huge range of *possible* sounds, however, only a very small subset are meaningful in human languages. Although we are capable of articulating an infinite variety of speech sounds, such as those produced by a child's babbling, only a very few are critical to language. The relatively few sounds perceived as meaningful by speakers and listeners in a particular language are called **phonemes.** Phonemes form a kind of perceptual category; each is a sound—or perhaps more precisely, a closely related cluster of sounds—that carries meaning (Anisfeld, 1984). In English, for instance, there are about 40 phonemes. Table 8-1 presents the phonemes of the English language.

Speech comprehension, of course, depends on an individual's distinguishing these phoneme-categories from one another (e.g., "*l*oad" from "*r*oad") in order to access the meaning the sounds carry. Although listeners typically make these discriminations easily and automatically, speech comprehension is by no means a simple task—in ordinary speech, phoneme production is extremely rapid, about nine phonemes a second (Liberman, 1982). Thus, to comprehend the oral discourse of the class-

TABLE 8-1.   Phonemes of the English Language.

Consonants		Vowels	
symbol	*example*	*symbol*	*example*
p	*p*it, s*p*it	i	h*e*, m*ea*t
b	*b*it, ta*b*	ɪ	b*i*d, s*i*t
m	*m*itt, s*m*all	e	b*ai*t, *eigh*t
t	*t*ip, s*t*ill	ɛ	b*e*t, *e*xact
d	*d*ip, ri*d*e	æ	b*a*d, b*a*t
n	*n*ip, pi*n*	u	wh*o*, b*oo*t
k	*k*in, s*ch*ool	ʊ	p*u*t, f*oo*t
g	*g*ive, bi*g*	ʌ	b*u*t, *u*tter
ŋ	si*ng*, thi*nk*	ə	*a*bout, en*e*my
f	*f*it, rou*gh*	o	b*oa*t, g*o*
v	*v*at, di*v*e	ɔ	b*ough*t, s*aw*
s	*s*it, p*s*ychology	a	p*o*t, f*a*ther
z	*z*ip, rou*s*e	:	Following a vowel indicates
θ	*th*igh, e*th*er		lengthening of the vowel;
ð	*th*y, ei*th*er		compare, for example, [bæ:d]
š	*sh*ip, ra*ti*o		(*bad*) and [bæt] (*bat*).
ž	plea*s*ure, vi*s*ion		
č	*ch*ip, ri*ch*	Liquids and Semivowels	
ǰ	*j*oy, gy*p*		
		l	*l*id, fi*ll*
		r	*r*ip, ca*r*
		y	*y*es, bu*y*
		w	*w*e, q*u*ick
		h	*h*igh, w*ho*

From *Language Development from Birth to Three*, by M. Anisfeld, 1984, Hillsdale, NJ: Erlbaum. Used by permission of the author and Lawrence Erlbaum Publishing Company.

room, students must exhibit a rather remarkable facility for processing the sounds of language.

Although their phonemes do overlap, each of the world's languages has its own distinct set; phonemes in one may not be phonemes in another. For instance, in the Thai language, the sound [v], which has meaning in English (e.g., *viper* and *wiper* are distinctly different words!), is not a phoneme. As a consequence, a native Thai speaker attempting to learn English words containing the sound [v] (such as *divide*) may hear the English /v/ as the familiar phoneme /w/ (/w/ is a phoneme in Thai) and perceive and pronounce such words incorrectly (e.g., as *de-wide*). He or she also would experience considerable difficulty in distinguishing between two words that differ only in these consonants. The tables are, of course, turned when English speakers encounter other languages. For instance, English speakers often experience difficulty in perceiving phonemes meaningful in, say, Spanish, Chinese, or Russian—differences obvious to native speakers of those languages.

By the time they enter school, most children have a relatively sophisticated knowledge about their language's sound system. Although their abilities to pronounce and perceive sounds are not fully mature, most can accurately produce and use the sound segments of their language; their pronunciation patterns conform closely to those of adults (Grunwell, 1986). They also have considerable knowledge about **prosody**—the use of speech rhythm, stress patterns (*And then do you know what HE did?*), and intonation (e.g., . . . *and he sounded REAL MAD. . . .*)—to convey meanings, emphases, and attitudes. Although the ability is far from completely developed, preschoolers also can make adjustments in their own speech patterns in different language contexts—using different accents and speech styles, for instance, in different settings (Grunwell, 1986; Lucas & Borders, 1987).

A capability only in its beginning developmental stages when children start school, however, is a form of metacognition—the capacity to **analyze** a language's sound system consciously. Such analytical skills have been called **metaphonological knowledge** (Grunwell, 1986)—knowledge about the sound system of the language. A number of authorities in reading, for instance, have argued that the ability to understand how sounds are combined to form words (e.g., *Cuh-ah-tuh . . . CAT*) and how specific words are similar or differ in sound structure (e.g., "How are *m*at and *s*at alike? How are they different?") is critical to learning to read (Chall, 1987). Although there is disagreement about how important these abilities are, there can be no doubt that important changes are taking place in this area around the time that children learn to read. At age 4, few children are able to understand how words can be broken down into phonemic segments; by age 6, however, many show some degree of phonemic awareness (Grunwell, 1986). When particular methods of reading instruction rely extensively on a child's knowledge that words are made up of constituent sounds and focus on their learning specific sound–symbol associations (e.g., phonics methods), a number of children may be at considerable risk for failure.

Language Structures

As we have noted, languages are structured—they are not mere collections of sounds into words, words into sentences, and sentences into larger units. Instead, at each level of structure, units combine meaningfully according to general organizational principles rather than randomly or idiosyncratically.

Languages typically are described as structured at three major levels: (1) at the level of combinations of sounds into words—the **morphology** of the language; (2) at the level of combinations of words into phrases, clauses, and sentences—the **syntax** of the language; and (3) at the level of combinations of sentences into higher order units such as paragraphs, narratives, and expository text (Zwicky & Kantor, 1980)—**language discourse.**

Morphology   The most basic level of organization is the province of **morphology,** a set of principles that describe how sounds are combined into words in a given language. Whereas phonemes are minimal meaningful distinctions in the sounds of a language, linguists define **morphemes** as combinations of sounds that are the minimal units of meaning (Prideaux, 1984). For example, the word *joyfully* is a combination of the sound units *joy + ful + ly,* each of which is a morpheme. Thus, each of the three morphemes in the word *joyfully* carries one of the dimensions of meaning of the word. The root word *joy* has a meaning of itself; adding *-ful* to the noun *joy* converts it to its adjectival form, and adding *-ly* to *joyful* transforms it to adverbial form. Of course, only certain combinations of morphemes are possible in a given language; for instance, we know immediately that utterances like *fuljoy, joylyful,* and *joyly* are not English. English morphology allows only a few of a near-infinite number of possibilities.

Use of morphological rules begins soon after children's speech moves beyond the single-word level, as children begin to add markers for pluralization and tense. Early on, children tend to "overapply" their morphological knowledge (e.g., *two sheepses, She goed home.*). Of course, like all aspects of language, morphological rules are extremely complex, and learning them continues throughout the entire period of formal schooling.

Syntax   The second major level of language structure is **syntax**—the grouping of words into larger units such as phrases, clauses, and sentences. The study of syntax always has been a major interest within linguistics, but especially so after the publication of Noam Chomsky's *Syntactic Structures* in 1957 and *Aspects of the Theory of Syntax* in 1965. These books transformed the way linguists looked at language learning, especially at how syntactical knowledge is acquired and used. Chomsky took a strongly nativist position, arguing that much syntactical knowledge is "hardwired" into the developing human and that syntactical structures are not acquired through processes of modeling, feedback, and the like.

Understanding the meaning of any language obviously depends on comprehension of its syntax. Syntactic speech is closely linked to propositional thought (Anisfeld, 1984); propositions ordinarily cannot be comprehended except through their expression in the syntax of language.

For instance, the information contained in word order in the sentence *The horse kicked Eddie* is essential to understanding what the sentence is saying, that is, to the encoding of the proposition underlying the sentence (see Chapter 4). Obviously, the sentences *Eddie kicked the horse* and *The horse kicked Eddie* carry very different meanings!

Syntactic regularity appears very early in children's speech, even earlier than morphology; children use consistent word order as soon as they begin to use two-word sequences (Anisfeld, 1984; R. Brown, 1973). Syntactic development, however, continues well into the school years. For instance, many children in the middle elementary grades and beyond have difficulty in comprehending the meaning of sentences with complex syntax. Especially troublesome are sentences with "embedded" syntactical forms (e.g., *Jerome Kern composed the song the girl sang in the contest that was held last Wednesday.*).

Discourse Structure   The most comprehensive level of language organization is **discourse structure.** Except for children just learning to talk, people typically do not communicate with one another in single words or even single sentences. Instead, talking and writing usually consist of extended sequences of clauses and sentences that form coherent stretches of discussion or writing.

In discourse, propositions take on a meaning in relation to one another. Discourse has the property of coherence, in which references forward or backward can give individual elements their meaning. For instance, consider the following sentence:

> *It was an extremely unlucky penetration.*

By itself, the sentence may not have any particular meaning to us. Let us, however, look at it when it is placed in context.

> *Air Force officials met today with members of the House Armed Services Committee. Perhaps the most pointed questions of the day came when Committee members began to inquire into the 23 October crash of a 28 million dollar B-1B bomber near LaMesa, California. "How," asked a member of the Committee, "could a single pelican take out 'the best warplane in the world?'" "It was an extremely unlucky penetration," replied the general. He described the accident as a fluke, but indicated that the Air Force will spend $38.5 million to put pelican-proof armor on the 99 remaining B-1B bombers. Because these planes fly very low and fast, he stated, they are more likely than most to meet birds, a fact the aircraft designers apparently overlooked.*

To comprehend discourse such as this, students must learn to tie discourse elements together, by referring either to what has gone before in the discourse or to what follows. They also must recognize, at least implicitly, the logical frameworks of a coherent utterance or well-written text. These underlying structures represent the fundamental relations that link propositions to one another—**cause and effect** between two events, **contiguity in time and place** of two or more events, and **resemblance,** correlations in appearance or function (Crombie, 1985)

Two discourse structures of particular interest to educators are **narratives** and **expository text.** Narratives are "stories," either oral or written, structured by a temporal sequence of events. Rudimentary knowledge of narrative structure appears very early in children's development (Applebee, 1983; McNamee, 1987). Here, for instance, is a first-grader's narrative about a set of events:

> *And then she got some ice cream.*
> *And then she put it in the cone.*
> *And then he . . . she went outside.*
> *And a . . . the kitty-cat scared her.*
> *And she dropped the cone.*
> *And she looked real mad.*

Many narratives, of course, are much more complex than this child's narration—narratives can range from very simple recountings like the one above to skilled dramatic performances (Romaine, 1984). The essential feature, however, of all narratives is a discourse structure based on the temporal sequence of events.

In contrast to narratives, expository text structure reflects the organization of abstract thought about a topic or body of information. Although expository text may contain narrative elements (and vice versa), the basic structure of exposition is logical, not temporal. Texts, essays, and persuasive arguments typically use expository structure.

Probably because expository structure is based more on logical than on directly observed temporal relationships, comprehension and use of exposition develop considerably later than that of narratives. Take a look at what a tenth-grader wrote when she was asked to "write all she could remember" about an article she'd read the day before:

> *There is a lot of radioactive waste around the U.S. It is building up.*
> *This waste comes from nuclear reactors. The problem is that it's very dangerous (radioactive) and lasts thousands of years. We've got to find somewhere to put it that keeps it away from people.*
> *Congress has decided it should be buried in Yucca Mountain, Nevada. It's supposed to be a good place to store it. Yucca Mountain is away from most people. It sits on a kind of rock that doesn't melt or anything. It's also dry in Nevada, which is good since the radioactive stuff could get into underground water.*

*Since the waste lasts 10,000 years, everybody is still worried. Yucca
Mountain sits between a bombing range and a place where they test A-
bombs. Will the bombs cause earthquakes? Will the dry climate last 10,000
years, because if it doesn't, it'll be a mess. Nobody really knows, but everybody hopes it's a good choice!*

As you can see, the student had a very well developed organization for
her response. Even without having the original essay, we can see that this
student recognized and used the underlying structure of the text to
encode and retrieve the text information. Many students at this age,
however, do not seem to use or even recognize text structure.

The use of expository text structure in learning and remembering
reading materials has considerable benefit. For instance, several studies
(see Andre, 1987b) have shown that students who use text structure
recall far more of the material than students who do not. Recognition of
expository text structure, however, often is a slowly developing skill. A
study conducted by Meyer, Brandt, and Bluth (1980) with ninth-graders
demonstrates this fact. In their study, Meyer et al. had students read
various passages and then, as a posttest, asked them to write all they
could remember about the passages. (These responses are called "free-
recall protocols.") They then analyzed students' responses to see if the
structure of the passages was used in writing the protocols. Their results
showed that only about a fourth of the students used text structure
consistently, and another quarter used it occasionally. Half the students
either did not or could not use text structure in writing their protocols.
These students recalled far less of what they read.

Children as young as 10, however, seem to profit from instruction
designed to help them recognize text structure. For example, Armbruster,
Anderson, and Ostertag (1987) examined the effects of carefully teaching
one very specific form of text structure, "problem/solution," to a group of
fifth-graders. The "problem/solution" format appears frequently in social
studies texts and is made up of three parts—an explanation of a problem
that an individual or group has encountered, the description of attempts
to solve the problem, and a discussion of how the attempts at solution
worked out. In their study, Armbruster et al. met with the children on 11
school days and had them work toward two goals—recognizing the
problem/solution structure in their reading passages and using it in writing summaries of reading passages. The results showed that the training
helped the children reach both goals. When they encountered new passages using the problem/solution format after their training, they showed
greater recall of main ideas and wrote better-organized passage summaries that contained more main ideas. Not only had they acquired a "macrostructure" for the text, but this macrostructure had important effects
on the organization and amount of their recall.

Recognizing text structures is a considerable achievement. As Hidi and Anderson (1986) have pointed out, the ability to identify and employ structural features of text ordinarily is a slow-developing process. To recognize and use a text's structure requires not only the formation of mental representations in a linear, forward-moving fashion, but overall processing of propositions at a whole-text level. Further, students must apply sophisticated metacognitive strategies in order to find the main points of expository text segments, consider their importance in the author's overall structure, and evaluate their connections to prior and subsequent text (Stevens, 1988).

Summary of the Dimensions of Language

Children know a great deal about language when they enter school. Their language knowledge, however, continues to develop along each of its major dimensions. Children acquire greater awareness of the intonation and stress patterns of the language. The development of metalinguistic ability to segment words into phonemes, for instance, is seen as critical to "sounding out" and reading words. The ability to deal with syntax likewise requires continuing development; many children have difficulty comprehending complex syntactic structures into the middle grades and beyond. At the level of discourse, most school-children are familiar with narrative structure, but even those at the high school level may fail to recognize the patterns of expository presentations. Students need not only to *use* language in a facile way, but to develop their metalinguistic capabilities to analyze and understand their own language use. They need to learn to take advantage of the many converging sources of information in language to understand the underlying meaning of communications.

Vocabulary Development

Vocabulary growth during the years children are in school is extraordinary. Although estimates of vocabulary size vary widely because of differences in definitions of what it means to "know a word" and in methodologies used to estimate vocabulary (see Nagy & Anderson, 1984), virtually all authorities agree that growth in word knowledge occurs at a phenomenal rate. Nagy, Anderson, and Herman (1987), for example, estimate that children may add as many as 3,000 words per year to their reading vocabularies between the third and the twelfth grades, with average vocabulary size reaching 40,000 words or more by the end of secondary schooling (Nagy & Herman, 1987).

The heart of any language is its words; for this reason alone, vocabulary acquisition has attracted the attention of educators and psychologists. Researchers also have noted for many years, however, that vocabulary is closely related to a large number of other educationally relevant variables. For instance, in an early but representative study, Conry and Plant (1965) found correlations of .65 and .46 between scores on the Vocabulary subtest of the Wechsler Adult Intelligence Scale (WAIS) and high school rank and college grades, respectively. Similarly, for many years researchers have observed that vocabulary can serve as a proxy for more-global measures of intelligence; correlations between vocabulary scores and intelligence test scores typically are very high, often +.80 or above. Vocabulary knowledge also is related to the fundamental language-based skills mentioned earlier, such as reading comprehension (e.g., Farr, 1969; Bruning & Dunlap, 1984; Stahl & Fairbanks, 1986; Sternberg, 1987) and writing quality (Grobe, 1981; Stewart & Leaman, 1983; Duin & Graves, 1987).

Despite the strong relationship of vocabulary to many important abilities, several questions remain unanswered. The exact role that vocabulary plays in these processes, for instance, is a matter of some debate. A continuing issue is whether it is useful to "teach vocabulary" or whether vocabulary is acquired more effectively through ordinary language experiences (e.g., McKeown & Curtis, 1987; Sternberg, 1987). Further, if vocabulary is to be taught, what vocabulary instruction methods are most effective? Finally, what does it mean to "know a word"? We examine these questions, beginning with the last, in the following section.

What Does It Mean to "Know a Word"?

Picture for a moment the variety of answers you might get if you asked a group of high school students the meaning of a relatively rare word, say, *ascetic*. Some would have no idea at all; some might venture a guess ("Is it something like 'clean'?"). Others would be more confident ("I think it means 'austere, self-denying.' ") and perhaps even add an instance of its use (*The monk lived an **ascetic** life, denying himself all but the most basic necessities.*). Still others might ask for clues before they ventured a guess ("Could you use it in a sentence for me?"). Given the example *He looked much like a student, thin and **ascetic,*** some of them might propose, "Well, it has something to do with a student and how he looks. It's either 'pale' or 'poor,' . . . could be either." Still others simply would be confused: "Isn't it something like 'art appreciation'?"

There obviously are many levels of "knowing a word," ranging from complete lack of knowledge to exquisitely detailed knowledge about a word, its origins, and the contexts in which it can be used most appropriately. As the previous discussion shows, "knowing a word" is not an all-

or-none phenomenon (Nagy & Anderson, 1984; Nagy & Herman, 1987).

One classification system for the stages leading to "knowing a word" is a simple continuum proposed by Beck, McCaslin, and McKeown (1980). At one end are **unknown** words, words not as yet established in semantic memory. At an intermediate level are words with which an individual is **acquainted,** in which the meaning is known only after deliberate attention is focused on the word. Thus, an eighth-grader at this level, encountering the word *gibber* in the sentence *The man began to **gibber** irrationally*, might say to herself, "Let's see—*gibber*—it must be something he's doing. It's like the word *gibberish*. Doesn't that mean 'nonsense'? Yes, that'd fit with 'irrationally.' It must be that he's talking nonsense." At the upper end of the continuum are **established** words, words about which the individual has solid knowledge.

Graves (1987) has pointed out that the continuum of "learning words" actually is a series of tasks that vary markedly depending on the learner's present knowledge and the depth of understanding required by the tasks. For instance, a first-grader may need to learn to read a word she already has in her oral vocabulary (e.g., *house*). A different challenge may be to learn a new meaning for a known word; many words (e.g., *run*) are **polysemous;** that is, they have multiple meanings. Yet a different vocabulary acquisition task arises when the student must learn a new word for a known meaning (e.g., a child may understand the ideas of *looking* and *keeping on* but does not know the word *stare*). In some instances, a student may know **neither** concept nor word, as when a teacher introduces a new concept (e.g., "impeachment," "entropy") in a subject area. Overall, of course, is the goal of moving words from students' receptive vocabularies—understanding words—to their expressive vocabularies—using the words actively and easily.

Definitional versus Contextual Word Knowledge

In thinking about goals for vocabulary instruction (Graves, 1987) and in describing word knowledge at any level—unknown, acquainted, or established—vocabulary researchers (e.g., Nagy, 1988; Stahl & Fairbanks, 1986) have found it useful to distinguish between **definitional** and **contextual** word knowledge. When we think of "knowing a word," for instance, we usually envision definitional knowledge first (Johnson & Bruning, 1984). Definitional knowledge refers to the relationship between a word and other known words, as in a dictionary definition (e.g. *An **octroi** is a tax paid upon certain goods entering a city.*). Obviously, placing a word within a semantic network by means of a definition is an important part of our word knowledge.

The knowledge developed from exposure to words **in context** also is critical, however. For example, a native speaker of English immediately recognizes the oddity of certain vocabulary choices in sentences like *She drove her plane to Austin, Texas, I suppose you are under my application now, He initiated his car's engine,* and *He despaired his hope of ever meeting her again.* Because words are individual units, we usually think of them as having independent status. With rare exceptions, however, word use in natural language is contextual—words virtually always are combined with others in speaking, reading, and writing. Because of this, our knowledge of word meanings necessarily needs to extend well beyond their "dictionary definition," leading many authorities (e.g., Nagy, 1988; Powell, 1988; Sternberg, 1984, 1987; Sternberg & Powell, 1983) to view vocabulary knowledge as organized in schema-like structures, containing not only the "meaning" of the word, but also a host of temporal, spatial, and grammatical cues. Look, for instance, at the following sentence:

> *As the mechanic tried to tighten the bolt one last turn, the bolt*
> _____, *and his wrench clattered to the cement.*

If we are asked to supply a word for this slot, we immediately draw on our knowledge of language and the world. Choices such as *cried, sensitive,* and *happily* are discarded as either unboltlike or grammatically nonsensical and we quickly focus on more acceptable possibilities.

In even a very short passage like the above, suitable choices typically are surprisingly constrained by the **external context** in which the word is embedded—word meaning clues coming from **outside** the word itself (Sternberg, 1984, 1987). Thus, we quickly surmise from the sentence context that the missing word must be a verb, something that might happen to a bolt when a mechanic tightened it one last time, and which, if it happened to a bolt, would result in the wrench's flying off and clattering to the floor.

In this case, a word was missing, but the process is similar when unknown words are encountered in context. With unknown words, however, **within-word** (morphological) cues also potentially are available to the reader (Drum & Konopak, 1987; Sternberg & Powell, 1983). Consider the following example:

> *To his dismay, the inventor found that his automatic bed-maker was* **unmarketable.**

Besides the external clues supplied by other words and by the syntax, a reader unfamiliar with the word *unmarketable* also has several within-word cues available. From earlier instruction or from other experiences with "prefixes" and "suffixes," the student may be able to analyze the components of the word and recognize *un-* as a prefix, *market* as the stem or root word, and *-able* as a suffix indicating an adjectival form of a word.

From contact with an array of more frequent words beginning with *un-,* such as *unsafe, unhappy, unclear,* and so forth, the student should have a sense of *un* as indicating negation. Knowledge of the root word *market* may enable the student to recognize that the word *unmarketable* has to do with buying and selling.

This assortment of cues, coupled with those from the external context, often make it possible for students to derive approximations of word meanings as they read. The presence of both within-word and external context cues, however, by no means ensures that they will be able to use them or even recognize them as potential clues to "figuring out" words. The less-sophisticated the reader, the fewer linguistic and metalinguistic cues that will be recognized. Also, some contexts in which new words are encountered are relatively "rich" in contextual cues, whereas others are not (Graves, 1987; Herman, Anderson, Pearson, & Nagy, 1987; Sternberg, 1987).

"Figuring out" a word from context is a conscious search for information about a word; more often, however, words simply trigger automatized procedural knowledge related to word recognition and use (see Chapter 4). For example, we automatically comprehend the meanings of the word *bank* as we read the following three sentences, *The river **bank** was eroded, You can **bank** on it,* and *The First National **Bank** opened a new branch in Greenwich.* When we speak, similarly, we do not pay any conscious attention to words' dictionary definitions. We simply use them, stating confidently, for example, *The boy dropped his piggy **bank,*** or *The pilot put the plane into a steep **bank.***

Thus, word knowledge is far from a simple "either–or" matter. In every instance "knowing a word" extends far beyond word definitions to subtle knowledge of the contexts of words' meanings and uses. Much vocabulary knowledge is tacit and unrecognized—knowing what words "go with" others, for instance. Much also is highly automatized, more procedural than declarative, as in the correct recognition and use of the polysemous (multiple-meaning) word *bank* in the examples just given.

Vocabulary Knowledge and Reading

As we indicated, among the most consistent findings of two generations of educational psychologists has been a link between vocabulary and reading. R.C. Anderson and Freebody (1981, 1983) suggested three ways in which this relationship might be explained. One possible explanation, a **verbal aptitude** hypothesis, is that vocabulary and reading comprehension are related because both depend on a third factor, general verbal ability. Individuals high in general verbal ability are likely to be strong vocabulary learners as well as individuals who have mastered the skills needed for reading comprehension. If this hypothesis is correct, vocabulary and reading need not be intrinsically linked; they simply go together in individuals—persons strong or weak in one are likely to be correspondingly strong or weak in the other. Vocabulary training would be unlikely to produce significant changes in reading comprehension, since underlying ability is the important factor.

A second perspective proposed by Anderson and Freebody is a **knowledge** hypothesis: Vocabulary and comprehension are linked because words serve as the external referents for underlying knowledge structures. Knowing a word well means that a person possesses not only well-developed schemata for that word, but also networks of associated concepts and principles that form large knowledge structures. The knowledge **underlying** the vocabulary, not the specific vocabulary itself, is the central factor associated with reading comprehension. The word is the "tip of the iceberg," so to speak. Thus, a person who can correctly explain the meanings of the words *font* and *point* as referring to type and size of print would be much more likely to have acquired underlying knowledge structures about printing. Because of this knowledge, a student would be able to read, say, a printer's manual with greater comprehension than another student who does not know these words, even though the specific words *font* and *point* might be relatively inconsequential to comprehension of that particular document. From an instructional standpoint, a focus on knowledge development, not specific vocabulary, would be likely to pay the greatest dividends.

The third hypothesis, the **instrumental** hypothesis, is the most straightforward and has had great appeal to educators. From this perspective, the connection between vocabulary knowledge and reading is direct—the more words known (and the fewer the number of unfamiliar words), the better reading comprehension will be. If this hypothesis is correct, the instructional implications also are considerably more clear-cut than those of the first and second hypotheses; instruction in vocabulary, particularly in passage-related vocabulary, should increase reading comprehension.

Although it is likely that all of these hypotheses have at least some validity (R.C. Anderson & Freebody, 1981; Mezynski, 1983), educators have stressed the third and many have attempted to improve reading comprehension through vocabulary instruction. Although the results of studies on direct vocabulary instruction have been somewhat mixed, at least some research has shown that instruction on passage-related vocabulary can improve reading comprehension significantly (see Stahl & Fairbanks, 1986). The difficulty with direct instruction, however, has been pointed out most forcefully by Nagy and his associates (Herman et al., 1987; Nagy, Herman, & Anderson, 1985; Nagy & Herman, 1987; Nagy et al., 1987). Only a small portion—perhaps 200–300 words per year—of the rapid growth in vocabulary during the school years can be attributed to **direct** vocabulary instruction. Learning word meanings to a level where they can be accessed quickly and usefully in reading takes considerable time (Wysocki & Jenkins, 1987). Although it is possible to design effective vocabulary instruction and such instruction may be critical, especially for poor readers (see Beck, McKeown, & Omanson, 1987), direct vocabulary teaching in school probably accounts for no more than a minority of vocabulary growth for most students (Nagy et al., 1985; Nagy & Herman, 1987).

If students learn most of their vocabulary words by ways other than direct instruction, how then is vocabulary acquired? The major competing explanation for the observed rapid vocabulary growth during the school years is that students learn most words incidentally from context—from conversation, from writing, and most especially from reading.

Acquisition of word meanings in this way is a slow, incremental process. A single contact with a word often produces a very small amount of learning; only after multiple encounters is there likely to be anything approaching full comprehension of a word's meaning and contexts of use. In a series of carefully designed studies examining the processes of learning words from context, Nagy and his co-workers have demonstrated the validity of both of these points: that incidental learning of word meanings does occur during normal reading and that the absolute amount of learning is in fact quite small; the probability of acquiring significant word knowledge from reading a word once in text is not more than 10 percent or so (Nagy et al., 1985; Nagy et al., 1987; Nagy & Herman, 1987). This small increment in word knowledge becomes important, however, when the amount of reading children do in and out of school is considered. R.C. Anderson, Wilson, and Fielding (1988), for instance, have shown that a typical fifth-grade student reads about 300,000 words from books outside school per year; other print materials, such as newspapers, comic books, and the like, increase the total to about 600,000 words. When a conservative estimate of 15 minutes a day of reading in school is added, the estimate for words read by the typical fifth-grader is upward of a million a year; some avid readers read many times this amount. Using data like these, Nagy has argued that learning words from reading is highly significant, representing a third or more of most students' annual vocabulary growth.

Vocabulary Knowledge and Writing

Most research on vocabulary instruction has examined its effects on reading; relatively little has been conducted on its role in writing. Recently, however, researchers have begun to stress the connectedness of reading and writing as communicative acts and as constructive processes involving general knowledge, language, and information manipulation (e.g., Birnbaum & Emig, 1983; Murphy & Bruning, 1987; Pearson & Tierney, 1984; Petrosky, 1982). Working from this general framework, Duin and Graves (1987) examined the question whether intensive vocabulary instruction might improve the quality of students' expository writing. Earlier research had shown that the choice of vocabulary in writing influences perceptions of writing quality (Grobe, 1981; Stewart & Leaman, 1983); passages written with "mature" vocabulary, for instance, are evaluated significantly more highly than passages with simple vocabulary. At the time of Duin and Graves' research, however, there had been almost no studies evaluating the possibility of a direct impact of vocabulary instruction on writing quality.

In their study, Duin and Graves compared three experimental treatments: (1) intensive vocabulary and writing instruction, (2) intensive vocabulary instruction alone, and (3) traditional vocabulary instruction. The intensive vocabulary and writing treatment consisted of six days of instruction designed to teach a set of 13 words. The instruction was intended to produce in-depth understanding of the words and skills in using the words in writing. Writing activities focused on word meaning, on associations and distinctions among words, and on their use in oral discussion and meaningful writing. The second treatment, intensive vocabulary alone, did not include the specific writing activities; and the third, traditional vocabulary treatment, consisted of completing worksheets, looking words up in the dictionary, writing new words and their definitions, and filling in open-ended sentences. When the effects of the three instructional patterns were compared, the results were clear: Not only were the words learned more effectively in the two intensive-vocabulary instruction conditions, the words were used much more frequently in writing by the two intensively instructed groups. Further, when the quality of student essays was rated, both groups were judged significantly better in quality than the traditional-vocabulary-instruction group, with the intensive-vocabulary-and-writing group the most effective. Additionally, there were large attitudinal differences favoring the intensive-vocabulary-and-writing group and the intensive-vocabulary-instruction group over the traditional-vocabulary-instruction group.

These results, especially when combined with earlier research by Duin and Graves (1986), show that intensive, focused vocabulary instruction, particularly when combined with writing practice keyed to meaningful use of words, not only can teach vocabulary effectively, but may improve writing quality significantly. Perhaps more importantly, the intensive-vocabulary-instruction-and-writing group showed much greater desire than those receiving traditional vocabulary instruction to learn new words by this method and use them outside of class and in their writing.

Vocabulary Instruction: Implications for Teaching

As Duin and Graves (1987, p. 33) have stated, "Words embody power, words embrace action, and words enable us to speak, read, and write with clarity, confidence, and charm." The underlying truth of this statement always has been apparent to educators; fluent vocabulary use in reading and writing underlies judgments of competence in most areas of education. As we indicated at the outset, however, our belief in the desirability of fluent vocabulary use is more certain than our knowledge about how best to help students expand their vocabularies. The following statements represent a distillation of findings from the research on vocabulary instruction and acquisition, drawing especially on the recommendations of Stahl and Fairbanks (1986) and Duin and Graves (1987):

1. **Build networks of words.** Effective vocabulary use almost certainly needs a solid foundation of declarative knowledge about the word meanings and their relationships to one another. Vocabulary instruction suffers when it becomes a rote activity devoid of purpose. However, when words are presented around a theme or topic (e.g., Beck, Perfetti, & McKeown, 1982; McKeown, Beck, Omanson, & Perfetti, 1983; McKeown, Beck, Omanson, & Pople, 1985; Duin & Graves, 1987), knowledge structures are developed that make effective word use in reading and writing more likely.

2. **Instruct intensively on fewer words.** Using vocabulary requires both procedural and declarative knowledge. Fluent vocabulary use is highly contextual and depends on automatic, rapid access. Quite obviously, words to which students are more frequently exposed will be more automatically available than those to which they have only a single or a few exposures (Beck et al., 1982; Mezynski, 1983; Jenkins, Stein, & Wysocki, 1984; Stahl & Fairbanks, 1986). Thus, multiple contacts with words are needed. Although there is little research about whether multiple exposures to the same information about a word (e.g., a word and its associate) or to varied information (e.g., a word used in several contexts) is best (Stahl & Fairbanks, 1986), multiple repetitions of both types are likely to be necessary before a word can be used effectively and automatically in natural language contexts.

3. **Encourage vocabulary use in other contexts.** Students need to be helped to generalize their classroom knowledge to other parts of their daily lives. In the intensive vocabulary instruction condition of Duin and Graves' (1987) study, for instance, students were asked to keep track of the times they read, spoke, or heard the words in outside activities. Because the students were actively encouraged to notice the new words, Duin and Graves found that they also were more inclined to use them on their own.

4. **Include both contextual and definitional information about word meanings.** In general, the research on vocabulary instruction has shown that approaches that include both contextual and definitional information will be more effective than either alone (Stahl & Fairbanks, 1986). When schemata for words are based only on one kind of information, word knowledge will be seriously deficient, and use of the word outside the context of instruction will be unlikely.

5. **Encourage students to use context to learn meanings of unknown words.** Learning to learn words is just as important as learning words; no matter how rich the vocabulary instruction, students still must learn most words independently (Graves, 1987). As we have seen, a significant proportion of new vocabulary words is acquired through incidental encounters with words in reading (Nagy et al., 1987; Nagy, 1988; Wysocki & Jenkins, 1987). Reading provides a rich context for learning vocabulary, but only if students are prepared to use this context. Potentially both morphological, within-word clues (Wysocki & Jenkins, 1987) and syntactical and discourse clues (Sternberg, 1987; Nagy & Herman, 1987; Nagy et al., 1987) are available for readers to use. Encouraging children to use their morphological, syntactic, discourse, and world knowledge to infer unknown word meanings can only be a positive factor toward vocabulary growth (Sternberg, 1987).

Classroom Discourse

Reading is one major route to learning in school. The oral discourse of the classroom—classroom talk—is the other. Achievement of many educational goals depends on the content of classroom talk, its sequencing, and how well the exchanges between teachers and students support instruction. Classroom discourse is the vehicle by which teachers guide, organize, and direct their pupils' activities. Classrooms are environments of communication (Green, 1983).

Classroom discourse serves at least two major aims of education. The first is the development of shared understanding (Edwards & Mercer, 1986; Green, 1983)—a body of common knowledge about the content of instruction, about classroom rituals and classroom language, and about one another. Classroom language—guided by the teacher—provides the context that supports or constrains participation and the amount of academic and social knowledge students gain (Green, 1983). If the discourse conveys the content of instruction effectively, is paced appropriately for student abilities and developmental levels, and has continuity, students will have the opportunity to learn. The direction that classroom discourse takes also shapes students' perceptions of self and learning; it can be supportive or threatening, uplifting or demeaning.

A second desired outcome of classroom discourse is student competence in communication (Green, 1983; Edwards & Mercer, 1986). If teachers guide classroom discourse effectively, students will have the opportunity to organize and express their new knowledge and to test it against meanings others have generated. They also will have learned to use speech to inform and persuade.

Challenges to Students

From the time students begin preschool or kindergarten until they complete their schooling, they need to adequately perform in the language environment of the classroom. Each level of development and each new classroom present new challenges to students. In this "foreign" setting in which the teacher is the only "native," students must learn how classroom communication takes place. Every classroom event—ranging from "show and tell" to "story time" to teacher–student interactions during reading instruction—has its own rules for participation and communication. Each context for language use is defined by what students are doing, where they are doing it, with whom, and the perceptions they have of what they are doing (Green, 1983).

Box 8-1 highlights some of the linguistic challenges students face.

Challenges to Teachers

Teachers need to use discourse processes to attract and hold their students' attention. As Stubbs has wryly put it, "Teachers' talk is very different from preachers' talk. Trying to control and teach a class full of children for forty minutes is very different from delivering a monologue to the converted" (Stubbs, 1983, p. 43).

The classroom, its features, and its activities also require unique types of discourse. Because teachers have so much more power and control than their students, for instance, much classroom talk has an unusual degree of domination by one speaker—the teacher—over the content of conversation, over judgments of what is and what is not relevant to conversations, and over when and how students may speak (Green, 1983; Stubbs, 1983). The discourse of the classroom also contains a higher-than-usual proportion of such acts as explaining, defining, prompting, requesting, and paraphrasing. In short, the typical classroom is a setting for a particular asymmetrical style of discourse, a style quite different from those students experience in their homes and neighborhoods.

Teachers have time to accomplish the goal of achieving effective classroom discourse. Discourse structures are built up over a period of days, weeks, and months. From the very beginning, however, the content, sequence, and process of the discourse shape the potential of subsequent dis-

Box 8-1

Developmental Challenges to Students in Classroom Discourse

Early Grades

Acquiring classroom linguistic rules. Classroom language has specialized rules, processes, and structures. In most primary classrooms children need to learn to speak only when called on ("I can't hear you when you don't have your hand raised."), not to interrupt others, to take turns in speaking, and to listen when the teacher speaks or reads. Only a few of these skills may be part of a child's prior oral language-experience.

Comprehending classroom vocabulary. Classroom language is specialized around new objects (e.g., a fish tank, books, chalkboard) and individuals, each of which needs to be labeled. Beyond these are arrays of unfamiliar activities (e.g., taking roll, coloring, working at a computer) that must be identified accurately. There also are a vast number of temporal (e.g., when, before, and) and spatial (inside, outside, on top of) markers critical to classroom communication.

Recognizing nonlinguistic cues for language. Language contexts include many cues not in the language itself. Teacher-related cues include movements (e.g., a teacher moving to her chair in the "reading circle"), facial expressions, and postures, as well as classroom events and objects. Children need to learn to recognize these cues quickly and to modify their language accordingly to fit the context (Lucas & Borders, 1987).

Acquiring basic metalinguistic abilities. From virtually their first moment in the classroom, students have to focus attention on and analyze language. To follow instruction in beginning reading, for instance, children need to understand metalinguistic concepts such as "word," "sentence," and "story." In some reading methods, they also may be asked to identify phonological aspects of language, such as component sounds within words (e.g., How are the words *stop* and *top* alike?).

Constructing narratives. Students in the primary classroom often are required to describe experiences from their lives outside of school or to make observations about classroom experiences, such as recounting events in a story the teacher has read. "Telling a story," for instance, is a narrative event that requires complex language use such as signaling to refer backward and forward between parts of the narrative (e.g., *The girl looked over the fence.* **She** [referring to "the girl"] *didn't see nothin'.* **So** (signaling a consequence of not seeing anything) *she decided to climb over.*). Many children will have only rudimentary skills of this type when they enter school (Norris & Bruning, 1988), and may need considerable encouragement and practice to develop them.

Later Grades

Developing thematic conversation skills. Younger children's conversations are notoriously disjointed, marked by rapid topic shifting and false starts. Here, for example, is a conversation among second graders:

1. Well, we . . . uh . . . have paper plates . . . with turkey on it and lots of [unintelligible]. *You know.*
2. Doo-doo-doo-doo-doo [singing].
3. I don't know what you're talking about.
4. You know what? My uncle killed a turkey.
5. Not frying pan?
6. No.
7. I seen a frying pan at Hulen's store!
(Dorval & Eckerman, 1984, p. 5)

Classroom discussion, however, requires that children stay on topic. When the teacher is involved, he or she can provide this topicality. For student–student discussions to succeed, however, children themselves must learn to be constrained by the topic under consideration. For mature discussion, they also must develop the ability to value others' judgments, to take others' perspectives, and to learn from what others are saying.

Acquiring advanced metalinguistic abilities. Language is enormously complex. Cues about meaning can be drawn from its phonology, its morphology, its syntax, and discourse structure. Students often need help to take advantage of the many cues that language offers. One approach is direct instruction. Another is for the teacher to model metalinguistic activities. Teachers can reveal their own thoughts, for instance, as they process a difficult section of text (e.g., *When I saw the word "he," I couldn't figure out who the author was referring to. Then I realized that it had to be Aquino, because later on it referred to "his struggle" against the landlords.*).

Developing knowledge of complex discourse structures. Both oral and written communication is patterned. Therefore, frames of reference for classroom communication, once learned, need not be relearned over and over. A discussion group, for instance, has typical roles for members. Other discourse modes, however, may be less structured, such as "persuasive communication" or "making a logical argument." One of the most-complex structures is that of exposition. As we have seen earlier, students who can recognize a teacher's or text's expository presentation and organize the information accordingly gain measurable benefits in the amount they will understand and later recall.

Drawn from Green (1983); Stubbs (1983); Durkin (1986).

course. This is not necessarily bad; links to earlier discourse can enhance later instruction. Reminders of earlier discussions (*I remember our having decided that . . .*), a review of content discussed during the previous days' lesson (*We talked about El Niño as a possible explanation for the current drought conditions, but some of you felt that . . .*), references to earlier comments by individuals (*Mark, here, was quite positive about the whole idea. Right, Mark? Everyone laughs, knowing that Mark has argued strenuously against the idea.*)—each is an attempt to link previous communication to the present one. By talking and doing things together over time, teachers and students build up a shared linguistic context on which further instructional discourse can be built. As Edwards and Mercer (1986) have put it:

> Throughout each lesson period, and across particular sessions, (teachers and students) are establishing jointly understood terms of reference, forms of discourse and knowledge, ways of thinking and doing things, criteria for recognizing and solving problems, which together constitute becoming educated. (p. 196)

The task of structuring a complex interaction in ways that are both effective and pleasurable falls to the teacher. Box 8-2 presents several key features of "teacher talk" that can be used to create an effective language context in the classroom. Each of these is used more-or-less constantly by most teachers as their contribution to the processes of classroom discourse.

These factors play a major role in effective teaching. For instance, the results of a large number of studies (e.g., Good, 1983; Brophy & Good, 1985) make it clear that teachers whose students make the greatest gains are those most effective in their classroom communication. Typically, successful teachers present and explain new concepts more actively and develop a context to give them meaning. They require responses from students and wait sufficiently long for students to respond. They also monitor student comprehension and use reviews and summaries frequently to check on and reinstate prior learning.

The Nonlinguistic Context for Classroom Discourse   Besides the teacher and students, a typical classroom contains seating, instructional aids such as chalkboards and overheads, demonstration articles, content materials such as books and papers, and other supplies. These items, although not directly related to language, do provide the physical stimuli for discourse. Edwards and Mercer (1986), for instance, provide the following example in which demonstrations with pendulums are used by the teacher of a group of 9-year-olds as the occasion for asking these students for hypotheses about the effects of lengthening the string or altering the weight of the bob on its period, or speed of motion of the pendulum:

Box 8-2

Typical Functions of Teachers' Classroom Talk

1. **Attracting attention.** Many teacher remarks are made to direct students' attention to what has been, is, or will be presented. Included here are teacher comments on students' responses that show that the teacher is paying attention to what they are saying.

2. **Controlling the amount of speech.** Teachers are the leaders of classroom discourse. They determine the quality of instruction when they create opportunities for speech, regulate taking turns, and promote periods of quiet.

3. **Checking understanding.** Teachers need to know whether they have been understood and whether students are following what has been said. Effective teachers monitor their students' comprehension consistently.

4. **Summarizing.** By literal restatement or by paraphrase of student responses, the teacher can confirm that he or she has understood what students have said.

5. **Defining.** Teachers frequently are called on to answer the question "What does this mean?" Good, clear explanations are vital.

6. **Correcting.** Teachers often correct student errors by means of discourse processes, commenting for instance on a student answer or writing comments on an essay examination.

Categories from *Discourse Analysis,* by M. Stubbs, 1983, Chicago: University of Chicago Press. Used by permission.

TEACHER: . . . *So you reckon it'll go faster.*
ADRIAN: *Yeh*
TEACHER: *Faster than David's?*
ADRIAN: *Yeh.*
TEACHER: *Faster than Jonathan's?*
ADRIAN: *Yeh, yeh.*
TEACHER: *What do you think, David?*
DAVID: *I reckon it'll go much faster.*
TEACHER: *Much faster?*
DAVID: *Well, not much faster, but faster.*
TEACHER: *Faster* [laughs]. *Jonathan?*
JONATHAN: *Er, I dunno. I think it might go slower.*

(Edwards & Mercer, 1986, pp. 187–188)

In this example, the physical props obviously are important determiners of what is being talked about. Through questioning, however, the teacher has moved the discourse to the level of general scientific principles. The students are doing far more than simply reporting on their direct observations.

Other nonlinguistic cues for discourse are present in the nonverbal repertoire of teacher and student. For example, consider the following sequence:

TEACHER: *Shannon, can you tell me what's going to happen when we turn the page* [of the storybook]?"
SHANNON: *Well, . . . maybe she's going to give her collection away.*
TEACHER: [looks quizzically at Shannon, raises eyebrows slightly]
SHANNON: *No, I think she's going to keep it.*

Students rely on a variety of gestural, facial, and postural cues when they make language choices. In the example above, the student was sensitive to the teacher's "look" in determining that her answer was not acceptable and that perhaps she should take another tack. Even minimal nonlinguistic cues, such as subtle changes in expression or posture, can signal to a student that the question is not yet completely answered. Similarly, a teacher waiting with book held in hand and continuing to look at a particular pupil after an initial response may cue the child that additional responding is appropriate.

The Classroom as a Setting for Discourse: A Summary   The classroom is a specialized linguistic community. Under the direction of a skilled teacher, it is an environment for purposeful communication in which learning is the goal. Both linguistic and nonlinguistic aspects of the classroom environment shape language use. Shared frames of reference for communication are built up over time by teachers and students; these frames of reference include a common vocabulary, meanings, and patterns of communication, as well as classroom furnishings and instructional materials. The responsibility for creating a productive context for language interactions in the classroom falls to the teacher; the teacher must orchestrate classroom communication. The attainment of each child's participation and instructional success depends on the teacher's skill in creating effective classroom discourse processes.

Linguistic Diversity in the Classroom

Most teachers today face classrooms of great linguistic diversity. A typical classroom may represent not only a range of developmental differences in language, but differences in dialect and even mother tongue. Somehow, teachers and schools must find ways to bridge the gaps that these language differences create.

In the United States, schools always have been the bastion of standard English, institutions with considerable power to enforce certain patterns of "proper" language use (Edwards, 1986). In doing this, the schools generally have reflected the views of society that certain kinds of language are better than others.

When all students speak English but some speak "nonstandard" English dialects, the contention is that the school has a duty to replace these deficient, "inferior" language forms with more standard, "correct" modes of expression. Another possibility, however, is that language use that diverges from that of the school is not deficient, but simply different. That is, the version of English some children use in their homes is not qualitatively inferior, but simply does not match the formal language of the school (see Heath, 1983; Romaine, 1984). Because of this mismatch, children may have difficulty accommodating to the requirements of the linguistic setting provided by the school. Such a perspective, we feel, reflects a more-positive view of language diversity—that all forms of language are legitimate. This view is based on the assumption that all humans are born with roughly similar language capabilities. That is, all languages are equally regular, rule-governed, and valid (Edwards, 1986). For cultural and political reasons, however, some language forms are more valued than others.

Children representing different social and ethnic communities quite obviously use language differently. The existence of these differences, however, does not necessarily lead to the conclusion that compensatory action is necessary. How do children from backgrounds in which the language of their home and community is a version of English other than "standard English" adjust to the linguistic requirements of the school? In a comprehensive examination of this question, Lucas and Borders (1987) used videotape, audiotape, and direct observation in kindergarten, fourth-grade, and sixth-grade classrooms in a Washington, DC, school. In these classrooms, all of the children were black; the kindergarten and fourth-grade teacher were black, and the sixth-grade teacher was white. Lucas and Border generally were interested in the question of whether teachers and students could "get things done" with language—that is, did communication problems arise in classroom interaction because of children's use of "black English" or "black vernacular"? To answer this question, the researchers observed a variety of classroom discourse settings, examining teachers interacting with their classes, small groups talking with and without the teacher, and one-on-one student conversations.

What Lucas and Borders found both confirmed earlier knowledge about classroom discourse and added new perspectives. As we saw earlier, teachers dominate classroom discourse. In teacher–student interactions, teachers talked considerably more than the students. Especially at the older ages, student comments tended to occur only in response to teacher initiations. By the fourth and sixth grades, the children had learned the prototypical discourse patterns for teacher–student interaction quite well—student talk had to be cued by the teacher. Self-initiations were rare; teachers elicited information and students responded to these elicitations.

Some very interesting findings emerged regarding student use of "dialect," however. When students interacted among themselves, dialect use was high; in interactions with the teacher, though, dialect use was very low and, by the upper grades, almost nonexistent. Also, when children interacted among themselves, the sheer volume of language also was considerably higher. These findings led the authors to conclude that elementary school children are keenly aware of situationally appropriate language use and are quite capable of altering their patterns of speech to fit the context. In general, Lucas and Borders concluded that because of the children's ability to use language in situationally appropriate ways and because of the awareness of dialect diversity by both teachers and children, the "production of dialect forms did not impede interaction in the classrooms . . . studied" (p. 136).

At the same time, however, Lucas and Borders had little doubt that the school, through its teachers, sought to promote the use of standard English as an appropriate form of expression. The following protocol is an example:

TEACHER: *What do you get for an allowance each week, L—?"*
STUDENT: *I don't get no allowance.*
TEACHER: *I don't get no allowance?*
SECOND STUDENT: [laughter]
TEACHER: *What was that?*
STUDENT: *I don't get . . . I don't get any allowance.*
TEACHER: *You don't get any allowance?*
STUDENT: *Nope. My grandmother get my money.*

(Lucas & Borders, p. 135)

That exchanges like these had some impact is revealed in the following excerpt from an interview with some of the sixth-graders in their study.

INTERVIEWER: *Do you think some people talk better than others?*
M: *Yeah.*
INTERVIEWER: *In what way?*
M: *Because some people say, like, you know, they'll say "I ain't got no more," like that, and some people say, "I haven't any more," like that.*
INTERVIEWER: *What is a good talker?*
R: *A person who speaks real good.*
INTERVIEWER: *Yeah, but how do you know they're speaking good? What are they doing that's different from a person who doesn't speak good?*

G: *Use a good **s** sound.*

P: *They put endings on their words.*

L: *Like sometime I think M talk well because every time I be saying the wrong words, she always correct me.*

INTERVIEWER: *What do you mean when you say the wrong word?*

L: *Like I be saying, "M, I ain't got none," like that. She say, "It's not ain't." She say, "You don't have any."*

(Lucas & Borders, p. 134)

Standard English has a high value in American culture. Since schools and teachers by and large represent its values, it seems highly unlikely that schools will abdicate their role of promoting it. What, then, is an appropriate view of language diversity? Perhaps first of all is a stance that variation within a language is simply that; there are no "substandard" and "superior" versions within a given language community. When some versions are judged superior, they are so judged for cultural, social-class, or even pragmatic reasons—not because of intrinsic qualities of the language varieties themselves. No matter what their linguistic background, children are widely competent language users (Norris & Bruning, 1988).

At the same time, children should be helped to acquire forms of linguistic expression and language use generally acceptable in our society. There are clear advantages to individuals who can express themselves in culturally acceptable ways. The danger, it would appear, lies in the **responses** of teachers and others to language variation. Although the presence or absence of dialect in children's speech may not be a crucial determinant of successful communication in school (e.g., Lucas & Borders, 1987), language patterns clearly do function as triggers for attitudes. As Edwards (1986) has put it, the process can be a viciously circular one: Children arrive at school speaking a language variety considered deficient; teachers, acting from good motives, try to replace this with a standard variety, but at the same time may make attributions, based on their perceptions of speech, about these children's intelligence, educability, and likely scholastic progress. Further, if the relationship between teacher and students is one of alienation, children can be made to feel inferior because their language use becomes the battleground on which conflicts between teacher and student are fought.

Children from Non-English-Speaking Backgrounds

Variations within a language community such as English create a challenge to both educators and students. When the languages of the home and the school are entirely different, however, the task of educating students becomes tremendously difficult. Without a common language, obviously, neither spoken nor written instruction is possible. Yet, this situation is faced increasingly by school systems across the United States. In large cities, it is not uncommon to have students with no entry knowledge of English who represent 50 or more distinct language communities.

What possibilities are available? One is to do nothing—a so-called **submersion** approach; simply bring the child into the classroom and hope that she or he somehow will adjust. This alternative obviously has little to recommend it on pedagogical, legal, or ethical grounds. A second alternative is English as a Second Language (ESL), intensive instruction in special English-language classes. The goal is to develop sufficient English-language skills to assist students in attaining a level of English-language competence that will permit them to succeed in other classes. ESL classes typically represent a wide diversity of first-language (native-language) backgrounds.

Where the number of individuals from a given first-language community is large (e.g., Spanish-speaking students in the American Southwest or south Florida), programs in transitional bilingual education (TBE) are common. In TBE programs, children typically receive their early instruction in their first language, coupled with intensive instruction in English. When students' English competence is judged sufficient for participation in classes with English-language instruction, students enter these classes. A final cluster of programs, called **immersion,** instruct *only* in the second language (Genesee, 1985). Such programs may alternate instruction in distinct time blocks (e.g., Spanish in the morning; English in the afternoon) or may have instruction only in the second language, a method sometimes called **structured immersion** (K. Baker & de Kanter, 1983).

The question of which approach is most effective is very difficult to answer (Secada, 1987; Willig, 1985); effectiveness depends on the goals being sought. To learn English, to succeed in subjects taught in English, to protect against loss of the native language and cultural identity, and to improve attitudes toward school are only a few of the many goals for U. S. programs. Goal selection depends on such factors as the circumstances under which the second language is being learned, the relationships between the minority and majority language/cultural groups, the relative social status of the groups in the culture, the size and political power of the minority group, and the desire of a minority group to maintain a cultural identity.

For even a given type of program, the experiences of minority-group children are likely to be dramatically different from those of children from "prestige" groups (Secada, 1987). For instance, whereas structured immersion may be highly successful for children of Canadian English-speaking parents who wish their children to become fluent in French and who volunteer their children's participation (see Genesee, 1985), an immersion approach may be disastrous for immigrant children of Hispanic background in San Diego or Los Angeles. Similarly, although well-designed TBE programs can be effective in producing higher English-language and subject-area achievement (see Willig, 1985), they also may create "subtractive bilingualism," in which the child's first language is lost by its being replaced with English. Thus decisions about programs need to be made with great wisdom and sensitivity to the goals of the language/cultural communities involved.

No matter what the program for children from other language backgrounds, a key factor from the standpoint of effective classroom discourse is the presence of a bilingual teacher, one who can effectively manage the "negotiation of meaning" in the classroom. Since receptive language competence (e.g., listening and comprehending) appears in advance of productive language competence (e.g., speaking, writing), a bilingual teacher affords non-English-speaking children the vital opportunity to express themselves. Even in immersion programs, a typical pattern early on will be for children to speak in their first language, and for the teacher to reply in the second (Genesee, 1985). Only later, as productive language capabilities increase in the second language, do two-way exchanges occur in the second language.

A second point is this: When there is great language diversity, teachers must take full advantage of the context of the classroom to foster language growth. Because the classroom environment is a specialized one with routines, patterned activities, and familiar objects, the classroom context can be highly supportive for learning functional language skills in which language use is linked to familiar frames of reference. The teacher, however, must use the patterns provided by activities and settings in a regular, predictable manner. There also is a great need to resist demands for premature language production and grammatical accuracy. Generally, language acquisition hinges more on comprehensible input than on early output (Krashen, 1982).

A final point is perhaps less cognitive than attitudinal. Language and culture are inextricably mixed. Linguists have led the way in asserting students' right to their own varieties and patterns of language; educators need to respect that diversity and to work to uphold their students' language rights (Romaine, 1984). This is not to say that there are not important, even compelling, reasons for learning the "majority" language of a country; even use of a nonstandard version of the majority language can index an inferior social or educational status (Romaine, 1984). But the goal of achieving fluency in the second language need not be achieved at the expense of driving a wedge between school and home and between members of the different language/cultural groups, nor need it be achieved at the cost of loss of first-language competence.

Classroom Discourse: Implications for Instruction

Teachers are responsible for leading and monitoring classroom communication. They need to consider language use as they plan and conduct instruction. They also need to exert control over ongoing discourse processes, including both their own and student speech, and to make "on-line" judgments of communicative success. The following points represent aspects of classroom discourse to which teachers might profitably attend.

1. **Recognize that choices about educational discourse are choices about instruction.** Classroom discourse is the hub of instructional activity; teaching can be viewed as monitoring discourse (Stubbs, 1983). If classroom talk is weak, so also will be the educational processes that rely on it—impoverished patterns of classroom discourse signal poor instruction. Cultivate and use productive discourse patterns.

2. **Prompt students to express themselves in extended discourse.** When students are asked to express themselves at length—not just in single words or sentences—they have to organize their thinking and develop their ability to express themselves. Often, unfortunately, students are not allowed communication beyond responding to "yes–no" questions or giving simple facts. Skill in using complex discourse structures can only develop through practice in their use.

3. **Check on shared cognitions.** The shared knowledge of a given classroom is built up little by little, bit by bit, over days, weeks, and months. Skilled teachers are "negotiators of meaning," checking frequently for the presence of understanding and clarifying what has been said (Petrosky, 1982). Explicit checks, such as solicitation of summaries or reviews of information, are critical. Equally important are the signals present in the ongoing discourse—do the responses of students lead you to believe that they are attaining the common understandings that you, as the teacher, are trying to develop?

4. **Value the language diversity students represent.** The language of students' homes is not necessarily the language of instruction. Although schools legitimately may model and teach the use of certain forms of language, students' language backgrounds must be respected. Teachers need to recognize that, even for many English-speaking students, the culturally based variations in language patterns and use may be substantial. What is polite and what taboo in speech, for instance, may be perceived quite differently by students and teachers who do not share a common subcultural background. For non-English-speaking students, the goal could be stated as that of "additive" and not "subtractive" bilingualism, in which the aim is to increase, not decrease, the child's total language competence.

Summary

Language is a key to classroom processes and critical to school success. The language-based skills of reading and writing underlie most instruction; instructional success also depends on effective oral language use by both teachers and students.

Languages are extraordinarily complex, structured at multiple levels. Sounds are organized into words, words into phrases and sentences, and sentences into discourse structures. Two major classes of discourse structure are narratives, in which the temporal sequence of events provides the organization, and exposition, in which text or speech is organized by the logical relationships between ideas. Narratives develop earlier; most children come to school with at least a rudimentary concept of story structure. By the middle grades, the ability to understand expository structure is beginning to become an important factor in understanding and recalling text materials.

Effective teaching depends on the quality of classroom discourse. Classroom discourse is unique, typically heavily dominated by the teacher and containing an unusual number of questions, directives, and the like. These discourse patterns may be quite different from those of students' homes and community; to be successful, students need to learn to adapt to the discourse style of the classroom. At the same time, teachers need to value the language diversity represented by students and to understand the regularity and rule-based nature of all language variants. For students who do not speak the language of the school, immediate steps are needed to permit instruction, however. Options in the United States include English as a second language (ESL) instruction; transitional bilingual education programs, in which students first are taught in the native language; and immersion programs, in which students are instructed exclusively in the second language. Bilingual teachers whose ability to speak the native language allows students to express themselves and to determine whether students are comprehending are vital to the success of any of these approaches.

CHAPTER 9

Learning to Read

At first glance, the act of reading seems simple. Words have meanings; reading, therefore, is a straightforward translation from symbol to thought or to speech. As we explore it more deeply, however, reading quickly reveals itself as a marvelously complex process, in which many cognitive activities must occur simultaneously—each affecting all others. Reading's consequences are also near-magical—through reading we can make contact with people removed in time and space, learn from them, and understand the meanings they have attempted to communicate.

These functional qualities make reading central to all levels of education. We begin early by teaching first-graders to read. Soon reading becomes instrumental for success in other areas of study. Without the ability to read, a child's likelihood of achievement in virtually any area of the school curriculum is seriously diminished. Beyond school, reading is critical to success in the workplace and is an important source of pleasure and entertainment for many adults.

In this chapter, we focus on beginning reading, the stage of reading called "learning to read." We look first at the psychological prerequisites of reading—that is, at what cognitive mechanisms must be in place in order for a child to learn to read. We then examine one current view of the transition into learning to read. In this section, we look at the stages children pass through as they move from prereaders to individuals with the skill to read unfamiliar work accurately and to understand what they have read. Finally, we move to reading instruction, highlighting the prominent methods and materials used to teach reading and summarizing key issues in the sometimes heated debates over teaching methods.

The Cognitive Prerequisites of Reading

Reading is a process of constructing meaning from text. As Mason and Au (1986) point out, reading is not word calling or "sounding out," but a special form of reasoning in which both the reader and the writer contribute perspective, inference, and logic.

In this section we highlight four factors on which children's success in learning to read depends: (1) world knowledge, (2) linguistic and meta-linguistic knowledge, (3) short-term and long-term memory capabilities, and (4) the ability to focus attention. These are not discrete, separable factors, of course; when readers read successfully, all of these dimensions operate at once. In discussing the beginning reader, however, it is useful to separate them. Some children may be well prepared on one dimension and not on the others; these factors do not necessarily develop simultaneously. Also, a beginning reader who had reasonably good skills overall may be relatively well prepared for some kinds of reading tasks, but not for others.

Knowledge of the World

We read to understand the meaning of written materials. This search for meaning—the process of comprehension—depends on both the writer and the reader. As we have stressed throughout this text, schema theory has had an especially important role in helping us better understand the nature of comprehension processes, including those in reading (Miller, 1988). With your indulgence, let us turn again to a "piggybank" passage, this one considerably simpler than the one you saw in Chapter 4:

> *Toby wanted to get a birthday present for Chris. He went to his piggybank. He shook it. There was no sound.*

As we know, the knowledge a young reader needs in order to comprehend even a brief passage like this is extraordinarily complex. For instance, the reader must know that *get a birthday present* means to buy one, that Toby went to his piggybank to get some money (the passage does not say so), that piggybanks contain money (the passage does not say so), that this money typically is in coin form, that coins in shaken piggybanks make noise, and that no rattling meant no money. For adults, comprehension comes without any special effort—all of these things are recognized automatically (and mostly without consciousness of their recognition). More than a few first-graders today, however, never have had experience with piggybanks, with buying and giving presents, or, for that matter, with birthday parties. With any part of this knowledge missing, the whole sequence of events in the passage can become incomprehensible. The main "point" of reading—getting meaning—would not be apparent to these first-graders.

As children read, they necessarily interpret the words and events in terms of what they know. Children who have helped care for a garden by watering, cultivating, and feeding the plants and who have gathered produce from the garden, for example, would be much more likely to make sense of a story about, say, a young Chippewa girl who works with her father harvesting wild rice than children who have not had these kinds of experiences.

Our knowledge directs attention in reading, guides interpretations, and makes comprehension possible (R. C. Anderson, 1984; Rumelhart, 1981; Schank & Abelson, 1977). The meaning that a beginning reader constructs, therefore, is not solely the meaning the author intended as he or she wrote the passage. Neither is it simply the reader's own mental constructions and inferences. Meaning is a joint construction of writer and reader.

Teachers and parents need to recognize that reading is a constructive process. As we'll see below, even when children mispronounce and misidentify words, teachers should continue to direct some of their attention to the meaning of what is being read. Although beginning readers undeniably need decoding skills such as letter, sound, and word identification, these skills in themselves do not add up to reading. To focus solely on "skills" with beginning readers misses the main point—meaning. Indeed, children can even be misled about the purposes of reading and can come to believe that "reading" is figuring out pronunciations, doing exercises with words, and completing worksheets (Cairney, 1988).

Linguistic and Metalinguistic Knowledge

A second general cognitive prerequisite for beginning readers is language knowledge. For most first-graders, expressive language has been developing rapidly since the second year of life; most already have extensive vocabularies of around 5,000 or 6,000 words (Chall, 1987). They also have a basic command of the morphology and syntax of their native language, as well as an ability to use language pragmatically in communicating with others (see Chapter 8).

Learning to read, however, presents a significant new challenge to most children's language development. In reading, children must link the language they already know to a new, visual system of symbols and combinations of symbols. To do so, children not only need to draw on their basic abilities to use and comprehend language (**linguistic knowledge**), but now must use **metalinguistic knowledge**—treat language as an object of analysis. That is, the ability to learn to read rests not only on basic language abilities such as vocabulary knowledge and expressive skills at the word, sentence, and narrative levels, but on children's knowledge *about* language at any of its many levels— knowledge about its sound system, words, sentence structure, and discourse structure. Good readers understand the skills they use in reading (Miller, 1988; Rayner & Pollatsek, 1989).

In alphabetic languages such as English, of course, individual letters and combinations of letters represent speech sounds. Furthermore, English pronounciation, although reasonably predictable, is not wholly so—letters are pronounced differently depending on their role in words and syllables (e.g., the *c* in *cat* and *face*), how they are combined with other letters (e.g., the *i* in *big* and *night*), and the presence of signals to their pronounciation (e.g., the *a* in *hat* and *hate,* as signaled by the "silent *e*"). Children must learn to recognize these unfamiliar new and highly abstract representations and map them in reasonably reliable and rapid ways onto the highly developed language system they already possess. Table 9-1 summarizes several linguistic and metalinguistic abilities that underlie early reading.

As we discuss later, many children lack the kinds of linguistic and metalinguistic knowledge listed in Table 9-1 when reading instruction begins. Not surprisingly, these children may view reading as an incomprehensible set of fragmented tasks (Norris, 1988). The problem is magnified when reading instruction relies heavily on metalinguistic abilities such as phonetic and word-analysis skills, particularly if these are taught in isolated drills.

Short-Term and Long-Term Memory Capabilities

Because it depends on use of world and linguistic knowledge, reading also is an act of memory. A child fixating on a particular word, for instance, must keep that word in mind long enough to build up the more-complex meaning of phrases, sentences, and whole passages. New meaning requires the continuing availability of earlier information; comprehension processes depend on the linkage between the words currently being processed and those processed earlier (Just & Carpenter, 1987).

As many studies have shown, young children's short-term memory capacity is quite limited. For example, the number of digits a 5-year-old can recall from a single presentation is only about four or five (Dempster, 1981). If the number presented exceeds this amount, the immediate memory span is exceeded and all or most of the information may be lost.

Reading, however, consists of sequential encounter of **related,** not isolated, elements—letters are clustered into meaningful words, words into phrases and sentences, and sentences into text. Thus, although it might appear that reading almost immediately would exceed the immediate memory span (e.g., after a child has read five or six words), it ordi-

TABLE 9-1. Some Linguistic and Metalinguistic Abilities Underlying Early Reading.[a]

	Word-Level Abilities
Print awareness	Understanding that print carries meaning; that reading is directional, can represent objects or speech, has special words (e.g., *word, letter*) to describe it.
Graphic awareness	Recognition of letter details (e.g., difference between *d* and *b*), that words are composed of letters.
Phonemic awareness	Ability to "hear" sound units; knowledge that spoken units can be analyzed and compared (e.g., *sh* and *ch*).
Awareness of grapheme/phoneme correspondence	Knowledge that letters and sounds "go together"; ability to apply that knowledge to decoding unknown words.
	Contextual-Level Abilities
Syntactic awareness	Recognition and use of sentence-level patterns, within-sentence context of words (e.g., correctly pronouncing *read* in the sentence *The girl **read** the book.*).
Text-structure awareness	Comprehension of relationships between parts of text, including recognition of cohesive elements in text, general knowledge of text structures (e.g., narratives).
Pragmatic awareness	Knowledge of purposes of written messages, uses of print.

[a]Word-level catergories adapted from Loman and McGee (1987).

most challenging

narily does not. The fact that words and sentences have meaning enable the reader to "chunk" information, or perhaps more accurately, to convert information into propositions (see Chapter 4). Each word is not a discrete, isolated unit but part of a stream of language.

Obviously, however, both short-term and long-term memory processes are fundamental to reading. Constructing meaning depends on an interaction of the two types of memory—new information must be "kept in mind" in short-term memory while previously encountered information is drawn from long-term memory. With this interaction in mind, some researchers and theorists who have examined reading from a memory perspective (e.g., Breznitz, 1987) have contended that slower-than-normal speeds of word decoding may place higher-than-normal demands on short-term memory and interfere with meaningful reading. Because words are encountered more slowly, the meaning of each must be held in memory longer in order for the reader to comprehend the meaning of a sentence or paragraph. At least some evidence has been presented in support of this position, although it would appear that conflicting demands on attention for the poor decoder (i.e., poor decoders lose comprehension because they must concentrate more on decoding; good decoders decode more automatically, allowing more attention to meaning) also is a plausible explanation of poor decoders' inability to comprehend and recall what they have read (LaBerge & Samuels, 1974; Samuels, 1988).

Attention

Reading requires that children's attention be focused on the materials to be read. Simply, if children are reading from a book, they must have the book out, be oriented toward the book, and be looking at it. Reaching this point with some children is not a trivial accomplishment. Teachers can take advantage, however, of a large array of behavioral management systems (e.g., see Axelrod, 1983; Kazdin, 1985) developed to help foster attentional skills.

Attention also is critical *within* the act of reading. Readers need to learn to direct their attention to the relevant elements of text in an organized, systematic way (e.g., *Look at the first letter. What is it, Sean?*). They need to control their eye movements, focus on specific words, and move their eyes in a left-to-right direction. Attention must move to each word successively and back to points in the text where comprehension has begun to falter. Attention must shift appropriately between text and text illustrations. During formal instructional periods, the problem of attention allocation become even more complex, as attention must be allocated in turn to the text, to classmates' responses, and to the teacher's directions and feedback.

Summary of Cognitive Prerequisites for Reading

At first glance, reading seems simply to be a matching task in which children learn to link visual cues to vocabulary. In fact, however, reading is a highly complex interaction with text requiring orchestration of a stream of sequential input of complex graphic information with several levels of language knowledge and with children's experiences with the world. Reading places demands on short-term memory and requires that children draw on their long-term memory to understand what they are reading. It also necessitates attention both at the broad-grained level of involvement with books and other reading materials and at the fine-grained level, in which attention must be directed appropriately toward details of letters, words, and text.

From Reading Readiness to Emergent Literacy

Almost everyone would agree there are developmental limits on how young children can profitably be taught to read. Today, most children in the United States learn to read during their first year in school, when they are about age 6 or 7. Fewer than 1 percent, according to Rayner and Pollatsek (1989), know how to read when they enter school. In the United States, our thoughts about when to begin to teach reading have been shaped by the concept of **reading readiness,** the idea that a certain level of mental maturity is necessary to begin reading instruction. The concept of reading readiness was given considerable impetus by the influential study of Morphett and Washburne (1931), who examined the relationship between general intellectual functioning and reading success. Their data led them to conclude that reading success was considerably greater for children who had a mental age of at least 6 years, 6 months when they started to school. Based on their analysis, Morphett and Washburne recommended that it was prudent to postpone reading instruction until children had reached this mental age.

Although the connection between teaching reading and the first grade has endured, the idea of reading readiness began to be defined more specifically as the subskills thought to underlie reading—such as letter name knowledge and visual, auditory, and perceptual readiness. A major influence in this transformation was the development of reading-readiness tests, which purported to measure critical factors underlying the ability to read (Teale & Sulzby, 1986a). The subskills view of reading readiness fit well with a conception of reading instruction as development of a carefully sequenced hierarchy of skills. This point of view also was closely aligned with the task-analysis approach to learning that dominated thinking about learning and instruction in the 1960s and 1970s (e.g., Gagne, 1965, 1970; see also Chapter 1). Hierarchical sequences of reading skills soon provided the framework for many basal reader series—the packages of texts, teacher guides, and student activities around which reading instruction still is organized.

One difficulty with the "reading readiness" concept is that children are placed in two discrete groups—readers and nonreaders. Also, reading is artificially isolated from other language skills as the "real" dimension of literacy to which the extensive language experiences of early

TABLE 9-2.   Contrasting Views: Reading Readiness and Emergent Literacy.

Reading Readiness	Emergent Literacy
Focus	
Reading as critical skill in literacy.	Literacy involves skills in reading, writing, listening, and speaking.
Prototypical view of reading	
Reading as a hierarchy of skills.	Reading as functional activity.
Function of preschool language activity	
Preparation for reading.	Part of multifaceted language-development process.
Focus in learning to read	
Formal instruction in reading.	Engagement with literate adults, adult modeling, self-exploration, formal instruction.
Sequencing of instruction	
Read first, write later.	Simultaneous use of all language forms—writing, reading, speaking, and listening.
Nature of curriculum	
Sequenced reading instruction, and hierarchical array of reading skills.	Variable language sources, language-based activities that include reading.

children are mere precursors. The concept of **emergent literacy,** however, provides an alternative point of view. From the perspective of emergent literacy, the most important consideration is that literacy development begins well before children actually being to read (Heath, 1986; Teale & Sulzby, 1986a). A prereader is neither "ready to read" nor "not ready to read." Instead, literacy development, like general language development, is seen as a continuous process that began far in advance of formal instruction. Table 9-2 summarizes some points of comparison between the reading-readiness and emergent-literacy perspectives.

   Children's movement into reading indeed does seem more continuous than discontinuous. As we saw in Chapter 8, the awareness of language so vital to reading—phonemic, morphemic, syntactic, and pragmatic—continues to develop throughout the preschool and primary school years. Also, although they cannot yet read, many prereaders already have discovered much *about* the process of reading: that its purpose is to get meaning, that the print context often provides cues for meaning, and that reading has functional uses (McGee, Lomax, & Head, 1988).

From the standpoint of emergent literacy, reading is not the *only* important language skill learned in school, but is one among a complementary array of critical language-based skills—reading, writing, speaking, and listening. Reading and writing are best learned from active engagement in meaningful communication activities, such as purposeful writing assignments and group projects. For most children, learning to read is not an unnatural act learned only by dint of extraordinary instructional effort, but rather a natural outgrowth of children's expansion of knowledge about language to include the medium of print.

The emergent-literacy perspective reminds us that the goal of "learning to read" might profitably be broadened to being competent in all forms of language expression. Reading is the key to literacy, but is not all there is to literacy. Critical literacy—linking thinking and expression through competent use of all forms of language—should be our goal, not simply functional literacy (Calfee, 1987a).

The Transition to Reading

The ability to read rests on a wide variety of linguistic and meta-linguistic skills, each of which is involved in learning to read. There is no single path from the point when children cannot read at all to a point where it can be said that they are "reading." A useful sequence of reading development based on decoding, however, has been proposed by Ehri and Wilce (1985, 1987a). They have argued that decoding skills develop in a predictable way and that children pass through at least four stages of decoding strategies as they begin to learn to read. Beginning as **nonreaders,** children typically first move into **visual-cue reading,** then **phonetic-cue reading,** and finally to **systematic phonemic decoding.** We begin first with the nonreader.

Nonreaders

Nonreaders are unable to read any primer or preprimer words in isolation (Ehri & Wilce, 1987a). Given a list containing such words as *bat, hit, go,* and *is,* nonreaders would be unable to read any of them. However, many of these same nonreaders would be aware that print carries meaning (McGee et al., 1988). They know, for instance, that newspapers, written advertisements, and books tell people something. They even may be able to "read" in the sense of identifying the names of products or businesses from signs. However, what these children are "reading" is more context than print. They cannot read the print materials when they are removed from context and pay little attention to the graphic (letter) cues.

A good example of this phenomenon can be seen in a study by Masonheimer, Drum, and Ehri (1984). Masonheimer et al. located a number of 3- to 5-year-olds who could identify "environmental words" (e.g., *Pepsi, Wendy's*) in their familiar context (i.e., as part of the logo). Most of these children, however, could not read these same words when they appeared in contexts other than the original ones (i.e., simply as printed words). They also were unable to detect alterations in the graphic cues (e.g., *xepsi*). Nonreaders may be able to "read" their environment, but not the print (Mason, 1980). In order to become a "real" reader, skills other than those acquired from simple exposure to the environment probably are required (Ehri & Wilce, 1985).

Visual-Cue Reading

Visual-cue reading is the first "real" reading. In this stage, children begin to rely less on the context in which words are embedded and more on the characteristics of words themselves. The word features to which many children first pay attention, however, seem to be predominantly **visual** ones. Examples of such cues might be the "tail" at the end of the word *dog* or the "look" of the word (Ehri & Wilce, 1987a). For children "reading" with a visual cue strategy, reading is a kind of paired-associate task (see Chapter 4) of linking a word's look with its pronunciation and meaning. Unfortunately, because words' distinctive visual features are exhausted quickly and because of the arbitrary nature of these associations, visual-cue readers are unable to read consistently over time. Simply, the memory task of reading this way soon becomes overwhelming. In Ehri and Wilce's judgment, this associative strategy soon is abandoned by most readers in favor of one relying more on generalizations based on phonetic information.

Phonetic-Cue Reading

Ehri & Wilce contend that a major step toward full word reading takes place when children begin to use phonetic cues. In **phonetic-cue reading,** words are read by "forming and storing associations between some of the letters in words' spellings and some of their sounds in pronunciation" (Ehri & Wilce, 1987a, p. 4). For example, a child may learn to read the word *fix* by associating the letter names *f* and *x* with the word's sounds. These associations, because they are not arbitrary, are much easier to remember and are more effective than the visual cues of word and letter shape.

Systematic Phonemic Decoding

Children become "expert" word readers and have unlocked an important key to reading when they can distinguish among similarly spelled words and read them with a reasonably high accuracy rate. These **systematic phonemic decoders** or "cipher readers," as they have been called by Ehri (Ehri & Wilce, 1987a) and Gough (Gough & Hillinger, 1980), have learned the alphabet, can hear the separate sounds in words, and understand that spellings more or less systematically correspond to pronunciations. In an alphabetic language such as English, this means that they are beginning to master a very complex mapping system linking more than 40 sounds (the phonemes of English) to a vast array of letters and letter combinations. Of course, these children are not yet "expert readers" in the more general sense. As we have pointed out, reading is a complex, interactive process focused on comprehension, not simply on decoding. Decoding is a vital "key" to reading, but it is not the only one. Reading places demands on the full range of a child's linguistic and world knowledge.

Knowledge and Skill in Decoding

As we have stated, virtually all authorities are in agreement that beginning readers must acquire decoding skills. Rapid and eventually automatic decoding is critical to the ability to read. Context cannot substitute for the ability to identify a word (Rayner & Pollatsek, 1989). There is less certainty, however, about where to place the emphasis in beginning reading instruction—on decoding, or on the more global meaning of what is being read? What should be the focus of beginning reading instruction? Samuels (1988) argues that the answer to this question may be analogous to the advice for a healthy diet—varied and balanced fare combining the acquisition of decoding skills with contextual analyses in meaningful reading activity.

Consider, for example, the passage in Table 9-3. Take a moment to try to make sense of it. Although the parallel to beginning reading is not exact because of your superior adult knowledge, we believe it is highly instructive. Think especially about the kinds of knowledge you use in reading it. If you are like most readers, reading a text such as this forces you to draw on a variety of kinds of knowledge. Some kind of letter and word decoding obviously is important. Like beginning readers, you probably made a rough correspondence between many of the letters and

TABLE 9-3

---

dɪlʌks bʌŋəloɀ. ɛksepšʌnlǫ prɛstɪž lʌkšurǫ lokešʌn ɪmidiʌt akypʌnciɀ
θri larǰ bɛdrumzɀ lɔts ʌv specɀ ʌtïčt gʌrɔǰ'. əplyʌnsʌz steɀ hy wʌnetɪzɀ
kal čïd at ʌfɔrdəbl riʌltiẓ. ṣsɹçβRẓẓ

---

sounds, but perhaps not all of them. You also used your knowledge of
syntax and your pragmatic knowledge that this passage probably means
something, however. At the same time, as soon as you were able to
decode your first word or two, your knowledge about the world—in this
case, your knowledge about real estate sales—was brought into play.

Just as it was for you in this "bungalow" passage, beginning readers'
word decoding is not simply a process of mapping symbols to phonemes
and words. As we've seen, it is a meaning-getting activity in which all
kinds of knowledge are used. Sentence and passage meaning assists in
decoding. Simultaneously, decoding unlocks sentence and passage meaning. Thus, instructional methods stressing only a single approach to
learning to read may handicap children who need multiple keys to un-
lock the meaning of words, sentences, and stories.

Skilled teachers draw on children's knowledge to help them read,
interweaving information from the text and its illustrations and from the
child's own memory to develop the ability to read. A demonstration from
Norris (1988) is a case in point. The illustrated text from Wagner (1971)
is about a friendly lion, Tony, and reads as follows.

> *Tony lived in a zoo.*
> *Tony was a lion.*
> *He was a friendly lion.*
> *"I need some hair for a nest," said a bird.*
> *"Take all you want," said Tony.*

The teacher begins by pointing back and forth between a picture of Tony
and the lion's name in print and says, "This is Tony." The teacher then
explains what the author wants the child to know about Tony. For example, in pointing to the first sentence, the teacher might say, "This tells
you where Tony lived." If the child is able to use the context cues available in the picture and the teacher's facilitation, the sentence is very
predictable without "knowing" any of the words. The teacher points to
the words as the child provides the information. If the child is unable to
make use of the context cues, more information can be provided to
direct the child's attention to them.

Each line of text is treated as an extension of the idea communicated in the first sentence, so that the child views reading as a series of integrated thoughts, rather than a series of disconnected ideas or words. For instance:

FACILITATOR: *Now it tells you what kind of zoo animal Tony was.*
CHILD: *Tony was a lion.*
FACILITATOR: *Oh, a lion! A lion who lives in a zoo* [pointing to relevant words in the text].

New or unpredictable words, such as *friendly,* are introduced by using them in context. Cohesive terms, such as the pronoun *he* (for Tony), are introduced. Similarly, the child's attention can be drawn to specific features of words, such as suffixes, that modify their meanings. For example:

CHILD: *He was a friend lion.*
FACILITATOR: *It's not telling you that Tony was a friend. It's telling you how he acted. He acted friendly* [pointing to the word]. *He was nice and did not bite or growl. Tell me about Tony.*
CHILD: *He was a friend—a friendly lion!*
FACILITATOR: *I'm glad he was friendly and not mean!*

(Norris, 1988, p. 670)

Similarly, misreadings of words are pointed out by repeating previous information and providing new cues.

CHILD: *He saw a friendly lion.*
FACILITATOR: *No, I don't think he saw a friendly lion. This is telling you about Tony: He's the one who was friendly.*
CHILD: *He was a friendly lion.*

When the child has finished "reading" the ideas on the page and understood their meaning, the child can be asked to tell the story using the words on the page, that is, by reading the words from the print. Context cues still can be provided as necessary, but the emphasis shifts strongly to decoding from the print. For instance:

FACILITATOR [pointing to the appropriate line in the text]: *Remember, this tells you where Tony lived.*
CHILD: *Tony lived in the—a zoo.*
FACILITATOR: *And this tells you what kind of animal Tony was.*
CHILD: *Tony was a lion.*
FACILITATOR: *And this tells you that he was nice.*
CHILD: *Tony was a friendly lion.*
FACILITATOR [pointing to the word *he*]: *When we know it is Tony, this is the other word we can use to talk about him.*
CHILD: *He was a friendly lion.*

Ideas in unpredictable and difficult sentences can be developed within the sentence one at a time, in a logical order.

FACILITATOR: *The bird needs to build something to keep her eggs in. I wonder what that is?*

CHILD: *A nest?*

FACILITATOR: *Oh, a nest* [pointing to those words in the sentence]. *And she needs something from Tony* [pointing to his hair in the picture] *that she can use to build her nest. . . .*

CHILD: *Hair?*

FACILITATOR: *Oh, I see, Hair . . .* [rising intonation, pointing to *for a nest*].

CHILD: *Hair for a nest!*

FACILITATOR: *Right! But she doesn't tell him that she wants all of it, just . . .* [pointing to the word *some*]

CHILD: *Some of it.*

FACILITATOR [pointing to the sentence within quotes]: *So tell me what the bird said she needed.*

CHILD: *She needs some hair for a nest.*

FACILITATOR: *Right, but it is the bird who is talking, so she doesn't say, "She needs some," she says . . .*

CHILD: *I need some hair for a nest.*

(Norris, 1988, p. 671)

The principal skills this teacher demonstrates are maintaining a clear focus on meaning and drawing out the child's considerable knowledge of language. Although some information is provided for the child, the teacher's major roles are focusing the child's attention on the text and eliciting text-relevant information from the child. In the preceding example, this information ranges from knowledge about zoos and zoo animals to information about how language is used. Included in the latter are the child's knowledge about sequencing of ideas, cohesiveness of text, and purpose in communication, plus specific aspects of sentence structure and vocabulary use. At the same time, the child is not allowed simply to continue to "read" the context; from the outset, attention is directed to the words and the need to decode their specific features (e.g., *friend/ friendly, was/saw, a/the*). Reading instruction is not unbalanced toward either "meaning" or "decoding." Instead, each aspect is used to create a source of information for the other. Reading instruction is not an abstract, decontextualized "drill and practice," nor is it solely "a guessing game" in which text features can be ignored. The strategy is to help the child find the meaning expressed in print and to begin to acquire an understanding of how letters and words represent meaning. The goal of increasingly rapid and fluent decoding—translating the printed word into speech and meaning—is embedded in a meaningful context. By skillfully helping children draw on all their available resources, decoding skills, sentence analysis, and text-comprehension abilities are developed simultaneously.

Methods of Teaching Reading

As can be seen from our example, a skillful reading teacher draws on several categories of children's knowledge in teaching reading. In the same way, teachers' overall objectives need to be broad-based, focusing on several dimensions of reading. Calfee and Henry (1986), for instance, have identified four broad areas important to reading:

1. **Decoding.** Translating printed words into their pronounceable equivalents.
2. **Vocabulary.** The assignment of meaning to words and activation of a network of associations.
3. **Sentence and paragraph comprehension.** Text units need to be "fit" to their functional roles (e.g., as the subject or predicate of a sentence, or as topic sentences).
4. **Text comprehension.** Complete texts need to be understood as entities—as "stories" (narratives), expositions, or dialogues, for instance.

A sensible reading curriculum must address each of these dimensions. The history of reading instruction, however, typically has not been one of balanced attention to all aspects of the process of learning to read. Instead, proponents of one method or another often have advocated, sometimes with near-religious zeal (e.g., Flesch, 1955), methods such as "systematic phonics" or "patterning." Others have favored a "meaning emphasis" with equal fervor. Over the years, numerous debates have raged about the efficacy of various methods.

A landmark event in this debate was Jeanne Chall's 1967 book, *Learning to Read: The Great Debate.* She divided reading methods into two broad categories, **code-emphasis** and **meaning-emphasis.** The former referred to approaches that initially emphasized decoding, learning the correspondence between letters and sounds. Prominent among code-emphasis methods was phonics, which stressed acquisition of basic letter–sound relationships and the rules for sounding out words (Weaver, 1988). Contrasted to these code-emphasis methods were meaning-emphasis approaches, which Chall judged to favor meaning over decoding in beginning reading. Included in the meaning-emphasis category were the "sight word" approaches (sometimes called "look–say"), which stressed the need for children to acquire at least a limited stock of familiar words they could recognize on sight. Another meaning-emphasis approach was language experience—a general method in which children's oral language such as their narratives about their experiences and observations is dictated and written down; what is written then becomes the basis for reading. Thus, in language experience methods, skills are taught in the context of the child's own direct experience with language and the world.

Chall's judgment was that code-emphasis approaches to beginning reading instruction generally produce superior achievement. Many (e.g., Carbo, 1988; K. S. Goodman, 1967; Goodman & Goodman, 1979; F. Smith, 1982; Weaver, 1988), however, have disagreed with her and have continued to advocate meaning-based instruction for beginning readers. Most current models of reading (e.g., Just & Carpenter, 1987; Mc-Clelland, 1986) appear to stake out a middle ground. Even Rayner and Pollatsek's (1989) model, described by its creators as primarily a "bottom-up" model, depicts top-down processes as interacting with bottom-up processes. These models suggest that reading is not best construed as "either–or"—that is, neither as an exclusively bottom-up, data-driven process (e.g., Gough, 1972), nor as a top-down process dominated by higher-level cognitive and language activity (e.g., K. S. Goodman, 1967; F. Smith, 1971).

With the rapid development of the phenomenon of the basal readers and the resurgence of code-emphasis approaches following the publication of Chall's book, meaning-based approaches languished in the 1970s. Also, in a climate that emphasized "reading subskills" and "skill development," reading instruction deteriorated in some instances into a pattern dominated by seatwork and worksheets, with teachers not so much providing reading instruction as managing the activities of assigning and checking worksheets. Further, in designing "controlled vocabulary" text materials for basals, frequent use was made of readability formulas to try to simplify text. Unfortunately, in the attempt to control "readability," which is a relatively mechanical measure typically depending on sentence length and word difficulty, other critical aspects of text that create "good stories" often were ignored, such as continuity, coherence, conflict, and surprise (Brennen, Bridge, & Winograd, 1986). The result was text that, although theoretically "readable"at the student's grade level, often was in fact disjointed, poorly formed, and quite unreadable.

In recent years, however, the picture seems to have begun to change for the better. By the early 1980s, analyses of classroom instruction and the contents of basal reading materials had begun to reveal the extent to which reading comprehension and the literary value of reading materials was being neglected (see, for example, D. Durkin, 1978–1979,

1981). Also, the development of more clearly articulated theories of comprehension in cognitive psychology (see Chapter 4) provided developers of curriculum and materials with a theoretical basis for emphasizing comprehension.

Compared to a decade ago, the teaching of reading now seems to be based in reading materials with greater literary value and better structure and places a greater emphasis on meaning and comprehension. More meaningful exercises are included for students, and most sexist portrayals of characters have been eliminated. To us, these changes generally seem to reflect the development of a more-coherent view of reading as an interactive, multifaceted process and to more nearly provide the desired "balanced diet" of meaningful reading instruction. That all is not yet completely well, however, is indicated in the recommendation of at least one author that basals contain "the perfect material for sentence combining—short, choppy sentences that can be combined to make more interesting, readable ones" (Reutzel, 1986). A recent study (Cairney, 1988) in Australia of children's perceptions of their basal reader experiences also is not particularly encouraging. Among a group of 178 primary school children who were interviewed, only 2 percent reported that gaining meaning or understanding was of major importance when they read their basals. Instead, these children saw much greater emphasis being placed on decoding, accuracy, and vocabulary. They viewed basal readers as largely of educational value, useful in "learning to read." The vast majority did not find them intrinsically interesting, however, and most showed no real awareness of the purpose of their worksheets.

Summary of Reading Methods

Reading instruction is a highly variable and often emotion-laden enterprise, representing many "philosophies" about how best to teach reading. Some methods more strongly emphasize decoding; others stress text meaning and using general and language knowledge to a much greater extent. In practice, however, most reading instruction has been dominated by the more eclectic perspective represented by basal reading series, packages of materials for reading instruction that include coordinated texts, teachers' manuals, and student worksheets. Basal reading series have been strongly criticized, however, especially for providing a less-than-coherent view of reading, poorly structured and uninteresting reading materials, and deadly "practice activities" that are boring and have little meaning for children. There now appears to be some movement toward improved literary quality in basal readers, as well as a greater emphasis on comprehension and on "whole language"—embedding reading instruction in a literate context of writing, speaking, and listening (K. S. Goodman, 1986). Such changes seem appropriate from both a theoretical and a practical perspective.

Implications for Reading Instruction

Whether or not reading is a "natural act," most would agree that the assistance of a skilled teacher in learning to read is important for most children. Reading rests on a child's language and world knowledge and depends on the acquisition of a system for mapping written symbols onto the spoken language the child already has. In alphabetic languages such as English, the child must learn an extraordinarily complex mapping from graphemes (letters and combinations of letters) to phonemes (the sounds of the language). As we have seen, however, reading is much more than decoding words; multiple levels of cognitive processes ranging from basic perception to the highest levels of cognition are involved. Thus, teaching reading cannot be a simple-minded, "by the book" activity—it requires the orchestration of many components into a meaningful whole if success is to be achieved. Following are themes we believe underlie successful reading instruction.

1. **Approach reading as a meaningful activity.** Reading is a meaning-getting act. This fact may be lost in some kinds of reading instruction. When reading is broken down into its constituent parts (e.g., reading "skills" or "subskills"), for instance, the overall context of reading can be lost. Children can come to perceive reading as a kind of training; its meaning can be obscured as we attempt to develop specific skills. We need to remind ourselves and our students of the basic reasons for reading—reading to learn and reading for enjoyment.

2. **Put reading into its proper context.** We believe that "critical literacy" (Calfee, 1987a) is a better goal than functional literacy. Critical literacy includes not only the ability to read, but the ability to use other forms of language effectively—writing, reading, listening, and speaking. Reading is the most important skill taught in the early grades, but our goal is to develop individuals who can use all forms of language effectively in thinking, reasoning, and communicating.

3. **Build on children's general knowledge.** A fundamental principle of cognition is the necessity of knowledge (see Chapter 2). All children have some knowledge about their worlds that can be accessed and used in reading. Unless relevant schemata are activated, reading is a meaningless exercise in word calling. Frames of reference enable children to give meaning to what they read.

4. **Encourage children to reflect on and use their language knowl-**

edge. Reading requires many dimensions of language knowledge—decoding, vocabulary, syntax, and text structure. For many children learning to read, this knowledge may be rudimentary or even lacking. Some children may not yet have developed metalinguistic abilities that would enable them to detect important distinctions about letters, words, or sounds. Others who do not share a background in the English-language community may have even more-basic language deficits. No matter what level of language skill the children bring, however, the teacher needs to draw on it for effective instruction.

5. **Help young readers move toward automatic decoding.** Rapid, fluent word decoding is a prerequisite to skilled reading. Although context can and should be used to provide beginning readers with decoding clues, nearly automatic responses are necessary for success. Good readers eventually rely little on context for their decoding (Perfetti & Hogaboam, 1975; Perfetti & Roth, 1981), although they _can_ use it very effectively. Poor readers typically have difficulty in automatic word decoding (Rayner & Pollatsek, 1989). Although it does not follow that children should be drilled endlessly on decoding exercises, word analyses, phonics rules, and the like, it does seem highly appropriate that decoding practice be an important part of any approach to reading instruction. This practice can be obtained in many ways, not the least of which is through guided meaningful reading. In such activities, the teacher directs students' attention to the revelant graphic and phonemic characteristics of words. Some structured decoding practice also may be beneficial, as long as this activity is not elevated to the status of "reading." Rereading passages to improve fluency (Samuels, 1988) and to attain automaticity also may be appropriate.

6. **Expect that some children will have serious difficulty in learning to read.** Although children may struggle with learning to read, most learn to read quite well. Others, however, will do poorly in reading, and some will grow to adulthood without ever becoming fluent in reading. In any given group of readers, for instance, as many as 10 to 15 percent will fall one to two years behind their peer group in reading level by third or fourth grade. Three to 5 percent will have more-serious problems; these children will lag two or more grade levels behind their peers.

For some children in the group with severe reading problems, the difficulty is low general ability. Others, however, will have normal or above-normal intelligence, but have a specific handicap in the area of reading. These children—called **dyslexic readers** or simple **dyslexics,** differ significantly from children who are simply poor readers. Many of them have notable speech and language delays, often coupled with difficulty in spelling and writing. In fact, the root problem for many dyslexics may well be one of language. A genetic basis seems probable for the disorder; dyslexia tends to occur more among males than females, among left-handers than right-handers, and to run in families (Rayner & Pollatsek, 1989).

Although intervention can help almost all poor readers improve, dyslexic children's prospects for becoming skilled readers are not particularly bright, even with special instruction. Poor reading skills, of course, can make school achievement very difficult. Yet many children with dyslexia do go on to high levels to accomplishment, both by using their own ingenuity to compensate for lack of reading skill and by drawing on the talents of teachers specially trained in methods designed to help dyslexic children learn to read. As teachers, we need to recognize the great difficulties that dyslexic children face and to be prepared to help them obtain the specialized assistance they need.

Summary

Learning to read is a prodigious linguistic and cognitive achievement. Reading superficially seems to be word-by-word decoding, but is in fact a multifaceted process in which all aspects of cognition and language must be orchestrated (R. C. Anderson et al., 1985). Beginning readers' success hinges on four major dimensions of ability—their knowledge of the world, their ability to use and analyze language, their short-term and long-term memory, and their capability of focusing attention. World knowledge enables comprehension; linguistic knowledge makes the mapping of the visual symbols of written language onto oral language and the creation of meaning possible. Short-term and long-term memory are critical processes as input is processed sequentially, kept in mind, and related to existing knowledge and language structures. Attention is equally important; developing readers must learn to focus on the appropriate aspects of words, letters, sentences, and texts in order to read effectively.

Learning to read once was seen as depending on "reading readiness." A more current view is that literacy grows out of the entire array of children's early language experiences. Even as nonreaders, most children know a great deal about the purposes of reading and its conventions. Some children can "read" environmental cues, such as signs and logos. True reading, however, requires attention to word and text features. As children begin to learn to read, many move through a step in which they first seem to rely on visual cues in text such as word shapes. Once children know the alphabet, however, they often begin to use partial phonetic cues supplied by letter names. Finally, children begin to "decipher"—to use the entire range of phonemic cues supplied by letters and letter combinations.

Although "deciphering" is important, it is only part of learning to read. Full ability in reading demands competence in four main areas: letter and word decoding, vocabulary recognition, syntactic mapping, and text-feature analysis. Competent reading instruction must balance all of these concerns. Instructional methods generally do include each of these areas; some, however, place far-greater emphasis on certain dimensions than on others. Some methods emphasize bottom-up processing and count on word decoding to lead to meaning. Others stress meaning, with the expectation that a top-down meaning emphasis will lead to skilled decoding. Because reading is an interactive process involving simultaneous processing at multiple levels of language and cognition, however, it is unlikely that either approach in an extreme form will be effective. What seems certain is that the emphasis on reading as a meaningful process must be maintained in any successful program of reading instruction, no matter what dimension of reading is being addressed.

CHAPTER 10

Reading to Learn

Reading assignments are among the most important instructional strategies teachers use to bring about new learning. Beginning in about the third grade, when most students have acquired basic reading skills, the emphasis in reading shifts from learning to read to "reading to learn." Third-graders, for example, may be given a brief essay about pioneer life with the expectation that they will learn and remember at least some of the essay's content. As students become more mature, the emphasis on reading as a way to learn new material becomes more pronounced. Ninth-graders may be expected to learn basic meteorological principles from a general science textbook; twelfth-graders may be assigned the first 20 pages of *A Midsummer-Night's Dream* prior to a discussion of Shakespeare's lighter works. In this course, no doubt, your instructor has assigned readings while he or she covers different materials in class. The assumption, of course, is that you will learn the content in this volume through your reading.

Learning from reading materials is such an important area of instruction that it has generated a massive research literature. Indeed, entire volumes have been devoted solely to how readers acquire the knowledge in text materials (e.g., Just & Carpenter, 1987; Spiro, Bruce, & Brewer, 1980). In this chapter, our focus is on **reading comprehension,** the construction of meaningful cognitive representations of text content growing out of readers' existing knowledge. We begin by examining three models of reading comprehension and then shift to a general schema theory perspective on comprehension processes that illustrates how readers construct representations of text material and retain these representations in memory. After examining a schema theory approach, we describe the role of readers' knowledge in comprehension—both general world knowledge and knowledge about reading comprehension. We then shift focus to an elaborative processing model that suggests how

readers give their attention to important aspects of text materials. Growing out of this model, we examine a series of external aids to reading
comprehension. We close with two sections designed to review general
approaches for facilitating reading comprehension.

Models of Reading Comprehension

In general, there are three distinct reading comprehension models
(see Andre, 1987a, for a cogent analysis of these models): data-driven,
conceptually driven, and interactive (see also Rumelhart, 1977; Rumelhart & McClelland, 1981). As you recall from Chapter 3, data-driven (or
bottom-up) processing refers to processing guided primarily by external
stimuli. Conceptually driven (or top-down) processing refers to processing guided by one's preexisting knowledge. In interactive processing,
reading is directed both by the text's data *and* readers' preexisting knowledge. In the next few pages we examine each of these kinds of reading
comprehension models more closely.

Data-Driven Models

As we have discussed in Chapter 9, reading comprehension may seem
like a simple phenomenon. Words have specific meanings, as can be
determined in a dictionary, and associations with other words or ideas.
To comprehend a reading passage, the meanings of the words (and their
associations) merely have to be identified and put into the proper order
set by the sentences. In such a basic perspective, reading comprehension
essentially is decoding.

Reading comprehension models that emphasize decoding and the
stringing together of word meanings are data-driven models (Andre,
1987a; Rumelhart, 1977; Rumelhart & McClelland, 1981). A well-
developed data-driven model was formulated by Gough (1973). We examine Gough's model as an example of data-driven models of reading
comprehension.

Gough's Model   To understand Gough's model, it is necessary to review some issues from
basic research on reading. Several researchers, Gough among them,
have used sophisticated eye-tracking equipment in order to follow the
movements of readers' eyes as they track across a page of printed text.
Typically, readers' eye movements consist of a series of stops and starts.
The eyes focus or fixate on one point of text and then move to another
point. (The movement is referred to as a saccade.) Vison is limited dur-

ing fixations to only a few letters. (The exact number is debated by researchers.) The eye essentially is blind during saccades.

Gough used the results of eye-tracking research as the basis for his model. In his view, readers proceed "through a sentence, letter by letter, word by word" (1973, p. 354). Reading processes begin with an eye fixation at the first segment of text, followed by a saccade, a second fixation, and so on through the text. Gough posited that each fixation placed about 15 to 20 letters in the iconic store (see Chapter 3, "Perception and Attention"). Once the information was placed in the iconic store (recall that such information is in raw and unprocessed form), pattern-matching processes begin, moving one letter at a time from left to right. Gough estimated that it would take about 10 to 20 msec for the identification of each letter. Gough further assumed that the information in the iconic store would last about .25 seconds and that readers could perform about three fixations per second. On the basis of these assumptions (which fit Gough's observations of readers' eye movements), Gough estimated that reading rates of about 300 words per minute were possible.

Once pattern-matching processes on each letter were complete, Gough envisioned the occurrence of a mapping response in which the representations of letters' sounds in a word were recalled and blended together to form the representation of the sound of the word. (Gough was careful to indicate it was not the sounds of the letter per se that were recalled. Instead, he argued that the memorial representation of the sound was activated.) When the sound representation of a word was complete, the word meaning was retrieved from memory and the process repeated with the next word. The decoded words are held in short-term memory. In short-term memory, the meaning of entire sentences is determined, and if clear meaning has been gained, the gist of the meaning passes on to long-term memory.

Although there are no *totally* data-driven models that exclude the role of long-term memory and presume meaning is completely determined by stimulus input (but see Gibson, 1969, for an attempt to construct such a model), Gough's model is a clear example of a contemporary data-driven approach. Each letter of each word is processed in serial fashion, and meaning is assigned to text on the basis of stored meanings in memory. As Gough himself foresaw, however, there are some serious problems with such strict data-driven models (see Andre, 1987a, and Brewer, 1973, for detailed critiques of data-driven models). Among the problems are the fact that recent research indicates that information is not gained from iconic store in a serial fashion (i.e., reading off the iconic store from left to right; see Chapter 3), that strict translations of letters into their sound representations would not allow readers to comprehend homonyms (or words in which spelling–sound correspondences are irregular, such as *though, slough, cough*), and that the context of words in sentences often determines their meaning (e.g., *Early in the inning he stole second.* versus *They admitted to the judge that Bob stole a car.*).

Conceptually Driven Models

Conceptually driven models of reading comprehension place their emphasis on the role of previous knowledge. Instead of describing reading as a sequential, detailed analysis of text to gain meaning, conceptually driven models are based on the premise that readers' expectations about a text and their previous knowledge of the subject matter determine the comprehension process. In this view, readers use the printed symbols on a page to construct meaning.

Just as no model of comprehension is totally data-driven, no model is completely top-down. Clearly, there must be some connection between what the writer intended (the meaning the writer meant to communicate with the words on the page) and the meaning constructed by the reader. Still, models vary in emphasis. One well-knowm model that has heavily emphasized conceptually driven processing is Goodman's.

Goodman's Model

Unlike Gough's model, which was based on analyses of eye movements during reading, Goodman's model grew out of observations of children's errors in oral reading. Goodman's initial research (see 1982a, 1982b) took place in natural settings (e.g., classrooms) in which he asked children to read stories aloud. Goodman chose stories that were somewhat difficult for the children and listened as they read. His analysis of the kinds of mistakes children made indicated to Goodman that reading was governed by processes that led readers to predict the contents of upcoming text. Further, Goodman believed that once readers were into a story, they used the text as a means of confirming or disconfirming their predictions.

Goodman's model of reading (1982a, 1982b) does not posit a sequence of invariant steps. Instead, Goodman believes that four cycles of processing occur simultaneously and interactively. In Goodman's terms, the four cycles are **optical** (picking up the visual input), **perceptual** (identifying letters and words), **syntactic** (identifying the structure of the text), and **meaning** (in which meaning is constructed for the input). Once a reader initiates the reading process, a meaning is constructed for the text. This meaning then is a prediction against which future input is judged. If the reader's prediction is confirmed, reading continues and the constructed meaning is enriched with new information. If the reader's prediction is incorrect, the reader may slow down, reread, or seek additional information in order to allow for the construction of a more accurate meaning.

Goodman's model suggests that errors or miscues should be fairly common in reading. Errors are not the result of poor reading. Instead, they stem from the same processes as good reading. For example, when children read the following material, many stumble over the last word in the second sentence: *The batter was firmly settled in the box. After a tremendous effort, the batter made a good pancake.* The reason for such an error, of course, is that many children use their knowledge of baseball to construct meaning for the sentences. They expect the last word to be *hit, double,* or another baseball-related term.

The strongest support for Goodman's idea that constructed meanings govern reading comes from his research on reading errors (Goodman, 1982c; Goodman & Goodman, 1982). When the children Goodman observed made errors in oral reading, they spontaneously corrected errors that interferred with meaning—typically by rereading and correcting themselves. However, when children made errors that did not affect meaning, these errors were seldom noticed or corrected. Apparently, if the word called out by the children fit the meaning they had constructed for the story, it was not seen as an error, regardless of whether or not the word was read correctly.

The strength of Goodman's model lies in its emphasis on conceptually driven processes. Further, its base in the analysis of children's reading errors makes it highly appealing. Andre (1987a), however, points out that the model overemphasizes conceptually driven processes. From Goodman's perspective, good readers should make less use of text information than poor readers, but this has not been verified by research (Leu, 1982). Andre also notes that Goodman's model is too vague to be helpful in guiding reading research or the development of applications. Still, the model is important for reminding us of the critical role of the readers' knowledge in reading.

Interactive Models of Reading

As we've seen, data-driven models of reading comprehension have problems accounting for the effects of readers' knowledge and the effects of context. Conceptually driven models do focus directly on the role of knowledge but tend to devalue the importance of data-driven processes in reading comprehension. Because of the shortcomings of data-driven and conceptually driven models, several models in which data-driven and conceptually driven processes interact have been proposed (e.g., Adams & Collins, 1977; Kintsch, 1986; Kintsch & van Dijk, 1978; Rumelhart & McClelland, 1981). One interactive model that has led to considerable research and applied interest is that of Just and Carpenter (e.g., 1987).

Just and Carpenter's Model

Like Gough's data-driven model, Just and Carpenter's interactive model of reading comprehension is based on eye-movement research. Unlike Gough, however, Just and Carpenter propose a highly interactive set of processes in which the stimulus material (the text) and the reader's knowledge base interact to result in a constructed meaning.

Just and Carpenter propose processes at the level of pattern matching, working memory, and long-term memory. These processes are not sequential; rather, they are highly interactive. Reading comprehension begins at the first fixation, at which visual stimuli enter the iconic store. Unlike Gough, who argued for a fixed number of letters in iconic store, Just and Carpenter suggest that the amount of input depends on several individual differences—reading ability, knowledge of the content area being read about, and the reader's purpose.

Once the visual input has been picked up in the iconic store, the next step is to extract the physical features of words. This process is largely data-driven, but it interacts with reading knowledge and the context of reading. For example, the **H** in **CHT** becomes an *a*, whereas the **H** in **THE** becomes an *h*. Meaning then is assigned, although predictions of meaning could precede and guide the extraction of physical features. For instance, when most people encounter the sentence, *Sarah stroked the long, silky fur of the* ⟨cat⟩. they read the word *cat* for the illegible scrawl appearing in its place. When this same scrawl appears in the following sentence, however, different features are extracted, *He* ⟨cut⟩ *his hand on a broken bottle.* The context of words guides our extraction of physical features.

Assigning meaning to a word, of course, depends on the extraction of physical features, the reader's long-term memory for words, and the reader's memory of the meaning constructed for the current passage. Unlike some interactive models (e.g., Kintsch, 1986), Just and Carpenter argue that almost every word in a passage is read and that the reader continuously integrates the meanings of new words with the constructed meaning in memory. If a sentence is completed, the reader assimilates the meaning of the sentence to the overall construction of meaning.

The Just and Carpenter model strikes a balance between data-driven and conceptually driven processes. Similar to Gough, a series of relatively automatic processes based on the input are described. However, these processes each are interactive with the reader's constructed meaning and general knowledge. Similar to Goodman, there is emphasis on predictions (predicting the meaning of a passage based on memory for what stories are like, predicting word meanings based on their context), but these are tempered by continuous decisions based on the interaction of input and reading knowledge.

A review of models of reading comprehension is helpful in focusing our thinking on the processes involved in constructing meaning for text materials. We see how the text and the reader's knowledge interact to form a unique representation of meaning. For us to consider research on reading comprehension and applications of this research to teaching, however, we need to examine a more-general perspective on memory that has guided a great deal of reading research in recent years.

A Schema Theory View of Reading Comprehension

As you recall from Chapter 4, schemata are hypothesized knowledge structures in memory that contain elements of related information and provide plans for gathering future information. Schema theory holds that the meaning of reading materials is constructed by readers based on the information they encounter, the information they already possess, and the way in which readers interact with new information. Consider the following paragraph drawn from a study performed by R. C. Anderson, Reynolds, Schallert, and Goetz (1977). As you read the paragraph, decide who or what Tony is.

> *Tony got up slowly from the mat, planning his escape. He hesitated a moment and thought. Things were not going well. What bothered him most was being held, especially since the charge against him had been weak. He considered his present situation. The lock that held him was strong, but he thought he could break it. He knew, however, that his timing would have to be perfect. Tony was aware that it was because of his early roughness that he had been penalized so severely—much too severely from his point of view. The situation was becoming frustrating; the pressure had been grinding on him for too long. He was being ridden unmercifully. Tony was getting angry now. He felt he was ready to make his move. He knew that his success or failure would depend on what he did in the next few seconds.*

If you are like many readers, you have decided that Tony was a prisoner in a jail cell. There are enough segments in ths paragraph that match up with people's "prisoner" schema so that this decision is reasonable. On the other hand, you may be like readers who decide that Tony is a wrestler. In this instance, too, there are several elements of the passage that fit "wrestler" schemata. As in the examples we gave in Chapter 4, the meanings readers construct for passages depend on the specific schemata activated during reading. These constructed meanings determine a great deal about what readers remember. Indeed, if we were to test people's memory for the "Tony" passage by giving them a free-recall test, we would find large differences in recall between those people who decided Tony was a prisoner and those who decided Tony was a wrestler.

As schema theory was discussed in depth in Chapter 4, we will not recapitulate it here. It is important to note, however, that schemata have at least six important functions in reading comprehension (Andre, 1987a; R. C. Anderson, 1984; R. C. Anderson & Pearson, 1985; Bransford, 1984). These functions are:

1. Providing the knowledge base for assimilating new text information.
2. Guiding the ways in which readers allocate their attention to different parts of reading passages.
3. Allowing readers to make inferences about text material.
4. Facilitating organized searches of memory.
5. Enhancing editing and summarizing of content.
6. Permitting the reconstruction of content.

The provision of a knowledge base for reading is a function of schemata that should be clear from your recent reading of the "Tony" passage. Even without unambiguous passages, the schemata activated during reading are those to which new information is assimilated. Recently, Glover et al. (1988a) found that signals in a second chapter of text asking readers to recall relevant information from a prior chapter activated readers' schemata formed during the reading of the earlier chapter and resulted in the assimilation of the new information in the second chapter to the signaled information in the prior chapter. Similarly, we have tried to provide several signals here to our section on schema theory in Chapter 4 (more about text signals later in the chapter). If we were successful in helping you activate your schemata for schema theory, this new information should be assimilated to what you already know about schema theory.

The ways in which schemata guide readers' attention during reading are more difficult to demonstrate. However, when we overtly attempt to activate certain schemata prior to reading, readers' selective allocation of attention can be seen. For instance, Glover et al. (1988a) performed an experiment in which "preview" sentences were embedded in a first chapter of text. These preview sentences (e.g., *As you will see in Chapter 23* . . .) were designed to alert readers that more about a specific topic mentioned in the chapter they were currently reading would appear in a later chapter. When Glover et al. observed readers working through the subsequent chapter, they noted that readers focused more of their attention on those parts of the subsequent chapter that had been signaled. Apparently, the activation of schemata guided readers in how they allocated their attention while reading. Likewise, if we gave some people the

"Tony" passage with the title "The Wrestler" while giving other people the same passage with the title "The Prisoner," we probably would see large differences in the ways by which readers in these two groups attend to specific elements of the passage. Probably, those people reading from the "wrestler" perspective would focus on elements of the passage germane to wrestling, and those individuals reading from the "prisoner" perspective would most closely examine materials congruent with a "prisoner" schema.

Drawing inferences requires the generation of knowledge not given in a reading passage. If you remember our example of "Piggo" in Chapter 4, you recall that we presented a brief passage about a girl breaking open a piggybank. Not stated in that passage were things like what Piggo was made of, what Piggo looked like, or what size Piggo was. Your knowledge (your schema) of piggybanks, however, lets you infer these things and construct a more complete meaning for the passage.

Schemata also facilitate organized searches of memory. To use R. C. Anderson and Pearson's (1985) example, if you are reading a passage about a ship's christening, your schema for ship christening represents a cluster of related instances of knowledge. These instances of knowledge are available in memory so that memory searches (e.g., *What kind of bottle is usually broken over a ship?* or *Where do they break the bottle on the ship?*) are guided by the schema activated during reading. The information in memory most relevant to the reading passage readily is available.

Schemata enhance the editing and summarizing of content. Since reading is guided by readers' schemata, new information constantly is being assimilated to the information in schemata. This assimilating and relating of new to previously known information allows readers to edit input (e.g., *That fits what I know about King George.* or *I know this stuff; I'll speed up until I see something new.*) in an efficient manner. Editing may involve marking certain segments of a passage as particularly important, registering disagreement with an author's position, determining that some content already has been mastered, and restructuring the content of a passage to put it in terms more meaningful to the reader.

Summarizing also can be seen as an editorial function of reading in which individuals consolidate the information in a passage into a readily remembered representation. Schemata facilitate summarizing by providing the knowledge structures into which the summary can be assimilated and stored.

Finally, schemata permit the reconstruction of content. As we saw in Chapter 6, there is compelling evidence that most of human memory is reconstructive. Indeed, only very rarely do readers recall the entirety of passages in verbatim form. Instead, most of us remember the gist of a passage and reconstruct its form on the basis of the other knowledge. So, if you were asked to recall the "Piggo" passage from Chapter 4, the probability is high that you could do a very fine job of describing a girl's destruction of a piggybank. It also is very likely, though, that you would reconstruct the passage on the basis of what you know about piggybanks—your piggybank schema—rather than remembering it verbatim.

General Knowledge and Reading Comprehension

An extremely important assumption of schema theory is that as to-be-learned information is linked more and more to what readers already know, their memory for the to-be-learned information should increase. This assumption has led to two very useful lines of inquiry and a widespread set of applications. In this section, we examine these two areas of research in some detail.

Advance
Organizers

Advance organizers are "appropriately relevant and inclusive introductory materials . . . introduced in advance of learning . . . and presented at a higher level of abstraction, generality, and inclusiveness" than subsequent to-be-learned reading materials (Ausubel, 1968, p. 148). Advance organizers are designed "to provide ideational scaffolding for the stable incorporation and retention of the more detailed and differentiated material that follows" (Ausubel, 1968, p. 148).

The idea of advance organizers has been one of the most intuitively appealing concepts in research on reading comprehension (Dinnel & Glover, 1985). Based on even a cursory review of cognitive psychology, advance organizers make sense. Anything that can serve to relate new information to what learners already know *ought* to be valuable. Indeed, early research on advance organizers seemed especially promising. For example, Ausubel and Fitzgerald (1961) had students read a passage about Buddhism and tested them for their mastery of the content in three conditions: a condition in which subjects first read a historical introduction, a condition in which the principles of Buddhism were first set forth in abstract and general terms, and a condition that first used a review of Christianity as an organizer designed to relate what the students already knew about religions to the material they were being asked to learn on Buddhism. The results were clear. On the posttest, students who read the advance organizer relating Christianity to Buddhism outperformed the students in the two other conditions.

Although Ausubel and his associates (e.g., Ausbuel, 1960; Ausubel & Fitzgerald, 1961, 1962; Ausubel & Youssef, 1963) continued to obtain positive results on the utility of advance organizers, many other researchers did not. By the mid 1970s, research on advance organizers was a jumbled mass of results both pro and con. Careful reviews of the advance organizer literature by Barnes and Clawson (1975) and Faw and

Waller (1976), however, began to clarify the area by pointing out problems in the research. In general, the definition of advance organizers was so vague that no standardization was possible. Everything from outlines to questions to pictures to graphs to paragraphs was used in one study or another as an advance organizer. Coupled with the often-severe methodological problems seen in early research (not keeping track of how long students studied material, not employing true control groups, poor development of posttests), the vagueness of what made for an effective advance organizer greatly limited research progress.

In the late 1970s and early 1980s, however, researchers began to clear up the methodological problems and tie their work into contemporary schema theory (Derry, 1984; Mayer, 1979; Mayer & Bromage, 1980). In these studies, advance organizers in the form of a paragraph or two of material prefacing the to-be-learned content showed consistent, if somewhat small, beneficial effects on readers' memory for materials. Still, the problem with defining organizers remained.

Recently, however, a series of studies has begun to suggest the characteristics of good, written organizers. In general, organizers that give readers an analogy for upcoming content, are concrete and use concrete examples, and are well learned by readers are far more beneficial than abstract, general, or poorly learned organizers (Dinnel & Glover, 1985; Corkill, Glover, & Bruning, 1988a; Corkill, Glover, Bruning, & Krug, 1988b).

Corkill et al. (in press), for example, contrasted the effects of concrete advance organizers in the form of a paragraph preceding text with abstract organizers and a read-only control condition. Across two experiments that employed to-be-learned materials of different lengths, Corkill and her associates found that even when the organizers were well learned by readers, only the concrete organizers benefited recall. Similarly, Dinnel and Glover (1985) found that well-learned organizers in analogy form had a beneficial effect on readers' recall.

In sum, the concept of advance organizers is theoretically appealing, and if properly developed, advance organizers are effective devices for enhancing readers' comprehension of text. A closely related idea, schema activation, has not yet received as much research attention.

Schema   As in the case of advance organizers, the concept of schema activation is
Activation   loosely defined. In general, **schema activation** refers to an array of activities designed to activate relevant knowledge in students' memory prior to encountering new, to-be-learned information (e.g., Alvermann, Smith, & Readence, 1985; Pearson, 1985; Peeck, 1982; Peeck, van den Bosch, & Kruepling, 1982; Rowe & Rayford, 1987). These activities typically have taken the form of having students answer questions germane to an upcoming topic, review previous learning, or develop a "schema

map" of related knowledge already in memory (R. C. Anderson & Pearson, 1985; Schumacher, 1987).

In many ways, it seems as though schema-activation procedures attempt to accomplish the goal of advance organizers (i.e., tying new information to what is already known) without resorting to the provision of written materials in advance of reading. The emphasis, instead, is on seeking means of helping students remember things they already know revelant to a new topic. Consider, for example, an early study conducted by Peeck and his colleagues.

Peeck et al. (1982) had a group of Dutch fifth-graders read a brief (125 words) passsage about a fictional fox. Prior to reading, half of the children activated relevant prior knowledge by generating ideas from memory about foxes. The remaining half of the children generated ideas about a topic not relevant to the fox passage, American farms. Immediately following reading, the children were tested via free recall. The results indicated that the children who activated their knowledge about foxes remembered significantly more of the passage content than the other children. More recently, Rowe and Rayford (1987) examined the effects of a specific form of schema activation in the reading performance of first-, sixth-, and tenth-grade students. They found that "purpose" questions—questions designed to prepare readers for the purpose of a passage by activating relevant background knowledge—had facilitative effects at all three grade levels.

Both advance organizers and schema activation are based on the idea that reading comprehension and students' memory for text can be improved by finding ways to help students relate new information to what they already know. Recent research on both topics suggests that such procedures are highly effective and ought to be a part of every teacher's repertoire of teaching strategies. Simply, the more ways teachers can find to help students relate new information to what they already know, the more that will be learned and retained from reading. Other aspects of readers' knowledge, however, also are critical in reading comprehension, especially what readers know about their own reading comprehension processes.

Metacognitive Reading Skills

An area of research on reading comprehension congruent with a schema theory perspective has emphasized readers' metacognitive reading skills (Cross & Paris, 1988; Jacobs & Paris, 1987; Palinscar, Brown & Martin, 1987; Waller, 1987). As you recall from Chapter 5, metacognition refers to thinking about thinking. Metacognitive reading skills specifically refer to knowledge readers have about reading and how this knowledge is used in the reading process. In the next few pages, we examine several metacognitive reading skills in detail.

Identifying Main Ideas An important skill directly related to reading comprehension is the ability of readers to locate the main ideas in a reading passage (Rosenschine, 1984; Yuill & Joscelyne, 1988). This metacognitive activity (see A. L. Brown, 1980) has received considerable research attention, although Andre (1987a) points out that most basal reading series provide students with almost no direct instruction in how to find main ideas (see also Hare & Milligan, 1984). Not surprisingly, a goodly number of readers, even those who can fluently "call out" the words in a passage, have trouble locating main ideas.

In an early study on teaching children to identify the main ideas in paragraphs, Glover, Zimmer, Filbeck, and Plake (1980) had students who scored below average on a test of reading comprehension attempt to identify the main ideas in a series of paragraphs. After determining that the students' performance was poor, training was provided through the simple procedure of having students underline the parts of paragraphs they believed were the main ideas. After underlining, students could turn a page and compare the portion of the paragraph they selected as representing the main idea with the main idea as determined by the experimenters. Across a training period of 25 days in which praise and other positive outcomes were given students for increases in their accuracy, students' abilities to identify the main ideas in paragraphs improved dramatically, as did their scores on a postexperiment test of reading comprehension.

More recently, Baumann (1984) and Taylor and Beach (1984) have reported similar results. In the current context, however, a particularly interesting approach to actively teaching students metacognitive skills for identifying main ideas was provided by Palincsar and Brown (e.g., A. L. Brown & Palincsar, 1982, 1989; Palincsar & Brown, 1984; Palincsar, Brown, & Martin, 1987). Although the focus of Palincsar and Brown's training program has been much broader than the identification of major ideas, we review it here because it is germane to much of what we discuss in the next few pages.

In Palincsar and Brown's approach, referred to as **reciprocal teaching,** a teacher (or student tutor) and student take turns talking about a reading passage. The teacher models reading comprehension activities aloud (including finding main ideas) and guides the student in performing comprehension activities. At the start of a lesson, the teacher begins by engaging the student in a short discussion designed to activate relevant prior knowledge. (See our earlier discussion of schema activation.) Then, both the teacher and student silently read a brief passage. Next, the teacher asks questions like those that might be on a test of the material. Finally, the teacher summarizes the passage, points out and clears up any problems in comprehension, and makes predictions about upcoming content (e.g., what might happen in a next chapter).

Gradually, across sessions, the teacher shifts responsibility more and more to the student so that the student asks questions, summarizes, clears up any misunderstandings, and predicts future performance. Highlighted through the process is how the teacher and student think about their reading comprehension. This may be fairly direct when the teacher guides the process (e.g., a teacher comments, "It helps me to guess what will happen next by putting myself in Hazel's place.") to rather informal (e.g., a tutor's comment to a student that "I like to check after each section to see if I can say what it's all about—the main idea, you know.") The technique also includes direct instruction in how to perform comprehension activities as well as tips for reading more effectively, as seen in this quotation taken from one of the seventh-grade tutors who participated in Palincsar et al.'s (1987) study:

> *Now let me see. . . . This is where I need to stop you. When you summarize as you read your paragraph, be gettin' your main idea formed in your mind and see if you can't remember it without lookin' back. At the very beginning it is difficult to do, and you may have to look back. But see if you can't get the main idea without goin' back and readin' bits and pieces of it.*

In general, research on training students to find the main idea of passages has been very positive. Students' abilities to find main ideas improve with practice and feedback, especially when the instruction focuses on metacognition.

Summarizing and Review

The ability to **summarize and review** a reading passage also is critical to reading comprehension. In fact, Winograd (1984) has reported that one of the major deficiencies among poor readers is their inability to adequately summarize content (see also Le Fevre, 1988). Recent research on teaching summarizing skills, however, suggests that this skill readily can be acquired by students. Palincsar et al. (e.g., 1987), for example, specifically emphasize this metacognitive skill in reciprocal teaching as teachers and students practice summarizing and reviewing the meaning of passages. At first, the teacher models summarization, but gradually he or she shifts the responsibility to the student. When the student is the primary summarizer, the teacher's role becomes more centered on providing feedback, prompts, and praise for good work. In Palincsar et al.'s method, the emphasis consistently is on acquiring and learning how to think about using the skill.

Another approach to teaching summarizing skills can be seen in a study by King, Biggs, and Lipsky (1984), which involved college students enrolled in a reading development course. As a part of their study, King et al. taught the students in the summarizing condition a set of rules for generating summaries drawn from Day's (1980) work. These rules (King et al., 1984, p. 210) were as follows:

1. Ignore *unimportant* information.
2. Ignore *repeated* information.
3. Group lists under *labels* (i.e., label lists).
4. Pick *topic* sentences.
5. Invent *topic* sentences (when missing).
6. Write down 3–5 topic sentences in abstracted form.
7. List important details.

Students in King et al.'s study practiced using the rules on two 5,000-word chapters. As the students read, they recorded their summaries on strips of paper fastened to their booklets. After training, students read an additional 5,000-word passage and were tested on their ability to recall the passage content two days later. Just prior to the testing, students were given 10 minutes to review their summaries. Students in the control condition were given the same materials and were instructed to take notes during reading but were given no rules for summarizing. They, too, were given 10 minutes to review their notes prior to the posttest. The results were impressive. Students in the summarizing condition recalled more than 25 percent more ideas on the posttest than students in the control condition. Apparently, even a brief training program emphasizing how to write summaries has a considerable impact on what students learn from text.

Other studies that have focused on teaching students rules for summarizing reading materials have obtained results highly similar to those reported by King et al. (1984). For example, Stevens (1988) found that middle and high school remedial students benefited greatly from training in finding main ideas. Taylor (1982) taught readers to focus on superordinate/subordinate relationships of ideas in passages and found that such training led to better summaries and heightened levels of recall. Long and Aldersley (1982) likewise had students attend to the relationship of ideas during summary construction and reported sizable benefits from training, as did Armbruster (1979). Recently, Armbruster et al. (1987) taught fifth-graders about a specific kind of text structure and how to use their knowledge of the text structure in summarizing the material. The results of later testing of readers' comprehension indicated that instruction in summarizing coupled with teaching students about text structure greatly improved students' reading comprehension.

Whether summarization training and the use of summaries for review has emphasized a tutoring approach (e.g., Palincsar et al., 1987) or a more didactic approach wherein rules for summarizing are taught directly (e.g., King et al., 1984), the results of research on the teaching of summarization skills have been highly positive. When students are taught to summarize text as they read and when they use their summaries in studying, significant improvements in learning are observed.

Self-Questioning   The metacognitive skill of **self-questioning** is a common part of good reading (Glover & Corkill, 1987). That is, good readers frequently ask themselves questions about the content of what they are reading in terms of assessing comprehension, determining the utility of the information, and deciding about the importance of ideas. As you recall, self-questioning and clarification of content are an integral part of Palincsar et al.'s reciprocal teaching. As self-questioning is embedded in their overall program, however, it is difficult to determine how this skill alone contributes to reading comprehension. King et al. (1984), however, have reported on the results of a self-questioning condition in contrast to the control and summarizing conditions we described earlier. As a part of their study, students in one condition were asked to form "higher-level" questions based on the text (students were first taught what *higher-level* meant based on a taxonomy of learning), to record them as notes, and then to read the passage to gain the answers. When the results were examined, the students who used self-questioning during reading did not recall as much content as did students who summarized, but they did recall nearly 20 percent more of the passage's ideas than the control group. Taken with the results of Palincsar et al.'s (e.g., 1987) studies of reciprocal teaching and earlier work (e.g., Andre & Anderson, 1978–79; Duell, 1978; Frase & Schwartz, 1975), King et al.'s results suggest that self-questioning directly enhances reading comprehension and that it is a relatively easy skill for students to learn.

Drawing   All texts leave things unsaid and depend on readers to **infer** information
Inferences   (as when a character's age is not mentioned, but his or her traits suggest youth). Drawing inferences about reading materials also includes the ability to infer ideas outside or beyond the realm of a reading passage (e.g., on the basis of reading this chapter, what have you inferred about how you can enhance the reading comprehension of your own students?) As we might expect, drawing inferences about reading materials is a skill possessed by good readers but tending to be absent in poor readers (Dewitz, Carr, & Patberg, 1987; Le Fevre, 1988).

Several studies have shown that students can be taught to make inferences about the materials they read and that this skill enhances reading comprehension (Dewitz et al., 1987). Perhaps the clearest findings on teaching inference skills comes from the work of Raphael and her colleagues (e.g., Raphael & Pearson, 1982; Raphael & McKinney, 1983; Raphael & Wonnacott, 1985).

Raphael and Wonnacott, for example, contrasted fourth-graders in a control condition with students of similar ability levels who received training in finding the answers to questions about reading materials. Three types of questions were used—those for which the answers were explicit in the text, those for which the answers were implicit in the text (inferences were needed much as the inference used in determining someone's age from his or her description), and those for which an integration of the reader's background knowledge and text information were required (the inferences required were similar to the inferences you might make in using the content of this chapter to aid your students' reading comprehension). Students in the experimental conditon received four days of training and practice in answering the three types of questions, with considerable attention given to showing students how to answer the questions. Although the study was complex, the results indicated that the training greatly facilitated students' abilities to draw inferences about text materials and significantly improved their comprehension of reading materials.

In a second experiment, Raphael and Wonnacott taught teachers how to train students to answer the three types of questions in an in-service program. Then, rather than conducting the experiment themselves, Raphael and Wonnacott looked at the results of the teachers' implementation of the training with students. The results again were highly positive. Showing students how to answer the different kinds of questions, coupled with practice and feedback, resulted in significant improvements in reading comprehension.

Finding Errors and Inconsistencies   One of the more remarkable findings in research on reading comprehension is how poorly even the best readers perform when they are asked to identify errors and inconsistencies in reading materials. Indeed, several studies suggest that readers identify as few as 20 percent of the errors in texts (e.g., L. Baker, 1984, 1985, in press; L. Baker & Anderson, 1982; L. Baker & Wagner, 1987). Consider, for example, the following passage taken from Baker and Wagner (p. 248):

> *Governors frequently go to great lengths to win legislators over to their side. They often spend many hours simply socializing with them. As governor of Montana, Ronald Reagan used to invite groups of legislators to his home. There, among other things, they would play with the model electric train network that he had set up in his basement.*

In Baker's (1985) study, only 24 percent of her participants (college students) asked to read a set of passages and underline anything "hard to understand" identified the misstatement about Montana. Further, only 51 percent of Baker's subjects who were told that there would be inconsistencies with prior knowledge in the passages identified the misstatement. Interestingly, when Baker later questioned the participants in her study, she found that the vast majority knew Reagan had been the governor of California and not Montana. Similarly, only 6 of 30 history majors recruited for a study in our laborabory found anything odd in the statement *Hitler, whose American mother left Baltimore in 1885, served in World War I.*

The results described above suggest that even fairly sophisticated readers often have trouble reading critically. Research on detecting errors and inconsistencies in text, however, suggests that students can be taught to be more critical and to do a better job of detecting errors. Grabe and Mann (1984), for instance, taught fourth-graders to detect inconsistencies through an activity they called the "Master Detective" game. In this approach, the children read a series of 10 statements displayed on a computer screen. The statements supposedly were made by 10 different suspects in a crime. In the first round of the game, the only one for which Grabe and Mann analyzed their data, five of the statements were consistent and five contained inconsistencies. The point of the game was for the children to find the inconsistencies, such as in the sample below taken from Grabe and Mann (p. 136):

> *All the people that [sic] work on this ship get along very well. The people that [sic] make a lot of money and the people that [sic] don't make much are still friends.* <u>The officers treat us like dirt.</u> *We often eat our meals together. I guess we are just one big happy family.* [Underlining of the inconsistent statement is added.]

The children in Grabe and Mann's experimental condition played the game once as a pretest, four times for practice (with different sets of statements each time), and once as a posttest. The children in the control conditon merely played the game twice as a pretest and posttest. The results were clear. The children who completed the four practice sessions far outperformed the children in the control condition on the posttest. Simple practice with feedback for identifying inconsistent statements (in a motivating, game situation) brought about significant improvement in the identification of inconsistencies.

More recently, Bullock and Glover (in press) examined the effects of schema activation and directions to look for errors on students' abilities to find factually incorrect statements in essays. The results indicated that seventh-graders who activated relevant schemata prior to reading with the expectation that they would encounter errors found nearly 90 percent of the errors in essays, whereas students in a control condition who merely were told to identify any errors or inconsistencies identified only about 45 percent of the errors. Together, the results reported by Grabe and Mann and Bullock and Glover suggest that fairly simple procedures may improve students' abilities to detect errors and inconsistencies in text. Appparently, a combination of practice with feedback and schema-activation procedures should result in a greater likelihood that students will critically read text.

Calibration of
Comprehension
Closely related to the ability to identify errors or inconsistencies in reading materials is how well students are able to estimate how much they have learned from reading. The correlation between what students believe they have learned from a reading passage and their actual test performance is referred to as their **calibration of comprehension** (Glenberg, Sanocki, Epstein, & Morris, 1987).

It seems reasonable that when students are given a reading assignment and told to expect a test, they should read and study until they believe they have mastered the material and then stop. Studying less would seem risky, as students probably would not meet the teacher's instructional goals and would perform poorly on the test. On the other hand, studying more than is needed to master the material could be seen as a waste of time. Students have many responsibilities and must divide their time among tasks wisely.

Our day-to-day experiences as teachers and psychologists suggest that students usually do have a good sense of how well they have mastered the material they study—an accurate calibration of comprehension. After all, a great number of students regularly succeed on tests. In contrast to this intuitively appealing belief are the findings of an impressive set of studies conducted by Glenberg and his associates (e.g., Glenberg, Wilkinson, & Epstein, 1982; Epstein, Glenberg, & Bradley, 1984; Glenberg & Epstein, 1985; Glenberg et al., 1987). In general, these studies have found that adult readers' beliefs about what they have learned from reading have little relationship to actual test performance.

Typically, studies of calibration of comprehension consist of having students read a series of brief passages, complete ratings of how confident they are in answering specific types of questions over the material, and, finally, take a posttest. In Glenberg et al.'s (1987) Experiment 1, for example, the correlation between college students' estimates of performance on an inference test and their actual test scores was nearly zero.

Despire the consistency with which studies show poor levels of calibration of comprehension, relatively simple procedures can be used to facilitate the accuracy of students' estimates of learning from text. For example, Pressley, Snyder, Levin, Murray, and Ghatala (1987) found that when readers have the opportunity to test their learning during reading, their estimates of performance improve substantially. Although research on procedures to influence the calibration of comprehension is yet very limited, activities such as self-questioning, summarizing, and other meta-cognitive skills also should aid students in estimating how well they have learned reading materials. In general, it seems that any program designed to improve reading comprehension should include a component focused on having students learn to make accurate judgments about their learning (see Vosniadou, Pearson, & Rogers, 1988).

Relating New Information to Previous Knowledge

We have come full circle back to one of the basic premises of schema theory. When new information can be related to what readers already know, the likelihood of learning and remembering new information increases. Not surprisingly, the process of looking for relations between what is known and what is to be learned is an integral part of Palincsar et al.'s reciprocal teaching. At the outset of each session in their program, the discussion begins by reviewing things the student already knows related to what is to come. Toward the end of the reciprocal teaching sessions, this responsibility shifts to the student as he or she finds ways to relate the content of reading material to what is already known.

Apparently, good readers almost automatically relate incoming information to their knowledge bases (Garner, 1987). This process can be facilitated among both good and poor readers through teaching students necessary background knowledge coupled with training in schema activation. Beyond general knowledge or domain-specific knowledge (consider how difficult it would be to make sense out of a passage about quarks with no knowledge of quantum mechanics), research has shown that even teaching students about the structure of different kinds of reading materials facilitates comprehension. For example, Fitzgerald and Spiegel (1983) taught average and below-average fourth-grade readers the typical structure of narrative stories and contrasted these children with another group of fourth-graders in a control condition who worked on dictionary skills. After the training, the children who learned about narrative structure outperformed the control children on measures of comprehension. Similarly, Barnett (1984) taught college students about the structure of reading materials. When contrasted to students in a control condition on later memory tests, the experimental-condition students recognized and recalled significantly more content.

Summary and Applications of Schema Theory

Schema theory holds that the meaning of reading materials is constructed by readers on the basis of the information they encounter, the information they already have in memory, and the way in which readers interact with new information. Both advance organizers and schema activation are approaches designed to facilitate the construction of meanings by bringing about a more-complete interaction of readers' general knowledge with the information in a reading passage. Readers' metacognitive skills also influence the construction of meanings, especially those skills central to reading comprehension.

To date, the results of research are clear. Techniques designed to relate new information to what readers already know help students learn and retain new information. Teachers should employ advance organizers and schema activation regularly. They should highlight the value of already acquired task-relevant knowledge for learning new information. Further, instructional programs should emphasize metacognitive reading skills including finding the main ideas in passages, summarizing what has been read, self-questioning, drawing inferences, finding errors and inconsistencies, checking on one's own learning from text, and relating new information to what is already known. Reciprocal teaching (e.g., Palincsar et al., 1987) is one highly effective approach for teaching a constellation of metacognitive reading skills. Research indicates, however, that each of the metacognitive skills described in this section may be taught alone or in combination with other skills. In general, as students master metacognitive reading skills, their reading comprehension improves. It seems that instructional strategies focusing on these skills are simple and direct and can be implemented in most classrooms.

When children make the transition from learning to read to reading to learn, teachers can facilitate the acquisition and use of metacognitive skills by providing practice with feedback on each of them. Further, teachers should borrow from the Palincsar et al. approach and directly model the skills for children with clear explanations of how and why each skill was implemented. During the course of instruction, the responsibility for initiating the skills should shift more and more to the students so that the teacher is in the position of helping them clarify their reading and providing feedback on the quality of their metacognition. There is no question but that teaching students how to learn from text is time-consuming (see Palincsar et al., 1987), but it it time well spent.

Memory for Prose

Even though schema theory is an extremely important perspective, a large amount of research on reading comprehension has been conducted from other theoretical positions. In this section of the chapter, we examine aspects of a body of research that has come to be known as "memory for prose" research. Because of the theoretical diversity of the area, we limit our theoretical discussions primarily to schema theory and elaboration of processing (see Chapter 5).

Text Signals

Text signals are devices designed to improve the cohesion of reading materials or to indicate that certain elements of the text are particularly important (Britton, 1986). There are several kinds of text signals used by writers, including number signals (e.g.,*The three most important points are (1) . . . , (2) . . . , and (3) . . .*), headings (see the heading at the top of this section), underlined, *italic*, or **boldfaced** text, preview sentences (e.g., *As we will see in Chapter 15, . . .*), and recall sentences (e.g., *Recall from Chapter 4, where we . . .*). The literature on text signals has some important implications for the construction of handouts, worksheets, and reading assignments.

One of the most-common forms of text signals is the **number signal** (Lorch & Chen, 1986). Number signals are exactly what they sound like. They amount to the use of numbers to enumerate a set of points, a set of steps in a process, a list of names, or other reading content. Number signals are especially effective for identifying important elements of a text students are to remember (e.g., four causes of the War of the Roses, five steps in readying a lathe for operation). When students read a brief passage such as a handout sheet, they tend to give more of their attention to the signaled content than to the unsignaled content and better remember the signaled material (Lorch & Chen, 1986).

Similar to number signals is the use of *italic* or **boldface print.** When either of these procedures is used sparingly, students pay more attention to the highlighted material than to the unhighlighted material and remember it better (Crouse & Idstein, 1972; Fowler & Barker, 1974; Glynn & DiVesta, 1979). **Headings** have a somewhat different effect in that they serve to improve the cohesion and readability of text (Wilhite, 1986).

Number signals, underlining, boldface print, and headings all are useful devices in constructing study materials for students. When specific elements of reading materials are critical, they should be underlined or boldfaced. Students pay more attention to such signaled content and are more likely to remember it. When a set or series of ideas, names, or steps is to be remembered, number signals should be used. Headings break up longer text into segments of thematically related content and reduce the amount of cognitive effort required to comprehend the material (Glynn & DiVesta, 1979; Lorch & Chen, 1986; Wilhite, 1986).

Two other types of text signals are preview sentences and recall sentences. **Preview sentences** signal upcoming contents, whereas **recall sen-**

tences signal back to previously learned material. Preview and recall sentences often are seen in textbooks but seldom show up in brief passages. However, they can have an important use in shorter reading assignments (Lorch, 1985; Glover et al., 1988a).

Preview sentences placed early in a reading passage tend to focus readers' attention on the upcoming material they signal and help students better remember it (Lorch, 1985). Preview sentences also have interesting effects when they signal contents in an upcoming assignment. Glover et al. (1988a), for example, had students read a brief assignment in which some preview sentences were embedded. These preview sentences signaled material the students would encounter in a later assignment. Then, when students read the second assignment, Glover et al. kept track of how readers allocated their attention to various parts of the material. Finally, when students were tested on the material, Glover et al. looked at how much students remembered and how they organized their recalls. The results indicated that students focused more of their attention on signaled text, confirming the findings of Lorch and Chen (1986). In addition, more of the signaled content in the second assignment was recalled than was the unsignaled material. Further, students tended to organize their recalls such that the material in which the signals had been embedded and the information the preview sentences signaled were recalled together.

These results are important to teachers for three reasons: (1) preview sentences help focus students' attention on important content, (2) information signaled by preview sentences is better recalled than unsignaled information, and (3) students tend to pull together the signaled content and the information in which the signal was embedded. For example, let us suppose we have two brief reading assignments for students we wish to assign on different days as classroom activities. Let us further suppose we want students to link together important information in the second day's assignment with some of the information given in the first day's assignment. One effective way of doing this is through the use of preview sentences. For instance, suppose at the end of a paragraph on, say, China's economy, we insert a preview sentence (*We will examine the reasons for China's reliance on imported technology in tomorrow's assignment.*). Then, during the next day we give the students a brief reading in which the signaled material appears. Not only are the students more likely to attend to the signaled information as a result of the preview sentences we placed in the first assignment, they are more likely to remember the signaled information *and* remember it in the context of the previous day's reading.

Preview sentences have not yet been examined in contexts other than reading materials. However, logic suggests to us that preview sentences should be effective in lectures and demonstrations as well. Even though simple in concept, preview sentences seem to be an effective means of influencing students' learning.

Recall sentences similarly have an interesting effect on students' processing of information. Unlike preview sentences, recall sentences signal back to previously learned material. Recall sentences are a commonly used device by textbook writers (Have you noticed a few in this chapter?), but they also have uses in shorter assignments. Across brief assignments, recall sentences have the effect of helping students remember information relevant to the content in which the signal is embedded. Further, recall sentences help students cluster in memory information that recall sentences refer back to and the information in which recall sentences are embedded. That is, it seems that students assimilate the information in which the signals are embedded to relevant knowledge they already possess (Glover et al., 1988a). As with preview sentences, recall sentences have been studied only in the context of reading. However, it seems reasonable that recall sentences in lectures, discussions, or demonstrations should have positive effects on students' memory for signaled information.

Adjunct Questions

In 1966, E. Z. Rothkopf published a paper that set the stage for research on the effects of adjunct questions on readers' memory for prose. In Rothkopf's study, participants read material taken from a textbook and were tested on their ability to remember the content. Some of the participants answered questions while reading (adjunct questions); others did not. The positioning of the questions was varied across the conditions in which participants answered questions. In addition, the adjunct questions were relevant to only some parts of the reading material. Much of the content was not surveyed via the adjunct questions.

When the participants in Rothkopf's study finished reading, they took a test on the material. Some of the test items were repeated versions of the adjunct questions; others covered content not related to the adjunct questions. We may refer to the repeated questions as tapping **intentional** learning, learning required by the adjunct questions. We may refer to the posttest questions not assessing content relevant to the adjunct questions as tapping **incidental** learning, learning not required by the adjunct questions.

There were four major findings in Rothkopf's (1966) study. First, adjunct questions had a powerful effect on intentional learning. That is, students' performances on the posttest questions that assessed their knowledge of content required for the adjunct questions was far superior to students' performance on questions assessing incidental learning. Second, when adjunct questions were placed *after* reading materials, they facilitated both intentional and incidental learning, although the impact on incidental learning was not large. Third, when adjunct questions prefaced reading materials, they enhanced intentional learning but did not facilitiate incidental learning. Indeed, on measures of incidental learning, a control group that received no adjunct questions but that was asked to study hard and remember the details of the passage outperformed the participants who received prefatory adjunct questions. Fourth, reading times (including the answering of adjunct questions during reading) seemed to vary directly with participants' performance on the posttest.

Rothkopf's study, both methodologically and conceptually, has had a powerful influence on subsequent research on the effects of adjunct questions on readers' memory for text. Since his seminal paper, there has been an explosion of research on adjunct questions (see Andre, 1987b; R. C. Anderson & Biddle, 1975; Faw & Waller, 1976; Hamaker, 1986; Hamilton, 1985; Rickards, 1979, for reviews). The results of these studies generally have painted a consistent picture. Following, we review the findings and highlight the practical applications of adjunct question research. Before proceeding, however, it is important to note that for all practical purposes, the findings on adjunct questions are identical to those on the use of instructional objectives given to students. That is, studies that have contrasted how instructional objectives (or learning objectives) and adjunct questions influence readers have indicated there is no difference between them (Peterson, Glover, & Ronning, 1980; Zimmer, Petersen, Ronning, & Glover, 1978).

Level of Questions Although many different hierarchies of questions have been proposed over the years, one widely used with a long history of research is that developed by Bloom et al. (1956). The Bloom et al. taxonomy posits levels of learning based on the sophistication and complexity of learning required by tasks. There are six major levels of learning described in the taxonomy that, from simple to complex, are as follows: knowledge, comprehension, application, analysis, synthesis, and evaluation. We will briefly describe the kind of learning required by questions at each of the levels of the Bloom et al. taxonomy.

Knowledge-level learning merely requires the retention of facts such as names or dates. It is akin to rote learning and is the level of question employed by Rothkopf in his 1966 study. Comprehension-level questions are more sophisticated, as they require students put the to-be-learned material into their own words. Application-level learning requires the use of information in some concrete form. It differs from comprehension-level learning in requiring the implementation of knowledge such as the distinction between when a student is able to **explain** alliteration (comprehension) and actually **use** alliteration in writing (application). Analysis-level learning is more complex yet, in that learners must be able to break information down into its component parts so the relationship among all the components is clear. For example, the request, "Compare and contrast levels of processing with schema theory," requires that students break down both schema theory and levels of processing into their component parts (encoding, storage, etc.) and relate them one to another. Synthesis-level learning demands that students put together old knowledge in new ways. For example, the request, "Using your knowledge of encoding specificity, construct a test over content you are teaching that will enhance students' test performance," requires the use of knowledge you already have (both how to construct tests and encoding specificity) in a new way. Evaluation-level learning involves students' making judgments about the value of methods or materials based on their knowledge. For example, if you were shown three videotapes of teachers giving a lesson and asked to determine how well each teacher employed the principles of cognitive psychology, you would be engaging in evaluation-level learning.

When we review the results of research on adjunct questions in terms of the level of learning required by the questions, some interesting findings emerge. Knowledge-level questions tend to facilitate only knowledge-level learning. Further, their effects are focused primarily on intentional learning (Andre, 1987b). Comprehension-level questions also have a strong effect on intentional learning and a limited but consistent effect on incidental learning (Hamaker, 1986; Muth, Glynn, Britton, & Graves, 1988).

Higher-order questions (at the application level or above) tend to enhance both intentional and incidental learning. Further, higher-order questions have their facilitative effect regardless of whether they preface or follow reading materials, although their greatest effect occurs when they preface text (Halpain et al., 1985). Higher-order questions also seem to enhance both lower-order (knowledge and comprehension) and higher-order learning (Halpain et al., 1985; Hamaker, 1986; Andre, 1987b).

In terms of applications, two lines of reasoning emerge. If teachers want students to learn very specific concepts in a reading passage, they should employ lower-order questions prefacing text. The problem with such an approach, however, is that it tends to result in a "post hole" effect. That is, students tend to learn in depth only those segments of test specifically indicated by the questions. The remainder of the text receives very little elaboration and, consequently, is poorly remembered.

The second line of reasoning emerges if teachers do not have specific elements of knowledge they want students to master but instead want students to learn a passage in depth. In this case, teachers should use higher-order questions. Higher-order questions cannot be answered by locating a specific term or phrase in a passage. Instead, they require that large segments of a passage be processed very elaborately. Consequently, students remember the entirety of passages better after answering higher-order questions than after answering lower-order questions (Benton, Glover, & Bruning, 1983a; Halpin et al., 1985).

Questions Requiring Decisions

There is no doubt that adjunct questions can have very facilitative effects on students' memory for prose. It turns out, however, that questions requiring students to make a decision are more effective than questions at the same level of the Bloom et al. taxonomy that do not require decisions. Apparently, the act of making a decision (yes/no) about some content in addition to answering the question results in considerably more elaborate processing (see Chapter 5), leading to better memory for the content (Benton et al., 1983a, 1983b). If student decision making is a reasonable part of a teacher's instructional goals, adjunct questions should be written so that students go beyond simply writing an answer to record a decision.

Location of Questions

In general, the results of research suggest that students' overall recall of content will be best if higher-order questions precede text and lower-order questions follow text (Hamaker, 1986; Hamilton, 1985). Since higher-order questions require such extensive and elaborate processing, they result in better learning when they preface materials. In this arrangement, students must carefully search and evaluate large segments of prose in order to determine their relevance to the questions. When higher-order questions follow reading, however, students must rely on their memories to answer the questions. Consequently, although the effect of higher-order questions following text is still greater than that of lower-order questions in any configuration, their impact is considerably less than that of higher-order questions prefacing text.

The issue of where to place lower-order questions is considerably different. As we've noted, prefacing text material with lower-order questions results in students' careful scrutiny of question-relevant material. This careful attention to answers, however, does not extend to other aspects of the passage (Reynolds & Anderson, 1982). Indeed, prefacing a passage with lower-order questions is almost a guarantee that material not relevant to the questions will be poorly learned. When lower-order questions *follow* text, however, the situation changes. Since students do not know which parts of a passage are relevant to questions, they must read all of it carefully. Then, when confronted with the questions after reading, they must recall the answers from memory. Lower-order questions following text have a less-beneficial effect on students' memory for specific answers, but they do not have a deleterious and may have a positive effect on students' memory for overall passage content.

Number of
Questions

Only a handful of studies have examined how different numbers of questions influence readers' memory for content (see Andre, 1987b). In general, it seems that only a few higher-order questions need to be employed to optimally enhance students' memory for text. Perhaps one higher-order question for every 1,000 words of text is sufficient to ensure elaborate processing of the text material. When lower-order questions are considered, the number of questions is less critical and should be determined on the basis of the teacher's specific instructional goals.

For Which
Students Are
Higher-Order
Questions
Appropriate?

One recurrent comment we have received from some teachers over the years is that their students "can't deal with higher-order questions." Although the research in this area is far afield from our current concerns (see Case, 1984a, 1984b, for cogent views of this and related issues), it is important for us to point out that the kinds of thinking required by higher-order questions are *not* restricted to high school or even junior high school students. Application, analysis, synthesis, and evaluation learning activities are well within the abilities of elementary school children, *if* the activities are structured in terms meaningful to them. Glover and Zimmer (1982), for example, gave fourth- and fifth-grade students practice in devising their own analysis-level questions about current affairs readings in the newspaper. With two weeks of daily practice in their 30-minute current affairs classes, the children all were able to formulate several analysis-level questions for each of their readings and were able to answer analysis-level questions without difficulty.

Elementary school children, by and large, do require practice in developing and answering higher-order questions. However, it seems to us that many elementary school teachers do not take the time to systematically model higher-order thinking or give children practice with feedback for application, analysis, synthesis, and evaluation. For that matter, our experience with many undergraduates (and some graduate students) suggests that our educational system often neglects higher-order thinking altogether in the rush to have students know and comprehend content. Currently, the literature suggests that higher-order questions are appropriate for the vast majority of students as long as the information is meaningful. However, it must be kept in mind that students, especially younger ones, will need to be taught *how* to respond to higher-order questions.

A General Approach to Improve Reading Comprehension: SQ3R

Over the years, a multitude of popular books and articles have been written on the general topic of how to improve one's reading comprehension. Many of these works contain a great deal of valuable information and can be very helpful to readers wishing to improve their performance. Because of our limited space, however, we have decided to highlight only one general approach to enhancing reading comprehension. The approach we emphasize was described several years ago by the late Frank Robinson in his book *Effective Study* (1972). Although there are critics of this approach (see Andre, 1987a, for a critique), we believe Robinson's general approach fits well within what we know about memory and reading processes. Indeed, studies have shown that Robinson's method helps students (above the elementary level) improve their reading comprehension (e.g., Carlisle, 1985; Graham, 1984). Further, Robinson's ideas have been the basis for several recent programs designed to improve reading and study skills. Personally, we have found Robinson's method to be particularly helpful for students engaged in independent study activities (such as learning the material in this text).

The procedures involved in Robinson's method can be taught to students as activities designed to help them improve their memory of what they study. Our experience (including teaching the method to our own children) suggests that students readily take to the approach, although younger students require reminders to continue to use the method and praise for following through with the steps on their own. As you examine the steps in Robinson's method, you'll see they are designed to relate upcoming information to what students already know, to keep students actively involved in comprehending material, and to provide occasions when students can get feedback on their learning.

Step 1: Survey. In Robinson's method, the first step is for students to look over—survey—the material. The purpose of an initial survey of the material is to familiarize the reader with the content and to help the reader gain a sense of what his or her reading task requires. From our perspective, the initial survey helps the reader establish the meaningfulness of the content by relating the material to what the reader already knows. Robinson suggested that a good strategy to follow during the survey step was to read chapter summaries as a means of gaining a general overview of the content.

Step 2: Question. Robinson's second step involves having the reader pose a series of questions about the reading material. Headings and subheadings can be converted into open questions. Later, during reading, the answers to the open questions formed from the headings help the reader determine how well the material has been comprehended. In addition, the reader should ask himself or herself questions about the content including the writer's goals, how the material in the chapter is related to knowledge the reader already possesses, and what relevant experiences the reader has had that relate to the material. These kinds of questions serve to increase the meaningfulness of the content and provide further checks on comprehension.

Step 3: Read. After surveying and questioning, it is time to read the material. The content should be read slowly and carefully, with attention given to answering the questions generated during step 2. Care also should be taken to link the contents of the reading material to what is already known.

Step 4: Recite. Once a section of reading material has been completed, the reader should stop and attempt to answer the questions raised during step 2. This recitation does two things: It helps the reader check comprehension, and if good questions were asked, it aids in making the material more meaningful. It also can be argued that reciting allows for a reprocessing of content in a way that strengthens memory for the content.

Step 5: Review. Robinson suggested that readers should focus their reviews primarily on material related to difficult-to-answer questions. This material should be reread until the questions can be answered. The review step is the last check on comprehension and provides for a final processing of the content.

A mnemonic, **SQ3R** (Survey, Question, Read, Recite, Review), can be used to help remember Robinson's approach. SQ3R and related techniques (which add steps, rename then, and so forth) are useful strategies for improving reading comprehension and should be a part of any program designed to help students improve their reading-comprehension skills.

Becoming a Flexible Reader

As adults, we understand there are different reasons for reading and adjust our processing activities accordingly. For example, the probability is high that you read this textbook and the evening paper in different ways. The reason is simple: You want to comprehend and remember the content of this text (and other similar materials) to the best of your ability, whereas remembering newspaper content is not critical. Further, you probably read the editorials and the advertisements in the newspaper differently. As a successful adult reader, the comprehension of different kinds of materials you read in a day is appropriate to what you want from them. This flexibility in reading can and should be taught to students (e.g., Harris & Sipay, 1983).

One approach to helping students develop flexible reading rates begins by locating different kinds of materials for which a word count has been made. (If such materials are not available, the words in various articles always can be counted the hard way.) Then, the teacher determines students' normal reading rates in words per minute (most people with a twelfth-grade education have a silent reading rate of about 200 words per minute) for different kinds of materials such as textbooks, short stories, and magazine articles. If the students' reading rates differ for the various kinds of reading, fine. If not, it is necessary for the teacher to consider whether students should speed up or slow down for different kinds of reading.

If a student is reading at about the same rate for various materials, it will be beneficial for him or her to become more flexible. A student's rates for careful reading (e.g., textbook materials) and normal reading (e.g., a short story) should be the starting point. Are the student's normal rates comfortable? Could the student easily remember the material he or she read? Was the student's normal reading rate faster than his or her careful reading rate? Did the student learn more by reading carefully than by reading normally? If the careful rate is not slower than the normal rate but if more was learned reading carefully than normally, the normal rate should be speeded up. On the other hand, if more was *not* learned during careful reading than normal reading, the careful rate should be slowed down. In general, normal reading should be about 25 to 50 percent faster than careful reading. Rapid reading (e.g., a newspaper article, reviewing previously read material) should be 25 to 50 percent faster than normal reading, and skimming (looking for key words in an advertisement, etc.) should be 50 to 100 percent faster than normal reading. If the student doesn't show differences roughly similar to those outlined above for different reading purposes, he or she should practice reading materials of a standard length with a timer set to go off that indicates a certain reading rate. The student's goal, of course, is to read as much of the passage as possible before the timer goes off while retaining as much comprehension as possible.

The program we've described above, simple as it sounds, must be individualized for each student. Comfortable normal reading rates may vary drastically in the same classroom, as may students' flexibility in reading for different purposes. Despite the fact that individualized programs are logistically difficult to implement, the benefits of flexible reading are great. Students can allocate their cognitive resources more wisely if they have different reading rates and they are better able to monitor their comprehension and mentally "shift" gears as needed. It seems to us that instruction in flexible reading should be included in any reading program.

Summary

At the outset of the chapter we reviewed three types of models of reading comprehension: data-driven, conceptually driven, and interactive. Data-driven models emphasize serial, word-by-word processing in which the meaning of a text is deciphered by readers. Conceptually driven models emphasize the construction of meaning based on readers' background knowledge. Interactive models envision both data-driven and conceptually driven processes interacting in the construction of meaning.

Schema theory provides a more general backdrop for thinking about reading comprehension. In a schema theory view, meaning is constructed as the reader's knowledge, the text material, and the context of reading interact to produce meaning. Closely tied to a schema theory perspective are research on advance organizers, schema activation, and metacognitive reading skills.

Advance organizers preface to-be-learned reading materials and are designed to help students tie the new material to what they already know. Schema activation is a process whereby students activate relevant knowledge prior to reading. Both advance organizers and schema activation have been shown to facilitate readers' comprehension of text. Several metacognitive reading skills also facilitate comprehension. These skills can be taught individually or presented in a comprehension training program such as the reciprocal teaching approach used by Palincsar et al. (1987).

A large body of research on memory for prose has proceeded from several different theoretical perspectives. Two aspects of this literature have focused on the influence of signals in text and adjunct questions on readers' memory for the content. In general, text signals serve to focus readers' attention on specific segments of text and help make reading materials more coherent. The effect of adjunct questions depends on the level of the questions and where they are placed with regard to the reading materials. The literature indicated that comprehension is best aided by a few higher-order questions prefacing text.

Readers can improve their comprehension by adopting techniques such as Frank Robinson's SQ3R (Survey, Question, Read, Recite, Review). The technique is readily taught to students and can have a very positive influence on reading comprehension. Of course, there are different purposes for reading and, consequently, different levels of comprehension are required. Students should be helped in the development of flexible reading strategies such that they match their reading speeds to the purpose of reading.

CHAPTER 11

Writing

In the past few years, there has been great concern over American students' writing abilities (Applebee, 1988; Applebee, Langer, & Mullis, 1986a; Cooper, 1988; DeConcini, 1988; Walberg & Fowler, 1987). Sparked by statements such as that of the National Commission on Excellence in Education (1983), careful analyses reveal that fewer than half of America's high school students are able to write proficiently (Applebee et al., 1986b). According to Applebee (1988), the quality of writing observed in our students has declined year by year since the mid 1960s. Consider the following excerpt from an undergraduate student's response to an essay question:

> *No. because I bilive that's not the way. The techer shuld condiser other. Ways don't have to de disipline. I think the techer is not known how to make class behavor. This is a important part of teching for me. All shuld know better ways. Espesly techers.*

Beyond the spelling and grammatical errors, this "paragraph" simply is incoherent. Whatever ideas the writer was trying to communicate cannot be determined from the words strung together into the "paragraph." Such a paragraph should be unacceptable among fifth-graders. To find college undergraduates (who presumably are surviving the college experience without being able to write) writing this way is intolerable.

Writing is a critical academic skill. Indeed, after reading, one is hard pressed to name a more-important skill. Writing is more than a school-oriented skill, however. The ability to communicate in writing is an important part of day-to-day life and is absolutely critical for many professions (e.g., law, teaching, business, architecture). Further, much of the intellectual and political life of Western civilization has been strongly influenced by writers who were able to clearly and forcefully express their ideas. Although we rarely consider the inability to write a disability in the same sense as the inability to read, poor writing skills are a distinct disadvantage. In contrast, people who write well find it an advantage in almost all areas of life—school (e.g., essays, exams), vocational (e.g., reports, memos, essays, position papers), and personal (e.g., love letters, diaries).

What can we do to improve the quality of student writing? Applebee (1988) argues that much of the reason for the observed decline in students' writing abilities is due to the poor quality and extremely small quantity of writing instruction students receive. If this reasoning is correct, then one simple and direct way to improve students' writing is to have teachers in all subject areas and at all grade levels require that their students write frequently and give feedback on their efforts.

Later in the chapter we go beyond the simple prescription just noted and describe a series of teaching strategies for improving the quality of students' writing. Before describing these strategies, though, it is important to examine the cognitive operations involved in writing.

A Cognitive Model of Writing

There are many forms of writing—fiction, biography, persuasive essays, poetry, business letters, and so on. Even in school, writing assignments vary in intent, length, topic, and amount of creativity expected of the writing. Writing also varies on the basis of students' ages (compare a third-grader's narrative about Christmas vacation with an eleventh-grader's essay on a Middle-Eastern peace plan), the subject matter under consideration, and the specific objectives of instruction. A good model of the writing process will take these variations into account and focus on components and processes that remain stable regardless of the type of writing under consideration. The best such model currently available is that proposed by Linda Flower and John Hayes (e.g., Carey & Flower, in press; Flower, Schriver, Carey, Haas, & Hayes, 1987; Hayes & Flower, 1986.) The Flower and Hayes model (see Figure 11-1) is in many ways a problem-solving model that helps us develop representation of the writing task. The representation includes determining the audience for the written product, the kinds of strategies the writer will use, and the ways in which the writer will evaluate the product. As you can see, three major components (task environment, long-term memory, and working memory) are envisioned. Each of these components further contains subcomponents characterized by specific processes. On the pages that follow we examine the various components of the model in detail.

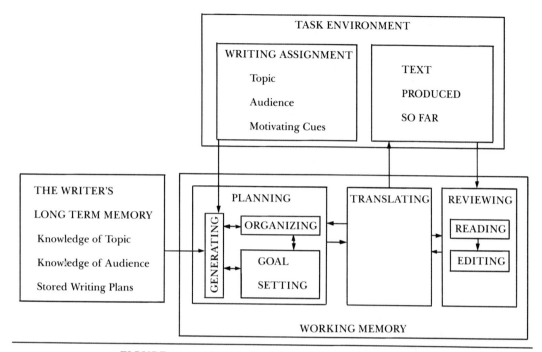

FIGURE 11-1. Structure of the writing model.

The Task Environment

A school writing task typically begins with the writing assignment—the rhetorical problem. The assignment permits the formation of a preliminary task representation since it usually describes the topic, its scope, the audience for whom the writing is intended, and some set of motivating cues. For example, a student may be asked to "write a two-page essay on the political problems involved in stopping acid rain." Such as assignment clearly specifies the topic and circumscribes the scope of the essay. Although audience is not mentioned, students presumably have some information about this (i.e., whether it is for the teacher's consumption, a judge in an essay contest, etc.). Motivating cues such as grades ("This essay will count for one-fourth of your term's grade.") or other outcomes ("Winners will receive a scholarship to a summer session at the Meatloaf School of Environmental Sciences.") also are significant aspects of the task environment.

Immediately obvious is the importance of knowledge in students' understanding of the writing task's demands. A student who possesses a great amount of knowledge about the topic is more likely to produce a good sample of writing than a student who has little knowledge (Durst, 1987). Beyond sheer knowledge of content, however, is knowledge of the audience. Although it may be argued that there is such a thing as "pure" writing done in and for itself, most writing is done for an audience (Lutz, 1987). Not surprisingly, the more writers know about the audience they are writing for, the better those audiences perceive the writing to be (Bertkotter, 1981; Lutz, 1987). For example, if a student knows that her instructor believes that local political issues are more important than national questions, likes the use of statistics to illustrate points, and dislikes anecdotal accounts, the student is likely to shape her essay to fit the teacher's tastes. Consequently, the essay is more likely to be judged by that teacher as a good essay than is one written by a student who has limited knowledge of the teacher's preferences.

Knowledge of the audience, of course, goes beyond learning about a specific teacher or editor. Professional writers spend substantial amounts of time learning who their audience will be prior to beginning writing (Bertkotter, 1981; Piazza, 1987). For example, if you intended to sell a story to a particular sports magazine, an important first step would be learning who reads the magazine. The best way to do this is by reading and studying the magazine, analyzing its editorial policy, and putting together a hypothetical "audience" based on the magazine's contents. One does not have to be a member of the literati to realize that the *Sporting News* and, say, *Atlantic Monthly* aim for vastly different audiences.

Before we can consider ways of providing writing assignments to help students improve their writing, one additional type of knowledge must be considered—knowledge of specific types of writing. Effective writers understand that journal articles, textbooks, short stories, plays, and letters each have different structures and components (Piazza, 1987). A good short story writer, for example, likely has read a multitude of short stories and understands the components of a short story and the devices short story writers use. This knowledge, of course, is vital when the writer is planning, writing, and revising the story.

Improving
Writing
Assignments

The task environment is critical to the quality of writing. An important part of providing students with a helpful task environment is making good writing assignments. What kinds of things can be done to improve writing assignments? A review of recent research findings (see, for example, Durst & Marshall, 1987; Marshall & Durst, 1987) suggests many strategies.

1. Make assignments for writing clear and concise. Students are most likely to benefit from writing activity if they know exactly what is expected of them.

2. Offer models of the type of writing expected. A good way to learn about writing short stories, for example, includes reading and studying short stories. Similarly, a good way to learn to write essays involves asking students to read essays and use good ones as models for their own. Generally, the so-called literature method (providing students with excellent models of specific kinds of writing) has had beneficial effects on students' writing abilities (Phillips, 1986).

3. Teach students to envision the audience for their writing. Although not strictly within the province of making assignments, learning to write for a specific audience is an important step in the development of writing skills. Beginning writers may have great difficulty with this task. However, activities such as asking children to work in pairs so that they write for each other's consumption may be helpful (Harris, 1986). With older students, emphasis may be placed on imagining who will read the material.

4. Have students write on topics about which they are knowledgeable. Even though there may be times when students write on topics about which they know little (e.g., to emphasize the use of imagination), the ability of students to express themselves and the quality of their writing almost inevitably will be better when they write about things they know. This is not to argue, in any sense at all, that students should not be pushed to expand their horizons or to gain new knowledge. Rather, this point relates to the simple dictum that one can write well only about those things one knows. Further, students can best concentrate on mastering new writing skills when they don't have to struggle with gaps in knowledge. Consider how difficult it is to give practice in, say, the use of analogies and similes in essay writing when students have no idea what acid rain is or what it has to do with political decisions.

External Storage   The task-environment component of Flower and Hayes' model includes an external storage—the written record writers put together as they work on a project. For example, a student working on an essay has the partially completed essay itself to look back on and perhaps notes she's written to herself about the assignment (e.g., "Be sure to mention Oliver Cromwell"). For longer assignments such as term papers, students may have several drafts of the paper, note cards, summaries of sources they've read, and their own evaluations of different parts of the paper.

External storage drastically reduces memory load. Simply, when students lose track of what they have written, they can reread their work and begin again. In addition, later parts of the writing model depend on external storage when the writing is reread, evaluated, and revised.

Long-Term Memory

A *good* writing assignment accesses knowledge in writers' long-term memories (G. E. Newell & MacAdam, 1987). This component of the model is seen as the source of knowledge about topics, audiences, and different kinds of writing. Long-term memory is not static—it continually changes as the writer reads and receives instruction (Bean, Singer, Sorter, & Frazee, 1987). In fact, it is important to conceive of an ongoing interaction between the external task environment (where reading materials, lectures, and so forth are available) and long-term memory.

Writing processes interact continually in working memory and long-term memory as writers search for ideas, vocabulary, and goals, and as they evaluate and review text. Writers do not simply check with long-term memory at the outset of their writing; long-term memory is an integral component of writing throughout the process.

The long-term memory component of the model also highlights the importance of knowledge once more. No matter how well developed a writer's composing abilities are, the ultimate quality of writing produced depends on the writer's knowledge germane to a particular writing assignment (Hayes & Flower, 1986). Even Shakespeare might have written poorly had he been assigned an essay on, say, nuclear physics.

Working Memory

Three major processes are envisioned by Flower and Hayes as occurring in working memory: planning, translating, and reviewing. Writers do not necessarily move from planning to translating to reviewing, however. Instead, most writers move back and forth interactively from process to process as the need arises. For instance, a writer may shift from reviewing back to planning and then to translating. More-complex arrangements in which a writer returns to the external task environment and long-term memory also seem likely. We begin our discussion of the processes in working memory with a closer examination of planning.

Planning   The planning process includes three subprocesses: goal setting, generating, and organizing. These subprocesses (see Hayes & Flower, 1986) interact vigorously and may be initiated at any time during writing. **Goal setting,** as the term implies, refers to establishing writing objectives. Goals may be long-term (e.g., "I'll write an A+ paper." or "This chapter has to fit into the rest of the book.") or short-term ("Here I want to give two examples." or "I need to do a summary that sets up the next section"). Goals also may be a part of preliminary planning prior to any writing (e.g., "I'll use lots of metaphors. Mr. Smudge likes 'em.") or they may be set after an initial writing session has been completed (e.g., "I think I'd better add something about Oliver North."). As can be envisioned, goal setting is not a one-time activity, but occurs many times during the course of writing.

The **generating** subprocess refers to the development of the ideas and content used in writing. Ideas may be generated from long-term memory (e.g., "Let's see, didn't we talk about that in class?") or from the external environment ("I know it's in my notes here somewhere."). Generation, as can be imagined, is an ongoing process that influences all other parts of the writing process. For example, let us suppose you are responding to an essay question about, say, presidential elections. At first you may plan to analyze the choice of the last three vice-presidents. As you write, however, you find that you can't remember their names. To continue, you will need to consult some source for this information, or some of your goals will have to change. Goals also may change, of course, as a result of generating unanticipated ideas, as when you hit on a good example or when exact statistics about some event are recalled.

The **organizing** subprocess is closely related to both generating and goal setting. In organizing, writers take their goals and ideas and integrate them into some sensible, coherent structure. Although organizing typically is seen as an early element of writing, writers return to it again and again as writing proceeds. Each new paragraph and new sentence requires organization. Also, any changes in goals or the ideas available for the text require a return to organizing.

Translating   In Flower and Hayes' model, translating refers to the process of transforming one's ideas into written text. Translating includes accessing semantic memory (including the lexicon), calling up vocabulary items, finding words for ideas, ordering the word string, and reading off the words as they are written. Translating typically puts an enormous strain on the capacity of writers' working memories. However, as many translating activities become automatic or nearly so among good writers, the load is greatly reduced (Hayes & Flower, 1986).

Reviewing   The reviewing subprocess involves a reexamination of what has been written and a comparison of this product to the writer's internal standards for acceptable writing. Although we often may think of reviewing occurring at the completion of a writing task, it may, in fact, happen at any time during writing, even when the initial plans for a passage are being stated (Hull, 1987).

Reviewing consists of two subprocesses: evaluating and revising. **Evaluating** amounts to rereading the text and comparing it to one or more criteria. Obviously, evaluating what has been written depends on the writer's knowledge about writing in general, but it also depends on knowledge of the particular form of writing the writer is attempting to produce (Hull, 1987).

Good and poor writers differ dramatically in their evaluation of text. For example, when confronted with samples of poor writing, good writers are apt to point to flaws in the writer's construction, coherence, and choice of words. Poor writers, in contrast, are likely to blame their own inability to decode the text as the source of the problem. In other words, good writers understand what good and poor samples of text are like and further understand causes for poor writing. Poor writers do not readily identify examples of bad writing. Instead, they tend to believe that their reading is at fault. This general pattern also is seen when writers critique their own products. Good writers often identify problems in their own work. Poor writers do not see shortcomings and seem surprised when others have comprehension problems.

Revising, the second subprocess involved in reviewing, amounts to the rewriting and restructuring of text. Revising may be limited to minor changes in wording, or it can involve the replacement of entire pages (Hull, 1987). Good writers are much more likely to revise materials they've written, viewing almost any sample of their work as preliminary and subject to editing. Poor writers, in contrast, often have great difficulty seeing that initial writing episodes are not carved in stone.

An Example of the Writing Model

The best way to capture the full flavor of the Flower and Hayes model is to follow a hypothetical individual through the task of completing a writing assignment. Let's try to keep up with Evelyn. She is enrolled in a high school journalism class and has been assigned the task of writing an article.

"Hmmm," reflects Evelyn, "Mr. Schmootz wants me to write a brief article describing the three candidates for senior class president. We had lots of examples of 'candidate descriptions' in class. I think I'll look at them first."

Evelyn pulled out her class folder and began flipping through it until she came to a set of "candidate descriptions." She examined them carefully, tapping her pencil on her desk. "Some of these are pretty fancy and use big words. Everybody in school has to be able to read the article. I won't try to impress anybody with my vocabulary. Also, when Mr. Schmootz says 'keep it brief,' he means 'keep it brief.' "

Evelyn pulled out a writing pad and glanced at a handout Mr. Schmootz had given out that day. She began to scratch together an outline and thought, "I'll begin by giving their names and listing the honors and awards they've won in high school. I can remember all that easily. Next, I'll take the responses to the questionnaire they filled out for Mr. Schmootz and describe how each person feels about the 'issues.' Last, I'll try to find one special thing to say about each person. Mr. Schmootz will like that."

Evelyn's reaction to the assignment is not especially unusual or striking, but it does allow us to see some elements of the model in action. The task environment (the assignment, the questionnaire, and Mr. Schmootz himself) seemed very clear to Evelyn. She immediately began using her long-term memory in planning at least a rough framework for the whole writing task (see Hull, 1987). Note that Evelyn used several sources of information in her planning—her knowledge of the content (i.e., her knowledge of the candidates), her knowledge of the audience (Mr. Schmootz and the students at her school), her knowledge of the kind of article she was to write, and the handout describing the candidates' responses to the "issues." Evelyn's brief thoughts also allow us to see that she was busy organizing the material she was going to write while specifying, at least loosely, her goals.

As we look back in on Evelyn, we see that she has begun writing and is working at a rapid pace, stopping now and again to think about her work. "No, that's not quite right," she thinks to herself. She erases and then starts again. "I don't want to make it sound like Susan doesn't like sports at all," she muses, "although it's pretty clear that she thinks sports shouldn't be so important. Instead, I'll try, 'Susan Smith believes sports are. . . .' "

Evelyn writes several more lines and then stops, putting the eraser of her pencil in her mouth and chewing on it gently: ". . . believe . . . ," she mutters to herself. "No, it's 'The group believes,' because group is one thing—singular. . . ."

This little segment of Evelyn's thinking lets us in on the translating process, in which she transforms her ideas into words. In addition, we can observe that she was reviewing her work as she proceeded with the task. She evaluated a sentence, found that it did not carry the meaning she wanted, erased it, and revised it. She then proceeded to translating again, producing an appropriate sentence.

Looking back at Evelyn one last time, we observe that she finally has completed her article and that she has begun to reread it, making minor changes as she moves along. "OK. That sounds right. Mmm. I think a comma goes there and, well, I'd better cut out that unneeded 'which.' I'd better capitalize 'Kappa.' I think this is a pretty good article, if I do say so myself."

In this final observation of Evelyn, we see that her review of the essay was typical of most good writers' reactions. That is, she carefully evaluated the material and made revisions where needed. Further, she made a last check of the mechanics of writing (punctuation, capitalization) *after* the task was complete.

Even a small sample of a writer's work, such as Evelyn's, tells a good bit about the dynamics of the writing process. Writing is not linear. We do not move from planning to translating to reviewing in a neat, orderly progression. Instead, writers cycle back and forth among all of the subprocesses involved in writing. In fact, some of the most important individual differences among writers seem to be based in their abilities to rapidly shift from operation to operation.

Individual Differences in Writing

Over the past several years, a great deal of research has focused on how good and poor writers differ in ways other than the obvious difference in ability to write (see, for example, Benton, Glover, Kraft, & Plake, 1984; S. Brown, 1986; Dickinson & Snow, 1986). Some surprising and not so surprising differences have been documented. In terms of traditional measures, good and poor writers at the same grade level do not differ widely in measures of intelligence, academic achievement, or motivation (Benton et al., 1984). They do differ, however, in reading ability (Benton et al., 1984; S. Brown, 1986) and, most strikingly, in the amount of writing they have been required to produce in academic settings (Mazzie, 1987).

Generally, good writers are better readers than poor writers. Correlational studies have indicated that measures of reading comprehension are positively related to writing ability (+.50) and to students' beliefs about their ability as writers (Shell, Murphy, & Bruning, 1989). These outcomes are not surprising when we consider that frequent and effective reading exposes students to more and more samples of writing. Such reading, in effect, teaches students a great deal about good writing.

That good writers generally have written far more than poor writers also is not surprising. Writing is a skill and, like any skill, will improve with practice and feedback. In general, we would expect that as students are asked to write more and more, their ability to write will improve. As one editor put it to one of the current authors several years ago: "If you want to write, you must write, write, write. No person ever mastered writing by talking about it."

Beyond reading ability and amount of practice in writing, there are other differences among writers. As one might suspect, these include the ways good and poor writers process information.

Information-Processing Differences

In recent years, several studies have looked for differences in how good and poor writers process information (e.g., Benton et al., 1984; Daiute, 1986; Kellogg, 1984). For example, Benton et al. contrasted good and poor college student writers (defined on the basis of how samples of their writing were scored by a panel of judges) on a series of information-processing tasks. They found no significant differences in the students' grade point averages or achievement test scores, which confirmed earlier work. In addition, they found no differences among the groups in the size of iconic store or the size of short-term memory. They did find differences, however, in how well good and poor writers manipulated information.

In one task, for instance, Benton et al. exposed subjects to a series of letters generated in random order on a computer screen. After the last letter was presented, subjects were instructed to reorder the letters they were holding in working memory into alphabetical order. All subjects completed several trials in order to obtain reliable estimates of their abilities to reorder the letters. The results indicated that good writers were both faster and more accurate than poor writers on this task.

Letter reordering might be seen as a rather trivial task, one not very related to writing skills. Other information-manipulation tasks much closer to actual writing activities, however, yielded highly similar results. On a word reordering task (presumed to be similar to actually forming a sentence from memory), for example, subjects were given sets of words (from 9 to 14 words in each set) in random order. Their task was to reorder the words into the one order that made a sentence for each string of words. Across several trials, good writers again proved to be faster and more accurate than poor writers. They also outperformed poor writers on a task that required them to put sets of randomized sentences into a proper paragraph (presumed to be similar to the activities required in assembling a paragraph during actual writing) and on a task that necessitated the organizing of sets of 12 sentences into three different paragraphs (presumed to be akin to the kinds of activities students engage in when organizing information for writing).

Benton et al.'s (1984) first experiment then was replicated with a sample of high school students. On each of the information-manipulation tasks, good writers again were significantly more rapid and significantly more accurate than poor writers. Similar results (Diamond, 1985; W. M. Reed, Burton, & Kelly, 1985) have since appeared in the literature, all confirming that good writers are better able to manipulate verbal information than poor writers. That is, they can reorder letters, words, sentences, and paragraphs far more efficiently than poor writers. Whether such information-manipulation abilities are innate or learned, however, cannot yet be determined. At least one study (W. M. Reed et al., 1985), though, suggests that the automaticity of some processes (e.g., punctuation, spelling) may be the cause for some of the differences. Such automatic processing, of course, is almost certainly linked to effective practice.

Directly related to the information-processing differences just described is the way in which good and poor writers allocate their attention during writing. Young writers, whether good or poor for their ages, often need to focus on manipulating the pencil and making proper letters. For very young writers, especially, the motor skill demands of writing are so great that children are likely to mouth each letter and each word as they write it. With practice, however, children begin to gain automatic control over the motor aspects of writing and no longer devote much of their attention to making letters (Robbins, 1986).

For older children there also may be a difference in attention while writing. Poor writers tend to focus on grammar, punctuation, capitalization, and spelling (Atwell, 1981; Birnbaum, 1982; Diamond, 1985; Pianko, 1979; Robbins, 1986), whereas good writers focus on the **meaning** they intend to impart (Diamond, 1985). Good writers either perform mechanical functions such as punctuation and spelling automatically or put off worrying about mechanical issues until a first draft of the ideas has been put onto paper.

Planning Differences

Beyond information-processing and attentional differences, there also are important differences in what writers attempt to accomplish with their writing. Gagne (1985) has organized writers' goals into three categories. In our terms, these categories are (1) expressing meaning, (2) avoiding errors, and (3) associative writing. Not all are equally useful. Effective writers focus on the communication of meaning as the primary goal of their writing. All other aspects of their generation of written products are secondary to this goal (Bates, 1984). This is not to say that good writers ignore grammar, spelling, punctuation, and the various parts of speech (among other things). Most demonstrate mastery of the mechanical aspects of writing precisely because some aspects of this knowledge are critical to clearly communicating meaning.

In contrast to good writers' goal of expressing meaning, avoiding errors tends to be the primary goal of poor high school and college writers (Bates, 1984; Birnbaum, 1982). When writers are asked to talk about their writing, good writers' comments overwhelmingly focus on entire blocks of text (e.g., an entire essay), with the emphasis on meaning. Poor writers, in contrast, tend to make comments at the level of individual words and sentences, with their focus on mechanics.

Younger students who write poorly for their ages also tend to write associatively (Bereiter, 1980) or, using the metaphor of the computer, to "core dump." That is, their goal seems to be writing all they know about some topic without any particular concern for mechanics, structure, or coherence. Although associative writing may be inadequate from an adult's perspective, it does have some advantages compared to the kind of writing generated by older students obsessed with mechanics. That is, the focus of associative writing *is* meaning, even though communication does not seem to be an important consideration. Consequently, it seems that associative writers could improve their writing through techniques such as peer editing that give feedback on communication effectiveness. In this technique, pairs of students write for each other's consumption and edit each other's work.

Idea Generation

As one might suspect, there are important differences in the number and quality of ideas for writing that people generate (Robbins, 1986). Generally speaking, older children have more ideas than younger ones, and adults develop more ideas than children. Differences in idea generation, however, are not limited to those associated with age. Among people in any age group, some will generate many ideas and others only a few.

The reasons for differences in idea generation are not completely clear. Knowledge about the topic (Carey & Flower, in press), knowledge about what makes for a good story (Root, 1985), knowledge of audience (Bates, 1984), and self-cuing or metacognitive writing strategies (Raphael, 1986) all may contribute to such differences. One of the most-interesting studies examining the idea-generation phenomenon in writing was conducted by Root (1985), who surveyed the idea-generation techniques of professional expository writers. The writers in this sample were people who wrote magazine and newspaper articles. Most focused their efforts on developing a wide range of marketable stories similar to those seen in general-interest magazines (such as "The Great Northern Line," a story about railroading, or "Three-Mile Island Revisited," a story about the aftermath of a nuclear accident), but a few emphasized book-length projects. Since these people made their living from writing, idea generation was critical. The results of Root's survey were both commonsensical and interesting at the same time. These professional writers spent a great deal of their time reading. Although they read about specific topics primarily while working on particular stories (e.g., reading about nuclear power when preparing a story on the dangers of nuclear reactors), their general tendency was to read widely and to look for ideas in varied places. Further, these professional writers typically kept newspaper and magazine clippings along with their own notes about ideas for later use—even when they had no idea that the notes ever would be helpful.

The results of Root's study parallel one of the major theses of this volume—knowledge plays a key role in effective cognitive functioning. There is no substitute for knowledge if idea generation is the goal. True creativity within any discipline, including writing, requires years of study—simply because so much must be known about a field before a person can generate truly unique and useful ideas.

Our students, of course, are not experts and will not have the broad range of knowledge possessed by professional writers. We can, however, increase their levels of idea generation through some straightforward techniques in which writers receive praise and other positive forms of descriptive feedback for heightened levels of idea generation (Corkill & Glover, in press; Glover, 1982; Goetz, in press).

Such an approach requires very frequent writing and careful attention from the teacher. The teacher must keep track of levels of idea generation from day to day (presuming the assignments are of similar complexity) and focus (in addition to whatever other goals the teacher has) specifically on improvement in idea generation. If the students are informed that idea generation is a critical goal and if the teacher systematically rewards new ideas, their idea generation is highly likely to improve. In short, if we want our students to generate ideas, we must tell them it is important, we must give them practice with feedback, and we should reward them for improvement.

Scardamalia, Bereiter, and Goelman (1982) have reported success in increasing elementary students' idea generation with an even simpler method. In their study, they merely waited until children appeared to be finished with their writing and then prompted them either by saying, "You're doing fine." or "Can you write some more?" Both comments increased children's efforts to write more, although some sixth-graders who experienced these prompts actually wrote less coherently than when no prompts were used. For some children, apparently, the prompts were too general and resulted in mere "word padding."

Differences in Organization

Good writers organize what they write more effectively than poor writers. Even though there are many ways in which we could discuss organization, one very striking organizational difference between good and poor writers is in cohesion.

Using **cohesive ties** refers to the skill of employing linguistic devices to pull together adjoining ideas (Halliday & Hasan, 1974; Mosenthal & Tierney, 1984; Norris & Bruning, 1988). There are many kinds of cohesive ties including, among the simplest, referential, conjunctive, and lexical. (For a more complete discussion, consult Halliday & Hasan, 1974, or Butterfield, 1986.) Referential ties may employ pronouns (e.g., *Roger fell asleep.* **He** *was tired.*) and definite articles (e.g., *There were three writers: the hack, the poet, and the playwright.* **The** *hack made the most money.*). Conjunctive ties, as one might imagine, employ conjunctions to add (*Sarah ate the pizza* **and** *Quinn's french fries.*), show causation (*Sarah tossed and turned all night* **because** *she ate too much pizza.*), and show the obverse of ideas (*Sarah had heard about pineapple pizza* **but** *couldn't believe anyone would actually eat such a concoction.*). Lexical cohesives bind together ideas through word choice. A simple form of lexical cohesion employs the same word or phrase on more than one occasion (e.g., *Royce found himself a* **sunny** *spot in the bleachers. He thought about two hours of* **sun** *would be perfect.*)

Good writers use more and a more-diverse array of cohesive ties than poor writers. Consider the following sample of an essay missing some cohesive ties:

> *Libby and Marissa went to town. She saw a store with pipes, glasses, and marbles in the window. She bought some from the woman at the counter. She was happy.*

Argh! The poor reader of such an essay has no idea whether it was Libby or Marissa who saw the store. Further, there is no way of knowing which of the three items was purchased. Finally, beyond not knowing who made the purchase, we don't know whether the buyer or the seller was the happy person. Good writers seem very sensitive to such problems in cohesion and avoid them. Poor writers have trouble seeing a problem in the first place.

Good writers also do other things to make their writing "considerate." For instance, they use transition sentences between paragraphs (notice how the first sentence in this paragraph cleverly tied back to previous material) and occasionally preface paragraphs with sentences that tie the upcoming content back to things discussed on previous pages. In addition, good writers use signals to subsequent content (e.g., *As you will see in the next chapter . . .*) and employ summaries of information at useful intervals. In general, good writers are aware of and constantly monitor the organizational quality of their writing, whereas poor writers seldom consider the issue.

Improving Students' Writing

To this point in the chapter, we've examined a model of the writing process and reviewed differences among writers. There also has been a great deal of research on how to help writers improve their skills. We begin our discussion of this topic by examining how the amount of writing required of students influences their writing skills.

Amount of Writing

More than 25 years ago, McQueen, Murray, and Evans (1963) performed an impressive study of the factors that led to proficient writing performance among entering college freshmen. Their findings pointed to one factor as the most-important determinant of writing skill—how much the students had been required to write in high school. This finding is corroborated every time another study examines the same issues (e.g., Applebee et al., 1986a). Since about the time of McQueen et al.'s study, however, there has been a consistent, year-to-year drop in the amount of writing students have been expected to complete in school (Applebee, 1988; Applebee et al., 1986b). At present, some students apparently proceed through high school without having to complete *any* significant writing assignments at all (Applebee et al., 1986a).

Why is it the case that we require so little writing? Part of the answer, we believe, lies in the demands writing assignments make on teachers. Consider an average high school English teacher who assigns 100 one-page papers each week. To read, grade, and comment on each paper requires a minimum of 10 minutes per paper, or 1,000 minutes of her time for the whole job. This comes to about 17 hours per week for grading papers. Seventeen hours a week doesn't seem too bad until we consider that the teacher probably is in class 25 hours per week and needs a minimum of 10 hours per week to prepare for lessons. Added up, we have 52 hours per week, not including sponsoring the Beta club (or student newspaper, debate teams, French club, etc.), taking tickets at the baseball game, managing a "homeroom" each morning, supervising study halls, or even grading other sorts of student work (e.g., examinations). Carefully grading two one-page papers per week from each student might cause a coronary.

Some relief, it seems, can be gained by not overloading English teachers until they burn out. Instead, writing should be required across *all* of the curriculum (Applebee et al., 1986a; Gray, 1988; Walberg & Fowler, 1987). In fact, at least one state (California) now requires writing in all parts of the curriculum (Gray, 1988). Still, a nationwide commitment is needed. Students' writing quality has dropped so low that all of us involved in education must make ourselves part of the solution. Unfortunately, there is no way to avoid a very stiff price for improving student writing, and that price is a large time and effort commitment from teachers.

There are some specific instructional techniques that can make a substantial difference, however. One approach that recently has gained considerable attention is peer editing.

Peer Editing

Peer editing has been referred to by several different names including diadic tutoring and shared composing (see Bissex, 1980; Dyson, 1983; D. Graves, 1975; Lamme & Childers, 1983). Peer editing consists of a process in which students in a class are paired together for a time. The students then write a set amount (a certain number of lines or words) on an assigned topic with the idea in mind that each person in the pair is the audience for the other. When the writing is completed, the students in each pair exchange papers. As "editors," each person reads and critiques the work of the other writer and gives feedback on how well meaning was communicated.

Peer editing may be varied in several ways. It can (and we suggest should, on occasion) include reading each other's paper aloud to one another, collaborating on revisions, trading papers and revising each other's work, and so on. Peer editing need not be limited to pairs of students, of course. Small groups of students may work together as a "community of writers" in the classroom. Peer editing may be used with very young writers and has been effective with college students as well. Overall, the results of research on peer editing appear very positive (Hilgers, 1986; Olson, Torrance, & Hildyard, 1985).

Beyond being an easily managed classroom activity, why has peer tutoring been so successful? Our analysis of the technique suggests several reasons. First, students are writing for a specific audience. Unlike much of the instruction in writing, peer editing puts a very real premium on audience awareness. Students are learning as directly as possible that good writing communicates meaning to another person.

A second factor involves the fact that students receive feedback on their writing almost immediately. Whereas a teacher may need several days to get through 100 essays, students readily can write a brief segment of prose, trade with their partners, and react to their partners' material all in the same class period. Further, it also seems that students may accept the judgments of their peers more readily than those of adults.

A third reason peer editing has been successful is its emphasis on editing skills. Peer editing puts the emphasis on detecting instances of poor writing and on correcting such errors. As they are used more and more frequently, these editing skills will generalize to more-critical evaluations of one's own writings. Especially when "read aloud" techniques are stressed, the improved editing skills lead directly to establishing standards for written communication and employing the standards for one's own writing.

A fourth variable influencing the success of peer editing is the stress on revision skills (of one's own or another's work). These skills involve using feedback from a reader to make changes in a text and learning to employ an external standard as the basis for reevaluating a writing project.

We highly recommend peer editing as part of any writing program. Beyond the instructional emphasis we've described above, the technique also has the advantage of freeing the teacher to concentrate on teaching specific knowledge and skills to students. In many ways, the English teacher who uses peer tutoring becomes a managing editor who is available to mediate disagreements and teach lessons to individual pairs of students (e.g., *Even though "flock" refers to many birds, it is a singular noun. There's just one flock of birds. When Bobby wrote "the flock was big," he was correct. You wouldn't say the "flock were big."*).

If the technique is used, we suggest that students trade partners after every two or three sessions in order to broaden their understanding of "audience." We also suggest peer editing not take the place of "teacher as editor." There is no substitute for having students write for a teacher, who then provides them with a descriptive and personal feedback.

Becoming One's Own Editor

One of the surest signs of very young or immature writers is the belief that once something has been written, no change can or should be made. Almost all professional writers, however, acknowledge that they typically revise and rewrite their materials and that revision is an important part of writing (Root, 1985). Indeed, most good writers make the editing and revising of their work an integral part of the writing process (Hull, 1987). Unfortunately, self-editing is one of the most difficult skills to teach. There are, however, a few things that can be done to facilitate self-editing.

First, have students set aside things they have written for a week or even longer before rereading them. Imposing a delay between the time something is written and when it is reread allows some forgetting to occur and facilitates the possibility of fully processing the material as if it has been written by someone else. (See Dellarosa & Bourne, 1985, for a discussion of this phenomenon.) A second aid to self-editing involves having students read what they have written out loud to a parent or sibling. Tell the students to trust their ears and to revise sentences that sound awkward. Our experience has been that students often use a "fix-up program" when reading silently to themselves (i.e., adding missing words, deleting unneeded words, fixing tenses, etc.), but that reading aloud makes errors much more obvious. Children quickly come to find that awkward writing "sounds wrong" and that good writing is pleasing to the ear. Reading aloud to parents or older siblings also is helpful because it puts another "editor" in the loop and provides the students with immediate feedback on the quality of their writing. Merely reading out loud isn't enough, of course; the students need to go back and rewrite the awkward places until they "sound right."

Rewriting

Ultimately, there is no substitute for frequent writing with feedback (Applebee, 1984, 1988). We've already noted how much time must be committed to the process by teachers, but at this point there seems to be no substitute for such levels of effort. Frequent writing with descriptive feedback, however, is not enough! To gain the full value of feedback, it must be used to make a correct response. Merely receiving a grade and comments about writing errors often is insufficient to alter writing habits. Rewriting, although not necessarily fun, provides an opportunity during which feedback may be used to alter a student's existing habits (Applebee et al., 1986b).

Rewriting should not be seen as a trivial activity or an afterthought. Rewriting provides an excellent teaching opportunity and a clear way to provide a correct practice opportunity. Further, students' explanations of how corrections were made and why the earlier drafts were incorrect also are helpful. Rewriting works only when it is an opportunity to learn to change one's writing habits.

Teacher–Student Conferences

Teacher–student conferences also may be used in writing instruction. The emphasis of teacher–student writing conferences should be on the quality of students' writing, the process by which the students arrived at their product, and the relationship between writing processes and the quality of writing (Olson et al., 1985). During the conferences, which are held with individual students, the teacher poses questions concerning the quality of the writing, the meaning the student wanted to convey, and the cognitive processes the student was using during writing. While this interaction is occurring, the teacher can single out important aspects of the writing for discussion.

Teacher–student conferences also are a time for the student to write directly in front of the teacher while talking about the process. The conference also may offer the possibility of the teacher's modeling effective writing behaviors. Having the students write while the teacher observes and interacts can be an effective means of teaching skills in a personalized manner. Consider, for example, the following exchange drawn from a tenth-grade composition class:

TEACHER: *I like how you described Fiver, but let me read the sentence about Hazel out loud. You listen critically.*

STUDENT: *OK.*

TEACHER: *"Hazel was leader material but he didn't know yet."*

STUDENT: *It doesn't sound so good, does it?*

TEACHER: *No, but I think you can do much better. Here* [points at note pad], *write another sentence and share your thinking as you do.*

STUDENT: *OK. Let's see . . . "Hazel had" . . . I mean a word that says he didn't know about . . . "undiscovered"?*

TEACHER: *That'd work.*

STUDENT: *Hazel had undiscovered leadership."*

TEACHER: *OK, but not just leadership. . . ."*

STUDENT: *I see. It doesn't fit just . . . Mmmm. "Hazel had undiscovered leadership abilities."*

TEACHER: *That's a good sentence!*

STUDENT: *Yeah. You don't just have it. It's like a skill or something, so you have to say "abilities."*

As you can see, the teacher was acting like an editor and gently nudging the student along as he constructed a clear sentence. The teacher also was careful to praise the student's efforts when positive change occurred. Modeling can be seen in an excerpt drawn from a conference the teacher had with another student.

STUDENT: *Sir Holger fought the followers of the evil mage.*

TEACHER: *That's a pretty good sentence. The meaning you want to share is very clear. I don't like the structure as well as I could, though. I prefer to avoid "of" the way you've used it. I like possessives instead. They save words. For example, "Sir Holger fought the evil mage's followers." It flows a little better.*

STUDENT: *It does sound better that way.*

TEACHER: *Some teachers might disagree, but I've always thought that if you can eliminate unnecessary words, you've helped your writing. Look here* [points to an assigned reading]. *I thought of this last night. Instead of "Bring me the swords that are sharp," I'd say, "Bring me the sharp swords."*

Given both positive and negative examples of writing samples, students are better able to discriminate between them and choose the good writing samples as their own standards.

Teacher–student writing conferences obviously are time-consuming and require preparation. Consequently, other activities must be developed for the remainder of the class and limits set on how many conferences can be held during a school year. Still, teacher–student conferences are a very valuable strategy for teaching writing skills.

Computers in Writing Instruction

As one might expect, there have been a number of recent studies focused on the value of writing on a microcomputer or word processor (e.g., Beesley, 1986; Klein, 1988). Some of the results have been impressive. Consider the following essay written by a first-grader near the end of the school year:

The Little Bear Goes Camping

Once there was a little bear. She had a mom and a dad. It was summer and little bear had nothing to do. Then her mother and father desited maybe to let little bear go camping with her big cousen. So they asked little bear if she wanted to. So they asked little bear and she said yes she thoaght that was a great idia. So little bear got all packed. Then her cousen came. So they went to the woods and started to camp. They had a wunderful time. They went fishing and they did a hole bunch of stoff. When they got home they started to talk all about what they did when they went camping. They had a wunderful time. Little bear broaght back flowers for her faimly pretty ones i mean it!!!!

THE! END!!!

There really isn't much doubt in our minds that a story the quality of "The Little Bear Goes Camping" would be far more difficult for a first-grader to write with paper and pencil rather than with a computer. Although a great deal of research still needs to be done in evaluating the utility of microcomputers as writing tools with beginning writers, preliminary evidence suggests that the early acquisition of writing skills is enhanced when children work with microcomputers (Sharples, 1985).

Computers also facilitate the acquisition of editing and revising skills (Daiute, 1986; Hawisher, 1987; Sharples, 1985). The ease with which segments of text can be rearranged and saved greatly reduces the logistic efforts involved in editing and revising materials. When students can rearrange a text, add words, delete words, and insert whole sentences into an essay with the touch of a few fingers, much less effort is required than when the entire product must be rewritten by hand or retyped on a conventional typewriter. Where writers once had to devote most of their energies to recopying their work, they can now focus their efforts on the quality of writing (Daiute, 1986).

Microcomputers, however, are not a "miracle cure" for problems in writing instruction. Students still must write frequently and get descriptive feedback on their writing. No computer program in existence can replace the teacher. Further, computer writing laboratories are expensive, and there are no cost-benefit data available showing that the use of computers is more cost effective than, say, decreasing the ratio of students per teacher. Finally, the research in this area is just beginning. It is unclear that the computer alone is the reason for improved writing skills and not increased attention, increased time on task, the novelty of working with computers, or increased teacher enthusiasm.

Creative Writing

Thus far, we have avoided the issue of "creative" writing and instead have emphasized the development of writing skills designed to enhance the communication of meaning. There is, however, a very large literature on creative writing. (See Carey & Flower, in press, for a brief overview.) Not much of this literature has dealt with the cognitive processes that might be involved in creative writing, and little has examined instructional procedures designed to make writing more creative. Still, there are some important issues worth reviewing.

Creativity and the Evaluation of Writing

One debate concerning creative writing has focused on issues involved in evaluation. Some have argued that creativity in writing and the evaluation of writing are antitheses. That is, writers cannot be creative if they are constrained by the possible evaluation of their work (Carey & Flower, in press; Glover, 1979b). The arguments supporting this position are based on reasoning that writers will not be willing to take risks and explore new paths if they are worrying about evaluation. From this perspective, the way to foster creative writing is to withhold all forms of evaluation from writing and to form a "psychologically safe" environment in which writers feel free to express their inner selves.

The argument that creative writing requires an evaluation-free, judgment-free environment led to the belief among some teachers that "creative writing" should not be graded. Further, many teachers gave up correcting spelling, punctuation, and grammar because they believed that correcting these elements of students' writing surely would delimit creativity (Applebee et al., 1986a). A careful analysis of this approach to teaching writing, however, suggests that it not only fails to enhance creativity, but it keeps students from improving the mechanics of their writing (Applebee et al., 1986a; Glover, 1979b).

Encouraging creativity and evaluating writing are not mutually exclusive. The entire publishing enterprise, for instance, requires the expression of creativity. However, no editor will even bother to read a manuscript unless it is mechanically correct. To write creatively in the world of editors and publishers, one must first be able to write correctly. Analogously to learning to play a musical instrument, a student must be able to play correctly before creativity becomes an issue.

Although evaluation has not been shown to restrict creativity, care should be taken to avoid quashing new ideas or attempts to be creative. Careful feedback can make very clear that you are not trying to have students stop being creative when you merely are correcting grammar. We advise that teachers *always* provide students with feedback designed to improve the quality of their writing without being needlessly critical. Further, teachers' expectations are important. Students are far more likely to strive for creativity if teachers expect it.

As we've emphasized throughout this volume, knowledge plays a critical role in cognition. Creative thought is no different. Carey and Flower (in press) point out that creative writing cannot occur without a great deal of knowledge about the topic and about writing. In terms of enhancing creative writing, then, teaching students about writing and having them learn about the topic on which they will write will increase the probability of writing creatively. In its most direct terms, our argument is highly similar to what writers and editors long have said to beginning writers: "To write well, one must write about what one knows."

A classic example of a highly successful writer who followed the dictum of writing about things he knew was James Michener. Michener, author of *Caravans, Tales of the South Pacific, Centennial, Space,* and many other novels, spent years of his life acquiring the knowledge he needed to write. Prior to beginning each of his later volumes (*Tales of the South Pacific* was based on his wartime experiences), Michener spent months and even years *learning* about the area and cultures he wanted to write about. In fact, as Michener became more successful, he hired an entire staff of researchers to travel with him and help him learn enough to write knowledgeably.

One can quibble over how creative Michener has been, but an examination of his habits and the results of research on other writers (e.g., Root, 1985) sheds light on a seldom-mentioned issue related to creativity. Gathering knowledge is in integral part of the writing process. Creation cannot occur in a vacuum—it must be based on content.

Grammar

One last topic must be addressed in a chapter on writing. How important is a knowledge of grammar to the ability to write? Must one know that gerund is not a small, white-and-brown furry animal related to hamsters in order to compose a good sentence? Is the skill of diagramming a sentence into its constituent parts important for today's young novelist? Research designed to shed light on such questions has been done since at least 1904 (De Boer, 1959). The results have been dramatic and consistent. There appparently is *no* relationship between knowledge of grammar and the ability to write. What? That's right; research dating back to 1904 shows no relationship between a knowledge of grammar on the one hand and an ability to write on the other (see Olson et al., 1985). The situation seems analagous to that of carpentry and structural engineering. One does not need to know the formal discipline of structural engineering in order to frame in a window.

There also is no evidence that teaching students grammar improves their ability to write (De Boer, 1959; Frogner, 1939; Kraus, 1957). In fact, the literature abounds with one failure after another of teaching grammar as a means of improving writing (see Olson et al., 1985). As long ago as 1939, Frogner contrasted teaching students grammar with teaching them a "thought" method (an approach based on analyzing meaning) as a means of improving their writing. Where teaching grammar made no difference, an emphasis on meaning brought about a very clear change in writers' abilities.

Many teachers continue to emphasize grammar at the expense of meaning, perhaps unaware of the overwhelming evidence showing that writers' knowledge of grammar is not critical to writing skill. Not that serious researchers in the area suggest that students should not be taught the basic mechanical skills involved in writing (punctuation, capitalization, spelling) or that some sense of grammar terminology may not be helpful (e.g., it is much easier to help polish a student's writing if both student and teacher understand the meaning of *split infinitive*). However, we must recommend that the communication of **meaning** should be the focus of instruction on writing and not the acquisition of grammar facts.

Summary

Writing is the process of expressing ideas in the printed symbols of a language. The most-complete model linking thought and language in writing is that developed by Linda Flower and John Hayes. This model describes three major components: the task environment, long-term memory, and working memory. The major cognitive processes—planning, translating, and reviewing—occur in working memory.

There are important individual differences between good and poor writers. Among these differences are the ability to manipulate information, to plan, to generate ideas, and to organize. Students' writing can be improved by increasing the amount of writing they do and providing them with high-quality feedback. Creating an environment for writing is a key feature of effective instruction. Teaching grammar seems to have little effect on the quality of students' writing. However, procedures such as peer editing and teacher–student conferences can bring about great improvements in the quality of students' prose. Creativity in students' writing can be facilitated by helping students gain knowledge about writing and about the topics on which they will write.

CHAPTER 12

Cognitive Approaches to Mathematics

Cognitive approaches to mathematics build on the basic model of cognition we described in the early chapters of this book. In this chapter, consequently, the general issues of knowledge acquisition, memory, and problem solving are addressed only as they apply to the specific domain of mathematics. As we described in Chapter 7, a major characteristic of problem solving in any domain is acquiring specialized and organized knowledge. Mathematics is no different. Students must acquire a body of domain-specific information and store it in memory in structures suitable for use.

Mathematical problem-solving skill acquired in schools is expected to generalize to tasks encountered outside the school. This expectation requires an understanding of mathematics based on the development of schemata with sufficient flexibility to permit analysis of "informal" problems that occur outside the boundaries of the conventional tasks presented in mathematics curricula. Furthermore, children must acquire a set of procedures for the operations of mathematics. Recent evidence from studies of simple addition and subtraction (e.g., Riley, Greeno, & Heller, 1983; Carpenter, 1985) suggest that even these apparently simple procedures are much more complex than most teachers and adults believe. Instruction in mathematics that permits students to use mathematics effectively both in and out of school is a challenging task.

Mathematics differs from many school subjects in that relatively little of its content is taught informally, that is to say, out of school. This is especially true of mathematics subjects commonly taught in junior and senior high school—algebra, geometry, calculus, and the like. Some children do enter kindergarten with a few arithmetic skills, most notably counting, since four-year-olds often are taught by parents, older siblings, or others to count to 10. In many cases, however, these children have not established conservation of number, that is, the critical idea of a one-to-one correspondence between a collection of objects and a particular number.

Before we begin a detailed discussion of mathematics problem solving in elementary school age children, a significant developmental issue must be addressed. The well-known work of Piaget describes a series of developmental stages through which all children pass. These stages are age-related, with most children of kindergarten age in the preoperational stage, whereas early elementary school children (grades 1–3) often have reached the concrete-operations stage. As educators have studied the implications of Piaget's stages for teaching, a general strategy has been to look at the curriculum in terms of the cognitive demands it places on children. The abstractness of arithmetic suggests that formal mathematics instruction should be delayed to as late as the fifth or sixth grade.

The reasons children may not be "ready" for formal mathematics are not clear. To say they are not cognitively prepared begs the question. However, developmentalists such as Case (1972) and Pascual-Leone (1976) have attempted to address that issue. Because of the demands many mathematical skills place on dealing with a variety of bits of information, Case and Pascual-Leone concentrated on issues for early school learning. Case (1972, 1978) has systematically examined the short-term memory capacity of young children, defining what he calls M-space (memory space). Short-term memory capacity in adults long has been estimated to be approximately seven plus or minus two chunks of information (see Chapter 4). Case's work suggests that young children are far below this adult level of performance. For example, Romberg and Collis (1987) recently carried out a systematic evaluation of short-term memory capacity in young children as a part of a larger study of mathematics competence. They proposed situations such as the following in which a child (age 6 or 7) is asked to find a sum as follows:

TEACHER: *What number equals 2 + 4 + 3?*
CHILD: *2 + 4 = 6, now what was the other number?*
TEACHER: *What number equals 2 + 4 + 3?*
CHILD: *Now, 2 plus, uh, what are the numbers?*

According to Romberg and Collis, this conversation reveals a short-term memory difficulty. They suggest the following explanation: The request for the third number implies not an operational failure, but a memory failure. The second response suggests that the child's effort to remember the third number results in a capacity overload that prompts the request for the remaining numbers. Using a series of memory tests,

Romberg and Collis have demonstrated that average M-space (memory capacity, in chunks) directly increases with grade level, although, as might be expected, with rather large within-grade variability. On their best measure of M-space, Romberg and Collis discovered that kindergarten children had M-space scores of almost exactly 1, whereas first-grader M-spaces equaled about 1.23 and the M-spaces of second-graders equaled just over 3. This suggests a considerable deficit in memory that might inhibit even simple arithmetic problem solving. A direct implication of these findings is that kindergarten and first-grade children are likely to face memory deficits in dealing with simple arithmetic. In order to remedy this potential difficulty, primary-grade teachers must be careful to provide visual presentations of number problems in order to avoid mistakes due *not* to lack of readiness to comprehend, but to short-term memory failures. As we'll see below when we examine addition and subtraction strategies in early elementary school children, these children, even without formal instruction, develop and use a variety of techniques to make simple arithmetic tasks visual, and hence reduce memory demands. For the present, at least, it seems reasonable to conclude that the apparent lack of "readiness" primary school children exhibit *may* more precisely be seen as a lack of short-term memory capacity. If this finding is valid, then instructional techniques that compensate for memory deficits may make instruction in mathematics at such early ages useful and appropriate. In point of fact, much of arithmetic learning in the primary grades *is* carried out with physical objects that reduce short-term memory demands.

As we just saw, recent research suggests the value of schemata-based approaches to learning mathematics. In this chapter, we pursue in considerable depth the teaching of two significant components of the mathematics curriculum: addition (and to a lesser extent, subtraction) and algebra, particularly algebra word problems. Each topic is examined in some detail to demonstrate its complexity as well as the usefulness of cognitive approaches for understanding the mathematical processes children acquire. In contrast to many adult views of arithmetic, we treat both addition and algebra as problem-solving processes.

The thrust of recent research in mathematics has been the attempt to represent mathematical concepts so as to permit clearer understanding of the processes children use to solve them (i.e., to become mathematicians). For instance, Riley et al. (1983) and Kintsch and Greeno (1985) proposed that representation through set schema provides a vehicle for such an understanding. A set schema, for instance, represents the idea of parts and a whole. To illustrate, the mathematics of addition may be presented as the presentation of two or more sets (i.e., parts) mathematically combined to form a whole (the superset). In addition to a set schema, addition also requires a change schema to show how parts may be combined. Much of arithmetic, and potentially much of other mathematics, can be described using these two schemata. In general, we argue that mathematics operations require the acquisition of multiple schemata that permit the class of operations we call, collectively, mathematics.

Much mathematics knowledge, particularly arithmetic, involves the formation of schemata that lead to a set of procedures. These procedures, more commonly called **algorithms,** guide the actions necessary to solve problems. A number of arithmetic algorithms (count all, count from larger, etc.) are briefly discussed below. In order for such algorithms to be flexible enough for use in problem solving, they must be linked to a network of conceptual knowledge. According to Greeno (1976) and Riley et al. (1983), when the appropriate algorithms are matched to conceptual knowledge, conceptual knowledge initiates appropriate algorithm selection. At the same time, the consequences (success or failure) of using certain algorithms often will result in changes in the conceptual framework. The interactive feedback of knowledge and procedures leads, ultimately, to sophisticated mathematics proficiency.

A key problem for mathematics students (and hence for their teachers) is to recognize that particular conceptual or procedural information is appropriate to a particular problem. Mathematicians (e.g., Polya, 1973; Schoenfeld, 1985) have argued for the need to teach heuristic (strategic) knowledge so that flexibility in problem solution is enhanced.

Heuristic Knowledge

Heuristics are the strategies problem solvers acquire for matching conceptual and procedural knowledge to the solution of a specific problem. Polya's 1973 book, *How to Solve It,* consists largely of general heuristic suggestions applicable to many mathematical problems. Polya suggests, for example, that to get started on a problem one should ask: "What is the unknown?" "What are the dates?" "What is the condition?" Unfortunately, Kantowski (1977) and Schoenfeld (1985) have shown that the value of such general heuristics is not impressive. Schoenfeld (1985, 1987) asserts that heuristics such as Polya suggests are in large part simply labels for categories of related strategies, and thus do not lead to specific procedures. Further, he argues, many mathematics algorithms are so complex, and consist of so many phases, that a general strategy is likely to be ineffective. Thus, Schoenfeld is arguing, as we have earlier, that general heuristics cannot replace domain-specific conceptual and procedural knowledge. The generalized heuristics (more properly called generalized schemata) Polya suggests may be similar to the general problem-solving strategies (see A. Newell & Simon, 1972) that seem to be of little value. General strategies cannot substitute for the specific information necessary for mathematics problem solving. Only after considerable mathematical conceptual and procedural knowledge is acquired do heuristics about mathematical problem solving appear to generate useful strategies (Schoenfeld, 1985).

Knowledge Acquisition

As students acquire a larger conceptual and procedural base in mathematics, and a greater linkage among these conceptual and procedural elements, they become more efficient and flexible problem solvers (Carpenter, 1986). Schoenfeld and Hermann (1982) and Silver (1979) suggest expert mathematicians use the **semantic** (meaning) aspects of a problem to encode its relevant features. Novice problem solvers in mathematics, however, likely lack semantic information and therefore must rely on problem form—the **syntactic** or surface features of problem presentations. In this same regard, Schoenfeld (1985) points out that many textbooks in arithmetic teach a kind of "keyword" problem-solving method based purely on syntactic structure. If this is the case, children may learn a set of rote operations based on the keywords without necessarily understanding the semantic structure of the problem. Consider the following arithmetic word problem:

> *Bill has six marbles and gives two to Joe. How many marbles does Bill have left?*

If a student is reacting only to "keywords," he or she would identify the two numbers in the problem and a keyword, in this case *left,* that elicits the schemata for subtraction. Focusing on keywords will give the correct response for this problem. Schoenfeld (1985) states that in one major textbook series, the "keyword method" will yield the "right" answer for virtually all problems (97 percent).

Real-life mathematical problems are not so neatly packaged, however. A teaching strategy permitting the student to solve a problem without a meaningful (semantic) representation of the problem statement seems unlikely to develop flexible and complex problem-solving strategies. Mathematics teachers need to help children extend their existing conceptual knowledge with new information extending the conceptual web of mathematics knowledge. Only if this information is meaningful will children develop algorithms appropriate to a wide variety of mathematical tasks.

In the past 10 years, empirical research in mathematics carried out from an information-processing perspective has burgeoned. The structure of mathematics provides a clear base from which to examine the development of problem-solving schemata in elementary and secondary school students. We examine this recent research by focusing on problem solving first in arithmetic, and then in algebra.

Arithmetic Problem Solving

At one time, mathematics educators distinguished between **computational** aspects of mathematics, which in many cases focused on learning rules such as the algorithms for addition and division, and **conceptual** aspects of mathematics, which presumably involved problem solving and understanding. Indeed, as recently as 1983, Doyle, in a review of academic tasks, stated:

> As students progress through the grades, the emphasis gradually shifts from basic skills to the content and the methods of inquiry embodied in academic disciplines. Older students are expected to learn algebra, history, biology, and literature rather than simply practice reading and *computational skills* [emphasis added]. (p. 160)

This distinction is rapidly disappearing. A wealth of recent theory-driven research with young children has shown the acquisition of the addition and subtraction algorithms, for example, to be substantive mathematical problems. Although it is true that these computational operations are so overlearned as to be "habitual for most adults," this should not obscure their basic problem-solving nature. The addition algorithm most adults use with such ease and competence was once, for all of us, a "problem" in the sense of our definition in Chapter 7. Furthermore, users of the common computational algorithms need to "understand" the rules in order to use them effectively in the varied situations that require mathematical competence. Consequently, we take the perspective that all mathematics is, at least initially, problem solving.

It is certainly true that in many elementary schools, arithmetic is treated as simply a "drill-and-practice" activity. The "facts" of arithmetic or the "times tables" are seen as discrete items to be stored in memory, with competence in arithmetic weighted toward rapid response rates. In this view of beginning arithmetic, the competent student is one who has acquired a large, readily available repertoire of "facts." We vividly recall "arithmetic races" from our elementary school experiences where expertise was demonstrated by running to the chalkboard and "solving" problems (such as summing several three-digit numbers) before an opponent could do the same. Such a tactic may well put a greater premium on speed than understanding. Still, even today accurate and rapid access to basic arithmetic "facts" is admired. However, whether or not such emphasis on procedural speed results in an "understanding" of arithmetic is not clear.

We argue that the distinction between arithmetic as a computation skill and algebra, trigonometry, and calculus as problem-solving skills ignores the problem-solving demands placed on young children as they develop basic arithmetic algorithms. Simply because arithmetic competence is taught in the elementary school whereas algebra is taught in junior high school does not make arithmetic less worthy of being called problem solving. The following analysis of "simple" addition and subtraction tasks reveals just how complex the problem-solving procedures of addition and subtraction are.

The Addition Algorithm

Although virtually all readers of this text can successfully add a column of three- or four-digit numbers, few of us can describe the rather-complex algorithm directing our behavior. Box 12-1 provides the sequence of productions (the addition algorithm) required to add such a column of numbers. J. R. Anderson (1983a) proposes this system to illustrate the nature of production systems rather than to directly illustrate young children's mathematics behavior, which serves to remind us of the complexity of the task assumed by mathematics teachers when they set out to "teach addition." Such production systems do in fact give a fairly accurate view of actual arithmetic behavior (see J. S. Brown & van Lehn, 1980). Brown and van Lehn have shown that many errors in children's subtraction performance can be explained as deletion or alteration of individual rules (subprocedures) in the production system. In most cases, of course, such changes result in failure to solve the problem.

The production system portrayal provides a picture of the surprisingly (at least to us as adults!) complex and long sequence of actions needed to simply "add" a column of numbers. The automaticity of our own well-developed addition algorithm belies the extensive knowledge and operations required. Note, for example, the amount of knowledge necessary to carry out such a production: (1) a large array of number "facts" (e.g., 7 plus 5 = 12); (2) conceptual-level understanding of such words as *column, iterate, carry, goal,* and *string digit,* all acquired in the context of their conceptual meaning in mathematics; and (3) the correct sequence in which these productions must be applied. Careful examination of the 12 productions listed in Box 12-1 reveals numerous distinctions the problem solver must make to deal with, for example, the presence or absence of a "carry" or the need to turn attention from the

Box 12-1

A Production (P) System for Performing Addition

P1   IF the goal is to do an addition problem,
     THEN the subgoal is to iterate through the columns of the problem.

P2   IF the goal is to iterate through the columns of an addition problem and the right-most column has not been processed,
     THEN the subgoal is to iterate through the rows of that right-most column
            and set the running total to 0.

P3   IF the goal is to iterate through the columns of an addition problem
            and a column has just been processed
            and another column is to the left of this column,
     THEN the subgoal is to iterate through the rows of this column to the left
            and set the **running total to the carry.**

P4   IF the goal is to iterate through the columns of an addition problem
            and the last column has been processed
            and there **is a carry,**
     THEN **write out the carry**
            and POP the goal.

P5   IF the goal is to iterate through the columns of an addition problem
            and the last column has been processed
            and there is no carry,
     THEN POP the goal.

P6   IF the goal is to iterate through the rows of a column
            and the top row has not been processed,
     THEN the subgoal is to add the digit of the top row to the running total.

P7   IF the goal is to iterate through the rows of a column
            and a row has just been processed
            and another row is below it,
     THEN the subgoal is to add the digit of the lower row to the running total.

P8　　　IF　the goal is to iterate through the rows of a column
　　　　　　　and the last row has been processed
　　　　　　　and the running total is a digit,
　THEN　write the digit
　　　　　　and delete the carry
　　　　　　and mark the column as processed
　　　　　　and POP the goal.

A Production System for Addition of Three-Digit Numbers

P9　　　IF　the goal is to iterate through the rows of a column
　　　　　　　and the last row has been processed
　　　　　　　and the running total is of the form "string digit,"
　THEN　write the digit
　　　　　　and set carry to the string
　　　　　　and mark the column as processed
　　　　　　and POP the goal.

P10　　　IF　the goal is to add a digit to another digit
　　　　　　　and a sum is the sum of the two digits,
　THEN　the result is the sum
　　　　　　and mark the digit as processed
　　　　　　and POP the goal.

P11　　　IF　the goal is to add a digit to a number
　　　　　　　and the number is of the form "string digit"
　　　　　　　and a sum is the sum of the two digits
　　　　　　　and the sum is less than 10,
　THEN　the result is "string sum"
　　　　　　and mark the digit as processed
　　　　　　and POP the goal.

P12　　　IF　the goal is to add a digit to a number
　　　　　　　and the number is of the form "string digit"
　　　　　　　and a sum is the sum of the two digits
　　　　　　　and the sum is of the form "1 digit"
　　　　　　　and another number sum is the sum of 1 plus string,
　THEN　the result is "sum digit"
　　　　　　and mark the digit as processed
　　　　　　and POP the goal.

From *The Architecture of Cognition* by J. R. Anderson, 1983a, Cambridge, MA: Harvard University Press. Used by permission.

present goal to one above it in the hierarchy of productions. Given this description, it should be no surprise that many persons, children *and* adults, perform at less-than-optimal levels with "simple" arithmetic.

Elementary school children face a formidable problem-solving task in acquiring the addition algorithm. At the same time, of course, children also are learning a subtraction algorithm as well as facing significant challenges in other domains of schooling, such as reading. For many children, a consequence of this bewildering array of demands is the acquisition of faulty algorithms (procedures) that result in errors. Interestingly, the study of errors children make in addition and subtraction has yielded considerable insight into arithmetic problem solving.

"Buggy" Algorithms

Many children fail to acquire mathematical algorithms easily. For instance, in examining the subtraction errors of a large number of children, J. S. Brown and Burton (1978) discovered that a sizable number had learned (and used consistently) one or more incorrect versions of the general subtraction algorithm. Many of the incorrect algorithms gave correct solutions part of the time, but in other applications gave incorrect ones. For example, some children consistently applied a subtraction algorithm that led them to subtract smaller numbers from larger ones *regardless* of which number was on top:

$$
\begin{array}{cccc}
8 & 23 & 47 & 52 \\
-\,3 & -\,16 & -\,35 & -\,17 \\
\hline
5 & 13 & 12 & 45
\end{array}
$$

Note that this incorrect algorithm (Brown and Burton described it and others as "bugs") gives the correct answer in the first and third problems—in fact, in those problems the child's subscription algorithm *seems* correct. Yet the algorithm used throughout these four problems—"Take the smaller number from the larger in each column."—gives the wrong answer in the second and fourth problems. A teacher, seeing all of the problems in sequence, may well dismiss the mistake in the second problem as a "careless error" and the one in the fourth as a "difficulty with 'borrowing,'" not recognizing that the child is using the same defective subtraction algorithm for all of the problems. Failure to diagnose this consistent error may well prevent the teacher from isolating the particular conceptual difficulty and therefore prevent the acquisition of a clear sense of the subtraction algorithm.

By analyzing the performance of thousands of schoolchildren, Brown and Burton and Burton (1981) have identified and classified more than 300 different subtraction bugs. This impressive array of bugs in subtraction alone has led to a closer examination of the processes children use in both addition and subtraction. A first step in this examination has been to classify different types of addition and subtraction problems so that meaningful analyses of algorithm errors can be pursued.

Problem Typologies

If we consider addition and subtraction as problem solving, what sorts of problems are possible? By treating addition and subtraction as open sentences and varying the unknown, six addition and six subtraction "sentences" can be created (Carpenter & Moser, 1983). These deceptively simple tasks provide the content for much of early elementary school arithmetic. The sentence types are shown in Table 12-1. For elementary school students, the numbers used in these sentences yield whole-number solutions drawn from the basic arithmetic facts. Research (e.g., Beattle & Deichmann, 1972) indicates that these problems (sentences) are not of equal difficulty to early elementary school children. In general, subtraction sentences are more difficult than addition sentences. Sentences of the form ($a + b = ?$ or $a - b = ?$) are easier than sentences of the form ($a + ? = c$ or $a - ? = c$). Sentences with the operation to the right of the equal sign ($c = ? - b$) are more difficult than parallel problems with the operation to the left of the equal sign. Exactly why this is so has not been determined; however, one plausible hypothesis is simply that teachers and textbooks tend to present problems in the "easier" form much more frequently than in the others. That is, students get much more practice with ($a + b = ?$) structures than those with operations on the right of the equal sign.

Addition and subtraction problems have been classified into four major categories: change, combine, compare, and equalize (Carpenter &

TABLE 12-1. Open Sentence Types [a]

a	$+$	b	$=$	$?$		$?$	$=$	a	$+$	b
a	$+$	$?$	$=$	c		c	$=$	a	$+$	$?$
$?$	$+$	b	$=$	c		c	$=$	$?$	$+$	b
a	$-$	b	$=$	$?$		$?$	$=$	a	$-$	b
a	$-$	$?$	$=$	c		c	$=$	a	$-$	$?$
$?$	$-$	b	$=$	c		c	$=$	$?$	$-$	b

[a]From "Acquisition of Addition and Subtraction Concepts," by T. P. Carpenter and J. M. Moser 1983, in R. Lesh, and M. Landau, *Acquisition of Mathematical Concepts and Processes*, p. 10. New York: Academic Press. Used by permission.

Moser, 1982; Riley et al., 1983). One example of a problem from each category follows. (Note that 20 different variations of these four types of problems are possible.)

CHANGE: *Heather had six apples. Chris gave her five more apples. How many apples does Heather have altogether?*

COMBINE: *Heather had six red apples and five green apples. How many apples does she have?*

COMPARE: *Heather has 12 apples. She has seven more than Chris. How many apples does Chris have?*

EQUALIZE: *Chris has five apples. If Heather loses eight apples, she will have the same number of apples as Chris. How many apples does Heather have?"*

Determining how children solve such problems requires an examination of counting skills, since primary children use counting to add and subtract. Examination of protocols of young children solving addition problems reveals three levels of counting strategies (see Carpenter & Moser, 1982) for such solutions. The counting strategies follow.

Counting All with Model

Carpenter and Moser (1982) indicate that in carrying out the simplest addition strategy, children use physical objects or their fingers to represent each number (set) to be combined, after which the union of the two sets is counted. Thus to add 4 and 7, a child represents each addend with a model of blocks or other objects (4 and 7, respectively), then counts the union of the two (in this case *1,2,3,4 (pause), 5,6,7,8,9,10,11*).

Counting on from First

In this somewhat more efficient addition strategy, the child recognizes that it is not necessary to begin from 1, but rather begins to count with the first addend and counts forward the extent of the second addend. Thus, in our example the child counts *4 (pause), 5,6,7,8,9,10,11*.

Counting on from Larger

Later, an even more efficient strategy appears: The child begins with the larger addend. Hence in the example 4 + 7, the child counts *7 (pause), 8,9,10,11*. This strategy is often used particularly when children are asked to add numbers greater than 10, numbers difficult to represent with their fingers.

Carpenter and Moser (1982) describe similar, though more complex, counting strategies for subtraction problems. For example, when using concrete objects children use a strategy called **separating from,** first constructing the larger set, then separating (one at a time) the appropriate set of objects from the larger one. A count of the objects remaining gives the answer to the problem.

Ultimately, of course, most children learn the basic addition and subtraction facts so that the counting strategies no longer are used. This is a surprisingly slow process, however. For subtraction, the majority of first-graders use some form of counting strategy. In second grade about one-third of such responses appear to be based on number facts, and by the third grade almost two-thirds of the responses are based on number facts (Carpenter & Moser, 1983). Yet a study by Lankford (1972) suggests that more than a third of seventh-graders still use counting strategies rather than stored arithmetic facts in solving addition and subtraction problems. Careful observation of adult addition and subtraction behavior also suggests that such counting strategies are not limited to children! Furthermore, all number combinations are not learned equally quickly. Thus in addition, doubles (6 + 6, 9 + 9, etc.) and numbers that sum to 10 are learned as addition facts earlier than other combinations.

Our description of the seemingly simple problem-solving behaviors of single-digit addition and subtraction reveals their true complexity. By now the reason for the complexity of the algorithm (Box 12-1) for adding columns of three-digit numbers should be clear. Most children do readily acquire these algorithms, however, and in our discussion of problem solving in Chapter 7, we identified a number of factors that facilitate problem solution. Primary among these is knowledge. The algorithms discussed so far provide persuasive evidence that children must acquire large amounts of knowledge for successful arithmetic problem solving. What specifically do children need to *know* in order to solve addition and subtraction problems?

Arithmetic Knowledge

Riley et al. (1983) have analyzed arithmetic tasks such as those we've described and have developed a theoretical model of the solution process. The model takes the form of a computer simulation that solves problems of the change, combine, compare, equalize form.

The problem text (i.e., the statement of the problem) provides the basis for task comprehension, which in turn leads to a problem representation. This representation is drawn from a set of problem schemata stored in long-term memory. When particular problem schemata are activated, an action schema (a **production**) then is represented in working memory and carried out as a solution attempt. Riley et al. propose that strategic knowledge (see Chapter 2) is required to generate a sequence among the production rules that permits top-down planning for efficient and accurate problem solving. In Riley et al.'s view, every arithmetic problem requires knowledge of three sorts: (1) problem schemata (derived from the semantic structure of the problem statement); (2) action schemata (stored actions for solving problems); and (3) strategic knowledge for sequencing (planning) solutions to problems.

Problem Schemata

Riley et al. suggest that a **problem schema** exists for every type of problem. Consider the following change problem:

> *Joe had eight marbles. Then he gave five marbles to Tom. How many marbles does Joe have now?*

Riley et al. propose that the problem representation for this task consists of three components. The first is the **start set,** the initial quantity—8 marbles. A second component, a change, must be recognized; this is called the **take-out set**—5 marbles. Finally, there must be recognition that the remaining marbles form the third component, the **result set**—3 marbles.

Action Schemata

Once a problem has been represented, solution requires knowledge of the **action schemata.** In the marble problem above, beginning with an empty set, the problem statement instantiates a schema (put-in) such that the start set equals eight marbles (representing the sentence *Joe had eight marbles.*). Then the action schema (take-out) indicates the change (i.e., removal of five marbles from the initial set). Finally, another action schema (count-all) counts the objects remaining—the result set, represented by the sentence *How many marbles does Joe have now?*

Strategic Knowledge

Note that since even simple addition and subtraction problems require differing action schemata, learners need **strategic knowledge** to choose schemata appropriate to different types of problems. Besides problem and action schemata, a top-down (strategic) approach must be acquired that matches existing schemata stored in memory to problem representations and, in turn, to action schemata. For children learning addition and subtraction, a continuing difficulty is to acquire enough flexibility in choice of schemata so that the right schema is applied to a particular problem at the right time.

Language: Another Factor

"Simple" problems in arithmetic may be more or less difficult depending on the nature of the language used in the problem statement. Hud-

FIGURE 12-1. Dogs and cats. Hudson used problems such as this one to determine children's difficulty with "How many more ——— than ——— are there" problems.

son (1980), for instance, gave children problems similar to that shown in Figure 12-1 and asked them one of the following two questions: (1) "How many more dogs than cats are there?" or (2) "Suppose the dogs all race over and each one tries to chase a cat! Will every dog have a cat to chase? How many dogs won't have a cat to chase?" Kindergarten children answered 25 percent of such problems correctly in response to the first question formulation, whereas they answered 96 percent correctly in response to the second type. Clearly the form of the question affects the problem representation and consequently the application of an appropriate solution schema. Question 1, cast in a more abstract manner, seems to lead to more problem-representation errors.

The question of level of abstraction of problem statement leads naturally to an issue of long-time concern in mathematics—word problems. Most of us remember the difficulty we had with "word" or "story" problems in algebra. Comprehending the text (an aspect of which Hudson's study touches on) as well as comprehending the appropriate mathematical schema apparently makes such problems especially difficult. Text comprehension as it relates to arithmetic problem solving recently has been the topic of careful study.

Text Comprehension and Arithmetic Problem Solving

Kintsch and van Dijk's (1978) theory of text processing (see Chapter 10) proposes that readers comprehend text by segmenting sentences into propositions that, depending on the text structure, are systematically related to one another. Kintsch and Greeno (1985), building on this work as well as on Riley et al.'s (1983), addressed this somewhat more general question: How does text processing (reading a word problem) interact with understanding the semantic information in the problem and the generation of appropriate mathematical schemata for problem solution? In other words, what is the interaction between text comprehension and problem solving in mathematics? Making sense out of a text apparently involves a set of schemata for reading comprehension that, in turn, are used to activate mathematics schemata.

Kintsch and Van Dijk (1978) suggest that memory representations of text have two components. The first is a propositional structure of information **specified** in the body of the text. The second component, a **situation model,** is derived from the text. Comprehending a word problem means constructing an appropriate conceptual representation from the text on which problem-solving processes can operate. For example, consider a "combine" arithmetic problem of the sort we described earlier:

Jill has three marbles. Jack has five marbles. How many marbles do they have altogether?

This problem provides information about two sets of marbles (Jill's and Jack's). It has an unknown—the superset (the sum, as we learned to call it) of the two given sets. Kintsch and Greeno (1985) suggest that one useful representation of this task involves the creation of a set schema.

TABLE 12-2.   A Schema for Representing Sets

Slot	Value
Object	(noun)
Quantity	(number), SOME, HOW MANY
Specification	(owner), (location), (time)
Role	start, transfer, result; superset, subset; largest, smallest, difference

From "Understand and Solving Arithmetic Word Problems," by W. L. Kintsch and J. G. Greeno, 1985, *Psychological Review, 92,* p. 114. Used by permission.

Table 12-2 represents a general set schema suitable for problems such as these. In the table, the **object** slot refers to a common noun labeling the sort of objects in the set. The **quantity** slot provides either the number of objects or a place holder (SOME, HOW MANY) denoting an indefinite statement or question. The **specification** slot distinguishes one set from others either by name of owner or by other description. Finally, the **role** slot provides a relational term that puts a particular set in the context or structure of the entire problem.

The slots and values given in Table 12-2 describe a set schema. Thus, for the three propositions contained in the first sentence in this problem (*Jill has three marbles.*), the schema slots and values (in the same order as Table 12-2) are: *object*—marbles; *quantity*—three; *specification*—Jill. Similarly, the three propositions in sentence 2 (*Jack has five marbles.*) take the form: *object*—marbles; *quantity*—five; *specification*—Jack. The last item in the schema (role) is unknown for these two sentences until the last sentence of the problem is read. To this point the problem solver has formed two sets, a set of three for Jill and a set of five for Jack. For the third sentence (*How many marbles do they have altogether?*), the propositions are: *object*—how many (marbles; *specification*—Jill and Jack together. At this point the *role* is determined (i.e., find the superset). This leads to an action strategy, making a superset for Jill and Jack combined.

The assignment of subset roles to both Jill's and Jack's marbles is not in the text statement, but is an inference the reader must make from the text. That is, the need to form these sets is not specifically mentioned in the problem. The necessity for such inferences intuitively suggests a potential source of error in correctly representing word problems. Finally, the solution to the problem is computed by a procedure such as a count-all strategy that counts the total of the two subsets taken together. The superset is formed.

This elongated description of "simple" processes—addition and subtraction—suggests the complexity of arithmetical learning and problem solving. The language of cognitive psychology—knowledge acquisition, problem representation, schemata—provides a way by which we may picture the task of mathematical problem representation. It seems clear that helping children achieve the schema of a set is vital to success in understanding problems such as those given in the examples above. Note, however, that carrying out such an activity does not mean children must acquire the **formal** language of sets and supersets, although at some point this may well be important for further instruction.

The schemata-formation process we've described should be especially useful for analyzing the problem solving of children who are having difficulty. A careful analysis of a child's representation of the schema for each part of a problem may well provide a diagnosis of a "bug" in the way the schema is formed. The specificity of this process can lead to very precise error determination and specific corrective action (see Brown & Burton, 1978, for a case in point).

Kintsch and Greeno (1985) assume that the propositions we've discussed are created as children read or hear a problem. Whenever a proposition triggers a set-building strategy, the set is formed and stored in working memory. Kintsch and Greeno also describe how this intricate process relates to working-memory capacity and the use of long-term memory. They conclude that models of text processing coupled with the hypotheses Riley et al. (1983) suggested about understanding word problems provide plausible descriptions of arithmetic word-problem solving.

A great deal of elaboration of these ideas will be necessary to provide a comprehensive description of addition and subtraction, however. Kintsch and Greeno point out that it is not enough simply to have knowledge (say, of the meaning of a superset). Problem solvers must have strategies for building such structures as they read a problem. In some cases, teachers may find that "arithmetic" problems actually are "reading" problems; they may need to provide support (such as reading a problem to a child) so attention may be focused on the arithmetic schemata activated by reading rather than on reading per se. How students in mathematics build such schemata is the topic of the next section of the chapter. In order to reflect the complexity of mathematics, however, we examine schemata formation in a more abstract type of mathematical problem solving—algebra word problems.

Problem Solving in Algebra

The schema approach described for arithmetic problem solving also has been applied to algebra word problems. For instance, researchers

(Hayes, Waterman, & Robinson, 1977; Hinsley et al., 1977; Mayer, 1982) have examined subjects who already have completed an algebra course for their recall of appropriate schemata for word-problem solution. Hinsley et al., for example, selected 76 algebra word problems from a high school algebra textbook, and gave them to a group of subjects who were asked to sort them into piles by problem type—with no definitions of problem type being supplied. Following the sort, the sorters were asked to describe the properties of the problems in each pile they had formed. The sorters found the task relatively easy—individually, each sorter identified about 14 problem categories of more than one problem each. Collectively, about 18 distinct problem categories were discovered that quite reliably sorted 64 of the 76 problems. Table 12-3 presents the 18 clusters of problems labeled by cluster and with a representative problem from each.

This table provides evidence that students quite readily categorize algebra problems, and do so with considerable agreement across persons about the categories. It also suggests that algebra word problems elicit a set of schemata common to most students who have completed an algebra course.

In a second experiment designed to more closely examine the schematic nature of student recall, Hinsley et al. chose problems from eight of the clusters shown in Table 12-3. They read each problem to students one part at a time. (Parts in most cases consisted of noun phrases of dependent clauses, but occasionally were entire sentences.) After each segment, the students were asked to attempt to categorize the problem and predict the nature of subsequent information in the problems as well as the question to be solved. Half of the subjects categorized the problems correctly into one of the eight clusters after hearing less than one-fifth of the text, in some cases requiring only 5 percent of the text before correctly categorizing the problem. For other problems as much as 31 percent of the text was required for categorization, but early correct classification of the problems was the rule. Apparently, much of the knowledge algebra problem solvers have about word problems is stored in clear and stylized schemata. Further keywords in the problems elicit appropriate schemata. Given our earlier discussion of keywords and arithmetic performance, however, it is not entirely clear that this finding is encouraging. Instead, students may be recalling schemata before they have enough information for a correct choice. Hinsley et al. quoted one subject who, after hearing the three words *A river steamer* form a problem, said: "It's going to be one of those river things with upstream, downstream and still water. You are going to compare . . ." (p. 97).

Further research by Hinsley et al. provided evidence consistent with Riley et al.'s findings (1983) that the schemata for differing types of problems direct the course of problem solving. Some subjects appeared to be

Table 12-3.   Problems Representative of Hinsley, Hayes, and Simon's 18 Clusters

1.	Triangle	Bob drives 1 mile west down a road and then 3 miles north to a convenience store. Jane starts at the same point but takes a diagonal road that dead ends at the convenience store. How far did Jane drive?
2.	Distance/rate/time	Two airplanes are being tested at the same time. The Silver Jet starts a timed course at 10:00 A.M. and averages 550 miles per hour. The new Purple Screamer starts 15 minutes later than the Silver Jet and averages 700 miles per hour. At what distance from the start will the Purple Screamer catch the Silver Jet?
3.	Averages	Driving west between two towns, a car's speed is 55 miles per hour. On the return trip, the driver breaks the law and drives at 62 miles per hour. Find the average speed for the whole trip.
4.	Scale converson	Robert is trying to understand two different scales of weight. In one, he weighs 150 VWs. In the other, he weighs 325 Zogs. Given the VW and Zog units are linearly related, find an expression that allows the conversion of Zogs to VWs.
5.	Ratio	A new softball league must choose between two types of balls. It is known that the distance a ball will travel when hit with a bat is directly related to its volume. If one of the new balls has a radius that is 9/10 the radius of the other one, what is the ratio of their volumes?
6.	Interest	A certain credit union charges 9.4 percent interest on automobile loans, compounded annually. How much will a $10,000 loan actually cost a consumer if the loan is paid off over five years in equal payments?
7.	Area	The town square is bordered by a sidewalk that is 180 feet long on one side and 320 feet long on the other side. What is the area of the town square?
8.	Maximum/minimum	A building contractor estimates that his profit p in putting up an office building x stories high is given by the equation $p = 2x**2 + 88x$. How many stories would be in the most profitable of buildings erected by this contractor?
9.	Mixture	Farmer Jones wants to maximize his yield in soybean production this year. He wants to plant both a drought-resistant variety of bean and one that is resistant to the fungus caused by too much moisture. He has determined that these should be mixed so that 30 percent of his seed is of the drought-resistant variety and 20 percent of the fungus-resistant variety. The remainder of the seeds will be the cheapest variety he can find. If he intends to plant a minimum of 235 bushels of the drought-resistant variety, how many bushels of the other varieties will he need to plant to maintain his mixture?

Table 12-3. *(Continued)*

10.	River current	A motorboat races 50 miles downstream in the same time it takes to travel 36 miles upstream. If the motorboat had been in still water (e.g., a lake), its engines would have driven it at 40 miles per hour. What is the rate of the river current?
11.	Probability	A gambler has been forced to use a perfectly balanced coin to make his last wager of the day. He has bet that he can flip the coin three times in a row and come up with heads. We don't think he can and have bet against him. What is the probability that he actually can obtain three heads in a row?
12.	Number	The 1s digit is four times the digit in the 10s place. If both added together make 10, what is the original number?
13.	Work	Ms. Smith and Ms. Jones are factory workers. It takes Ms. Smith 30 seconds less to pack a crate than it does Ms. Jones. How many more crates can Ms. Smith pack than Ms. Jones in a typical eight-hour day?
14.	Navigation	A hot-air balloonist leaves his recovery team and flies south at 13 miles per hour. If the propane tank for his heater (used to keep the air in the balloon hot enough to fly) is enough for six hours of flying and the recovery team (because of starts, stops, and the many zigzags needed to keep up with the balloonist) can average 30 miles per hour, how far south can the balloonist fly if he intends to land in sight of his recovery team?
15.	Progressions	Two joggers set out from two different houses 12 miles apart. If Jane average seven minutes a mile and Robert averages 10 minutes a mile, when will they meet?
16.	Progressions-2	Find the sum of the first 32 even integers.
17.	Physics	A baseball is thrown at 98 miles per hour. If the pitcher released the ball at 5 feet above the ground and the force of gravity pulls the ball to the ground at the rate of 1.22 feet per second, how far will the ball travel before it hits the ground?
18.	Exponentials	The area of each green in a golf course decreases from hole number 1 to hole number 18. If the area of each is .90 of the one before and first green has an area of 500 square feet, what is the total area of all the greens?

This table is based on "From Words to Equations: Meaning and Representation in Algebra Word Problems," by D. A. Hinsley, J. R. Hayes, and H. A. Simon, 1977, in P. A. Carpenter and M. A. Just (Eds.), *Cognitive Processes in Comprehension,* Hillsdale, NJ: Erlbaum.

formulating the problem as they read it, since immediately on completion of reading, they provided either a formula for solution or the solution itself. The subjects seemed to have used early parts of the problem as cues for use of a particular solution schema stored in memory.

Most of us recall—sometimes painfully—our first encounter with algebra "story" problems such as those in Table 12-3. Such problems in algebra typically follow a brief initial period of instruction in algebra providing basic information dealing with equations, unknowns, and so forth, and in most cases follows seven to eight years of instruction in various aspects of arithmetic. Thus, story problems would appear to be built on a substantial knowledge base of prior instruction in mathematics. It is unfortunate that the knowledge base is such that in many cases algebra word problems are perceived as "new" rather than growing out of and extending prior schemata.

Apparently, in algebra word problems the situation where a representation of the problem must be constructed by the reader while reading a problem may make the task "new" and difficult. Student performance with algebra word problems, coupled with expressed dislike for such tasks, suggests that the issues raised by Kintsch and Greeno (1985) are real. That is, the dual task of reading (comprehending) the text of an algebra problem and at the same time constructing the appropriate schema for problem solution is difficult for many students. A correct representation of a problem is, of course, critical since it leads to a particular, appropriate solution schema. In some arithmetic curricula, however, students may have little experience with comprehension processes such as those described by Kintsch and Greeno. Story problem solving is likely to be difficult unless algebra students have had extensive prior work with text comprehension and mathematical problem solving.

Mayer (1981) analyzed algebra word problems in a number of high school algebra textbooks. He found over 100 problem types, with many of them being variations on the problem categories found by Hinsley et al. For instance, Mayer found 12 different kinds of distance/rate/time problems. He also discovered that problems differed in frequency of appearance in the textbooks, and when he asked students to read and then recall a series of eight story problems, they remembered high-frequency problems more successfully (Mayer, 1982). It would seem that students store story schemata for common algebra problems in long-term memory.

Silver (1981), in an interesting application of these studies of schema development, asked seventh-graders to sort 16 story problems into piles, and then compared the sorting performance of good and poor problem solvers. Good problem solvers tended to sort the stories based on some underlying algebra schema structure. The poor problem solvers, however, tended to group the stories based on the surface structure of the

problems. This finding is consistent with those reported earlier (Schoenfeld & Herrmann, 1982; Silver, 1979) that distinguish between semantic and syntactic understanding of mathematical problems.

Thus, one may conclude from these studies that problem solution is
related to the formation of a wide variety of problem schemata types.
However, Mayer's (1981) finding of a variety of problems types (as many
as 12) within a problem category suggests that rather than needing to
learn and store perhaps 16–18 clusters of schemata, algebra problem
solvers must develop and store as many schemata as there are varieties of
problems within a cluster. According to Mayer (1981), this may be as
many as 100 types. Alternatively, a problem solver might develop a production system for each cluster of problem types that has sufficient flexibility to deal with variations of problems within the cluster.

Explaining Algebra Errors

The implication that students may need to store a very large number
of schemata seems disconcerting. If algebra problems demand a new
schema for each subtype, then sheer numbers make it likely that not all
will be learned. Furthermore, as the size of the pool of schemata increases, the chances of learning and storing faulty schemata (bugs) also
must increase. Reed's work on algebra errors suggests that this may
indeed be the case.

Using
Inappropriate
Schemata

Just as appropriate schemata can help a problem solver represent and
solve word problems, so can inappropriate schemata hinder correct problem representation and solution. S. K. Reed and his colleagues (Reed,
1984, 1987; Reed, Dempster, & Ettinger, 1985) have carried out a number of studies of students' ability to estimate answers to algebra word
problems. Consider the following problem from Reed (1984):

> *Flying east between two cities that are 300 miles apart, a plane's speed is
> 150 mph. On the return trip, it flies at 300 mph. Find the average speed
> for the round trip.* (Answer, 200 mph.)

Working with college students, Reed (1984) found that 84 percent estimated 225 mph as the average speed. Only 9 percent gave the correct
response. Why the high failure rate? Student responses clearly showed
the problem elicited the average-speed schemata (see Table 12-3, number 3) that Hinsley et al. (1977) and Mayer (1981) had discussed. The
overwhelming majority of students, however, saw the problem as one of
a *simple* average (i.e., Find the sum of the two speeds and compute the
mean; 450/2 = 225 mph.). In other words, for many students the prob-

lem elicited a schema (find the simple average) that yields an incorrect response. Note that implied in the problem is the fact that the plane flew twice as long at the slower speed. Thus, it took 3 hours to fly the 600 miles, and hence the average speed was 200 mph. Many students, unfortunately, apparently failed to make that inference.

As the work of Kintsch and Greeno (1985) and Riley et al. (1983) suggests, the need to develop such inferences from text may activate inappropriate schemata. To test that hypothesis, Reed gave the following version of the same problem to a group of students:

> *A plane flies 150 mph for 2 hours and 300 mph for 1 hour. Find its average speed.*

Note that in this version the fact that the plane flew slowly for 2 hours is made explicit. Forty percent of students gave the correct response in this version and only 19 percent chose the incorrect 225 mph response. Although a substantial number still did not solve the problem correctly, making the problem more explicit apparently evoked the appropriate schema for estimating a weighted average in a much larger number of students.

Making Faulty Estimates   A major question growing out of Reed's (1984) research was students' ability to estimate the appropriateness of answers. For mathematics teachers and tutors, evaluating the appropriateness of an answer is almost axiomatic. Yet, Reed's data suggest that few students have adequate schemata for making useful estimates. This may be illustrated more clearly with an example of a "work schema" problem such as the following:

> *It takes Bill 12 hours to cut a large lawn. Bob can cut the same lawn in 8 hours. How long does it take them to cut the lawn when they both work together?*

Thirty percent of students estimated the simple average—10 hours. Note the inconsistency—this answer implies that it takes longer for the two boys to mow the lawn together than for Bob to do it alone! These students apparently lacked an intuitive schema for when and how to compute weighted averages. Furthermore, they didn't seem to have an "estimation schema" for evaluating the reasonableness of their estimates. Reed has pointed out the value of estimation as a tool for detecting a student's intuitive problem-solving schema. He further has argued that students develop schemata for a particular type of algebra problem that translate into an algorithm for solution. If the student does not estimate well, then Reed takes this as at least partial evidence for lack of understanding of the algorithm; that is, it is applied by rote rather than meaningfully (Carpenter, Corbitt, Keponer, Lindquist, & Reys, 1980).

Failure to Use
Analogies
Effectively

One way to increase the meaningfulness of an algorithm is to show how it relates to an already more completely understood algorithm. That is, new learning may occur more readily if it is seen as analogous to previously mastered concepts. For instance, Gick and Holyoak (1980, 1983) used analogies to help problem solvers represent tasks. They did so by giving general problems (and solutions) to subjects, who then were asked to solve related problems. Although the procedure generally was helpful, many students didn't use the first problem to solve the second until they were given an explicit hint that it was valuable for solving the second problem.

S. K. Reed et al. (1985) hypothesized that in a domain-specific area such as algebra word problem solution with a limited number of problem types, analogies might prove more directly useful. Thus, they predicted that solvers given a practice problem from a particular cluster of problems would use information from that problem to solve similar problems from the same cluster. Reed et al. carried out an elaborate set of experiments to test this hypothesis, but the results were, in the main, disappointing. Students were able to use a practice problem as an analogy for solving subsequent **equivalent** problems, but only when the practice problem was carefully analyzed and summarized for them. When students were given problems **similar** but not equivalent to the practice problems, they failed to see them as analogous, and could not solve them. Instead, most students attempted to match the solution of the practice problem to the new problem exactly. This resulted in failure, of course, since the problems were not identical.

Such careful research efforts suggest that reducing errors in algebra word problem solving is difficult. Apparently, students' schemata often are incompletely understood or stored so specifically they are not perceived as useful for solving other problems. Further, if a match *is* made with their stored schema, solvers often appear to use it almost by rote; thus, problems not identical to stored schemata often are not solved.

To summarize, a schema-based approach to mathematics may be useful both to explain learning and as a means for diagnosing errors. Learners may or may not use schemata effectively, however. In arithmetic, schema approaches seem to work well. In contrast, the research in algebra suggests that although students do form schemata, the schemata by themselves often are not sufficient for problem success. One critical difference between the two subject areas may be the number of schemata that must be learned. Another difference may be the extent to which the schemata are learned meaningfully. The evidence supplied by Reed and his colleagues suggests that in too many cases algebra instruction produces rote acquisition of schemata that cannot be applied to problems even slightly different from those on which the schemata were based. Such findings have broad implications for the teaching of mathematics.

Cognition and Mathematics Instruction

In a chapter titled "Strategic Teaching in Mathematics," Lindquist (1987) asserts: "Just as there is a need for a new definition of reading, there is a need for cognitively based mathematics programs" (p. 112). In keeping with the theme of this book, our discussion of arithmetic and algebra in this chapter has taken a cognitive approach. In both areas, a cognitive perspective appears to provide useful conceptualizations. Thus, the thrust of a cognitive approach in mathematics is to argue for treating all of mathematics instruction as cognitive and, in particular, as problem solving. This does *not* lead to the inclusion of a chapter on problem solving in mathematics, but rather to make problem solving the instructional method for all topics in the mathematics curriculum. Is this approach viable? Is it necessary?

Carpenter (1985) asserts that prior to formal instruction in arithmetic, ". . . almost all children exhibit reasonably sophisticated and appropriate problem-solving skills in solving simple word problems. They attend . . . they model the problem; they invent more efficient procedures . . ." (p. 37). He goes on to say: "Contrast this with performance several years later, when many children solve any problem by choosing a single arithmetic operation based on surface details of the problem" (p. 37). In other words, he argues, as a result of traditional instruction children abandon their earlier problem-solving approach for a more-mechanical application of rote skills. Carpenter believes that traditional instruction teaches young children that mathematics is merely an exercise in manipulation of symbols and does *not* relate it to problem solving. Unfortunately, acquiring that belief may create tremendous obstacles in learning mathematics. Once students divorce mathematics from problem solving, difficulties in later course work are inevitable.

Is Carpenter correct? By the eighth or ninth grade, many students do appear to apply algebra schemata in highly specific, inflexible ways, suggestive of a rote process. Furthermore, analysis of NAEP (National Assessment of Educational Progress) (1983) data for children aged 9 and 13 shows actual **declines** in the performance of tasks requiring thinking or understanding. In fact, the increase in performance from 9 to 13 is almost entirely accounted for by increased accuracy of performance on "routine" exercises. Thus, the body of evidence already cited provides considerable support for Carpenter's contention.

At the same time, the research in arithmetic problem solving (e.g., Riley et al., 1983) provides reasonable evidence that possession of more powerful and **flexible** schemata leads to improved problem solving. These schemata—not computational skills—permit problem solving. Although increasing knowledge leads to more powerful mathematics performance, the critical knowledge appears to be at the level of strategy—schemata—rather than in mathematics "facts."

The production system illustratied in Box 12-1 represents a schema for addition that includes an array of procedures and subprocedures linked in a particular sequence. Like any procedure, of course, this production system *can* be taught essentially by rote. The challenge for all teachers and, in the context of this chapter, the challenge to mathematics teachers especially, is to teach the conceptual web of information underlying the procedures in such a way that Carpenter's criticism does not hold. The problem-solving approach young children bring to the learning of mathematics must be nurtured and built on, rather than extinguished (see Hiebert, 1986).

In 1980, the National Council of Teachers of Mathematics (NCTM) proposed that problem solving be the focus of mathematics instruction. The references cited in this chapter, virtually all to research carried out since then, suggest that this proposal has had a great impact on mathematics research. The view of simple addition and subtraction as problem solving rather than algorithm memorization is a case in point. On the other hand, the limited success algebra students have with word problems that do not match their stored schemata suggest that all too many students' schemata have been acquired by rote. Such schemata lack flexibility and lead to the development of production systems appropriate to only a few of the wide variety of mathematics problems. Virtually all mathematics instruction emphasizes the development of procedures. Although procedures (production systems) are necessary, Reed's work with algebra suggests that one undesirable outcome of such an emphasis is the development of highly specific schemata and procedures that apply to only a small class of problems. From this perspective, students faced with algebra problems requiring procedures slightly different from their rote-memorized ones quickly display the inadequacy of their problem-solving skills. Such inadequate problem solving is not inevitable, however. According to S. K. Reed (1984; see also Chipman, 1988), detailed analyses of the relevant semantic features of algebra word problems would help many students develop a richer and more-flexible conceptual knowledge that in turn would lead to the formation of more-flexible problem schemata and procedures. Similarly, a study by Jones, Krouse, Feorene, and Saferstein (1985) provides evidence that an instructional sequence dealing with different types of problems within a cluster, coupled with emphasis on the relevant semantic features that show the similarities *and* the differences between problems, significantly improves student problem solving.

In sum, accurate and flexible performance in algebra, like that of arithmetic performance, grows out of the acquisition of a web of conceptual understandings. This conceptual structure in turn leads to the acquisition of schemata on which solution procedures can be built. Students' algebra word problem performance suggests that mathematics instruction must provide for clear **semantic** understandings of problems. Only when there is understanding will there be the development of a large set of schematic structures adaptable to a wide variety of problems. Rote memorization of a limited number of schemata yields predictable results—a focus on surface features of problems and, most particularly, a failure to solve even slightly different problems.

Implications

What do cognitive approaches to learning mathematics imply for mathematics instruction? The following suggestions summarize current thinking.

1. All mathematics should be taught from a problem-solving perspective. Specific facts and concepts, procedures, algorithms, and schemata should be learned in the context of problem solving, not as isolated items.

2. Mathematics instruction should focus on process and structure, not answers. Students need to be encouraged to examine their own thinking, their own work—searching not simply for right answers, but for reasons **why** a procedure is or is not useful in a particular situation. The lack of flexibility many students exhibit in solving algebra problems suggests that they have learned algorithms only by rote.

3. Teachers need to spend more time verbally modeling thoughtful problem-solving behavior. They especially need to detail the processes they use to solve a problem and show the importance of the processes. Teachers also need to make explicit the **sequence** of thinking as well as the relationships among bits of semantic information in problems that validate that thinking. Along with the processes leading to "correct" solutions, they should demonstrate potential errors in solution strategy and how such errors can occur.

4. Students need more exercises that require the verbalization and, if possible, visualization of processes used in solution attempts. When mistakes occur and students "get stuck," teachers can enhance problem solving by asking them to examine the existing problem-solving process and to look for errors or new approaches rather than providing the "correct" answer. In other words, teachers should be coaches rather than solution givers.

5. In any domain, students construct meaning from their experience. Although agreement on how this construction takes place is far from

universal, the evidence for meaning construction is quite clear. Consequently, instructional techniques that emphasize constructive proceses are likely to enhance student learning.

6. Processes students use to construct a problem representation are a source of valuable information revealing both strengths and weaknesses. Errors are an especially rich source of information teachers can use to search for specific misunderstandings. Close examination of student problem-solving processes may reveal errors attributable to a student's lack of strategic (schematic), factual, or even linguistic knowledge. The work on arithmetic "bugs" indicates that errors cannot be taken lightly—superficial examination of error patterns may lead teachers to inappropriate conclusions about the nature of student problem-solving performance.

7. The common practice of "grouping" together all problems solvable with a particular schema seems ill advised. A better practice is to provide a mixture of problems. Such a mixture gives students practice in recognizing different problem types within and across problem clusters. Exposure to a variety of problems leads both to discrimination between problem types and to appropriate generalization of schemata.

8. Implicit in all of the preceding suggestions is the requirement for teachers who are well prepared in mathematics and comfortable with the topic. Children enter elementary school with well-developed and usable problem-solving skills that must be enhanced by a skilled teacher rather than extinguished.

Summary

A major purpose of this chapter was to demonstrate the value of the information-processing perspective for understanding how students learn mathematics. An extensive body of research on arithmetic operations such as counting, addition, and subtraction has shown that success in arithmetic seems to depend on the acquisition of a body of conceptual knowledge that is organized (translated) into schemata. These schemata lead to a set of procedures (algorithms). Treating the content of addition and subtraction and other arithmetic operations as problems to be solved rather than as sets of facts to be stored in memory appears to be a productive approach to the learning of arithmetic content.

An examination of how students solve algebra word problems suggests that difficulties stem from students' failures to learn flexible and powerful schemata. Without such schemata, students do not develop procedures adaptable to a wide range of problems. Many students appear to acquire procedures applicable to only a very narrow range of problems. Consequently, when they are faced with problems beyond that range, they have no basis for understanding the task. Carpenter (1985), in a trenchant critique of mathematics instruction, argued that traditional instruction (which is focused on content acquisition rather than problem solving) turns productive, problem-solving primary school children into rigid, unproductive middle school and secondary school students. Although Carpenter may be accused of overstating the facts of the matter, there is little doubt that mathematics instruction focusing on schemata development and problem solving is likely to be more effective than methods based on rote learning of "math facts."

CHAPTER 13

Problem Solving in Science

The goals of science are ambitious: to understand the physical, biological, and social worlds. Such complex goals present great challenges to science teachers. Helping students acquire an understanding of these three worlds and of the methodology of science is a formidable task.

Problem solving is an integral part of attaining the goals described above. For example, to fully appreciate the methodology of science (the development and testing of hypotheses), one must learn science as a problem-solving process. Unfortunately, however, many elementary and secondary school science textbooks place a premium on vocabulary development rather than problem solving. Indeed, S. Carey (1986) argues that junior and senior high school science texts introduce more new vocabulary per page than foreign-language texts! She goes on to say that "science as a vocabulary lesson is a recipe for disaster, especially if understanding is the goal" (p. 1124). Understanding science *is* more than memorizing vocabulary. Understanding science means using its concepts to solve problems—problems not only from the science curriculum and the science laboratory, but also in real life.

Recognizing that domain-specific knowledge is essential to problem solving and that general problem-solving strategies are ineffective in knowledge-rich domains quickly led psychologists to the choice of science as a knowledge domain in which to study problem solving (Bhaskar & Simon, 1977; Shavelson, 1973; Simon & Simon, 1978). Early studies in this area involved collaboration of cognitive scientists and college science instructors, particularly in introductory college physics courses. Thus, the early research focused on several areas of classical physics (mechanics, kinematics, statics), chosen because the areas are clearly specified and the basic information, principles, and criteria for effective problem-solving performance all are well defined.

To examine the effects of differing amounts of domain-specific information on problem-solving success, researchers (e.g., Chi, Feltovich, &

Glaser, 1981; Larkin et al., 1980; Simon & Simon, 1978) contrasted the performance of experts (typically, college physics instructors) and novices (undergraduate physics majors). They made the reasonable assumption that extensive physics knowledge differences existed between the two groups and, further, that this knowledge (expertise) difference would be reflected in different problem-solving processes. To test this assumption, physics problem-solving protocols (see Chapter 7) were obtained from novices and experts. Strikingly different patterns of performance emerged when the protocols were analyzed. As expected, experts and novices differed widely in extent of knowledge, but they differed in other ways as well. One startling difference was the finding that many novices had a number of erroneous beliefs or preconceptions that made understanding basic physics experiments difficult.

Naive Science Conceptions

McCloskey, Caramazza, and Green (1980) asked college students to respond to situations like that shown in Figure 13-1. They then used students' reactions to these situations to determine the extent to which they understood Newtonian (classic) physics. As you can see in the figure, for example, students encountered two drawings of a coiled tube. Each drawing shows a marble leaving the "exit" of a coiled tube. The students' task was to determine which line (straight or curved) best depicts what would happen if someone rolled a marble through the tube. As you know, one of the solutions (the straight line) represents what the laws of physics say will happen in the situation and, indeed, what actually will happen.

Surprisingly, McCloskey et al. found that even students who had taken a course in high school physics gave answers that showed naive conceptions of physical laws. For example, on the coil-and-marble task shown in Figure 13-1, one-third of the students indicated that the ball would continue in a curved line. Of course, such an outcome violates Newton's first law (inertia), which states that any object continues either in a state of rest or in uniform, straight-line motion unless acted on by another force.

The errors observed by McCloskey et al. and those reported in a similar study that used gravity problems (Champagne, Klopfer, & Anderson, 1980) seem to show that incorrect responses represent people's naive, "intuitive" conceptions of physics. Such naive conceptions are not isolated events restricted to a few unusual physics problems, however. McCloskey (1983) has argued that people develop remarkably well-articulated naive theories of scientific phenomena on the basis of their

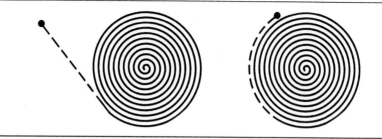

FIGURE 13-1.   Balls leaving coiled tubes. McCloskey et al. (1980) used figures like this one to determine students' understanding of Newtonian physics.

everyday experiences. These theories provide people with causal explanations for how the world operates (see McCloskey, 1983, p. 321).

The ordinary experiences of everyday life (even prior schooling) are a
source of data that seem to support naive theories. Consequently, the
presence of well-developed but incorrect theories coupled with everyday
experiences that seem consistent with these theories leads to a set of
beliefs about how the world operates that is very difficult to change. In
fact, many students find their naive concepts superior to the abstract
and, in many cases, seemingly counterintuitive principles of Newtonian
physics.

To illustrate, Clement (1983) presented data on naive beliefs about
motion involving a coin toss. In this problem, an object such as the block in
Figure 13-2 is tossed into the air and caught by the tosser. The problem
solver is asked to draw a diagram using arrows to show the direction of the
force acting on the block at any particular point. The left side of Figure 13-
2 shows an expert's response; the right side shows a typical incorrect
response.

The "simple" expert drawing (see Figure 13-2) appears to ignore (and
hence contradict) the intuitive, and incorrect, "upward motion" illustrated in the right part of the figure—what students call the "force of the
throw." Clement (1983) reported that only 12 percent of engineering
students responded correctly to this question prior to taking a college
physics course. He gave the same problem to two more-experienced
groups of students. Only 28 percent of a group who had **completed** the
introductory course in mechanics (where motion is a prominent topic)
responded correctly. Furthermore, only 30 percent of a second group,
who had completed two semesters of physics (including mechanics),
solved the problem correctly. Although these data suggest that instruction improves class performance somewhat, a remarkably high percentage (more than 70 percent) continued to display naive responses. Teach-

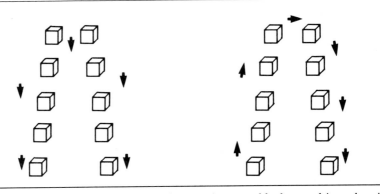

FIGURE 13-2.   Conceptions of the force acting on a block tossed into the air (arrows indicate direction of force). An expert's conception of the force acting on a block tossed into the air is presented on the left. The right side is a novice's response. This task is similar to that used by Clement (1982).

ing effectiveness aside, these data suggest the difficulty teachers may have in overcoming naive beliefs.

Another example of the naive concepts students have about the workings of the world can be seen in Osborne and Freyberg's (1985) study in which, among other questions related to biology, children were asked whether certain objects were plants. Amazingly, only 60 percent of the 12- and 13-year-olds in the study identified carrots as plants and only 80 percent of the 14- and 15-year-olds agreed that oak trees were plants. In fact, 10 percent of the 12- and 13-year-olds thought that grass was not a plant. It was not clear from the study what the dissenting children thought carrots, oaks, and grass were, but there is no question that their conceptual systems related to plants were rudimentary.

Still another instance of poorly developed conceptual systems can be seen in an experiment reported by Osborne and Freyberg that focused on a typical elementary school science problem, electrical flow. In this experiment, Osborne and Freyberg presented children with a simple electrical circuit problem (see Figure 13-3) in which a battery was used to light a lamp. When the students were asked to show how the electric current flows in the circuit, about 35 percent of the 10- to 14-year-old participants reported that current in **both** wires flowed **from** the battery **to** the light. In fact, only 80 percent of the 17- to 18-year-old participants were able to make the correct response and indicate that current flows through the wire in one direction with the same current level in both wires. Further, when asked to explain the amount of current in various parts of the circuit, many students erroneously stated that since the lightbulb emits light and heat, some of the current is "used up." There-

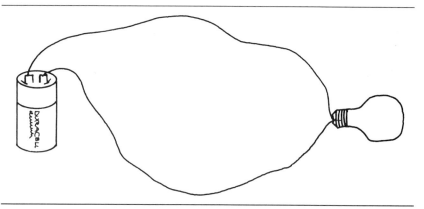

FIGURE 13-3.   A simple electrical circuit. A figure such as this one was shown to children in Osborne and Freyberg's study.

fore, these students concluded, there is less current going back to the battery than leaving it.

A final experiment taken from Osborne and Freyberg's volume will serve to help us close this section. In this instance (see Figure 13-4) students were asked questions about the physics concept "force." Please stop reading at this point and indicate the forces acting on the football in Figure 13-4 at points A, B, and C. The rest of our description depends on your understanding the figure.

Finished? Good. According to Osborne and Freyberg, the answers to such questions provide a basis for distinguishing between students who understand "force" in Newtonian terms and those who have naive conceptions of "force." In their experiment, of 800 13- to 17-year-olds, fewer than 22 percent **at any age level** chose the correct (Newtonian) response pattern (down, down, down; after the ball has been thrown up, the only force acting on it is gravity). Astonishingly, three-quarters of the high school aged students who participated in Osborne and Freyberg's study—even those who had completed a physics course—could not correctly identify the forces acting on such an object.

The overwhelming evidence indicates that students not only **lack** scientific information, but they also bring misinformation that affects the manner in which they try to understand problems. Students' misconceptions tend to be very powerful—in some areas negating direct evidence they observe in experimental and classroom settings. Some researchers (e.g., see McDermott, 1984) argue that this misinformation is more than a simple set of false beliefs. Instead, they argue that most students lack a coordinated and consistent conceptual system for understanding the world. They appear to have a set of incomplete and uncoordinated sche-

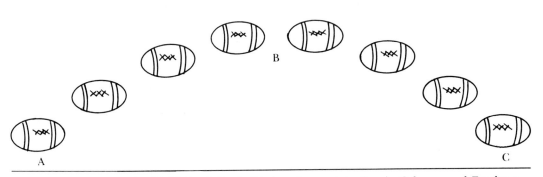

FIGURE 13-4. A football being thrown into the air. Osborne and Freyberg employed a figure such as this one to test students' knowledge of force. The students were asked to indicate the direction of force acting on the football at points A, B, and C.

mata that arise primarily from unguided experience—what we may refer to as uncontrolled observation.

Other researchers, however, hold alternative views that suggest the presence of well-organized but incorrect conceptual systems. For example, S. Carey's (1985) analysis of 10-year-olds' intuitive biology theories suggests that children have rich conceptual frameworks. These frameworks are not simply fragmentary, unconnected false beliefs. Instead, they are conceptual systems—incorrect, but nevertheless reasonably coherent and consistent with typical real-life observations.

Regardless of which view of children's misinformation is correct, there is no question that students bring considerable erroneous information to science classes. This information must be unlearned before appropriate conceptual systsems can be acquired. Unfortunately, since students' incorrect conceptual systems are the result of a life's worth of personal, unguided observations of the world, these systems may be strongly held and difficult to change. Teachers must **expect** children to have incorrect conceptions and, indeed, search them out. Since children's beliefs have developed out of their life experiences, children are not likely to abandon them unless they are presented with instruction that shows that "new" ideas are "more intelligible, more plausible, and more fruitful" than old, incorrect beliefs (Osborne & Freyberg, 1985, p. 48).

To summarize, as a consequence of long periods of informal knowledge accumulation, many and perhaps most students acquire misconceptions about science that formal instruction may not always modify. The acquisition of new and more-appropriate scientific conceptual systems is likely to be slow. Moreover, the process is more than simply correcting errors. You can demonstrate the tenacity of incorrect belief systems by giving any of the examples used by McCloskey et al. (1980) or Osborne and Freyberg (1985) to naive adults (i.e., your friends in other classes). If the problems are presented in a nonauthoritarian manner, denial of Newtonian explanations will be common, and existing belief systems will be maintained in the face of evidence of the "correct" answers. Indeed, many "naive" scientists appear to trust their intuitions rather more than they do "laboratory experiments" that appear to contradict those intuitions.

Thus expert–novice differences are much more complex than simple differences in the amount of information people possess, and teachers must be aware of "intuitive" (and often incorrect) science knowledge students bring with them. Substantial instructional time must be used to present students with situations that expose their naive beliefs so that they may be confronted.

Confronting Naive Beliefs

In contrast to mathematics, where much of the content is first taught in school settings, children enter school with a wealth of science knowledge based on uncontrolled observations made as part of their daily experience. Children learn physical "laws" as they throw a ball, do a "sit-up," play on a slide, turn on a lamp, and so on. However, these uncontrolled experiences permit the development of inadequate, incomplete, and often-incorrect conceptions of how the world operates. Much of this knowledge is tacit, unarticulated information embedded in the actions of the child. These conceptions (schemata) are stored in memory and, quite naturally, provide the basis for explanations when children are faced with science "problems." Teachers not only should expect to find these naive beliefs, but they must find ways of seeking them out before systematic instruction in science can begin.

The best way to eliminate naive, incorrect beliefs is to expose them and confront them directly (Resnick, 1983). Such confrontation, though, requires more than the mere teaching of vocabulary. Instead, instruction in science must be experience-based. One possibility is laboratory experience.

Several laboratory-based approaches to teaching science have been developed over the years, but none have been remarkably successful. Particularly at the elementary level, such programs (e.g., "Science: A Process Approach"—SAPA) have failed because they did not include the three essential ingredients for adequate instruction in science. That is, these programs haven't worked because (1) teachers themselves do not understand the concepts, (2) laboratory materials are insufficient, and (3) the schools have not committed enough regular curricular time to laboratory instruction. Regrettably, "quick fixes" are not on the horizon. Instead, improvement in science instruction (particularly at the elementary level) will require a long-term effort.

What needs to be done to improve the quality of laboratory-based instruction in the schools? We recommend a three-pronged approach involving teacher-training institutions, the public schools, and the schools' relations with the public. First and foremost, the requirements of students studying to become elementary school teachers must be drastically revised. Currently, many colleges and universities allow elementary-education students to complete their undergraduate degrees with no more than one "real" science course. Science requirements must be increased. Elementary school teachers must attain a basic level of literacy in biological, physical, and earth sciences that will allow them to model the kind of expert conceptions science instruction requires. It may very well be that new college-level science curricula will need to be developed nationwide—curricula designed not for those who strive to become scientists themselves, but for those who must have the expert knowledge necessary to teach science to our children.

A second point focuses on the schools and their relationships with their communities. Essentially, the schools—faculty, administration, school boards—will have to educate their communities on science instruction matters. Such educational efforts will have to be every bit as rigorous as the changes we prescribe for higher education. The reason is economic. Laboratory-based educational experiences are expensive. The monies needed to provide laboratory experiences must come from taxpayers. The schools and those who support the schools must begin an education campaign to provide a solid base of intellectual and economic support in the community—the best-prepared teachers will come up short if they do not have the laboratory facilities and materials needed for instruction.

Our third point also has a clear school orientation. Science instruction must be given **time.** The most excellent teachers employing the finest methods and materials will not succeed if science is not a regular part of each child's school day. Sadly, the one area of instruction most likely to be cut out of the elementary school day is science (Kowalski, Glover, & Krug, in press).

One final issue also needs to be addressed. The widespread misconceptions about scientific knowledge suggest that we need to examine school curricula carefully. If students who have been through a year of physics still cannot understand simple force problems, we are doing something wrong. A reasonable approach to this issue is to begin by examining the problem-solving behavior of expert problem solvers in science and from these observations derive goals for curricula that teach science.

Problem-Solving Expertise in Science

Clearly, few elementary or secondary school students will achieve the expertise of physicists, chemists, or biologists. Nor, we think, is it reasonable to think that they should. Still, elementary and secondary school science instruction, at a minimum, should help students progress toward expertise—toward becoming expert science problem solvers. But just what are the characteristics of expert problem solvers in science?

Studies of Expert–Novice Differences

Studies of experts show that they possess substantially more information than novices (e.g., Chi, Glaser, & Rees, 1982). Experts also solve problems much more quickly than novices. According to D. P. Simon and Simon (1978), for example, time differences to solution for experts and novices are of the order of 4:1. This suggests, of course, that experts, even though they have far more relevant knowledge to search in memory, are much more efficient at searching a particular solution space. Furthermore, studies of solution time (e.g., Larkin, 1979, 1980) reveal that experts' recall is "chunked." For example, a number of equations all linked to a particular physics principle may be recalled by an expert in a single configuration or "bundle," followed by a pause, and then the recall of another "bundle" of equations appropriate to another relevant principle. Novices, in contrast, show no such chunking patterns. The presence of bursts of recall among experts suggests, consistent with our discussion of mathematics problem solving, the presence of meaningfully linked schemata elicited as "bundles" when appropriate problem demands are encountered (but see Chi et al., 1982).

Research contrasting experts and novices in science also has revealed some differences that are harder to describe. For instance, a significant difference between novices and experts is experts' use of what Larkin (1977) has referred to as "qualitative analysis" and what Simon and Simon (1978) called "physical intuition." In both cases, the authors were referring to the development of rather elaborate problem representations, often representations that include the construction of a sketch or other physical version of the problem. Such elaborate problem representations, whether visual or verbal or both, typically are constructed as a first (or early) step in problem solving. They apparently serve to locate ambiguity in problem descriptions and to clarify or make specific aspects of the problems that must be deduced or inferred. Once constructed, these sophisticated task representations serve to generate succeeding solution steps, such as the generation of particular solution equations.

Still another difference between experts and novices is in their choice of strategies. As described in Chapter 7, experts consistently use a "working-forward" strategy, whereas novices use a "working-backward" approach (Simon & Simon, 1978). Experts appear to identify problem variables and then move forward to generate and solve equations that use existing information. Novices, in contrast, seem to **begin** the solution process with an equation that contains the problem unknown (the desired end product). If the equation contains a variable that was not given, novices work **backward** from that equation searching for an equation that yields (they hope) the variable they need, and so on. For example, suppose that the solution to a physics problem required solving the equation $V = mgh$, where the several values in the equation are unknown, but h is the unknown asked for by the question. The novice typically works **backward** from that equation, seeking to generate other equations that will give the values of m, g, and V so that ultimately the equation can be solved for h. The expert, on the other hand, apparently understanding the problem in a more fundamental way, works forward from a set of equations generated from the problem statement, concluding the solution sequence with the equation $V = mgh$ in a fashion so that all of the relevant values are known and are placed in the equation, and the solution to h is calculated. It seems that the rich network of information experts possess is organized into schemata that use key concepts from problem statements and from their own knowledge base to instantiate forward-moving solution procedures. These science schemata seem very similar to the algebra schemata we described in Chapter 12.

Related to the ways in which information is organized in memory, there are differences between experts and novices in terms of the information they use to solve problems. Chi et al. (1982), for example, found that experts are more likely to generate **necessary** inferences (i.e., those essential for solution) from problem statements than were novices. Similarly, there are differences in problem representation—novices tend to organize their problems in knowledge around the "surface structure" of the explicit statements in problems, whereas experts organize their knowledge schematically around fundamental science principles (e.g., Newton's laws) that often are only **implied** by problem statements.

Once schemata related to the fundamental principles are activated, experts use stored procedural knowledge to generate solution attempts that are then tested against the requirements of the problem statement. Experts possess substantially more procedural knowledge than novices. This difference in procedural knowledge may account for the differences in problem-solving strategies chosen by experts (working forward) and novices (working backward).

A Model for Teaching Science

The differences between novices and experts suggest a model for science instruction. Teachers need to help students acquire *both* declarative and procedural science knowledge. Instruction should help students think about science problems in terms of the underlying scientific laws of the discipline. This is not to say, however, that "doing" science in the elementary and secondary schools should focus simply on knowledge acquisition. Rather, novices need a great deal of support in acquiring skill and in making inferences from the context of particular problem statements. These inferences, for experts, lead to the activation of schemata that trigger procedures that move the solver toward solution. Knowledge, independent of appropriately organized schemata, is not sufficient to generate procedures for successful problem solving. Furthermore, since school-age students may have a large storehouse of incorrect or incomplete science schemata (Carey, 1985; Osborne & Freyberg, 1985), tasks and assignments must be chosen carefully first to confront these naive beliefs and then to lead students to develop and store schemata related to fundamental scientific laws.

Science instruction, according to this view, should be directed at building knowledge structures (schemata) that allow learners to react to problems with appropriate solution procedures. The trick is to help students **organize** their knowledge into schemata that are productive and related to fundamental scientific concepts. Such organization is critical. Perfetto, Bransford, and Franks (1983) have demonstrated that the mere presence of knowledge does not necessarily lead to the use of that knowledge in problem solving. To be used, knowledge must be well organized in memory.

In their study, Perfetto et al. gave students a set of very obvious clues that provided strong hints about the solution of a set of verbal problems. For example, one problem is as follows:

A man who lived in a small town in the United States married more than 20 different women in the same town. All are still living, and he has never divorced one. Yet he has broken no law.

The very blatant clue was "A minister marries several people each week." In the experiments, a list of 12 clues (one for each of 12 problems) was studied by the experimental subjects. Then one group of subjects received 12 problems, each problem related to one of the clues, as in the example above. However, they were not told that the clues were related to the problems. A second group was informed that the clues were relevant to the problems. A third group (the control) received the problems without seeing the clues. Over a series of variations of this basic design, the findings were unmistakable. The group that studied the clues and then attempted the problems **without instruction that the clues were related to the problems** performed no better than the control group that did not see the clues at all. On the other hand, the informed group performed significantly better on the problems.

More recently, Krug and Glover (1989) have demonstrated that the way in which clues are organized at the time students study them is of critical importance. After replicating Perfetto et al.'s basic findings, Krug and Glover contrasted a list of clues with different versions of embedding the clues in expository texts. When the clues were embedded in the expository texts, students recalled them at a much higher rate than when the clues merely were presented in lists. Further, with no instructions that the clues were related to later problems, clues embedded in well-organized texts still were much more likely to be used in problem solving than when the clues merely were listed. Krug and Glover argued that the well-organized expository texts provided students with much-better organizational structures at the time of encoding, leading to more useful memory structures and, consequently, more-useful knowledge for problem solving.

Clearly, knowledge must be organized into appropriate schemata before it is useful for problem solving. Without explicit instruction or presentation in extremely well organized contexts, however, many students fail to understand how information (knowledge) given by the text or the teacher relates to problems they are asked to solve.

Glaser (1984) points out one additional issue. In many cases schemata for solution are not themselves contained in the problem statement, but instead must be derived from knowledge *and* procedures stored in memory. For novice students, whose scientific schemata frequently are incomplete or faulty, successful problem solving without careful instruction is rare.

To review, schemata represent structured knowledge, acquired through experience, of the interrelationships among events, situations, and so forth. The information contained in slots within a schema may change, but the basic schema, if it proves useful for problem solution, will not. For successful instruction to occur, research suggests that teachers must first discover a student's present state of knowledge (the schemata currently possessed in a domain). The teacher then should propose a new state of knowledge (a schema) that is close to, but different from, the learner's theory (Glaser, 1984). Encouraging students to evaluate their existing schemata against the new state leads them to modifications that incorporate information from the new state. With a succession of tasks, each selected so as to just challenge existing schemata, the student will gain more-complex and mature schemata and develop better methodologies for acquiring new knowledge.

Our argument focuses on the need for knowledge in specific subject domains and implies that the general programs (IDEAL, Instrumental Enrichment) for teaching problem solving described in Chapter 7 have limited value in knowledge-rich domains such as mathematics and science. Research in these domains provides strong support for the crucial role of specific knowledge for problem solving. Consequently, the programs described in Chapter 7 are likely to be useful only when the domain-specific demands of the problems are small.

It may well be that general problem-solving skills should be taught students as they begin to study a particular domain. At that point, these general skills may provide students with initial approaches for attacking problems. As the domain is mastered, however, specific knowledge structures—science schemata—need to replace the weak general domain-free problem-solving schemata as well as the incorrect or incomplete knowledge-specific schemata students often bring to a subject. Given the misconceptions possessed by so many students, this indeed can be a daunting task.

Learning and Teaching Strategies

Students come to instructional settings with learning strategies acquired from school experience as well as from unstructured settings. One goal of formal education is to teach students new learning strategies that help them acquire and organize information. The evidence suggests that this goal is not always met, however. Some students actually acquire learning strategies that **interfere** with learning new material.

Learning Strategies

Roth (1985) asked middle school students to read science materials (written at their grade level) and examined how they thought about it. As a result, she identified five "learning" strategies used by the children, only one of which, unfortunately, resulted in restructuring and refining naive schemata. The five strategies are briefly described below.

Overreliance on the Sufficiency of Prior Knowledge   Students who exhibited the strategy of "overreliance on prior knowledge" read the assignment and then reported that they understood the text; in fact, many reported that they had "known this stuff" before they even read the material. Thus one student, after reading a passage that used milk as an example of how all food ultimately can be traced back to green plants (the food producers), reported that the passage was "about milk." When pressed, he reported that it was how we get milk from cows. The point of the reading—that plants make food that cows convert to milk— was missed entirely. In this student's view, he already "knew" the content. Instead of using the knowledge just acquired from the text to answer questions, students of this type tend to use associations of the new material with prior knowledge to report that the text simply was repetitious.

Overreliance on Text Vocabulary

In the "overreliance on vocabulary" strategy, students isolated new words or phrases in the assignment, often out of context, but expressed feelings of comprehension if they could state that the text was about a specific word, for example, "photo-something" (*photosynthesis*). According to Roth, the children reported feeling confused about the text only if they could not decode the new words. For these children, answering questions about the text simply required recall of "new" or "big" terms and a phrase or sentence around them. Often the new words were not put into the context of the students' own experiences. Surprisingly, this strategy often pays off when the questions teachers ask about text materials con- sist of requests for definitions or identifications of "new" words. This is the kind of almost mindless vocabulary acquisition we referred to in the opening of the chapter.

Overreliance on Unrelated Facts

Many other students have adopted a view of science as the accumulation of facts (air expands when heated; water boils at 212° Fahrenheit). Such students see science learning as demanding recall of facts and other natural phenomena. In Roth's study, for instance, such students dis- played quite-accurate recall of these bits of information. The ideas were not linked into meaningful schemata, however, nor was there differentia- tion of major from trivial points. These students especially "benefited" from teachers who displayed a vocabulary-oriented view of science. Just as some students see science as vocabulary acquisition, other students see it as mere fact acquisition.

Overreliance on the Adequacy of Prior Knowledge

Large numbers of students in Roth's study used this strategy. For these students, new topics were understood in terms of prior knowledge. These well-motivated students sought to link text knowledge to existing prior knowledge. However, the goal of students using this strategy was not to modify the structure of prior knowledge, but rather to confirm its correctness. In many cases, students distorted or even ignored informa- tion inconsistent with existing knowledge. Given the existence of "naive" beliefs in many children, this strategy poses special difficulty for teach- ers. Student efforts to make new knowledge conform to existing, often incomplete or incorrect knowledge may well interpret the outcome of an experiment in ways very different from those anticipated by the teacher. In contrast to the "overreliance on the sufficiency of prior knowledge" learning strategy, these students realized that the information was new; however, they did not appear to understand that it might challenge their existing knowledge structures.

Conceptual-Change Students   "Conceptual-change students" see text materials as a vehicle for changing existing schemata. In Roth's study, they worked to reconcile old ideas with new material. As a result, they not only identified and learned the main ideas in the text, but they also were able to state where the text or other materials conflicted with their existing schemata. Further, they saw the text as a source of new knowledge and were willing to revise their old schemata in light of new information. Interestingly, but not surprisingly, this group of students was most often likely to admit to being confused or puzzled by the text.

It is not clear why there are such differences in learning strategies. Nonetheless, teachers need to anticipate them. If students report new material as "old stuff," the teacher must provide a teaching situation that shows how the new material challenges old beliefs, making it clear that the material is, in fact, new, and must be accommodated by students into revised schemata. Similarly, students who see science as vocabulary or fact acquisition may be presented with situations (experiments, demonstrations, field studies) that require the linking of words and facts into schemata that help the student better understand and explain the world.

Teaching Strategies

Given the range of possible student learning strategies, what **instructional** strategies might help students learn and understand science at more mature and "scientific" levels? Four of the five learning "strategies" we described above permit children to avoid learning new information by classifying it as already known. That is, children mistakenly fit the new information into already existing and inadequate schemata or treat it as isolated facts or terms to memorize. Simply assigning these students material to read, as a consequence, is unlikely to lead to the sorts of accommodation new schemata require. Instead, it may be more appropriate to introduce students to new concepts by first finding out what they already believe to be true about them. However, many writers (Carey, 1985; Nussbaum & Novick, 1982; Osborne & Freyberg, 1985) correctly point out the difficulty of this easy-sounding first step.

Obtaining Student Views of Science   The best way to find out what students know is from individual interviews. According to Osborne and Freyberg, the questions teachers use in interviews should be posed in a personal way—"Will you explain to me the way **you think** our eyes work?"—rather than impersonally—"How do people's eyes work?" (The second question suggests that there is a correct answer the child **should** know and provide—an answer the child may neither fully understand nor agree with.) Further, questions should represent a balance of easy-to-answer (often factual) questions and more-penetrating ones such as "Why do you think that?" The point of questioning individuals is to lead them to reveal their own sense of how science works.

Many researchers interested in elementary and secondary school science believe that individual interviews are necessary to establish the beginning point for science instruction. However, since the individual interview may take more time than teachers can afford, other techniques have been proposed. For example, Nussbaum and Novick (1982) suggest that one useful way to obtain children's conceptions (and misconceptions) is through what they call an "exposing event"—a situation or demonstration posed to a group of children that evokes student comment. It is not enough, though, simply to expose preconceptions; means must be found to challenge the preconceptions and help children construct new and more-adequate science schemata. As an example of how this process may be put into action, the Nussbaum and Novick approach is described in detail.

A Model for Teaching Science   Nussbaum and Novick have proposed a threefold strategy for teaching science to children: (1) reveal and understand student preconceptions, (2) create conceptual conflict with those preconceptions, and (3) encourage the development of revised or new schemata about the phenomena in question. We examine each step below.

REVEALING STUDENT PRECONCEPTIONS.   Teachers first must engage students in activities that reveal their naive beliefs. Figure 13-5, based on the work of Nussbaum and Novick, presents the responses of some elementary students at a laboratory school to an "exposing event" whose content deals with the particle theory of gases. In this event, students were shown a flask and a vacuum pump. They were told that half of the air in the flask was drawn out of the flask with the pump. The children were then asked to imagine that they possessed magic spectacles that permitted them to see the air remaining in the flask. Finally, they were asked to draw a picture on the chalkboard of the air remaining in the flask. On completion of the drawings, students were asked to describe and explain them. This class activity thus generated both verbal and pictorial accounts of student preconceptions.

Figure 13-5 shows that students hold a wide range of conceptions about the nature of gases. Obviously, all members of the class do not

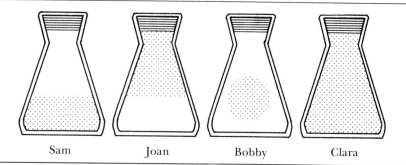

FIGURE 13-5. Children's depictions of a science problem. These depictions are representative of those made by elementary students at Burris Laboratory School.

share the same view of the properties! During this first stage of instruction, the teacher's major role is to help students express their ideas clearly and concisely. The teacher also encourages confrontation of ideas among the students, but does *not* judge the adequacy of student responses. The teacher's expectation is that exchanging views with other students about **student-generated ideas** not only has intrinsic interest, but also serves to clarify each student's own thinking. These activities serve to move the students to the next phase.

CREATING CONCEPTUAL CONFLICT.   The drawings and explanations generated by the class are posed as alternatives to whatever view each child holds. (If it happens that the "correct" or "scientific" view is not posed by the children, the teacher may wish to supply it as one given by a student in another class.) The teacher must, of course, resist student appeals for "which is the right one?"

Pupil-to-pupil discussion in itself may change some students' conceptions. Children with differing views may be paired and asked to choose the "best" drawing and to give a rationale for their choice. After allowing substantial time for discussion, the teacher then leads the students to see the need for an "empirical" test to determine the merits of the alternatives. Teacher questions such as "How can we decide which is better?" or "What can we do to decide?" may help students see the need to gather evidence for decision making. (If the teacher is very lucky, a student spontaneously will suggest such a test.)

The test must be selected so that after careful examination it will eliminate all but the "scientifically correct" alternative. In the example from Nussbaum and Novick, the teacher diverted the children to a different task altogether. She took a syringe, closed the openings at the end, and then drove the plunger halfway into the barrel. She asked the class to describe the nature of the contents of the apparently empty syringe, to which they responded "Air." She then asked what happened to the air when she pushed the syringe halfway home. Students readily generated answers that included some version of "squeezing" or "compressing" the air. As a technique for generalizing the meaning of the concept "compression" the teacher then reminded the children of earlier work with liquids and solids that had demonstrated their relative lack of compressibility. She then asked them to speculate about the special characteristics of air that permitted it to be compressed. Following discussion of this question, she returned their attention to the "exposing event," the (partially) evacuated flask, and asked the children to think about the air in the flask and the syringe. According to Nussbaum and Novick, in a number of replications of this experience, some child **always** made a comment such as "Maybe the air is made up of little pieces with empty space between." The class then reviews the drawings made during the exposing event and begins to make inferences and eliminate various of the alternatives. In this process, students raise questions that lead to the final phase.

ENCOURAGING COGNITIVE ACCOMMODATION.   When the empirical test has been completed and discussed, the teacher needs to give students support, new information, and elaboration of existing information that will help them restructure their ideas about the situation in question. In the "gas" example, prior to accepting the "scientific" explanation, students frequently asked questions such as "What holds the particles apart?" This question permitted the teacher to bring in another property of gases—the inherent motion of the particles. To complete the teaching example, the teacher drove the plunger still farther into the syringe, and asked students to comment. Finally, she asked if she could compress the air to zero volume. These additional steps permitted her to give further information about compression, but to remind students that a limit of compressibility is reached when there is no space left between the particles.

We presented the "air" example to provide you with some sense of the complexity of obtaining student explanations of physical phenomena, and how those naive explanations can, **by use of the students' own questions and comments,** be used to lead students toward more-scientific conceptual structures. When student discussions are followed by "empirical tests" that permit students to "discover" a more nearly scientific explanation, many (though by no means all) students acquire more-accurate science schemata.

Student Learning   Students' cognitive structures *do* change as a result of science instruction. Champagne, Klopfer, Desena, and Squires (1981) carried out an instructional sequence in which they evaluated the effects of a four-week individualized instructional sequence for changing schema structure in a junior high school geology lesson. Champagne et al. first constructed an integrated structure (a schema) for 13 words in a unit of material on rocks. This was saved for reference and not used in the instruction. Prior to instruction, Champagne et al. (1981) gave a junior high school group the same 13 words and asked each person to arrange them on a sheet of paper to show "how you think about the words" (p. 100). They then were asked to explain their arrangement. Following the four-week period of instruction, the students were given the 13 words and asked to sort them a second time. A comparison of students' responses after the unit with their first responses, as well as a comparison to an expert's responses, indicated that the introduction brought about more complex, expert-like, and complete schematic structure concerning rocks. In this test of the effectiveness of instruction, 18 of a class of 30 students achieved substantial improvement in schematic structure as an apparent result of the instructional sequence. Not only does this experiment show the effectiveness of instruction, it also suggests an interesting technique for assessing student schema structures before and after instruction. This sorting technique seems particularly appropriate when the subject matter is a set of concepts whose relationships are readily classified.

Research on a problem of electrical current flow carried out by Osborne and Freyberg (1985) in a manner similar to the work of Nussbaum and Novick revealed that although a significant proportion of 11-year-olds finally accommodated to a scientific view of electric current flow, 15 to 35 percent did not. Some children (similar to adults!) held to their preconceptions in the face of seemingly incontrovertible evidence.

Why do students cling to naive beliefs? At a basic level, they simply may reject the "empirical test," in which case different "exposing" events might be attempted. In addition, Osborne and Freyberg suggest that teachers should ask students about their views of the empirical test and its purpose. What appears to the teacher to be a clear and strong link between the empirical task and the exposing event may not seem at all clear to some students. Thus, in the Nussbaum and Novick teaching example we described, some students simply may not see any relationship between compression of gases using the syringe and the original event, evacuating the flask. To identify students for whom this is a possibility, teachers may well wish to finish each instructional unit with a series of open-ended questions thoughtfully designed (in advance!) to determine students' views of the activity's objective, how it was accomplished, and what conclusions they may have drawn.

Instructional sequences such as those described above take a great deal of classroom time. Teachers may well argue that since time available for science already is limited, it is not feasible to put such a three-phase teaching program into action, except occasionally for "demonstration" purposes. Clement (1983), in discussing the difficulties of tackling naive physics beliefs of college students, takes issue with this point of view and has argued that much **more** instructional time at the college level should be devoted to examining such preconceptions. He asserts that attempts to "cover" many physics topics, especially while using formal scientific/ mathematical language, may make it impossible for students to gain an intuitive understanding of Newtonian concepts of physics. If Clement is correct, arguments made at the beginning of this chapter against treating science as "vocabulary acquisition" gain additional strength, and the use of student (rather than textbook or teacher) language to confront naive beliefs is further supported.

The instructional approach we've described is not the only teaching technique science teachers should use. Students and teachers need and value variety. Yet the research evidence provided by Osborne and Freyberg as well as the work of Driver, Guesne, and Tiberghien (1985) provides strong support for its frequent use. Thoughtful teachers will find many variations of this approach that will serve to meet the basic goals the model proposes: expose naive beliefs, create conceptual conflict, and encourage cognitive accommodation to more-mature views of science.

Extending the Breadth of Learning

Challenging students' naive beliefs through a succession of experiments or demonstrations is not the final goal of teaching. The more-general goal is to help children acquire more expert-like views of science and use those views to make sense of the world in which they live. As a consequence, teachers must find ways to generalize from instructional episodes to "real-world" situations.

Application as an Aid to Learning

J. R. Anderson (1987) asserts that initial learning in any domain begins with very specific task contexts. One implication of this assertion is that students see explanations as applying only to a narrow range of phenomena. Thus, Anderson argues that every new concept should be taught in the context of a variety of tasks and that the significance of each task to the scientific concept in question must specifically be pointed out. For instance, a series of instructional sessions where children have opportunities to assess how newly gained schemata apply to related scientific topics in other contexts may help children see the power of scientific schemata. It also appears that students should use their own language to show their understanding of how a particular concept may be generalized to situations other than the one in which it was originally taught.

The Learning Community

Anderson suggests the "learning community" as a potentially useful device in science instruction. In science, the learning community is a classroom where students, sometimes individually, but often in groups, actively engage in the activities of a scientist: description, prediction, explanation, control. Such a community gathers evidence from its work with "real-life" objects and events to evaluate alternative conceptualizations and explanations. The community learns to use the authority of teacher and textbook but, perhaps more importantly, to use their own activities with discussion and confrontation to reach conclusions about scientific issues. Conflicting student explanations for a phenomenon coupled with the group's attempts at empirical verification not only permits free exchange of ideas, but also provides opportunity for treating scientific misconceptions in a nonthreatening manner.

Much of the research on "learning communities" has been carried out primarily with elementary and junior high school students, but other work suggests that senior high school and college students will benefit from similar approaches (see Clement, 1983; McDermott, 1984). Even more than in the elementary school, secondary and college laboratory experiences sometimes emphasize formal procedure and methodology as ends in themselves, rather than as means for verifying the value of scientific explanation. This emphasis leads some students to view the goal of science as use of a method rather than understanding that the scientific method is simply a **tool** (albeit a powerful one) to aid in the discovery and validation of new knowledge about the world. Informal activities that expose and challenge the preconceptions revealed in college students will serve as vehicles to help students acquire a sense of the significance and value of the methodology of science.

It is important to keep in mind, however, that instruction should result in more than knowledge acquisition. Useful schemata contain not only knowledge, but procedures as well—actions that permit problem solving. Further, students need strategic knowledge (see Chapter 2) for planning in problem solving.

According to DeJong and Ferguson-Hessler (1986), a difference between expert and novice problem solvers is that, for experts, problem statements elicit schemata organized according to problem types. Stored with problem types are declarative and procedural knowledge that lead to a successful problem-solving process.

DeJong and Ferguson-Hessler compared the problem schemata of good novice physics problem solvers with those of ineffective novice problem solvers. They reasoned that good novice problem solvers would have problem schemata more like those of experts; consequently, physics problems would elicit appropriate solution procedures more often. To test the accuracy of this reasoning, DeJong and Ferguson-Hessler compared the problem schemata of an expert in electricity and magnetism to those of a group of university students who had successfully passed an examination on those topics and a second group who failed the examination. As one might predict, the schemata of successful students were significantly more like the expert's than were those of the unsuccessful students. These findings are similar to those discussed in Chapter 12 on algebra word problem schemata: Successful students are those whose organized problem schemata, including procedures, resembled those of experts. Just as algebra students need to acquire problem schemata for different sorts of algebra word problems, science students need to acquire schemata for different sorts of science problems. Since the nature of these problem schemata is not clear to novices, science instructors need to be specific in pointing out the problem types and the differences in procedures appropriate to each.

A substantial research base indicates that carefully conceived instructional sequences *do* change students' science schemata. Helping students see the generality of new knowledge requires understanding the concepts in expert-like ways. Instruction also must provide students with a wide range of situations to which the concepts are applicable so that scientific knowledge becomes organized into schemata that include not only declarative knowledge, but the procedures for solving science problems in settings other than the classroom.

Implications for Teaching

1. The ambitious goals science sets for itself—understanding the physical, biological, and social worlds as well as the methodology of science—provide great challenges to teachers. Cognitive approaches to learning science recommend that science be presented to students as a problem-solving process rather than simply as a knowledge (vocabulary or fact) acquisition process.

2. Students bring to science a wealth of preconceptions, many of which are incomplete or incorrect. Before effective instruction can occur, these preconceptions must be identified. The identification process often is slow and uncertain. It requires considerable teaching time, accompanied by a careful choice of instructional materials that elicit the

student's own thinking, not just verbalization of information the student thinks a teacher desires. Particularly difficult to expose are the naive beliefs students have about scientific phenomena. If instructional time permits, carefully conducted individual interviews seem to be the best way to reveal these preconceptions. If time does not permit extensive work with individuals, however, the class as a group may serve as a learning community (J. R. Anderson, 1987) that will become a useful vehicle for identifying preconceptions. A three-pronged approach to science instruction (exposing events, conceptual conflict, and cognitive accommodation) (Nussbaum & Novick, 1982) is effective in eliciting and confronting students' preconceptions.

3. Since scientific schemata often appear to be in conflict with experience-based schemata (naive beliefs), experiments or demonstrations usually are necessary to challenge the preconceptions. These demonstrations must be chosen thoughtfully so that they require children to examine their own thinking (preconceptions) about concepts in ways that lead them to consider and adopt more-scientific views. Substantial teacher patience and openness is necessary so that students feel free to verbalize their own thinking and use their own language to come to grips with inconsistencies or inadequacies in their thinking. Although students quite readily memorize "correct" explanations, observations of explanatory behavior following such memorization suggests that students frequently return to explanations consistent with earlier preconceptions. As we have pointed out before, knowledge alone is insufficient to change habits of thought. Students must have experience-based activities that encourage them to construct new understandings (accommodations) consistent with more-mature, expert views of science.

4. Expert task representations differ from those of novices not only in amount of knowledge, but in the nature and complexity of representations. To help students progress toward competence in science, teachers must understand the nature of expert schemata. In the elementary grades, this often is difficult because of inadequate science preparation among teachers. Many, if not most, elementary school teachers have not developed adequate conceptions of science and the methods of science. It is likely that some (even many) elementary school teachers possess the same naive preconceptions as their students. The specialization of teaching fields possible at the junior and senior high school levels reduces, but does not eliminate, the likelihood of problems in teacher expertise.

5. Because they are directly tied to fundamental scientific concepts and contain substantial procedural information, the expert problem solvers' schemata are more sophisticated than those of novices. On the other hand, novices' schemata more frequently reflect a problem's "surface" and the naive beliefs students have acquired from uncontrolled prior experience. Laboratory experiences as well as classroom discussion must

move students toward the acquisition of schemata that reflect more fundamental (i.e., more expert-like) understandings of scientific concepts. Laboratory experiments also must involve confrontation of novices' naive beliefs so that they may discover the contradictions and inadequacies of their prescientific beliefs.

6. Instructors with high levels of expertise must be particularly sensitive to inaccurate preconceptions of students, who often repeat the terms and concepts experts presented to them in a rote fashion. Unless carefully constructed opportunities are available to students, they may not display their naive beliefs. Instead, they may remain silent or parrot the text or the teacher. In order to ascertain children's level of understanding of scientific concepts, teachers need to contrive laboratory and field experiences and experiments as well as logical analyses and extensions of these experiences to broaden the usefulness of scientific concepts and deal with the potential reappearance of naive beliefs.

7. Conceptual change in children is a slow, long-term process. Students need opportunities to see for themselves that their scientific views of the world are inadequate. Progress in science teaching should be assessed over relatively lengthy periods of time—many weeks—rather than at the close of each class period. This is not to say that teachers should not evaluate the effectiveness of their instruction frequently, but rather that expecting rapid changes in students is unrealistic. If expectations are too high, both student and teacher may become discouraged.

8. Science curricula should not begin with the structure of subject matter. Rather, curricula should begin with a focus on the ideas that children hold prior to instruction. Curricula then are constructed to provide children with a set of experiences that ask them to confront their preconceptions in ways that lead to more-scientific conceptions. The magnitude of this task should not be underestimated. Historically, science curricula have been written from the perspective of the expert, not the novice. To write materials that challenge the naive beliefs of children in productive ways and lead them, ultimately, to more expert-like knowledge structures will require massive efforts.

9. By the middle school years, many children have acquired a number of dysfunctional strategies for reading science texts (K. J. Roth, 1985). Students may, for example, erroneously conclude that they already know a topic. Others simply see science as vocabulary or fact acquisition and read accordingly. Such dysfunctional reading strategies may be countered by using problems that help students see the shortcomings of their approaches. Teachers also may need to generate sophisticated interviewing and questioning techniques in order to discover the extent to which students hold such beliefs.

10. Techniques that effectively confront children's naive beliefs and inadequate study patterns include introduction of exposing events, intro-

duction of discrepant events, generation of a range of conceptual responses to an exposing event, and practice extending new conceptual responses to a broad range of situations. These activities are most valuable when accompanied by direct student involvement with science materials and with other students.

11. In both science and mathematics, schema-based views of knowledge-acquisition and problem-solving strategy development are linked to effective teaching. Effective teachers find means to assess student schemata prior to instruction, and then develop instructional materials that confront naive preconceptions and enhance the acquisition by students of more expert-like understandings of science.

12. Present conceptions of expertise in science problems suggest (just as with algebra word-problem solving) that teachers must help students acquire a rather large array of science schemata. These permit students to represent problems quickly and evoke the procedural information that makes problem solving possible. Teachers can help students by making explicit references to these schemata and giving them a wide array of problems for which these frames of reference are appropriate.

Summary

Science involves gathering data, making and verifying predictions, and producing explanations of scientific events. Within science, the domain of physics served as a vehicle for the initial attempts of cognitive scientists to study how people solved problems in knowledge-rich domains. Cognitive scientists used protocol analysis to examine the differences in problem-solving behavior between novices (beginning students in a science) and experts (usually Ph.D.-level instructors). As one might expect, there were large differences in the extent of scientific knowledge. Furthermore, experts revealed task representations quite different from those of novices. Examinations of reasons for these differences led to the recognition that novices not only know less than experts, but they approach many scientific tasks with a set of preconceptions that, in many cases, make expert-like task representations impossible.

A significant part of science instruction in virtually any domain is to help students reveal their preconceptions about that domain. Then students need to be exposed to carefully chosen empirical and scientific events that lead them to examine the value of their preconceptions and to revise these preconceptions in the direction of more-scientific (expert-like) conceptions. The process of confronting naive beliefs and making accommodations to these beliefs that permit construction of more expert-like schemata is lengthy. Teachers not only should present challenging experiences to children, but they also must take care to allow students sufficient time to examine their naive beliefs. Following this confrontation, children must discover means for accommodating their naive beliefs in the direction of more-scientific views.

According to K. J. Roth (1985), middle school students exhibit a number of dysfunctional learning strategies. Most of these dysfunctional strategies appear to be aimed at finding a rationale for concluding that one already knows new material or that new material is simply facts to be learned in isolation. The use of demonstrations, followed by carefully guided and constructed discussions and questions, appears to help students confront and change these misconceptions. Teachers must be cognizant of such student strategies and provide instruction that challenges these unproductive approaches to studying science.

At present, considerable consensus exists that confronting students' naive schemata is best accomplished via a three-fold instructional process. Extensive opportunities (most practically in group settings) must be taken to expose naive beliefs. Then empirical events (experiments, demonstrations, field trips) must be presented to challenge these naive beliefs and lead students to change their schemata so as to incorporate more scientific (expert) schemata. Some evidence suggests that the feedback children give each other is particularly effective in leading them to confront their own naive beliefs.

Studies of expertise in science suggest not only that scientists possess more knowledge of science, but that their knowledge is represented differently. Whereas novices appear to organize their knowledge around surface features of problems, experts organize their knowledge around fundamental physics concepts that may not be present in the problem statement, but rather are inferred by the nature of the problem. Thus, instruction must lead to the development of problem schemata organized around the fundamental concepts and procedures of a scientific discipline.

Novice science student performance is characterized not only by lack of knowledge, but also by lack of expert-like schemata in which knowledge is organized by problem type. Expert schemata include procedural as well as declarative information. Similar to the findings about algebra word-problem solution (see Chapter 12), the problem schemata of most novices appear to lack useful procedural components.

Effective science instruction involves a view of science as problem solving rather than simple declarative knowledge acquisition. Students' naive beliefs (at all levels of instruction) need to be transformed into more expert-like schemata that permit them to accurately represent science problems and to use procedural knowledge to solve the problems. Teachers, themselves, must be well versed in the schemata of science.

CHAPTER 14

Social Science Problem Solving

Problem solving in the social sciences appears to differ markedly from that in mathematics and science. In mathematics and science, many problems have a single representation and one solution mutually agreed on by knowledgeable experts. In contrast, experts in the social sciences frequently disagree not only on the way a problem is to be represented, but also on the appropriateness of a solution deriving from a particular representation. For example, economics experts disagree widely on the significance of the United States' enormous national debt. Some represent the debt as a severe economic burden that will affect the economic well-being of future generations. Others argue that the national debt is at a reasonable level relative to the magnitude of our gross national product. Furthermore, even if economists agree the debt is too large, methods for reducing it (solving the problem) are vigorously argued and no consensus has emerged.

Cognitive approaches to problem solving provide some clarification of this issue (see H. A. Simon, 1973; Voss, in press; Voss et al., 1983a) by conceiving of two classes of problems: well-structured (single-solution) problems, such as those common in college mathematics and science courses, and ill-structured (multiple-representation and hence multiple-solution) problems, such as those found in political science, economics, history, the humanities, and the arts.

In **well-structured** problems, the "givens" of the problem either are carefully specified in the problem or are known by the solver as a result of prior experience with similar problems. Any constraints on solutions are equally well known. Thus, in solving algebra equations with two unknowns, for example, the equations are specified and the permissible operations (that is, the constraints) are (or should be) known so that a single "correct" solution emerges. Experts in the field of algebra will be in agreement on the solution. Contrast a typical algebra problem to an ill-structured social science problem such as the following:

What adjustments to the nation's economy are necessary so that inflation remains as low as possible consistent with healthy economic growth?

Obviously, this "problem" contains many terms definable in different ways—for instance, what are "healthy" economic growth and "low" inflation? Further, what adjustments of the economy are meant? Even among expert economists, definitions of these terms are likely to vary depending on one's political affiliation, economic theory, or level of knowledge, or perhaps even on one's age or station in life. It may even be that the greater the expertise in relevant social science domains such as economics or political science, the less the between-expert agreement on the "best" representation of the problem, much less common agreement on the "best" solution. Similar disagreements also occur in other fields—art, music, and literature, for example—where problems arise such as that of judging quality of work.

As James Voss (in press) states, not only must the solutions to ill-structured problems be justified, so also must the representations. The problem solver needs to explain why the task representation proposed is the "best" or the most nearly correct. Given a particular representation, of course, it still remains to be seen if the solution growing out of the representation is "correct" according to some outside criterion. Voss and his colleagues have struggled with these problems in a series of recent papers.

Problem Representation in Political Science

Voss et al. (1983a) have examined problem solving in political science, especially policy problems with respect to Soviet agricultural productivity. In these problems, experts and novices were presented with the existence of an undesirable state of affairs (i.e., inadequate agricultural productivity) requiring improvement. How does problem solving in areas such as these proceed?

Voss et al. carried out a problem-solving protocol analysis of six experts on the Soviet Union (university faculty) and 10 novices (students in a course on Soviet domestic policy). The problem presented for solution was:

Suppose you were the Minister of Agriculture in the Soviet Union and assume that crop productivity has been low over the past several years. You have the responsibility to increase crop production. How would you go about solving this problem?

All individuals were asked to "think out loud" while constructing their solution. The sessions were tape recorded for later analysis.

Expert Solution Attempts

Consider initial statements from two experts. Expert A began:

> I think that as Minister of Agriculture, one has to start out with the realization that there are certain kinds of special agricultural constraints within which you are going to work. The first one, . . . is that by almost every count only ten percent of the land in the Soviet Union is arable . . . and secondly, even in that arable area . . . you still have climate, for instance, problems over which you have no direct control. (p. 175)

Expert A went on to look at the problem historically and concluded that a major factor was inadequate technological development. Thus the "problem to be solved" was represented as a technological one.

Expert B, on the other hand, began as follows:

> I think the most difficult part of this sort of problem for a Soviet leader is that the objective is not as clear as your question hints, because solving the productivity of agriculture in technical terms, even in economic terms, is no big problem, given that you can get the land fertile and can rotate it. But in the Soviet Union all these economic problems are political issues. . . . You can not raise agriculture productivity . . . without damaging certain political priorities. . . . (p. 179)

Expert B went on to say, "So our problem really is not technological, but it is social—how to make labor work harder on the collective, as opposed to the private plot" (p. 179). Expert A posed constraints on the problem representation that had to do with improving the technological aspects of farming. Expert B, on the other hand, explicitly rejected the technological factors and saw the problem as constrained and defined by political realities of the Soviet system.

Expert C incorporated parts of the problem representations of both A and B. A number of technological problems were listed for solution by the Ministry of Agriculture; however, the political issue was brought in as follows:

> There is the whole political angle. That is, how does the Minister of Agriculture actualize whatever he sees as problem areas involved with other areas? To a certain extent that is going to depend on how powerful he is . . . on how much pull he has. . . . What kind of access does he have to the Politburo? . . . What kinds of favors do they (heads of ministries) owe each other? So there is the whole political thing. (p. 184)

Expert D took yet another approach, decomposing the same problem into five pieces: the constraints of climate and politics and three subproblems of bureaucracy, peasant mentality, and lack of organizational substructure.

The excerpts presented here suggest common themes—agricultural issues of technology and climate, and political issues of power and influence. Which representation is more nearly correct? Must all be taken into account for a "better" or a "best" problem representation? Until each is tried, of course, one cannot tell—and, in reality, no country can take the time or devote the resources to try out each solution prior to adopting one. Thus, at present, one cannot know which is correct. The inability to reach agreement on problem representations and solutions makes research in social science problem solving difficult. Voss et al. (1983a) argue that such difficulty is exacerbated by two factors: the lack of agreement on the value (correctness or appropriateness) of solutions, and the often-long delay in implementing solutions.

Expert Problem Solving Consistency

Voss, Tyler, and Yengo (1983b) were properly concerned about the consistency of social science experts in solving problems within their specializations. As a result, they asked social science experts to solve additional problems in their areas of expertise. Across a number of different problems, the experts tended to use similar representation strategies at about the same level of abstractness on each. This finding suggests that expertise in a given area leads the expert to use similar problem approaches to solving problems in the area of expertise. The question still remains, however, as to whether social science expert solutions are the most appropriate and workable ones. It is at least theoretically possible that the tendency to use similar problem representations may lead the problem solver to overlook other, more productive representations.

Novice Solution Attempts

Novice responses were much more specific than those of experts. In most cases, they took the form of decomposing the problem into low-level specific subproblems for which they provided suggested solutions. One novice essentially argued as follows: There is a lack of land—so find more land—maybe from other countries. Need trade—set up trade exchange. Poor irrigation—set up irrigation systems. Poor technology—do technological studies, and get information from other countries. Lack certain items—get a surplus in other areas to make up for lack. Not enough labor—hire more people. These "solutions" gave no consideration to the political issues implicit in, for example, finding more land.

Although some novices exhibited relatively more sophisticated problem decompositions, there was a consistent lack of recognition of the problems that might occur as solutions were put into action. The listings of subproblems showed little recognition of the political and economic realities within which agriculture in the Soviet Union operates. Nor do they suggest the sort of coordinated effort required both within the Ministry of Agriculture and with other parts of the government if solutions are to be put in place.

In another interesting study, Voss, Blais, Means, Greene, and Ahwesh (1986) examined the economics problem-solving behaviors of novice students (those with some training in economics) and a naive group (whom they defined as persons with no formal instruction in economics). The study examined the variables of college experience, formal training in economics, and practical experience with economics in terms of job or avocation. Members of the two groups were equated for level of college experience as well as related vocational or avocational work in an area related to economics. The economics problems used were "practical" problems related to costs of an automobile (9 problems), the federal deficit (9 problems), and interest rates (10 problems). One finding was that college-educated novice student performance was indistinguishable from that of college-educated naive students. This suggests that the knowledge acquired in one or two economics classes was not yet sufficiently synthesized or organized to lead to superior performance on the practical economics problems attempted. On the other hand, college-trained individuals (whether naive or novice) outperformed groups who had no college education. No differences were found that related to the experience factor.

In effect, the major finding of the study was that college experience generally was a significant predictor of problem-solving success. The particular advantage given by "college experience" is difficult to sort out, however; differential intelligence, for example, may well be involved. On the other hand, the college experience simply may give students general skills in problem analysis and answer generation. (Note the similarity of this statement to our earlier description of general problem-solving skills.) For purposes of this chapter, we should emphasize that the lack of difference between the naive and novice college-trained groups lends credence to the claims of other writers (Alvermann, 1987; Newmann, 1986) that social science instruction at the secondary level overemphasizes knowledge at the expense of opportunity for reasoned problem solving.

Constraints in Social Science Problem Solving

All problems have constraints. In well-structured problems, problem constraints typically are well known to experts in the domain. In ill-structured problems, the constraints not only are more numerous, they also are less well defined and agreed upon. In many cases the constraints will include, at least in part, judgments based on personal beliefs and goals. Thus, a political scientist with a strongly held belief that a nation has responsibility for caring for its elderly may, in considering budget-balancing efforts, set a constraint on recommending any reductions in aid to the elderly. Another social scientist, less committed to the elderly, may deem cuts in Medicare or other support for the elderly as perfectly appropriate. Still another may view cuts in Medicare as appropriate, but because of the political power of the elderly as a voting group, may establish a constraint that cutting funding for such programs is not politically feasible.

Voss and Post (in press) suggest that in ill-structured problems, *both* the problem representation and the solution require justification. Arguments must be generated to "prove" a particular representation is correct. Further arguments are required to substantiate the claim that the solution proposed is appropriate. Thus, one can disagree with a particular solution because the problem has not been properly represented; or alternatively, one might accept the representation, but argue that the solution does not properly address the causes built into the problem. Both representation and solution may be satisfactory—but the solution is unworkable because it does not take into account one or more constraints. In many cases in the social sciences, justification includes appeal to what may be considered non–social science variables such as values and morality. One may well argue that such variables should be made **explicit** elements of the problem representation since it is readily apparent that such values act to shape both problem representation and solution.

Problem Solving in Other Social Sciences

The view of problem solving about the Soviet Union readily can be extended to other social science areas. History textbook writers who assert, for example, that the westward spread of settlement of the United States occurred because Americans "loved freedom" are, in effect, proposing an explanation (a solution) for a major phenomenon in American history. However, this explanation ignores competing explanations such as those arising, for example, from economic issues. Whether such an explanation is correct (wholly or in part) depends on the importance a historian ascribes to various historical data. Since historical data often are fragmentary and incomplete and open to multiple interpretations, a clear and unequivocal verification of a historical explanation often is difficult. Perhaps it is impossible. The weight given to those data that do exist is likely to vary from expert historian to expert historian depending on matters such as knowledge level and personal values.

As a result of difficulties in both problem formulation and solution verification, historical interpretation of important trends of the past may differ markedly. Recently, for example, a number of "revisionist" educational historians have attacked the widely held view that the American educational system was developed in the hope that an educated populace could more effectively govern itself. Some historians now argue, for instance, that the educational system was established to provide well-trained and docile workers for the American free-enterprise system. Surprisingly to some, perhaps, considerable documentation can be found to support both problem representations. Acceptance of either view (or rejectance of both) depends on one's knowledge of the data and, equally importantly, how one interprets those bits of data. Of course, related social science areas such as foreign policy, international relations, and the like face the same difficulties in evaluating problem representations as well as possible problem solutions.

Social Science Expertise

As we've noted, because of the lag time to "solution," it is virtually impossible in many instances to evaluate the effectiveness of social science expert solutions. Frequently, implementation and consequent evaluation of such solutions would require major societal restructuring, accomplished over relatively long periods of time—often decades. One might argue, however, that problem solutions posed by social science experts should be different from and, at least intuitively, appear better than solutions to the same problems posed by novices or by non–social science experts. Thus, one may compare and contrast social science expert solutions to those generated by non–social science groups. Differences between experts and novices have been described on the preceding pages. However, other comparisons also are possible. For example, how do the solutions of social science experts in a particular field compare to those of other social scientists whose expertise is in other fields? How do the solutions compare to those of experts from other non–social science areas? Some information is available to provide tentative answers to both questions.

Voss et al. (1983a, 1983b) asked faculty members and advanced graduate students whose field of expertise was not the Soviet Union (instead, it was the Third World or Latin America) to solve the "Soviet agriculture" problem described earlier. These "nonexpert experts" (i.e., persons expert in a subject matter of social science not directly related to the task) presumably share with the experts on Soviet agriculture general knowledge about problem solving in the social science area; however, there would be differences in extent and depth of knowledge about the Soviet Union. The "nonexpert" protocols in some ways resembled the expert protocols, with considerable time spent in problem representation at an abstract level as well as the development of constraints on possible solutions. The proportion of the protocol spent on problem representation, however, was considerably less for the nonexpert group. The Soviet Union experts, as expected, possessed substantially more specific, declarative knowledge about the agriculture task. This additional knowledge apparently resulted in establishing constraints that tied directly to Soviet Union agriculture, whereas constraints posed by the nonexperts were more general in nature.

Voss and his colleagues (1983b) also asked four expert chemists to solve the Soviet agriculture problem. Protocols of these experts (but in this case, persons whose expertise was in a non–social science field) more closely resembled those of novices than they did those of the social science experts. The chemists tended to go quickly to solutions, spending little time developing an abstract representation of the problem or in consideration of constraints on problem solution. Apparently, the expertise of chemists as chemists did not readily transfer to social science. It is not difficult to understand why. Not only did the chemists lack specific, declarative knowledge about the social science area, they also failed to represent the problem in an abstract manner, with appropriate attention to constraints on both representations and solutions.

In summary, the available evidence clearly indicates that social science experts do differ from novices in the extent of declarative knowledge with which they create and elaborate a problem representation. Beyond that, the evidence suggests that social science experts from different specializations, although differing to some degree in their base of declarative knowledge, tend to use similar problem-solving strategies, spending substantial time on problem representation at an abstract level. This representation typically is accompanied by a listing of the constraints that lead, finally, to the generation of potential solutions consistent with the constraints of the problem as they have represented it. At a minimum, this seems to imply that social science experts share a common approach to problem representation and solution generation. Of course, social science experts with differing specializations will display predictable differences in problem representation and generate potential solutions consistent with differential amounts of knowledge about a specialty.

In contrast, the problem-solving efforts of non–social science experts asked to deal with social science problems reveal relatively little time spent in problem representation. Instead, they tend to develop a series of low-level solutions that do not give much consideration to practicality, such as issues of politics in a country devoted to a particular ideology. Thus, their efforts at problem solving have more elements in common with those of novices in the field than they do with those of the social science experts.

Instruction in the Social Sciences

As indicated in Chapter 7, skill in problem solving depends on the presence of a substantial knowledge base. Newmann (1986) asserts that a recurring issue for social studies is lack of common agreement on priorities for social studies education. This lack of agreement leads to lack of focus for knowledge acquisition. Examination of the characteristics of experts and novices shows that to a marked degree, experts in any field possess a greater fund of relevant knowledge than do novices. What do students in the United States know about the social sciences?

Recently, Ravitch and Finn (1987) wrote a book entitled *What Do Our 17-Year-Olds Know?* The book reports the results of a national assessment of the knowledge about history and literature possessed by a carefully selected sample ($N = 7,812$) of 17-year-olds in the United States. Of particular interest for this chapter are the findings about knowledge of history. The findings are indeed dismal. On an examination prepared by the staff of the National Assessment of Educational Progress (NAEP), students averaged just over 54 percent correct in the history portion. Their performance might not be of great concern were it not for the large number of errors on seemingly elementary questions. For example, only 32 percent of the sample could locate the time of the Civil War in the correct half-century. Indeed, 26 percent located it prior to 1800, and 38 percent between 1800 and 1850. Although 60–80 percent of students could correctly identify historic individuals such as Alexander Hamilton, Richard Nixon, and George Washington, fewer than 50 percent could identify such American figures as Andrew Carnegie or Joseph McCarthy. Only 31 percent could satisfactorily identify the Magna Carta, and only 44 percent realized that the Constitution divides powers between states and the federal government.

Summarizing the results of the examination, Ravitch and Finn grouped the 141 history items into clusters relating to rather-specific topics. They then gave the average percentage correct for each cluster. Following are the scores for a few of the clusters: chronology—51 percent, the Constitution—54 percent, international affairs—58 percent, post–World War II to the present—55 percent. The highest score for any clusters was 71.3 percent for maps and geography and for science and technology. Lowest cluster scores were for pre–national and Colonial history (49 percent) and Reconstruction to World War I history (49.5 percent). Converting the average percentage correct to a letter grade, Ravitch and Finn gave American 17-year-olds a D.

Although results such as these need to be viewed with some caution, these findings suggest that at least in American history, high school students may not have the knowledge base necessary for effective problem solving in the social sciences. Since most states require, by law or statute, at least a year-long study of American history and American government, it is not likely that knowledge of world history and other social science courses is greater, since they too are studied for periods of a year or less. Furthermore, prospects for increases in instructional time devoted to the social sciences are not bright. A recent historical study of secondary school curriculum by Goldenstein, Ronning, and Walter (1988) revealed that student choices of social science course offerings have decreased over the past three decades. For a sample of Nebraska students, social science offerings made up 18 percent of the total school curriculum in 1953. That figure has steadily declined such that by 1983 only a little more than 13 percent of the courses selected by students were from the social science areas.

Some (e.g. Bennett, 1987) have suggested a **required** curriculum for secondary schools that includes three years of social studies instruction. Although this might offer some hope of more adequate time for acquisition of social science knowledge, such a requirement also demands thoughtful, analytical teachers, each dealing with small enough numbers of students so the knowledge students obtain can be organized and synthesized. Without this, even simple social science problem solving would seem improbable. We would not argue that present secondary school students are, or should be expected to become, expert problem solvers in social sciences. Yet students' rote learning of social science data (e.g., dates, names), acquired for no apparent use, is unlikely to yield thoughtful, satisfied, and productive students and, ultimately, citizens. Some compromise must be found between fact acquisition and the levels of expertise described earlier so that secondary school students can organize the information they acquire to permit at least some significant problem solving. Finally, because of the emphasis on reading and language arts in the elementary school, the elementary curriculum is not likely to provide a solid base of social science information; thus, the junior and senior high schools will need not only to provide information, but to develop whatever problem-solving expertise is possible. There appears, unfortunately, to be no clear social science analog to the counting and addition problem-solving activities so much a part of the mathematics curriculum in the elementary school.

The decline in social studies course selections we mentioned earlier is quite surprising, given the widespread acceptance of the belief that we live in a "small world" that demands knowledge of other cultures and countries. Perhaps some of the explanation for this decline lies in the current status of the social studies curriculum. A recent review by Armento (1985) reveals little agreement among experts on goals for social studies education and little change in social studies in the 20-year period reviewed. Alvermann (1987), on the other hand, suggests a somewhat more optimistic outlook. She cites three recent changes in social studies instruction:

1. Increased focus on the development of reasoning skills, as opposed to acquisition of purely factual knowledge.
2. General agreement that new learning in social studies must be linked to students' existing knowledge.
3. Improved research in social studies instruction that may lead to better understanding of how teachers may help students construct meaning from social science text material.

The changes suggested by Alvermann certainly are consistent with the cognitive view we espouse in this text. Viewing meaning as a constructive process rather than as a teacher-supplied dimension would appear to make social science instruction more effective. The existence of a cognitive thrust revealed in Alvermann's review of K–12 social studies curricula and instruction is supported by an examination of advanced-text materials in at least some of the social sciences. In a chapter on reasoning and international relations, for instance, Voss (in press) cites a wide array of text materials concerned with the role of cognitive processes in formulating foreign-policy decisions. Such a cognitive emphasis in graduate-level texts on foreign-policy issues provides hope that more-cognitive approaches to social studies education ultimately will be delivered in the secondary and elementary schools.

According to Voss, social scientists now argue that since governments are people, then decision making in government must take into account cognitive and affective qualities of the individuals involved in decision making. This view has implications for how social science content should be taught. Of particular relevance to this discussion are the following points from Voss' chapter:

1. **A change in orientation is required.** Problem solving and informal reasoning must play a larger role in social science instruction. Rather than simply acquiring facts about, say, the Civil War, students should be asked to use those facts to attempt to understand and predict decisions that occurred in the conduct of the war. This change requires acquisition of a substantial knowledge base prior to attempting problem solution.

2. **Several constraints on learning in the social sciences must be addressed.** Voss argues that higher expectations must be held for knowledge acquisition, that teachers of social studies must be more broadly prepared in social sciences, and that textbooks that treat social science topics in depth are needed. He also asserts that social sciences must tackle "controversial" topics, using the conflict to heighten student learning.

3. **A substantial data base must be acquired.** For effective informal reasoning, students must learn a substantial body of knowledge. As we have argued earlier, there is no substitute for knowledge. This knowledge should not be viewed as accumulation of facts, or as an end in itself, but rather as an organized, systematic body of information on which problem solving and decision making can be based.

Newmann (1986) makes much the same argument from a social studies expert point of view. He states that the key issues in social studies instruction are (1) lack of teacher agreement on priorities, (2) student disengagement, that is, students' boredom with social studies, and (3) mediocre teaching in the social studies areas. Without posing direct solutions for dealing with these three very-difficult issues, he does consider the knowledge issue from the perspective of both teacher and student. Consistent with a cognitive view, he argues that social science skills in reasoning cannot be taught without knowledge. On the other hand, the curriculum of the secondary school as presently constituted often requires too much knowledge acquisition before problem-solving skills can be developed, and so students disengage.

As an alternative, Newmann suggests a strategy that emphasizes depth over breadth so that students realize the factual knowledge they are asked to acquire can be organized and **used** in problem solving. Students will more quickly acquire and practice skills if they can see that skills will be used meaningfully.

Recent research suggests that cognitive approaches to the study of social sciences have much to offer to instruction. Increased clarity and structure in the social sciences may result by making sure that social science knowledge is useful for developing problem representations and potential solutions. At the same time, the issue of student disengagement might be addressed by providing greater opportunity for significant problem solving. Whether the constraints of time, lack of agreement on goals, or level of social studies teachers' expertise make such approaches feasible remains to be seen.

Summary

Cognitive approaches to social science instruction are of fairly recent origin. These approaches suggest the desirability of using the extensive knowledge base of the social sciences for posing problems and solutions to social science problems. At the same time, the fact that many, perhaps most, social science problems are ill-structured (i.e., multiple possible problem representations and hence multiple solutions) suggests the importance of helping students construct a view of social science problem solving that differs markedly from that of the physical sciences and mathematics. Not only must solutions to social science problems be justified, but also the representations of the problems themselves. Further, the nature of social science data seems to lead more naturally to the development of informal rather than formal problem solving and decision making. At the same time, pleas abound for making the study of the social sciences more rigorous and concerned with the integration and use of social science information.

References

ABELSON, R. P. (1981). Psychological status of the script concept. *American Psychologist, 36,* 715–729.

ACREDOLO, L. P., PICK, H. L., & OLSON, M. C. (1975). Environmental differentiation and familiarity as determinants of children's memory for spatial location. *Developmental Psychology, 11,* 495–501.

ADAMS, M. J., & COLLINS, A. (1977). *A schema-theoretic view of reading* Champaign: University of Illinois, Center for the Study of Reading. (Technical Report No. 32)

ADELSON, B. (1981). Problem solving and development of abstract categories in programming language. *Memory & Cognition, 9,* 422–433.

AHSEN, A. (1987). The new structuralism. *Journal of Mental Imagery, 11* (whole No. 1).

ALBA, J. W., & HASHER, L. (1983). Is memory schematic? *Psychological Bulletin, 93,* 203–231.

ALVERMANN, D. E. (1987). Strategic teaching in social studies. In B. F. Jones, A. S. Palinscar, O. Sederburg, & E. G. Carr (Eds.), *Strategic teaching and learning: Cognitive instruction in the content areas* (pp. 92–110). Alexandria, VA: Association for Supervision and Curriculum Development.

ALVERMANN, D. E., SMITH, L. C., & READENCE, J. E. (1985). Prior knowledge activation and the comprehension of compatible and incompatible text. *Reading Research Quarterly, 20,* 420–436.

ANDERSON, C. W. (1987). Strategic teaching in science. In B. F. Jones, A. S. Palinscar, D. S. Ogle, & E. G. Carr (Eds.), *Strategic teaching and learning: Cognitive instruction in the content areas* (pp. 213–256). Alexandria, VA: Association for Supervision and Curriculum Development.

ANDERSON, J. R. (1976). *Language, memory, and thought.* Hillsdale, NJ: Erlbaum.

ANDERSON, J. R. (1982). Acquisition of cognitive skill. *Psychological Review, 89,* 369–406.

ANDERSON, J. R. (1983a). *The architecture of cognition.* Cambridge, MA: Harvard University Press.

ANDERSON, J. R. (1983b). A spreading activation theory of memory. *Journal of verbal learning and verbal behavior, 22,* 261–295.

ANDERSON, J. R. (1985). *Cognitive psychology and its implications* (2nd ed.). New York: Freeman.

ANDERSON, J. R. (1987). Skill acquisition: Compilation of weak-method problem solutions. *Psychological Review, 94,* 192–210.

ANDERSON, J. R., & BOWER, G. H. (1973). *Human associative memory.* Washington, DC: Winston.

ANDERSON, J. R., & REDER, L. M. (1979). An elaborative processing explanation of depth of processing. In L. S. Cermak & F.I.M. Craik (Eds.), *Levels of processing in human memory* (pp. 385–404). Hillsdale, NJ: Erlbaum.

ANDERSON, R. C. (1984). Role of the reader's schema in comprehension, learning and memory. In R. C. Anderson, J. Osborn, & R. J. Tierney (Eds.), *Learning to read in American schools: Basal readers and content texts* (pp. 243–258). Hillsdale, NJ: Erlbaum.

ANDERSON, R. C., & BIDDLE, W. B. (1975). On asking people questions about what they are reading. In G. H. Bower (Ed.), *The psychology of learning and motivation, Vol. 9* (pp. 175–199). New York: Academic Press.

ANDERSON, R. C., & FREEBODY, P. (1981). Vocabulary knowledge. In J. T. Guthrie (Ed.), *Comprehension and teaching: Research reviews* (pp. 77–117). Newark, DE: International Reading Association.

ANDERSON, R. C., & FREEBODY, P. (1983). Reading comprehension and the assessment and acquisition of word knowledge. In B. Hutson (Ed.), *Advances in reading/language research* (pp. 231–256). Greenwich, CT: JAI Press.

ANDERSON, R. C., HIEBERT, E. H., SCOTT, J. A., & WILKINSON, I.A.G. (1985). *Becoming a nation of readers: The report of the Commission on Reading.* Champaign, IL: Center for the Study of Reading.

ANDERSON, R. C., & ORTONY, A. (1975). On putting apples into bottles—a problem of polysemy. *Cognitive Psychology, 7,* 167–180.

ANDERSON, R. C., & PEARSON, P. D. (1984). A schema-theoretic view of basic processes in reading comprehension. In P. D. Pearson (Ed.), *Handbook of reading research* (pp. 255–291). New York: Longman.

ANDERSON, R. C., REYNOLDS, R. E., SCHALLERT, D. L., & GOETZ, E. T. (1977). Frameworks for comprehending discourse. *American Educational Research Journal, 14,* 376–382.

ANDERSON, R. C., SPIRO, R., & ANDERSON, M. C. (1978). Schemata as scaffolding for the representation of information in connected discourse. *American Educational Research Journal, 15,* 433–440.

ANDERSON, R. C., WILSON, P. T., & FIELDING, L. G. (1988). Growth in reading and how children spend their time outside of school. *Reading Research Quarterly, 23,* 285–303.

ANDRE, M.L.D.A., & ANDERSON, T. H. (1978–1979). The development and evaluation of a self-study technique. *Reading Research Quarterly, 14,* 605–623.

ANDRE, T. (1987a). Questions and learning from reading. *Questioning Exchange, 1,* 47–86.

ANDRE, T. (1987b). Processes in reading comprehension and the teaching of reading comprehension. In J. A. Glover & R. R. Ronning (Eds.), *Historical foundations of educational psychology* (pp. 259–296). New York: Plenum.

ANGLIN, J. M. (1977). *Word, object and conceptual development.* New York: Norton.

ANISFELD, M. (1984). *Language development from birth to three.* Hillsdale, NJ: Erlbaum.

APPLEBEE, A. N. (1983). *The child's concept of story.* Chicago: University of Chicago Press.

APPLEBEE, A. N. (1984). Writing and reasoning. *Review of Educational Research, 54,* 577–596.

APPLEBEE, A. N. (1988). The national assessment. Paper presented to the annual meeting of the American Educational Research Association, New Orleans.

APPLEBEE, A. N., LANGER, J. A., & MULLIS, I.V.S. (1986a). Writing: Trends across the decade. 1974–1984. Princeton, NJ: National Assessment of Educational Progress. (ERIC Document Reproduction Service No. ED 273 680)

APPLEBEE, A. N., LANGER, J. A., & MULLIS, I.V.S. (1986b). *Writing report cards.* Princeton, NJ: The Nation s Report Card, National Assessment of Educational Progress.

ARMBRUSTER, B. (1979). An investigation of the effectiveness of "mapping" text as a studying strategy of middle schools. Unpublished doctoral dissertation, University of Illinois, Urbana.

ARMBRUSTER, B. (in press). Metacognition in creativity. In J. A. Glover, R. R. Ronning, & C. R. Reynolds (Eds.), *Handbook of creativity.* New York: Plenum.

ARMBRUSTER, B., ANDERSON, T. H., & OSTERTAG, J. (1987). Does text structure/summarization instruction facilitate learning from expository text? *Reading Research Quarterly, 22,* 331–346.

ARMENTO, B. J. (1985). Research on teaching social studies. In M. C. Wittrock (Ed.), *Handbook of research on teaching.* New York: Macmillan.

ATKINSON, R. C. (1975). Mnemotechnics in second-language learning. *American Psychologist, 30,* 821–828.

ATKINSON, R. C., & RAUGH, M. R. (1975). An application of the mnemonic keyword method to the acquisition of a Russian vocabulary. *Journal of Experimental Psychology: Human Learning and Memory, 104,* 126–133.

ATKINSON, R. C., & SHIFFRIN, R. M. (1968). Human memory: A proposed system and its control processes. In K. W. Spence and J. T. Spence (Eds.), *The psychology of learning and motivation: Advances in research and theory, Vol. 2.* New York: Academic Press.

ATKINSON, R. C., & SHIFFRIN, R. M. (1971). The control of short-term memory. *Scientific American, 225,* 82–90.

ATWELL, M. (1981). The evolution of text: The interrelationship of reading and writing in the composing process. Paper presented to the annual meeting of the National Council of Teachers of English, Boston.

AUBLE, P. M., FRANKS, J. J., & SORACI, S. A. (1979). Efforts toward elaboration: Elaboration or "aha!"? *Memory and Cognition, 7,* 426–434.

AUSUBEL, D. P. (1960). The use of advance organizers in the learning and retention of meaningful verbal material. *Journal of Educational Psychology, 51,* 267–272.

AUSUBEL, D. P. (1963). *The psychology of meaningful verbal learning.* New York: Grune & Stratton.

AUSUBEL, D. P. (1968). *Educational psychology: A cognitive view.* New York: Holt, Rinehart & Winston.

AUSUBEL, D. P., & FITZGERALD, D. (1961). The role of discriminability in meaningful verbal learning and retention. *Journal of Educational Psychology, 52,* 266–274.

AUSUBEL, D. P., & FITZGERALD, D. (1962). Organizer, general background, and antecedent learning variables in sequential learning. *Journal of Educational Psychology, 33,* 243–249.

AUSUBEL, D. P., & YOUSSEF, M. (1963). Role of discriminability in meaningful parallel learning. *Journal of Educational Psychology, 54,* 331–336.

AXELROD, S. (1983). *Behavior modification for the classroom teacher.* New York: McGraw-Hill.

BAARS, B. J. (1986). *The cognitive revolution in psychology.* New York: Guilford Press.

BADDELEY, A. D. (1978). The trouble with levels: A re-examination of Craik & Lockhart's framework for memory research. *Psychology Review, 85,* 139–152.

BAER, D. M., WOLF, M. M., & RISLEY, T. R. (1968). Some current dimensions of applied behavior analysis. *Journal of Applied Behavior Analysis, 1,* 91–97.

BAKER, K. (1987). Comment on Willig's "A meta-analysis of selected studies in the effectiveness of bilingual education." *Review of Educational Research, 57,* 351–362.

BAKER, K., & DE KANTER, A. (1983). Effectiveness of bilingual education. In K. Baker & A. de Kanter (Eds.), *Bilingual education: A reappraisal of federal policy* (pp. 33–86). Lexington, MA: Lexington Books.

BAKER, L. (1984). Spontaneous versus instructed use of multiple standards for evaluating comprehension: Effects of age, reading proficiency, and type of standard. *Journal of Experimental Child Psychology, 38,* 289–311.

BAKER, L. (1985). Differences in the standards used by college students to evaluate their comprehension of expository prose. *Reading Research Quarterly, 20,* 297–313.

BAKER, L. (in press). Metacognition, comprehension monitoring, and the adult reader. *Educational Psychology Review.*

BAKER, L., & ANDERSON, R. I. (1982). Effects of inconsistent information on text processing: Evidence for comprehension monitoring. *Reading Research Quarterly, 17,* 281–294.

BAKER, L., & WAGNER, J. L. (1987). Evaluating information for truthfulness: The effects of logical subordination. *Memory & Cognition, 15,* 279–284.

BARNES, B. R., & CLAWSON, E. U. (1975). Do advance organizers facilitate learning? *Review of Educational Research, 45,* 637–660.

BARNETT, J. E. (1984). Facilitating retention through instruction about text structure. *Journal of Reading Behavior, 16,* 113.

BARTLETT, F. C. (1932). *Remembering: A study in experimental and social psychology.* Cambridge: Cambridge University Press.

BATES, P. T. (1984). Writing performance and its relationship to the writing attitudes, topic knowledge, and writing goals of college freshmen. *Dissertation Abstracts International, 56,* 02A. (University Microforms No. DA 8508248)

BAUMANN, J. F. (1984). The effectiveness of a direct instruction paradigm for teaching main idea comprehension. *Reading Research Quarterly, 14,* 93–112.

BEAN, T. W., SINGER, H., SORTER, J., & FRAZEE, C. (1987). Acquisition of hierarchy organized knowledge and prediction of events in world history. *Reading Research and Instruction, 26,* 99–114.

BEATTLE, I. D., & DEICHMANN, J. W. (1972, April). Error trends in solving number sentences in relation to workbook format across 1st and 2nd graders. Paper presented at the American Educational Research Association annual meeting, Chicago. (ERIC Document Reproduction Service No. ED 064 170).

BECK, I. L., McCASLIN, E., & McKEOWN, M. G. (1980). The rationale and design of a program to teach vocabulary to fourth grade students. Pittsburgh: University of Pittsburgh Press, Learning Research and Development Center.

BECK, I. L., & MCKEOWN, M. G. (1985). Teaching vocabulary: Making the instruction fit the goal. *Educational Perspectives, 23,* 11–15.

BECK, I. L., MCKEOWN, M., & MCCASLIN, E. (1983). All contexts are not created equal. *Elementary School Journal, 83,* 177–181.

BECK, I. L., MCKEOWN, M. G., & OMANSON, R. C. (1987). The effects and uses of diverse vocabulary instructional techniques. In M. G. McKeown & M. E. Curtis (Eds.), *The nature of vocabulary acquisition* (pp. 117–156). Hillsdale, NJ: Erlbaum.

BECK, I. L., PERFETTI, C. A., & MCKEOWN, M. G. (1982). The effects of long-term vocabulary instruction on lexical access and reading comprehension. *Journal of Educational Psychology, 74,* 506–521.

BEESLEY, M. S. (1986). The effects of word processing on elementary students' written compositions. *Dissertation Abstracts International, 47,* 11A. (University Microfilms No. 87-04, 015)

BELLEZZA, F. S. (1981). Mnemonic devices: Classification, characteristics, and criteria. *Review of Educational Research, 51,* 247–275.

BENNETT, W. J. (1987). *James Madison High School: A Curriculum for American Students.* Washington, DC: U. S. Department of Education.

BENTON, S. L., GLOVER, J. A., & BRUNING, R. H. (1983a). The effect of number of decisions on prose recall. *Journal of Educational Psychology, 75,* 382–390.

BENTON, S. L., GLOVER, J. A., KRAFT, R. G., & PLAKE, B. S. (1984). Cognitive capacity differences among writers. *Journal of Educational Psychology, 76,* 820–834.

BENTON, S. L., GLOVER, J. A., MONKOWSKI, P. G., & SHAUGHNESSY, M. (1983b). Decision difficulty and recall of prose. *Journal of Educational Psychology, 75,* 727–742.

BEREITER, C. (1980). Development in writing. In L. W. Gregg & E. R. Steinberg (Eds.), *Cognitive processes in writing* (pp. 73–93). Hillsdale, NJ: Erlbaum.

BERNSTEIN, B. (1971). *Class, codes and control. Vol. 1: Theoretical studies towards a sociology of language.* London: Routledge & Kegan Paul.

BERTKOTTER, C. (1981). Understanding a writer's awareness of audience. *College Composition and Communication, 32,* 153–167.

BHASKAR, R., & SIMON, H.A. (1977). Problem solving in semantically rich domains: An example from engineering thermodynamics. *Cognitive Science, 1, 193–215.*

BIRNBAUM, J., & EMIG, J. (1983). Creating minds, created texts: Writing and reading. In R. Parker & F. Davis (Eds.), *Developing literacy: Young children's use of language* (pp. 87–104). Newark, DE: International Reading Association.

BIRNBAUM, J. C. (1982). The reading and composing behaviors of selected fourth- and seventh-grade students. *Research in the Teaching of English, 16,* 241–260.

BISANZ, G. L., VESONDER, G. T., & VOSS, J. F. (1978). Knowledge of one's own responding and the relation of such knowledge to learning. *Journal of Experimental Child Psychology, 25,* 116–128.

BISSEX, G. (1980). *GNYS AT WRK: A child learns to write and read.* Cambridge, MA: Harvard University Press.

BJORK, R. A. (1975). Short-term storage: The ordered input of a central processor. In F. Restle, R. M. Shiffrin, N. J. Castellan, H. R. Lindman, & D. B. Pisoni
(Eds.), *Cognitive theory* (pp. 45–72). Hillsdale, NJ: Erlbaum.

BLOOM, B. S., ENGLEHART, M. D., FURST, E. J., HILL, W. H., & KRATHWOHL,
D. R. (1956). *Taxonomy of educational objectives: The classification of educational
goals. Handbook I: Cognitive domain.* New York: McKay.

BOBROW, D. G., & NORMAN, D. A. (1975). Some principles of memory schemata.
In D. G. Bobrow & A. M. Collins (Eds.), *Representation and understanding:
Studies in cognitive science.* New York: Academic Press.

BOLTWOOD, C. R., & BLICK, K. A. (1978). The delineation and application of
three mnemonic techniques. *Psychonomic Science, 20,* 339–341.

BOURNE, L. E. (1982). Typicality effects in logically defined categories. *Memory &
Cognition, 10,* 3–9.

BOURNE, L. E., JR. (1970). Knowing and using concepts. *Psychological Review, 77,*
546–556.

BOURNE, L. E., JR. (1974). An inference model of conceptual rule learning. In R.
Solso (Ed.), *Theories in cognitive psychology.* Potomac, MD: Erlbaum.

BOURNE, L. E., JR., DOMINOWSKI, R. L., & LOFTUS, E. F. (1979). *Cognitive processes.*
Englewood Cliffs, NJ: Prentice-Hall.

BOUSFIELD, W. A. (1953). The occurrence of clustering in randomly arranged
associates. *Journal of General Psychology, 49,* 229–240.

BOWER, G. H. (1970). Analysis of a mnemonic device. *American Scientist, 58,* 496–
510.

BOWER, G. H., & CLARK, M. C. (1969). Narrative stories as mediators for serial
learning. *Psychonomic Science, 14,* 181–182.

BOWER, G. H., MONTEIRO, K. P., & GILLIGAN, S. G. (1978). Emotional mood as a
context for learning and recall. *Journal of Verbal Learning and Verbal Behavior,
17,* 573–587.

BRAINERD, C. J., & PRESSLEY, M. (EDS.) (1985). *Basic processes in memory development.* New York: Springer-Verlag.

BRANSFORD, J. D. (1984). Schema activation and schema acquisition: Comments
on Richard C. Anderson's remarks. In R. C. Anderson, J. Osborn, & R. J.
Tierney (Eds.), *Learning to read in American schools* (pp. 259–272). Hillsdale,
NJ: Erlbaum.

BRANSFORD, J. D., ARBITMAN-SMITH, R., STEIN, B. S., & VYE, N. J. (1985). Improving thinking and learning skills: An analysis of three approaches. In J. W.
Segal, S. F. Chipman, & R. Glaser (Eds.), *Thinking and learning skills: Relating
instruction to basic research, Vol. 1* (pp. 133–206). Hillsdale, NJ: Erlbaum.

BRANSFORD, J. D., BARCLAY, J. R., & FRANKS, J. J. (1972). Sentence memory: A
constructive versus interpretive approach. *Cognitive Psychology, 3,* 193–209.

BRANSFORD, J. D., & JOHNSON, M. K. (1972). Contextual prerequisites for understanding: Some investigations of comprehension and recall. *Journal of Verbal
Learning and Verbal Behavior, 11,* 717–726.

BRANSFORD, J. D., & JOHNSON, M. K. (1973). Considerations of some problems of
comprehension. In W. G. Chase (Ed.), *Visual information processing.* New York:
Academic Press.

BRANSFORD, J. D., & STEIN, B. S. (1984). *The IDEAL problem solver.* New York:
W. H. Freeman.

BRANSFORD, J. D., STEIN, B. S., VYE, N. J., FRANKS, J. J., AUBLE, P. M., MEZYNSKI, K. J., & PERFETTI, C. A. (1982). Differences in approaches to learning: An overview. *Journal of Experimental Psychology: General, 111,* 390–398.

BRAUNE, R., & FOSHAY, W. R. (1983). Towards a practical model of cognitive information processing task analysis and schema acquisition for complex problem-solving situations. *Instructional Science, 12,* 121–145.

BRENNAN, A. D., BRIDGE, C. A., & WINOGRAD, P. N. (1986). The effects of structural variation on children's recall of basal reader stories. *Reading Research Quarterly, 21,* 91–104.

BREWER, W. F. (1973). Is reading a letter-by-letter process? A discussion of Gough's paper. In J. F. Kavanagh & I. G. Mattingly (Eds.), *Language by ear and by eye* (pp. 359–365). Cambridge, MA: MIT Press.

BREZNITZ, Z. (1987). Increasing first graders' reading accuracy and comprehension by accelerating their reading rates. *Journal of Educational Psychology, 79,* 236–242.

BRITTON, B. K. (1986, April). Signalled text effects on learning of six expository texts. Paper presented at the annual meeting of the American Educational Research Association, San Francisco.

BRITTON, B. K., GLYNN, S. M., & SMITH, J. W. (1985). Cognitive demands of processing expository text: A cognitive workbench model. In B. K. Britton & J. Black (Eds.), *Understanding expository text* (pp. 271–302). Hillsdale, NJ: Erlbaum.

BROADBENT, D. E. (1958). *Perception and communication.* London: Pergamon Press.

BROOKS, L. W., & DANSEREAU, D. F. (1983). Effects of structural schema training and text organization on expository prose processing. *Journal of Educational Psychology, 75,* 811–820.

BROPHY, J. E., & GOOD, T. L. (1985). Teacher behavior and student learning. In M. Wittrock (Ed.), *Handbook of Research on Teaching* (3rd ed.) (pp. 236–271). New York: Macmillan.

BROWN, A. L. (1980). Metacognitive development and reading. In R. J. Spiro, B. C. Bruce, & W. F. Brewer (Eds.), *Theoretical issues in reading comprehension* (pp. 458–482). Hillsdale, NJ: Erlbaum.

BROWN, A. L., BRANSFORD, J. D., FERRARA, R. A., & CAMPIONE, J. C. (1983a). Learning, remembering, and understanding. In J. H. Flavell & E. M. Markman (Eds.), P. H. Mussen (Series Ed.), *Handbook of child psychology. Vol. 3: Cognitive development* (pp. 263–340). New York: Wiley.

BROWN, A. L., DAY, J. D., & JONES, R. S. (1983b). The development of plans for summarizing texts. *Child Development, 54,* 968–979.

BROWN, A. L., & PALINCSAR, A. S. (1982). Inducing strategic learning from texts by means of informed, self-control training. *Topics in Learning and Learning Disabilities, 2,* 1–18.

BROWN, A. L., & PALINCSAR, A. S. (1989). Guided, cooperative learning and individual knowledge acquisition. In L. Resnick (Ed.), *Cognition and instruction: Issues and agendas* (pp. 117–161). Hillsdale, NJ: Erlbaum.

BROWN, A. L., & SMILEY, S. S. (1978). The development of strategies for studying texts. *Child Development, 49,* 1076–1088.

BROWN, J. A. (1958). Some tests of the decay theory of immediate memory. *Quarterly Journal of Experimental Psychology, 10,* 12–21.

BROWN, J. S., & BURTON, R. B. (1978). Diagnostic models for procedural bugs in basic mathematical skills. *Cognitive Science, 2,* 155–192.

BROWN, J. S., McDONALD, J. L., BROWN, T. L., & CARR, T. H. (1988). Adapting to processing demands in discourse production: The case of handwriting. *Journal of Experimental Psychology: Human Perception and Performance, 14,* 45–59.

BROWN, J. S., & VAN LEHN, K. (1980). Repair theory: A generative theory of bugs in procedural skills. *Cognitive Science, 4,* 379–426.

BROWN, R. (1973). *A first language: The early stages.* Cambridge, MA: Harvard University Press.

BROWN, R., CAZDEN, C., & BELLUGI, U. (1968). The child's grammar from I to III. In J. P. Hill (Ed.), *Minnesota symposia on child psychology, Vol. 2* (pp. 70–126). Minneapolis: University of Minnesota Press.

BROWN, S. (1986). Reading–writing connections: College freshman basic writers' apprehension and achievement. (ERIC Document Reproduction Service No. ED 274 965)

BRUCE, V., & GREEN, P. (1985). *Visual perception.* Hillsdale, NJ: Erlbaum.

BRUNER, J. S., GOODNOW, J. J., & AUSTIN, G. A. (1956). *A study of thinking.* New York: Wiley.

BRUNING, R. H., & DUNLAP, K. (1984). Background knowledge, interest, and vocabulary knowledge as predictors of reading passage comprehension. Paper presented at the National Reading Conference, St. Petersburg, FL.

BUCHANAN, B. G., & SHORTLIFFE, E. H. (1984). *Rule-based systems.* Reading, MA: Addison-Wesley.

BUGELSKI, B. R., KIDD, E., & SEGMEN, J. (1968). Image as a mediator in one-trial paired-associate learning. *Journal of Experimental Psychology, 76,* 69–73.

BULLOCK, R., & GLOVER, J. A. (in press). Detecting false statements in text: The role of schema activation and external standards. *Journal of Educational Psychology.*

BURBULES, N. C., & LINN, M. C. (1988). Response to contradiction: Scientific reasoning during adolescence. *Journal of Educational Psychology, 80,* 67–75.

BURTON, R. B. (1981). DEBUGGY: Diagnosis of errors in basic mathematical skills. In D. H. Sleeman & J. S. Brown (Eds.), *Intelligent tutoring systems* (pp. 62–81). London: Academic Press.

BUTTERFIELD, J. (ED.) (1986). *Language, mind, and logic.* New York: Cambridge University Press.

CAELLI, T., & MORAGLIA, G. (1986). On the detection of signals embedded in natural scenes. *Perception & Psychophysics, 39,* 87–95.

CAIRNEY, T. H. (1988). The purpose of basals: What children think. *The Reading Teacher, 41,* 420–428.

CALFEE, R. C. (1987a). The school as a context for assessment of literacy. *The Reading Teacher, 40,* 738–743.

CALFEE, R. C. (1987b). The structural features of large texts. *Educational Psychologist, 22,* 357–375.

CALFEE, R. C., & HENRY, M. K. (1986). Project READ: An inservice model for training classroom teachers in effective reading instruction. In J. V. Hoffman (Ed.), *Effective teaching of reading: Research and practice* (pp. 199–299). Newark, DE: International Reading Association.

CAMPBELL, D., & STANLEY, J. (1963). *Experimental and quasi-experimental designs for research.* Skokie, IL: Rand McNally.

CARBO, M. (1988). Debunking the great phonics myth. *Phi Delta Kappan, 70,* 226–240.

CAREY, L., & FLOWER, L. (in press). In J. A. Glover, R. R. Ronning, & C. R. Reynolds (Eds.), *Handbook of creativity.* New York: Plenum.

CAREY, S. (1985). *Conceptual change in childhood.* Cambridge, MA: MIT Press.

CAREY, S. (1986). Cognitive science and science education. *American Psychologist, 41,* 1123–1130.

CAREY, S. T., & LOCKHART, R. S. (1973). Encoding differences in recognition and recall. *Memory & Cognition, 1,* 297–300.

CARLISLE, K. P. (1985). Learning how to learn. *Teaching and Development Journal, 39,* 75–80.

CARLSON, L., ZIMMER, J. W., & GLOVER, J. A. (1981). First-letter mnemonics: DAM (don't aid memory). *The Journal of Genetic Psychology, 104,* 287–292.

CARMICHAEL, L., HOGAN, H. P., & WALTER, A. A. (1932). An experimental study of the effect of language on the reproduction of visually perceived forms. *Journal of Experimental Psychology, 15,* 73–86.

CARPENTER, T. P. (1985). Learning to add and subtract: An exercise in problem solving. In E. A. Silver (Ed.), *Teaching and learning mathematical problem solving: Multiple research perspectives* (pp. 123–161). Hillsdale, NJ: Erlbaum.

CARPENTER, T. P. (1986). Conceptual knowledge as a foundation for procedural knowledge: Implications from research on the initial learning. In J. Hiebert, (Ed.), *Conceptual and procedural knowledge: The case of mathematics* (pp. 135–176). Hillsdale, NJ: Erlbaum.

CARPENTER, T. P., & MOSER, J. M. (1982). The development of addition and subtraction problem-solving skills. In T. P. Carpenter, J. M. Moser, & T. A. Romberg, (Eds.), *Addition and subtraction: A cognitive perspective* (pp. 42–68). Hillsdale, NJ: Erlbaum.

CARPENTER, T. P., & MOSER, J. M. (1983). Acquisition of addition and subtraction concepts. In R. Lesh & M. Landau (Eds.), *Acquisition of mathematical concepts and processes* (pp. 106–113). New York: Academic Press.

CASE, R. (1972). Learning and development: A neo-Piagetian interpretation. *Human Development, 15,* 339–358.

CASE, R. (1978). A developmentally based theory and technology of instruction. *Review of Educational Research, 48,* 439–463.

CASE, R. (1984a). The process of stage transition: A neo-Piagetian view. In R. J. Sternberg (Ed.), *Mechanisms of cognitive development* (pp. 19–44). New York: Freeman.

CASE, R. (1984b). *Intellectual development: A systematic reinterpretation.* New York: Academic Press.

CASE R. (1985). *Intellectual development, birth to adulthood.* New York: Academic Press.

CERASO, J. (1967). The interference theory of forgetting. *Scientific American, 179*(4), 117–124.

CHALL, J. S. (1967). *Learning to read: The great debate.* New York: McGraw-Hill.

CHALL, J. S. (1987). Two vocabularies for reading: Recognition and meaning. In

M. G. McKeown & M. E. Curtis (Eds.), *The nature of vocabulary acquisition* (pp. 7–17). Hillsdale, NJ: Erlbaum.

CHAMPAGNE, A. B., KLOPFER, L. E., & ANDERSON, J. H. (1980). Factors influencing the learning of classical mechanics. *American Journal of Physics, 48,* 1074–1079.

CHAMPAGNE, A. B., KLOPFER, L. E., DESENA, A. T., & SQUIRES, D. A. (1981). Structural representation of students' knowledge before and after science instruction. *Journal of Research in Science Teaching, 18,* 97–111.

CHARNESS, N. (1979). Components of skill in bridge. *Canadian Journal of Psychology, 33,* 1–50.

CHASE, W. G. (1987). Visual information processing. In K. R. Boff, L. Kaufman, & J. P. Thomas (Eds.), *Handbook of perception and human performance. Vol. 2: Information processing* (pp. 28-1 to 28-60). New York: Wiley.

CHASE, W. G., & SIMON, H. A. (1973). *The mind's eye in chess.* In W. G. Chase (Ed.), *Visual information processing.* New York: Academic Press.

CHEN, H. (1986). Effects of reading span and textual coherence on rapid-sequential reading. *Memory & Cognition, 14,* 202–208.

CHI, M.T.H., FELTOVICH, P. J., & GLASER, R. (1981). Categorization and representation of physics problems by experts and novices. *Cognitive Science, 5,* 121–152.

CHI, M.T.H., GLASER, R., & REES, E. (1982). Expertise in problem solving. In R. Sternberg (Ed.), *Advances in the psychology of human intelligence* (pp. 161–183). Hillsdale, NJ: Erlbaum.

CHIPMAN, S. (1988, April). Cognitive processes in mathematics. Paper given at the annual meeting of the American Educational Research Association, New Orleans.

CHOMSKY, N. (1957). *Syntactic structures.* The Hague, The Netherlands: Mouton.

CHOMSKY, N. (1965). *Aspects of the theory of syntax.* Cambridge, MA: MIT Press.

CLEMENT, J. (1983). A conceptual model discussed by Galileo and used intuitively by physics students. In D. Gentner & A. L. Stevens (Eds.), *Mental models* (pp. 206–251). Hillsdale, NJ: Erlbaum.

COFER, C. N., BRUCE, D. R., & REICHER, G. M. (1966). Clustering in free recall as a function of certain methodological variations. *Journal of Experimental Psychology, 71,* 858–866.

COHEN, R. L. (in press). A review of SPT research. *Educational Psychology Review.*

COLLINS, A. M., & LOFTUS, E. F. (1975). A spreading-activation theory of semantic processing. *Psychological Review, 82,* 407–428.

COLLINS, A. M., & QUILLIAN, M. R. (1969). Retrieval time from semantic memory. *Journal of Verbal Learning and Verbal Behavior, 8,* 240–248.

COLLYER, S. C., JONIDES, J., & BEVAN, W. (1972). Images as memory aids: Is bizarreness helpful? *American Journal of Psychology, 85,* 31–38.

CONRY, R., & PLANT, W. T. (1965). WAIS and group test prediction of an academic success criterion: High school and college. *Educational and Psychological Measurement, 25,* 493–500.

COOPER, C. R. (1988). Statewide writing assessment. Paper presented to the annual meeting of the American Educational Research Association, New Orleans.

COOPER, L. A., & SHEPARD, R. N. (1973). Chronometric studies of the rotation of mental images. In W. G. Chase (Ed.), *Visual information processing* (pp. 56–82). New York: Academic Press.

CORKILL, A. J., BRUNING, R. H., & GLOVER, J. A. (1988a). Advance organizers: Concrete vs. abstract. *The Journal of Educational Research, 82,* 76–81.

CORKILL, A. J., & GLOVER, J. A. (in press). Cognitive correlates of creative abilities. *Creative Adult and Child Quarterly.*

CORKILL, A. J., GLOVER, J. A., BRUNING, R. H., & KRUG, D. (1988b). Advance organizers: Retrieval context hypotheses. *Journal of Educational Psychology, 80,* 304–311.

COVINGTON, M. C., CRUTCHFIELD, R. S., DAVIES, L. B., & OLTON, R. M. (1974). *The productive thinking program: A course in learning to think.* Columbus, OH: Charles E. Merrill.

COX, S. D., & WOLLEN, K. A. (1981). Bizarreness and recall. *Bulletin of the Psychonomic Society, 18,* 244–245.

CRAIK, F.I.M. (1979). Human memory. *Annual Review of Psychology, 30,* 63–102.

CRAIK, F.I.M., & LOCKHART, R. S. (1972). Levels of processing: A framework for memory research. *Journal of Verbal Learning and Verbal Behavior, 11,* 671–684.

CRAIK, F.I.M., & LOCKHART, R. S. (1986). CHARM is not enough: Comments on Eich's model of cued recall. *Psychological Review, 93,* 360–364.

CRAIK, F.I.M., & TULVING, E. (1975). Depth of processing and the retention of words in episodic memory. *Journal of Experimental Psychology: General, 104,* 268–294.

CRAIK, F.I.M., & WATKINS, M. J. (1973). The role of rehearsal in short-term memory. *Journal of Verbal Learning and Verbal Behavior, 12,* 599–607.

CROMBIE, W. (1985). *Process and relation in discourse and language learning.* Oxford: Oxford University Press.

CROSS, D. R., & PARIS, S. G. (1988). Developmental and instructional analyses of children's metacognition and reading comprehension. *Journal of Educational Psychology, 80,* 131–142.

CROSSMAN, E.R.F. (1959). A theory of the acquisition of a speed-skill. *Ergonomics, 2,* 153–166.

CROUSE, J. H., & IDSTEIN, P. (1972). Effects of encoding cues on prose learning. *Journal of Educational Psychology, 63,* 309–313.

CROWDER, R. G. (1976). *Principles of learning and memory.* Hillsdale, NJ: Erlbaum.

DAEHLER, M. W., & BUKATKO, D. (1985). *Cognitive development.* New York: Knopf.

DAIUTE, C. (1986). Physical and cognitive factors in revising: Insights from studies with computers. *Research in the Teaching of English, 20,* 141–159.

DARWIN, G. J., & BADDELEY, A. D. (1974). Acoustic memory and the perception of speech. *Cognitive Psychologist, 6,* 41–60.

DARWIN, G. J., TURVEY, M. T., & CROWDER, R. G. (1972). An auditory analogue of the Sperling partial report procedure: Evidence for brief auditory storage. *Cognitive Psychology, 3,* 255–267.

DAVIS, R. (1986). Knowledge-systems. *Science, 231,* 957–963.

DAVISON, A., & GREEN, G. (1987). *Linguistic complexity and text comprehension.* Hillsdale, NJ: Erlbaum.

DAY, J. D. (1980). Teaching summarization skills: A comparison of training methods. Unpublished doctoral dissertation, University of Illinois, Urbana.

DE BOER, J. J. (1959). Grammar in language teaching. *Elementary English, 36,* 413–421.

DE BONO, E. (1973). *CoRT thinking materials.* London: Direct Education Services.

DECONCICI, D. (1988). America's little red schoolroom: How is it holding up today? *American Psychologist, 43,* 115–117.

DEGROOT, A. D. (1965). *Thought and choice in chess.* The Hague: Mouton.

DEJONG, T., & FERGUSON-HESSLER, M.G.M. (1986). Cognitive structures of good and poor novice problem solvers in physics. *Journal of Educational Psychology, 78,* 279–288.

DELLAROSA, D. (1988). A history of thinking. In R. J. Sternberg & E. F. Smith (Eds.), *The psychology of human thought* (pp. 1–18). New York: Cambridge University Press.

DELLAROSA, D., & BOURNE, L. E. (1985). Surface form and the spacing effect. *Memory and Cognition, 13,* 529–537.

DELOACHE, J. S. (1986). Memory in very young children: Exploitation of cues to the location of hidden objects. *Cognitive Development, 1,* 123–137.

DELOACHE, J. S., CASSIDY, D. J., & BROWN, A. L. (1985). Precursors of mnemonic strategies in very young children's memory. *Child Development, 56,* 125–137.

DEMPSTER, F. N. (1981). Memory span: Sources of individual and developmental differences. *Psychological Bulletin, 89,* 63–100.

DENIS, M. (1986). Visual imagery: Effects or role in prose processing? In F. Klix & H. Hafgendorf (Eds.), *Human memory and cognitive capabilities: Mechanisms and performances* (Part A, pp. 237–244). Amsterdam: North-Holland.

DERRY, S. J. (1984). Effects of an organizer on memory for prose. *Journal of Educational Psychology, 76,* 98–107.

DEUTSCH, D. (1987). Auditory pattern recognition. In K. R. Boff, L. Kaufman, & J. P. Thomas (Eds.), *Handbook of perception and human performance. Vol. 2: Information processing* (pp. 32-1 to 32-55). New York: Wiley.

DEWITZ, P., CARR, E. M., & PATBERG, J. P. (1987). Effects of inference training on comprehension and comprehension monitoring. *Reading Research Quarterly, 22,* 99–119.

DIAMOND, B. J. (1985). The cognitive processes of competent third grade writers: A descriptive study. *Dissertation Abstracts International, 46,* 05A. (University Microfilms No. DA 8513892)

DICKINSON, D. K., & SNOW, C. E. (1986). Interrelationships among pre-reading and oral language skills in kindergarteners from two social classes. (ERIC Document Reproduction Services No. ED 272 860)

DILOLLO, U., & DIXON, P. (1988). Two forms of persistence in visual information processing. *Journal of Experimental Psychology: Human Perception and Performance, 14,* 601–609.

DINNEL, D., & GLOVER, J. A. (1985). Advance organizers: Encoding manipulations. *Journal of Educational Psychology, 77,* 514–521.

DIVESTA, F. J. (1987). The cognitive movement and education. In J. A. Glover & R. R. Ronning (Eds.), *Historical foundations of educational psychology* (pp. 203–236). New York: Plenum.

DOOLING, D. J., & LACHMAN, R. (1971). Effects of comprehension on retention of prose. *Journal of Experimental Psychology, 88,* 216–222.

DORE, J. (1985). Children's conversations. In T. A. Van Dijk (Ed.), *Handbook of discourse analysis. Vol. 3: Discourse and dialogue* (pp. 84–98). London: Academic Press.

DORVAL, B., & ECKERMAN, C. O. (1984). Developmental trends in the quality of conversation achieved by small groups of acquainted peers. *Monographs of the Society for Research in Child Development, 49* (2, Serial No. 206).

DOYLE, W. (1983). Academic work. *Review of Educational Research, 53,* 159–199.

DRIVER, R., GUESNE, E., & TIBERGHIEN, A. (1985). *Children's ideas in science.* Philadelphia: Open University Press.

DRUM, P. A., & KONOPAK, B. C. (1987). Learning word meanings from written context. In M. G. McKeown & M. E. Curtis (Eds.), *The nature of vocabulary acquisition* (pp. 7–17). Hillsdale, NJ: Erlbaum.

DUELL, O. K. (1978). Overt and covert use of different cognitive levels. *Contemporary Educational Psychology, 3,* 239–245.

DUIN, A. H., & GRAVES, M. F. (1986). Effects of vocabulary instruction used as a prewriting technique. *Journal of Research and Development in Education, 20,* 7–13.

DUIN, A. H., & GRAVES, M. F. (1987). Intensive vocabulary instruction as a prewriting technique. *Reading Research Quarterly, 22,* 311–330.

DUNCKER, K. (1945). On problem solving (L. S. Lees, Trans.). *Psychological Monographs, 58,* 407–416.

DURKIN, D. (1978–1979). What classroom observations reveal about reading comprehension instruction. *Reading Research Quarterly, 14,* 481–533.

DURKIN, D. (1981). Reading comprehension instruction in five basal reading series. *Reading Research Quarterly, 16,* 515–544.

DURKIN, K. (ED.). (1986). Language and social cognition during the school years. In K. Durkin (Ed.), *Language development in the school years* (pp. 203–261). Cambridge, MA: Brookline Books.

DURKIN, K., CROWTHER, R. D., & SHIRE, B. (1986). Children's processing of polysemous vocabulary in school. In K. Durkin (Ed.), *Language development in the school years* (pp. 105–132). Cambridge, MA: Brookline Books.

DURST, R. K. (1987). Cognitive and linguistic demands of analytic writing. *Research in the Teaching of English, 21,* 347–376.

DURST, R. K., & MARSHALL, S. D. (1987). Annotated bibliography of research in the teaching of English. *Research in the Teaching of English, 21,* 422–443.

DYSON, A. (1983). The role of oral language in early writing processes. *Research in the Teaching of English, 17,* 1–30.

EBBINGHAUS, H. (1885). *Uber das Gedachtnis* [Memory]. Leipzig, Germany: Duncker and Humblot.

EBERTS, R., & SCHNEIDER, W. (1986). Effects of training of sequenced line movements. *Perception & Psychophysics, 39,* 87–95.

EDWARDS, J. (1986). Language and educational disadvantage: The persistence of linguistic "deficit" theory. In K. Durkin (Ed.), *Language development in the school years* (pp. 139–154). Cambridge, MA: Brookline Books.

EDWARDS, J., & MERCER, R. (1986). Context and continuity: Classroom discourse and the development of shared knowledge. In K. Durkin (Ed.), *Language development in the school years* (pp. 172–202). Cambridge, MA: Brookline Books.

EGAN, D., & SCHWARTZ, B. (1979). Chunking in recall of symbolic drawings. *Memory & Cognition, 7,* 145–158.

EHRI, L. C., & WILCE, L. S. (1985). Movement into reading: Is the first stage of printed word learning visual or phonetic? *Reading Research Quarterly, 20,* 163–179.

EHRI, L. C., & WILCE, L. S. (1987a). Cipher versus cue reading: An experiment in decoding acquisition. *Journal of Educational Psychology, 79,* 3–13.

EHRI, L. C., & WILCE, L. S. (1987b). Does learning to spell help beginners learn to read words? *Reading Research Quarterly, 22,* 47–65.

ELMES, D. G., & BJORK, R. A. (1975). The interaction of encoding and rehearsal processes in the recall of repeated and nonrepeated items. *Journal of Verbal Learning and Verbal Behavior, 14,* 30–42.

EMIG, J. (1971). *The composing process of twelfth graders.* Urbana, IL: National Council of Teachers of English.

EMMERICH, H., & ACKERMAN, B. (1979). A test of bizarre interaction as a factor in children's memory. *The Journal of Genetic Psychology, 134,* 225–232.

ENGLERT, C. S., & HIEBERT, E. (1984). Children's developing awareness of text structures in expository materials. *Journal of Educational Psychology, 76,* 65–74.

EPSTEIN, W., GLENBERG, A. M., & BRADLEY, M. M. (1984). Coactivation and comprehension: Contribution of text variables to the illusion of knowing. *Memory & Cognition, 12,* 355–360.

ERICSSON, K. A., CHASE, W. G., & FALOON, S. (1980). Acquisition of a memory skill. *Science, 208,* 1181–1182.

ERVIN, S. M. (1964). Imitation and structural change in children's language. In E. H. Lenneberg (Ed.), *New directions in the study of language* (pp. 163–189). Cambridge, MA: MIT Press.

FARR, R. (1969). *Reading: What can be measured?* Newark, DE: International Reading Association.

FAW, H. W., & WALLER, T. G. (1976). Mathemagenic behaviors and efficiency in learning from prose materials. Review, critique and recommendations. *Review of Educational Research, 46,* 691–720.

FERSTER, C. B., & SKINNER, B. F. (1957). *Schedules of reinforcement.* New York: Appleton-Century-Crofts.

FEUERSTEIN, R., RAND, Y., HOFFMAN, M. B., & MILLER, R. (1980). *Instrumental enrichment: An intervention program for cognitive modifiability.* Baltimore: University Park Press.

FISHER, D. L., DUFFY, S. A., YOUNG, C., & POLLATSEK, A. (1988). Understanding the central processing limit in consistent-mapping visual search tasks. *Journal of Experimental Psychology: Human Perception and Performance, 14,* 253–266.

FITTS, P. M., & POSNER, M. I. (1967). *Human performance.* Belmont, CA: Brooks/Cole.

FITZGERALD, J., & SPIEGEL, D. L. (1983). Enhancing children's reading comprehension through instruction in narrative structure. *Journal of Reading Behavior, 15,* 1–17.

FLAVELL, J. H., FRIEDRICHS, A. G., & HOYT, J. P. (1970). Developmental changes in memorization processes. *Cognitive Psychology, 1,* 324–340.

FLESCH, R. (1955). *Why Johnny can't read.* New York: Harper & Row.

FLEXSER, A. J., & TULVING, E. (1978). Retrieval independence in recognition and recall. *Psychological Review, 85,* 153–171.

FLOWER, L., SCHRIVER, K., CAREY, L. J., HAAS, C., & HAYES, J. R. (1987). Planning in writing: A theory of the cognitive process. ONR Technical Report, No. 1. Pittsburgh: Carnegie-Mellon University.

FOGIEL, M. (ED.) (1976). *The physics problem solver.* New York: Research and Education Association.

FOWLER, R. L., & BARKER, A. S. (1974). Effectiveness of highlighting for retention of text material. *Journal of Applied Psychology, 59,* 358–364.

FRASE, L. T., & SCHWARTZ, B. J. (1975). Effect of question production and answering in prose recall. *Journal of Educational Psychology, 67,* 628–635.

FREDERIKSEN, C. H. (1975). Representing logical and semantic structure of knowledge acquired from discourse. *Cognitive Psychology, 7,* 371–458.

FREEBODY, P., & ANDERSON, R. C. (1983). Effects of vocabulary difficulty, text cohesion, and schema availability on reading comprehension. *Reading Research Quarterly, 18,* 277–294.

FRIEDMAN, A., POLSON, M. C., & DAFOE, C. G. (1988). Dividing attention between the hands and the head: Performance trade-offs between rapid finger tapping and verbal memory. *Journal of Experimental Psychology: Human Perception and Performance, 14,* 60–68.

FROGNER, E. (1939). Grammar approach vs. thought approach in teaching sentence structure. *English Journal, 28,* 518–526.

FURST, B. (1954). *Stop forgetting.* New York: Garden City Press.

GAGNE, E. D. (1985). *The cognitive psychology of school learning.* Boston: Little, Brown.

GAGNE, R. M. (1965). The analysis of instructional objectives for the design of instruction. In R. Glaser (Ed.), *Teaching machines and programmed learning. II: Data and direction* (pp. 32–41). Washington, DC: National Education Association.

GAGNE, R. M. (1970). *The conditions of learning* (2nd ed.). New York: Holt, Rinehart & Winston.

GAGNE, R. M. (1977). *The conditions of learning for instruction* (3rd ed.). New York: Holt, Rinehart & Winston.

GARNER, R. (1987). Monitoring of passage consistency among poor comprehenders: A preliminary test of the "piecemeal processing" explanation. *Journal of Educational Research, 74,* 159–162.

GEARY, D. C., & WIDAMAN, K. F. (1987). Individual differences in cognitive arithmetic. *Journal of Experimental Psychology: General, 116,* 154–171.

GENESEE, F. (1985). Second language learning through immersion: A review of U.S. programs. *Review of Educational Research, 55,* 541–561.

GETZELS, J. W., & CSIKSZENTMIHALYI, M. (1976). *The creative vision: A longitudinal study of problem finding in art.* New York: Wiley.

GHATALA, E. S., LEVIN, J. R., PRESSLEY, M., & LODICO, M. G. (1985). Training cognitive strategy monitoring in children. *American Educational Research Journal, 22,* 199–216.

GIBSON, E. J. (1969). *Principles of perceptual learning and development.* New York: Prentice-Hall.

GIBSON, E. J., & SPELKE, E. S. (1983). The development of perception. In J. H. Flavell & E. M. Markman (Eds.), P. H. Mussen (Series Ed.), *Handbook of child psychology. Vol. 3: Development* (pp. 1–76). New York: Wiley.

GICK, M. L., & HOLYOAK, K. J. (1980). Analogical problem solving. *Cognitive Psychology, 12,* 306–355.

GICK, M. L., & HOLYOAK, K. J. (1983). Schema induction and analogical transfer. *Cognitive Psychology, 15,* 1–38.

GLASER, R. (1984). Education and thinking: The role of knowledge. *American Psychologist, 39,* 93–104.

GLAZE, J. A. (1928). The association value of non-sense syllables. *Journal of Genetic Psychology, 35,* 255–269.

GLENBERG, A. M., & EPSTEIN, W. (1985). Calibration of comprehension. *Journal of Experimental Psychology: Learning, Memory, and Cognition, 11,* 702–718.

GLENBERG, A. M., SANOCKI, T., EPSTEIN, W., & MORRIS, C. (1987). Enhancing calibration of comprehension. *Journal of Experimental Psychology: General, 116,* 119–136.

GLENBERG, A. M., SMITH, S. M., & GREEN, C. (1977). Type I rehearsal: Maintenance and more. *Journal of Verbal Learning and Verbal Behavior, 16,* 339–352.

GLENBERG, A. M., WILKINSON, A. C., & EPSTEIN, W. (1982). The illusion of knowing: Failure in the self-assessment of comprehension. *Memory & Cognition, 10,* 597–602.

GLOVER, J. A. (1979a). Levels of questions asked in interview and reading sessions. *The Journal of Genetic Psychology, 135,* 103–108.

GLOVER, J. A. (1979b). Procedures to enhance the creative writing of elementary school children. *Journal of Applied Behavior Analysis, 12,* 483.

GLOVER, J. A. (1982). Implementing creativity training of students through teacher inservice training. *Educational Research Quarterly, 6,* 13–19.

GLOVER, J. A. (in press). Longer, long-term memory for prose.

GLOVER, J. A., BRUNING, R. H., & PLAKE, B. S. (1982a). Distinctiveness of encoding and recall of text materials. *Journal of Educational Psychology, 74,* 522–534.

GLOVER, J. A., & CORKILL, A. (1987). The spacing effect in memory for prose. *Journal of Educational Psychology, 79,* 198–200.

GLOVER, J. A., & CORKILL, A. J. (in press). Applications of cognitive psychology. In C. R. Reynolds & T. B. Gutkin (Eds.), *Handbook of school psychology.* New York: Wiley.

GLOVER, J. A., DINNEL, D. L., HALPAIN, D., MCKEE, T., CORKILL A. J., & WISE, S. (1988a). Effects of across-chapter signals on recall of text. *Journal of Educational Psychology, 80,* 3–15.

GLOVER, J. A., HARVEY, A. L., & CORKILL, A. J. (1988b). Remembering written instructions: Tab A goes into slot C, or does it? *British Journal of Educational Psychology, 58,* 191–200.

GLOVER, J. A., PLAKE, B. S., & ZIMMER, J. W. (1982b). Distinctiveness of encoding and memory for learning tasks. *Journal of Educational Psychology, 74,* 189–198.

GLOVER, J. A., RANKIN, J., LANGNER, N., TODERO, C., & DINNEL, D. (1985). Memory for sentences and prose: Levels-of-processing or transfer-appropriate-processing? *Journal of Reading Behavior, 17,* 215–234.

GLOVER, J. A., & RONNING, R. R. (EDS.) (1987). *Historical foundations of educational psychology.* New York: Plenum.

GLOVER, J. A., TIMME, V., DEYLOFF, D., & ROGERS, M. (1987a). Memory for student performed tasks. *Journal of Educational Psychology, 79,* 445–452.

GLOVER, J. A., TIMME, V., DEYLOFF, D., ROGERS, M., & DINNEL, D. (1987b). Oral directions: Remembering what to do when. *Journal of Educational Research, 81,* 33–53.

GLOVER, J. A., & ZIMMER, J. W. (1982). Procedures to influence levels of questions asked by students. *Journal of General Psychology, 107,* 267–276.

GLOVER, J. A., ZIMMER, J. W., FILBECK, R. W., & PLAKE, B. S. (1980). Effects of training students to identify the semantic base of prose material. *Journal of Applied Behavior Analysis, 13,* 655–667.

GLYNN, S. M., & DIVESTA, F. J. (1979). Control of prose processing via instructional and typographical cues. *Journal of Educational Psychology, 71,* 595–603.

GODDEN, D. R., & BADDELEY, A. D. (1975). Context-dependent memory in two natural environments: On land and under water. *British Journal of Psychology, 66,* 325–331.

GOETZ, E. M. (in press). In J. A. Glover, R. R. Ronning, & C. R. Reynolds (Eds.), *Handbook of Creativity.* New York: Plenum.

GOLDENSTEIN, E. H., RONNING, R. R., & WALTER, L. J. (1988). Course selection across three decades as a measure of curriculum change. *Educational Leadership, 46,* 56–59.

GOLDMAN, S. R., & VARNHAGEN, C. K. (1986). Improving comprehension: Causal relations instruction for learning among handicapped learners. *Reading Teacher, 39,* 898–904.

GOLDSTEIN, E. B. (1988). Geometry or not geometry? Perceived orientation and spatial layout in pictures viewed at an angle. *Journal of Experimental Psychology: Human Perception and Performance, 14,* 312–314.

GOOD, T. L. (1983, April). Classroom research: A decade of progress. Paper presented at the meeting of the American Educational Research Association, Boston.

GOODMAN, C., & GARDINER, J. M. (1981). How well do children remember what they have recalled? *British Journal of Educational Psychology, 51,* 97–101.

GOODMAN, K. S. (1967). Reading: A psycholinguistic guessing game. *Journal of the Reading Specialist, 6,* 126–135.

GOODMAN, K. S. (1982a). Reading: A psycholinguistic guessing game. In F. V. Gollasch (Ed.), *Language and literacy* (Vol. 1, pp. 19–31). Boston: Routledge & Kegan Paul.

GOODMAN, K. S. (1982b). The reading process: Theory and practice. In F. V. Gollasch (Ed.), *Language and literacy* (Vol. 1, pp. 33–43). Boston: Routledge & Kegan Paul.

GOODMAN, K. S. (1982c). Miscues: Windows on the reading process. In F. V. Gollasch (Ed.), *Language and literacy* (Vol. 1, pp. 64–79). Boston: Routledge & Kegan Paul.

GOODMAN, K. S. (1986). *What's whole in whole language?* Richmond Hill, Ontario: Scholastic–TAB.

GOODMAN, K. S., & GOODMAN, Y. (1979). Learning to read is natural. In L. B. Resnick & P. A. Weaver (Eds.), *Theory and practice of early reading* (pp. 51–94). Hillsdale, NJ: Erlbaum.

GOODMAN, K. S., & GOODMAN, Y. M. (1982). Learning about psycholinguistic processes by analyzing oral reading. In F. V. Gollasch (Ed.), *Language and literacy* (Vol. 1, pp. 149–168). Boston: Routledge & Kegan Paul.

Goss, A. E. (1961). Verbal mediating response and concept formation, *Psychological Review, 68,* 248–274.

Gough, P. B. (1972). One second of reading. In F. Kavanagh & I. G. Mattingly (Eds.), *Language by ear and by eye* (pp. 331–358). Cambridge, MA: MIT Press.

Gough, P. B., & Hillinger, M. L. (1980). Learning to read: An unnatural act. *Bulletin of the Orton Society, 30,* 180–196.

Grabe, M., & Mann, S. (1984). A technique for the assessment and training of comprehension monitoring skills. *Journal of Reading Behavior, 16,* 131–144.

Graham, K. G. (1984). *Study skills handbook.* Springfield, IL: IRA.

Graves, D. (1975). An examination of the writing processes of seven-year-old children. *Research in the Teaching of English, 9,* 227–242.

Graves, M. F. (1987). The roles of instruction in fostering vocabulary development. In M. G. McKeown & M. E. Curtis (Eds.), *The nature of vocabulary acquisition* (pp. 165–181). Hillsdale, NJ: Erlbaum.

Graves, M. F., & Duin, A. H. (1985). Building students' expressive vocabularies. *Educational Perspectives, 23,* 4–10.

Gray, D. J. (1988). Writing across the curriculum. *Phi Delta Kappa, 52,* 729–733.

Green, J. (1983). Research on teaching as a linguistic process: A state of art. In E. Gordon (Ed.), *Review of research in education, Vol. 10* (pp. 151–252). Washington, DC: American Educational Research Association.

Greeno, J. G. (1974). Hobbits and orcs: Acquisition of a sequential concept. *Congitive Psychology, 6,* 270–292.

Greeno, J. G. (1976). Cognitive objectives of instruction: Theory of knowledge for solving problems and answering questions. In D. Klahr (Ed.), *Cognition and instruction* (pp. 123–155). Hillsdale, NJ: Erlbaum.

Grobe, C. H. (1981). Syntactic maturity, mechanics, and vocabulary as predictors of quality ratings. *Research in the Teaching of English, 15,* 75–85.

Grossberg, S. (1986). The adaptive self-organization of serial order in behavior: Speech, language, and motor control. In E. C. Schwab & H. C. Nusbaum (Eds.), *Pattern recognition by humans and machines* (pp. 1–42). New York: Academic Press.

Grunwell, P. (1986). Aspects of phonological development in later childhood. In K. Durkin (Ed.), *Language development in the school years* (pp. 34–56). Cambridge, MA: Brookline Books.

Halliday, M., & Hasan, R. (1974). *Cohesion in English.* London: Longman.

Halpain, D., Glover, J. A., & Harvey, A. L. (1985). Differential effects of higher- and lower-order questions: Attention hypotheses. *Journal of Educational Psychology, 71,* 703–715.

Hamaker, C. (1986). The effects of adjunct questions on prose learning. *Review of Educational Research, 56,* 212–242.

Hamilton, R. J. (1985). A framework for the evaluation of the effectiveness of adjunct questions and objectives. *Review of Educational Research, 55,* 47–85.

Handel, S. (1988). Space is to time as vision is to audition: Seductive but misleading. *Journal of Experimental Psychology: Human Perception and Performance, 14,* 315–317.

Hare, V. C., & Milligan, B. (1984). Main idea identification: Instructional explanations in four basal reader series. *Journal of Reading Behavior, 16,* 169–203.

HARRIS, A. J., & SIPAY, E. R. (1983). *Readings on reading instruction* (2nd ed.). New York: Longman.

HARRIS, J. (1986). A silent voice, an absent ear: The role of the reader in theories of composing. *Dissertation Abstracts International, 47,* 08A. (University Microfilms No. 86-25, 625)

HAUCK, P., WALSH, C., & KROLL, N. (1976). Visual imagery mnemonics: Common vs. bizarre mental images. *Bulletin of the Psychonomic Society, 7,* 160–162.

HAWISHER, G. E. (1987). The effects of word processing on the revision strategies of college freshmen. *Research in the Teaching of English, 21,* 145–159.

HAWKINS, H. L., & PRESSON, J. C. (1987). Auditory information processing. In K. R. Boff, L. Kaufman, & J. P. Thomas (Eds.), *Handbook of perception and human performance. Vol. 2: Information processing* (pp. 26-1 to 26-48). New York: Wiley.

HAYES, J. E., & MICHIE, D. (1983). *Intelligent systems.* New York: Halstead.

HAYES, J. R. (1981). *The complete problem solver.* Philadelphia: Franklin Institute Press.

HAYES, J. R. (1988). *The complete problem solver* (2nd ed.). Hillsdale, NJ: Erlbaum.

HAYES, J. R. (in press). A cognitive model of creative problem solving. In J. A. Glover, R. R. Ronning, & C. R. Reynolds (Eds.), *Handbook of creativity.* New York: Plenum.

HAYES, J. R., & FLOWER, L. S. (1986). Writing research and the writer. *American Psychologist, 41,* 1106–1113.

HAYES, J. R., & SIMON, H. (1974). Understanding written problem instructions. In L. W. Gregg (Ed.), *Knowledge and cognition.* Hillsdale, NJ: Erlbaum.

HAYES, J. R., WATERMAN, D. A., & ROBINSON, C. S. (1977). Identifying relevant aspects of a problem text. *Cognitive Science, 1,* 297–313.

HAYGOOD, R. C., & BOURNE, L. E., JR. (1965). Attribute- and rule-learning aspects of conceptual behavior. *Psychological Review, 72,* 175–196.

HEATH, S. B. (1983). *Ways with words: Language, life and work in communities and classrooms.* Cambridge: Cambridge University Press.

HEATH, S. B. (1986). Separating "things of the imagination" from life: Learning to read and write. In W. H. Teale & E. Sulzby (Eds.), *Emergent literacy* (pp. 156–172). Norwood, NJ: Ablex.

HEBB, D. O. (1949). *The organization of behavior.* New York: Wiley.

HERMAN, P. A., ANDERSON, R. C., PEARSON, P. D., & NAGY, W. E. (1987). Incidental acquisition of word meaning from expositions with varied text features. *Reading Research Quarterly, 22,* 263–284.

HIDI, S., & ANDERSON, V. (1986). Producing written summaries: Task demands, cognitive operations, and implications for instruction. *Review of Educational Research, 56,* 473–493.

HIEBERT, J. (ED.) (1986). *Conceptual and procedural knowledge: The case of mathematics.* Hillsdale, NJ: Erlbaum.

HIGBEE, K. L., & KUNIHIRA, S. (1985). Cross-cultural applications of yodai mnemonics in education. *Educational Psychologist, 20,* 57–64.

HILGERS, T. C. (1986). How children change as critical evaluators of writing. Four three-year care studies. *Research in the Teaching of English, 20,* 36–55.

HINSLEY, D. A., HAYES, J. R., & SIMON, H. A. (1977). From words to equations: Meaning and representation in algebra word problems. In P. A. Carpenter & M. A. Just (Eds.), *Cognitive processes in comprehension.* Hillsdale, NJ: Erlbaum.

HINTON, G. E., MCCLELLAND, J. L., & D. E. RUMELHART (1986). Distributed representations. In D. E. Rumelhart & J. L. McClelland (Eds.), *Parallel distributed processing: Explorations in the microstructure of cognition: Vol. 1, Foundations* (pp. 77–109). Cambridge, MA: MIT Press.

HOLLAND, J., & SKINNER, B. F. (1961). *The analysis of behavior.* New York: McGraw-Hill.

HOLYOAK, K. J. (1985). The pragmatics of analogical transfer. In G. H. Bower (Ed.), *The psychology of learning and motivation, 9.* Pp. 59–87. New York: Academic Press.

HOLYOAK, K. J. (1987). A connectionist view of cognition (Review of *Parallel distributed processing*). *Science, 236,* 992–996.

HOMME, L., CSANYI, A. P., GONZALES, M. A., & RECHS, J. R. (1968). *How to use contingency contracting in the classroom.* Champaign, IL: Research Press.

HUDSON, T. (1980, July). Young children's difficulty with "How many more _____ than _____are there?" questions. Doctoral dissertation, Indiana University, 1980. *Dissertation Abstracts International, 41.*

HULL, C. L. (1934). The concept of the habit-family hierarchy and maze learning: Part I. *Psychological Review, 34,* 33–54.

HULL, C. L. (1952). *A behavior system: An introduction to behavior theory concerning the individual organism.* New Haven, CT: Yale University Press.

HULL, G. (1987). The editing process in writing: A performance study of more skilled and less skilled college writers. *Research in the Teaching of English, 21,* 8–29.

HUNT, E. (1987). Science, technology and intelligence. In R. R. Ronning, J. A. Glover, & J. Conoley (Eds.), *The impact of cognitive psychology on measurement* (pp. 156–178). Hillsdale, NJ: Erlbaum.

HYDE, T. S., & JENKINS, J. J. (1969). Recall for words as a function of semantic, graphic, and syntactic orienting tasks. *Journal of Verbal Learning and Verbal Behavior, 12,* 471–480.

INHELDER, B., & PIAGET, J. (1958). *The growth of logical thinking: From childhood to adolescence.* New York: Basic Books.

ISAACS, E. A., & CLARK, H. H. (1987). References in conversations between experts and novices. *Journal of Experimental Psychology: General, 116,* 26–37.

JACOBS, J. E., & PARIS, S. G. (1987). Children's metacognition about reading: Issues in definition, measurement, and instruction. *Educational Psychologist, 22,* 255–278.

JACOBY, L. L. (1978). On interpreting the effects of repetition: Solving a problem versus remembering a solution. *Journal of Verbal Learning and Verbal Behavior, 17,* 649–667.

JACOBY, L. L., & CRAIK, F.I.M. (1979). Effects of elaboration of processing at encoding and retrieval: Trace distinctiveness and recovery of initial context. In L. S. Cermak & F.I.M. Craik (Eds.), *Levels of processing in human memory* (pp. 1–22). Hillsdale, NJ: Erlbaum.

JACOBY, L. L., CRAIK, F.I.M., & BEGG, I. (1979). Effects of decision difficulty on recognition and recall. *Journal of Verbal Learning and Verbal Behavior, 18,* 585–600.

JAMES, W. (1890). *The principles of psychology.* New York: Holt, Rinehart & Winston.

JEFFRIES, R., POLSON, P. G., RAZRAN, L., & ATWOOD, M. E. (1977). A process model for missionaries–cannibals and other river-crossing problems. *Cognitive Psychology, 9,* 412–440.

JENKINS, J. J. (1974). Remember that old theory of memory? Well, forget it! *American Psychologist, 25,* 785–795.

JENKINS, J. J., & RUSSELL, W. A. (1952). Associative clustering during recall. *Journal of Abnormal and Social Psychology, 47,* 818–821.

JENKINS, J., STEIN, M., & WYSOCKI, K. (1984). Learning vocabulary through reading. *American Educational Research Journal, 21,* 767–788.

JENKINSON, E. B. (1988). Learning to write/Writing to learn. *Phi Delta Kappan, 69,* 712–717.

JOHNSON, C. N., & WELLMAN, H. M. (1980). Children's developing understanding of mental verbs: Remember, know, and guess. *Child Development, 51,* 1095–1102.

JOHNSON, C. W., & BRUNING, R. H. (1984). Keywords and vocabulary acquisition: Some words of caution about words of assistance. *Educational Communications and Technology, 33,* 125–138.

JONES, E. D., KROUSE, J. P., FEORENE, D., & SAFERSTEIN, C. A. (1985). A comparison of concurrent and sequential instruction of four types of verbal math problems. *Remedial and Special Education, 6,* 25–31.

JUSCZYK, P. W. (1987). Speech perception. In K. R. Boff, L. Kaufman, & J. P. Thomas (Eds.), *Handbook of perception and human performance. Vol. 2: Information processing* (pp. 27-1 to 27-66). New York: Wiley.

JUST, M. A., & CARPENTER, P. A. (1987). *The psychology of reading and language comprehension.* Boston: Allyn & Bacon.

KAIL, R. V., JR. (1984). *The development of memory in children* (2nd ed.). New York: Freeman.

KANTOWSKI, M. G. (1977). Processes involved in mathematical problem solving. *Journal for Research in Mathematics Education, 8,* 163–180.

KAZDIN, A. E. (1985). *Treatment of antisocial behaviors in children and adolescents.* Homewood, IL: Dorsey Press.

KELLAS, G., FERRARO, F. R., & SIMPSON, G. B. (1988). Lexical ambiguity and the timecourse of attentional allocation in word recognition. *Journal of Experimental Psychology: Human Perception and Performance, 14,* 601–609.

KELLOGG, R. T. (1984). Cognitive strategies in writing. (ERIC Document Reproduction Service No. ED 262 425)

KILPATRICK, J. (1985). Doing mathematics without understanding it: A commentary on Higbee and Kunihira. *Educational Psychologist, 20,* 65–68.

KING, J. R., BIGGS, S., & LIPSKY, S. (1984). Students' self-questioning and summarizing as reading study strategies. *Journal of Reading Behavior, 16,* 205–218.

KINTSCH, W. (1970). Models for free recall and recognition. In D. A. Norman (Ed.), *Models of human memory* (pp. 177–236). New York: Academic Press.

KINTSCH, W. (1974). *The representation of meaning in memory.* Hillsdale, NJ: Erlbaum.

KINTSCH, W. (1977). *Memory and cognition* (2nd ed.). New York: Wiley.

KINTSCH, W. (1986). Learning from text. *Cognition and Instruction, 3,* 87–108.

KINTSCH, W. (1988). The role of knowledge in discourse comprehension: A construction-integration model. *Psychology Review, 95,* 163–182.

KINTSCH, W., & GREENO, J. G. (1985). Understanding and solving arithmetic word problems. *Psychological Review, 92,* 109–129.

KINTSCH, W., & VAN DIJK, T. A. (1978). Toward a model of text comprehension and production. *Psychological Review, 85,* 363–394.

KLATZKY, R. L. (1984). *Human memory: Structures and processes* (2nd ed.). San Francisco: Freeman.

KLEIN, F. (1988). The potential utilization of microelectronic technology in accomplishing the major goals of schooling. Paper presented to the annual meeting of the American Educational Research Association, New Orleans.

KOFFKA, K. (1933). *Principles of Gestalt psychology.* New York: Harcourt Brace Jovanovich.

KOLERS, P. A. (1975). Memorial consequences of automatized encoding. *Journal of Experimental Psychology: Human Learning and Memory, 1,* 689–701.

KOSSLYN, S. M. (1980). *Image and mind.* Cambridge, MA: Harvard University Press.

KOSSLYN, S. M. (1981). The medium and the message in mental imagery: A theory. *Psychological Review, 88,* 46–66.

KOSSLYN, S. M. (1987). Seeing and imagining in the cerebral hemispheres: A computational approach. *Psychological Review, 94,* 148–175.

KOWALSKI, T., GLOVER, J. A., & KRUG. D. (in press). The role of the laboratory school in developing curriculum. *Contemporary Education.*

KRAFT, R. G., & GLOVER, J. A. (1981). The effects of individual differences in ability to image on recall of nonmeaningful information. *Bulletin of the Psychonomic Society, 18,* 139–141.

KRASHEN, S. D. (1982). *Principles and practice in second language acquisition.* Oxford: Pergamon.

KRAUS, S. (1957). A comparison of three methods of teaching sentence structure. *English Journal, 46,* 275–281.

KREUTZER, M. A., LEONARD, C., & FLAVELL, J. H. (1975). An interview study of children's knowledge about memory. *Monographs of the Society for Research in Child Development, 10*(1, Serial number 59).

KROLL, N.E.A., SCHEPLER, E. M., & ANGIN, K. T. (1986). Bizarre imagery: The misremembered mnemonic. *Journal of Experimental Psychology: Learning, Memory, and Cognition, 12,* 42–53

KRUG, D., & GLOVER, J. A. (1989). Use of cues embedded in text in problem solving. Research report, Ball State University, Muncie, Indiana.

LABERGE, D., & SAMUELS, S. J. (1974). Toward a theory of automatic information processing in reading. *Cognitive Psychology, 6,* 283–323.

LAMME, L., & CHILDERS, N. (1983). The composing processes of three young children. *Research in the Teaching of English, 17,* 31–50.

LANKFORD, F. G. (1972). Some computational strategies of seventh grade pupils. (U.S.O.E. Project No. 2-C-013)

LARKIN, J. H. (1977). Skilled problem solving in experts. (Technical Report) Group in Science and Mathematics Education. University of California, Berkeley.

LARKIN, J. (1979). Processing information for effective problem solving. *Engineering Education, 70,* 285–288.

LARKIN, J. (1980). Teaching problem solving in physics: The psychological laboratory and the practical classroom. In D. T. Tuma & F. Reif (Eds.) *Problem solving and education: Issues in teaching and research* (pp. 26–51). Hillsdale, NJ: Erlbaum.

LARKIN, J. H. (1985). Understanding, problem representations, and skill in physics. In S. F. Chipman, J. W. Segal, & R. Glaser (Eds.), *Thinking and learning skills, Vol. 2* (pp. 141–159). Hillsdale, NJ: Erlbaum.

LARKIN, J., McDERMOTT, J., SIMON, D. P., & SIMON, H. A. (1980). Expert and novice performance in solving physics problems. *Science, 208,* 1335–1442.

LeFEVRE, J. (1988). Reading skill as a source of individual differences in the processing of instructional texts. *Journal of Educational Psychology, 80,* 312–314.

LEU, D. J. (1982). Oral reading error analysis: A critical review of research and application. *Reading Research Quarterly, 17,* 420–437.

LEVIN J. R. (1981). The mnemonic '80s: Keywords in the classroom. *Educational Psychologist, 16,* 65–82.

LEVIN, J. R. (1985). Yodai features = mnemonic procedures: A commentary on Higbee and Kunihira. *Educational Psychologist, 20,* 73–77.

LEVIN, J. R. (1986). Educational applications of mnemonic pictures: Possibilities beyond your wildest imagination. In A. A. Sheikh (Ed.), *Imagery in the educational process* (pp. 202–265). Farmingdale, NY: Baywood.

LEVINE, M. (1966). Hypothesis behavior by humans during discrimination learning. *Journal of Experimental Psychology, 71,* 331–338.

LEVINE, M. (1975). *A Cognitive theory of learning: Research on hypothesis testing.* Hillsdale, NJ: Erlbaum.

LIBERMAN, A. M. (1982). On finding that speech is special. *American Psychologist, 37,* 148–167.

LILES, B. Z. (1985). Cohesion in the narratives of normal and language-disordered children. *Journal of Speech and Hearing Research, 28,* 123–133.

LINDQUIST, M. M. (1987). Strategic teaching in mathematics. In B. F. Jones, A. S. Palinscar, D. S. Ogle, & E. G. Carr (Eds.), *Strategic teaching and learning: Cognitive instruction in the contents areas* (pp. 116–131). Elmhurst, IL: North Central Regional Educational Laboratory.

LOFTUS, E. T., GREENE E., & SMITH, R. H. (1980). How deep is the meaning of life? *Bulletin of the Psychonomic Society, 15,* 282–284.

LOMAX, R. G., & McGEE, L. M. (1987). Young children's concepts about print and reading: Toward a model of word reading acquisition. *Reading Research Quarterly, 22,* 237–256.

LONG, G. L., & ALDERSLEY, S. (1982). Evaluation of a technique to enhance reading comprehension. *American Annals of the Deaf, 127,* 816–820.

LORCH, R. F. (1985). Effects on recall of signals to text organization. *Bulletin of the Psychonomic Society, 23,* 374–376.

Lorch, R. F., & Chen, A. H. (1986). Effect of number signals on reading and recall. *Journal of Educational Psychology, 78,* 263–270.

Lucas, C., & Borders, D. (1987). Language diversity and classroom discourse. *American Educational Research Journal, 24,* 119–141.

Luchins, A. S. (1942). Mechanization in problem solving: The effect of Einstellung. *Psychological Monographs, 54* (Whole No. 6).

Lutz, J. A. (1987). A study of professional and experienced writers revising and editing at the computer and with pen and paper. *RITTYE, 21,* 398–421.

MacLeod, C. M. (1988). Forgotten but not gone: Savings for pictures and words in long-term memory. *Journal of Experimental Psychology: Learning, Memory, and Cognition, 14,* 195–212.

Madigan, S. A. (1969). Intraserial repetition and coding processes in free recall. *Journal of Verbal Learning and Verbal Behavior, 8,* 828–835.

Maier, N.R.F. (1931). Reasoning in humans I: The solution of a problem and its appearance in consciousness. *Journal of Comparative Psychology, 12,* 181–194.

Mandler, J. M. (1984). *Stories, scripts, and scenes: Aspects of schema theory.* Hillsdale, NJ: Erlbaum.

Mansfield, R. S., Busse, T. V., & Krepelka, E. J. (1978). The effectiveness of creativity training. *Review of Educational Research, 48,* 517–536.

Marr, D. (1982). *Vision.* San Francisco: Freeman.

Marr, D. (1985). Vision: The philosophy and the approach. In A. M. Aitkenhead (Ed.), *Issues in cognitive modeling* (pp. 26–61). Hillsdale, NJ: Erlbaum.

Marshall, J. D., & Durst, R. K. (1987). Annotated bibliography of research in the teaching of English. *Research in the Teaching of English, 21,* 202–223.

Martindale, C. (in press). Personality, situation, and creativity. In J. A. Glover, R. R. Ronning, & C. R. Reynolds (Eds.), *Handbook of creativity.* New York: Plenum.

Martlew, M. (1986). The development of written language. In K. Durkin (Ed.), *Language development in the school years* (pp. 117–138). Cambridge, MA: Brookline Books.

Mason, J. (1980). When do children begin to read? An exploration of four-year-olds' letter and word reading competencies. *Reading Research Quarterly, 15,* 203–227.

Mason, J. M., & Au, K. H. (1986). *Reading instruction for today.* Glenview, IL: Scott, Foresman.

Masonheimer, P. E., Drum, P. A., & Ehri, L. C. (1984). Does environmental print identification lead children into word reading? *Journal of Reading Behavior, 16,* 257–271.

Mastropieri, M., & Scruggs, T. (in press). A review of the use of mnemonics with learning disabled students. *Educational Psychology Review.*

Masur, E. F., McIntyre, C. W., & Flavell, J. H. (1973). Developmental changes in appointment of study time among items in a multitrial free recall task. *Journal of Experimental Child Psychology, 15,* 237–246.

Mayer, R. E. (1979). Can advance organizers influence meaningful learning? *Review of Educational Research, 49,* 371–383.

Mayer, R. E. (1981). Frequency norms and structural analysis of algebra word problems into families, categories, and templates. *Instructional Science, 10,* 135–175.

MAYER, R. E. (1982). Memory for algebra story problems. *Journal of Educational Psychology, 74,* 199–216.

MAYER, R. E. (1984). Twenty-five years of research on advance organizers. *Instructional Science, 8,* 133–169.

MAYER, R. E., & BROMAGE, B. K. (1980). Different recall protocols for technical texts due to advance organizers. *Journal of Educational Psychology, 72,* 209–225.

MAZZIE, C. A. (1987). An experimental investigation of the determinants of implicitness in spoken and written discourse. *Discourse Processes, 10,* 31–42.

McCANN, R. S., BESNER, D., & DAVELAAR, E. (1988). Word recognition and identification: Do word-frequency effects reflect lexical access? *Journal of Experimental Psychology: Human Perception and Performance, 14,* 693–706.

McCLELLAND, J. L. (1986). The programmable blackboard model of reading. In D. E. Rumelhart & J. L. McClelland (Eds.), *Parallel distributed process: Explorations in the microstructure of cognition. Vol. 2: Psychological and biological models* (pp. 122–169). Cambridge, MA: MIT Press.

McCLELLAND, J. L. (1988). Connectionist models and psychological evidence. *Journal of Memory and Language, 27,* 107–123.

McCLELLAND, J. L., RUMELHART, D. E., & HINTON, G. E. (1986). The appeal of parallel distributed processing. In D. E. Rumelhart, J. L. McClelland, & PDP Research Group (Eds.), *Parallel distributed processing: Explorations in the microstructures of cognition. Vol. 1: Foundations* (pp. 3–44). Cambridge, MA: MIT Press.

McCLELLAND, J. L., RUMELHART, D. E., & PDP RESEARCH GROUP (EDS.), (1986). *Parallel distributed processing: Explorations in the microstructures of cognition. Vol. 2: Psychological and biological models.* Cambridge, MA: MIT Press.

McCLOSKEY, M. (1983). Naive theories of motion. In D. Gentner & A. L. Stevens (Eds.), *Mental models* (pp. 71–94). Hillsdale, NJ: Erlbaum.

McCLOSKEY, M., CARAMAZZA, A., & GREEN, B. (1980). Curvilinear motion in the absence of external forces: Naive beliefs about the motion of objects. *Science, 210,* 1139–1141.

McCORMICK, C. B., & LEVIN, J. R. (1984). A comparison of different prose-learning variations of the mnemonic keyword method. *American Educational Research Journal, 21,* 379–398.

McDANIEL, M. A., & EINSTEIN, G. O. (1986). Bizarre imagery as an effective memory aid: The importance of distinctiveness. *Journal of Experimental Psychology: Learning, Memory, and Cognition, 12,* 54–65.

McDANIEL, M. A., & EINSTEIN, G. O. (in press). Material appropriate processing. *Educational Psychology Review.*

McDANIEL, M. A., EINSTEIN, G. O., DUNAY, P. K., & COGG, R. S. (1986). Encoding difficulty and memory: Toward a unifying theory. *Journal of Memory and Language, 25,* 645–656.

McDERMOTT, L. C. (1984). Research on conceptual understanding in mechanics. *Physics Today, 37,* 24–29.

McDOUGALL, R. (1904). Recognition and recall. *Journal of Philosophical and Scientific Methods, 1,* 229–233.

McELROY, L. A., & SLAMECKA, N. J. (1982). Memorial consequences of generating nonwords: Implications for semantic memory interpretations of the generation effect. *Journal of Verbal Learning and Verbal Behavior, 21,* 249–259.

McGee, L. M., Lomax, R. G., & Head, M. H. (1988). Young children's written language knowledge: What environmental and functional print reading reveals. *Journal of Reading Behavior, 20,* 99–118.

McGeoch, J. A., & Irion, A. L. (1952). *The Psychology of Human Learning* (2nd ed.). New York: Longman, Green.

McKeown, M. (1985). The acquisition of word meaning from context by children of high and low ability. *Reading Research Quarterly, 20,* 482–496.

McKeown, M. G., Beck, I. L., Omanson, R. C., & Perfetti, C. A. (1983). The effects of long-term vocabulary instruction on reading comprehension: A replication. *Journal of Reading Behavior, 15,* 3–18.

McKeown, M. G., Beck, I. L., Omanson, R. C., & Pople, M. T. (1985, April). Some effects of the nature and frequency of vocabulary instruction on the knowledge and use of words. *Reading Research Quarterly, 20,* 522–535.

McKeown, M. G., & Curtis, M. E. (1987). *The nature of vocabulary acquisition.* Hillsdale, NJ: Erlbaum.

McKoon, G., & Ratcliff, R. (1986). Inferences about predictable events. *Journal of Experimental Psychology: Learning, Memory, and Cognition, 12,* 82–91.

McKoon, G., Ratcliff, R., & Dell, G. S. (1986). A critical evaluation of the semantic–episodic distinction. *Journal of Experimental Psychology: Learning, Memory, and Cognition, 12,* 295–306.

McNamee, G. D. (1987). The social origins of narrative skills. In M. Hickmann (Ed.), *Social and functional approaches to language and thought* (pp. 287–304). Orlando, FL: Academic Press.

McQueen, R., Murray, A. K., & Evans, F. (1963). Relationships between writing required in high school and English proficiency in college. *Journal of Experimental Education, 31,* 419–423.

Medin, D. L., Dewey, G. I., & Murphy, T. D. (1983). Relationships between item and category learning: Evidence that abstraction is not automatic. *Journal of Experimental Psychology: Learning, Memory and Cognition, 9,* 607–625.

Medin, D. L., Wattenmaker, W. D., & Hampson, S. E. (1987). Family resemblance, conceptual cohesiveness, and category construction. *Cognitive Psychology, 19,* 242–278.

Melton, A. W. (1963). Implications of short-term memory for a general theory of memory. *Journal of Verbal Learning and Verbal Behavior, 2,* 1–21.

Merry, R. (1980). Image bizarreness in incidental learning. *Psychological Reports, 46,* 427–430.

Mewhort, D.J.K., Butler, B. E., Feldman-Stewart, D., & Tramer, S. (1988). "Iconic memory," location information, and the bar-probe task: A reply to Chow. *Journal of Experimental Psychology: Human Perception and Performance, 14,* 729–736.

Meyer, B.J.F. (1975). *The organization of prose and its effects on memory.* Amsterdam: North-Holland.

Meyer, B.J.F., Brandt, D. M., & Bluth, G. J. (1980). Use of top-level structure in text: Key for reading comprehension of ninth-grade students. *Reading Research Quarterly, 16,* 72–103.

Meyer, B.J.F., & Rice, G. E. (1984). The structure of text. In P. D. Pearson (Ed.), *Handbook of reading research* (pp. 316–342). New York: Longman.

Mezynski, K. (1984). Issues concerning the acquisition of knowledge: Effects of vocabulary training on reading comprehension. In P. D. Pearson (Ed.), *Handbook of reading research* (pp. 255–291). New York: Longman.

MILLER, G. A. (1956a, August). Information and memory. *Scientific American.*

MILLER, G. A. (1956b). The magical number seven, plus-or-minus two: Some limits on our capacity for processing information. *Psychological Review, 63,* 81–97.

MILLER, G. A. (1981). *Language and speech.* San Francisco: Freeman.

MILLER, G. A. (1988). The challenge of universal literacy. *Science, 241,* 1293–1299.

MILLER, G. A., GALANTER, E., & PRIBRAM, K. H. (1960). *Plans and the structure of behavior.* New York: Holt, Rinehart & Winston.

MINSKY, M. (1975). A framework for representing knowledge. In P. Winston (Ed.), *The psychology of computer vision.* New York: McGraw-Hill.

MITCHELL, D. B., & BROWN, A. S. (1988). Persistent repetition priming in picture naming and its disassociation from recognition memory. *Journal of Experimental Psychology: Learning, Memory, and Cognition, 14,* 213–222.

MOESER, S. D. (1983). Levels-of-processing: Qualitative differences or task–demand hypotheses? *Memory & Cognition, 11,* 316–323.

MONTAGUE, W. E., ADAMS, J. A., & KIESS, H. D. (1966). Forgetting and natural language mediation. *Journal of Experimental Psychology, 72,* 829–833.

MORPHETT, M. V., & WASHBURNE, C. (1931). When should children begin to read? *Elementary School Journal, 31,* 496–503.

MORRIS, C. D., BRANSFORD, J. D., & FRANKS, J. J. (1977). Levels of processing versus transfer appropriate processing. *Journal of Verbal Learning and Verbal Behavior, 16,* 519–533.

MORRIS, P. E., & COOK, N. (1978). When do first letter mnemonics aid recall? *British Journal of Educational Psychology, 48,* 22–28.

MOSENTHAL, J. M., & TIERNEY, R. J. (1984). Cohesion: Problems with talking about text. *Reading Research Quarterly, 24,* 240–244.

MURDOCK, B. B., JR. (1961). The retention of individual items. *Journal of Experimental Psychology, 62,* 618–625.

MURPHY, C., & BRUNING, R. H. (1987, December). Examining classroom "talk": A measure of students' comprehension of literary texts. Paper presented at the National Reading Conference, St. Petersburg Beach, FL.

MURPHY, G. L., & MEDIN, D. L. (1985). The role of theories in conceptual coherence. *Psychological Review, 92,* 289–316.

MUTH, K. D., GLYNN, S. M., BRITTON, B. K., & GRAVES, M. F. (1988). Thinking out loud while studying text: Rehearsing key ideas. *Journal of Educational Psychology, 80,* 315–318.

NAGY, W. E. (1988, April). Some components of a model of word-learning ability. Paper presented at the annual meeting of the American Educational Research Association, New Orleans.

NAGY, W. E., & ANDERSON, R. C. (1984). How many words are there in printed school English? *Reading Research Quarterly, 19,* 304–330.

NAGY, W. E., ANDERSON, R. C., & HERMAN, P. A. (1987). Learning word meanings from context during normal reading. *American Educational Research Journal, 24,* 237–270.

NAGY, W. E., & HERMAN, P. A. (1985). Incidental vs. instructional approaches to increasing reading vocabulary. *Educational Perspectives, 23,* 16–21.

NAGY, W. E., & HERMAN, P. A. (1987). Breadth and depth of vocabulary knowledge: Implications for acquisition and instruction. In M. G. McKeown & M. E. Curtis (Eds.), *The nature of vocabulary acquisition* (pp. 19–35). Hillsdale, NJ: Erlbaum.

NAGY, W. E., HERMAN, P. A., & ANDERSON, R. C. (1985). Learning words from context. *Reading Research Quarterly, 20,* 233–253.

NATIONAL ASSESSMENT OF EDUCATIONAL PROGRESS. (1983). *The third national mathematics assessment: Results, trends, and issues.* Washington, DC: National Institute of Education. Report ED (1.118-13-MA-01)

NATIONAL COMMISSION ON EXCELLENCE IN EDUCATION. (1983). *A Nation at Risk: The imperative for educational reform.* Washington, DC: U.S. Government Printing Office.

NATIONAL COUNCIL OF TEACHERS OF MATHEMATICS (NCTM). (1980). *An agenda for action: Recommendations for school mathematics of the 1980's.* Reston, VA: NCTM.

NEISSER, U. (1967). *Cognitive psychology.* New York: Appleton-Century-Crofts.

NEISSER, U. (1982). *Memory observed.* San Francisco: Freeman.

NEISSER, U., & WEENE, P. (1962). Hierarchies in concept attainment. *Journal of Experimental Psychology, 64,* 640–645.

NELSON, T. O. (1977). Repetition and depth of processing. *Journal of Verbal Learning and Verbal Behavior, 16,* 151–171.

NELSON, T. O. (1985). Ebbinghaus's contribution to the measurement of retention: Savings during relearning. *Journal of Experimental Psychology: Learning, Memory, and Cognition, 11,* 472–479.

NEVES, D. M., & ANDERSON, J. R. (1981). Knowledge compilation: Mechanisms for the automatization of cognitive skills. In J. R. Anderson (Ed.), *Cognitive skills and their acquisition* (pp. 86–102). Hillsdale, NJ: Erlbaum.

NEWELL, A., & ROSENBLOOM, P. S. (1981). Mechanisms of skill acquisition and the law of practice. In J. R. Anderson (Ed.), *Cognitive skills and their acquisition* (pp. 251–272). Hillsdale, NJ: Erlbaum.

NEWELL, A., & SIMON, H. A. (1972). *Human problem solving.* Englewood Cliffs, NJ: Prentice-Hall.

NEWELL, G. E., & MACADAM, P. (1987). Examining the source of writing problems: An instrument for viewing writers' topic-specific knowledge. *Written Communication, 4,* 156–174.

NEWMAN, F. M. (1986). Priorities for the future: Toward a common agenda. *Social Education, 50,* 240–250.

NICKERSON, R. S., PERKINS, D. N., & SMITH, E. E. (1986). *The teaching of thinking.* Hillsdale, NJ: Erlbaum.

NILSSON, L., LAW, J., & TULVING, E. (1988). Recognition failure of recallable unique names: Evidence for an empirical law of memory and learning. *Journal of Experimental Psychology: Learning, Memory, and Cognition, 14,* 266–277.

NOBLE, C. E. (1952). An analysis of meaning. *Psychological Review, 59,* 421–430.

NORMAN, D. A. (1976). *Memory and attention* (2nd ed.). New York: Wiley.

NORMAN, D. A., & BOBROW, D. G. (1976). On the role of active memory processes in perception and cognition. In C. N. Cofer (Ed.), *The structure of human memory* (pp. 123–156). San Francisco: Freeman.

NORMAN, D. A., & RUMELHART, D. E. (1975). *Explorations in cognition.* New York: Freeman.

NORRIS, J. A. (1988). Using communication strategies to enhance reading acquisition. *The Reading Teacher, 26,* 668–673.

NORRIS, J. A., & BRUNING, R. H. (1988). Cohesion in the narratives of good and poor readers. *Journal of Speech and Hearing Disorders, 53,* 416–424.

NUSBAUM, H. C., & SCHWAB, E. C. (1986). The role of attention and active processing in speech perception. In E. C. Schwab & H. C. Nusbaum (Eds.), *Pattern recognition by humans and machines* (pp. 113–157). New York: Academic Press.

NUSSBAUM, J., & NOVICK, N. (1982). Alternative frameworks, conceptual conflict and accommodation: Toward a principled teaching strategy. *Instructional Science, 11,* 183–200.

O'LOONEY, J. A., GLYNN, S. M., & BRITTON, B. K. (in press). Cognition and writing: The idea generation process. In J. A. Glover, R. R. Ronning, & C. R. Reynolds (Eds.), *Handbook of creativity.* New York: Plenum.

OLSON, D. R., TORRANCE, N., & HILDYARD, A. (1985). *Literacy, language, and learning.* New York: Cambridge University Press.

OLTON, R. M., & CRUTCHFIELD, R. S. (1969). Developing the skills of productive thinking. In P. Mussen, J. Langer, & M. Covington (Eds.), *Trends and issues in developmental psychology.* New York: Holt, Rinehart & Winston.

OSBORNE, R., & FREYBERG, P. (1985). *Learning in science.* Portsmouth, NH: Heinemann.

PAIVIO, A. (1971). *Imagery and verbal processes.* New York: Holt, Rinehart & Winston.

PAIVIO, A. (1975). Imagery and long-term memory. In A. Kennedy & A. Wilkes (Eds.), *Studies in long-term memory* (pp. 64–110). London: Wiley.

PAIVIO, A. (1986a). *Mental representations: A dual coding approach.* New York: Oxford University Press.

PAIVIO, A. (1986b). Dual coding and episodic memory: Subjective and objective sources of memory trace components. In F. Klix & H. Hafgendorf (Eds.), *Human memory and cognitive capabilities: Mechanisms and performances* (Part A, pp. 225–236). Amsterdam: North-Holland.

PAIVIO, A., CLARK, J. M., & LAMBERT, W. E. (1988). Bilingual dual-coding theory and semantic repetition effect on recall. *Journal of Experimental Psychology: Learning, Memory, and Cognition, 14,* 163–172.

PAIVIO, A., & CSAPO, K. (1975). Picture superiority in free recall: Imagery or dual coding? *Cognitive Psychology, 5,* 176–206.

PAIVIO, A., & SMYTHE, P. C. (1971). Word imagery, frequency and meaningfulness in short-term memory. *Psychonomic Science, 22,* 333–335.

PAIVIO, A., SMYTHE, P. C., & YUILLE, J. C. (1968). Imagery versus meaningfulness of nouns in paired-associate learning. *Canadian Journal of Psychology, 22,* 427–441.

PAIVIO, A., YUILLE, J. D., & MADIGAN, S. A. (1968). Concreteness, imagery, and meaningfulness values for 925 nouns. *Journal of Experimental Psychology Monograph Supplement, 76,* 1–25.

PALINCSAR, A. S., & BROWN, A. L. (1984). Reciprocal teaching of comprehension-fostering and comprehension-monitoring activities. *Cognition and Instruction, 1,* 117–175.

PALINCSAR, A. S., BROWN, A. L., & MARTIN, S. (1987). Peer interaction in reading comprehension instruction. *Educational Psychologist, 22,* 231–254.

PALMERE, M., BENTON, S. L., GLOVER, J. A., & RONNING, R. R. (1983). Elaboration and recall of main ideas in prose. *Journal of Educational Psychology, 75,* 898–907.

PARIS, S. G., CROSS, D. R., & LIPON, M. Y. (1984). Informal strategies for learning: A program to improve children's reading awareness and comprehension. *Journal of Educational Psychology, 76,* 1239–1252.

PASCUAL-LEONE, J. (1976). A view of cognition from a formalist's perspective. In K. F. Riegel & J. Meacham (Eds.), *The developing individual in a changing world, Vol. 1* (pp. 306–330). The Hague: Mouton.

PEARSON, P. D. (1984). Guided reading: A response to Isabel Beck. In R. C. Anderson, J. Osborn, & R. J. Tierney (Eds.), *Learning to read in American schools* (pp. 21–28). Hillsdale, NJ: Erlbaum.

PEARSON, P. D. (1985). The comprehension revolution: A twenty-year history of process and practice related to reading comprehension. Urbana-Champaign: University of Illinois, Center for the Study of Reading. (Reading Education Report No. 57)

PEARSON, P. D., & TIERNEY, R. J. (1984). On becoming a thoughtful reader: Learning to read like a writer. Urbana-Champaign: University of Illinois, Center for the Study of Reading. (Reading Education Report No. 50)

PEECK, J. (1982). Effects of mobilization of knowledge on free recall. *Journal of Experimental Psychology: Learning, Memory, and Cognition, 8,* 608–612.

PEECK, J., VAN DEN BOSCH, A. B., & KRUEPELING, W. (1982). The effect of mobilizing prior knowledge on learning from text. *Journal of Educational Psychology, 74,* 771–777.

PEPPER, S. C. (1942/1961). *World hypotheses: A study in evidence.* Berkeley: University of California Press.

PERFETTI, C. A., & HOGOBOAM, T. (1975). Relationship between single word decoding and reading comprehension skill. *Journal of Educational Psychology, 67,* 461–469.

PERFETTI, C. A., & ROTH, S. (1981). Some of the interactive processes in reading and their role in reading skill. In A. M. Lesgold & C. A. Perfetti (Eds.), *Interactive processes in reading* (pp. 269–297). Hillsdale, NJ: Erlbaum.

PERFETTO, G. A., BRANSFORD, J. D., & FRANKS, J. J. (1983). Constraints on access in a problem solving context. *Memory and Cognition, 11,* 24–31.

PETERS, E. E., LEVIN, J. R., McGIVERN, J. E., & PRESSLEY, M. (1985). Further comparison of representational and transformational prose learning imagery. *Journal of Educational Psychology, 77,* 129–136.

PETERSEN, C. H., GLOVER, J. A., & RONNING, R. R. (1980). An examination of three prose learning strategies on reading comprehension. *The Journal of General Psychology, 102,* 39–52.

PETERSON, L. R., & PETERSON, M. J. (1959). Short-term retention of individual verbal items. *Journal of Experimental Psychology, 58,* 193–198.

PETROSKY, A. (1982). From story to essay: Reading and writing. *College Composition and Communication, 33,* 19–36.

PHIFER, S. J., McNICKLE, B., RONNING, R. R., & GLOVER, J. A. (1983). The effect of details on the recall of major ideas in text. *Journal of Reading Behavior, 15,* 19–29.

PHILLIPS, L. M. (1986). Using children's literature to foster written language development. (ERIC Document Reproduction Service No. ED 276 027)

PIAGET, J. (1929). *The child's conception of the world.* Totowa, NJ: Littlefield, Adams.

PIAGET, J. (1969). *The mechanisms of perception.* New York: Basic Books.

PIANKO, S. (1979). A description of the composing processes of college freshmen writers. *Research in the Teaching of English, 13,* 5–22.

PIAZZA, C. L. (1987). Identifying context variables in research on writing: A review and suggested directions. *Written Communication, 4,* 107–138.

PICHERT, J. W., & ANDERSON, R. C. (1977). Taking different perspectives on a story. *Journal of Educational Psychology, 69,* 309–315.

PISONI, D. B., & LUCE, P. A. (1986). Speech perception: Research, theory, and the principal issues. In E. C. Schwab & H. C. Nusbaum (Eds.), *Pattern recognition by humans and machines* (pp. 1–42). New York: Academic Press.

POINCARE, H. (1913). *The foundations of science.* Lancaster, PA: Science Press.

POLSON, P. G., & JEFFRIES, R. (1985). Instruction in general problem solving skills: An analysis of four approaches. In J. W. Segal & S. F. Chipman (Eds.), *Thinking and learning skills, Vol. 1* (pp. 417–455). Hillsdale, NJ: Erlbaum.

POLYA, G. (1973). *How to solve it* (2nd ed.). New York: Doubleday.

POMERANTZ, J. R. (1985). Perceptual organization in information processing. In A. M. Aitkenhead & J. M. Slack (Eds.), *Issues in cognitive modeling* (pp. 157–188). Hillsdale, NJ: Erlbaum.

POSNER, M. I., & BOIES, S. J. (1971). Components of attention. *Psychological Review, 78,* 391–408.

POSNER, M. I., & KEELE, S. W. (1968). On the genesis of abstract ideas. *Journal of Experimental Psychology, 77,* 353–363.

POSNER, M. I., & KEELE, S. W. (1970). Retention of abstract ideas. *Journal of Experimental Psychology, 83,* 304–308.

POSTMAN, L., THOMPKINS, B. S., & GRAY, W. D. (1978). The interpretation of encoding effects in retention. *Journal of Verbal Learning and Verbal Behavior, 17,* 681–706.

POSTMAN, L., & UNDERWOOD, B. J. (1973). Critical issues in interference theory. *Memory and Cognition, 1,* 19–40.

POWELL, J. S. (1988, April). Defining words from context: Is helpfulness in the eyes of the beholder? Paper presented at the annual meeting of the American Educational Research Association, New Orleans.

PRESSLEY, M. (1977). Children's use of the keyword method to learn simple Spanish vocabulary words. *Journal of Educational Psychology, 69,* 465–472.

PRESSLEY, M. (1985). More about Yodai mnemonics: A commentary on Higbee and Kunihira. *Educational Psychologist, 20,* 69–73.

PRESSLEY, M., LEVIN, J. R., & DELANEY, H. D. (1982). The mnemonic keyword method. *Review of Educational Research, 52,* 61–92.

PRESSLEY, M., SNYDER, B. L., LEVIN, J. R., MURRAY, H. G., & GHATALA, E. S. (1987). Perceived readiness for examination performance (PREP) produced by initial reading of text and text containing adjunct questions. *Reading Research Quarterly, 22,* 219–235.

PRIDEAUX, G. D. (1984). *Psycholinguistics: The experimental study of language.* London: Croom Helm.

PUFF, C. R. (1970). Role of clustering in free recall. *Journal of Experimental Psychology, 86,* 384–386.

PYLYSHYN, Z. W. (1973). What the mind's eye tells the mind's brain: A critique of mental imagery. *Psychological Bulletin, 80,* 1–24.

PYLYSHYN, Z. W. (1981). The imagery debate: Analogue media versus tacit knowledge. *Psychological Review, 88,* 16–45.

QUILLIAN, M. R. (1962). A revised design for an understanding machine. *Mechanical Translation, 7,* 17–29.

QUILLIAN, M. R. (1967). Word concepts: A theory and simulation of some basic semantic capabilities. *Behavioral Science, 12,* 410–430.

QUILLIAN, M. R. (1968). Semantic memory. In M. Minsky (Ed.), *Semantic information processing* (pp. 21–56). Cambridge, MA: MIT Press.

RABINOWITZ, J. C., & CRAIK, F.I.M. (1986). Specific enhancement effects associated with word generation. *Journal of Memory and Language, 25,* 226–237.

RABINOWITZ, J. C., MANDLER, G., & PATTERSON, K. E. (1977). Determinants of recognition and recall: Accessibility and generation. *Journal of Experimental Psychology: General, 106,* 302–329.

RAPHAEL, T. E. (1986). Students' metacognitive knowledge about writing. Research Series No. 176. (ERIC Document Reproduction Service No. ED 274 999)

RAPHAEL, T. E., & MCKINNEY, J., (1983). An examination of fifth and eighth grade children's question answering behavior: An instruction study in metacognition. *Journal of Reading Behavior, 15,* 67–86.

RAPHAEL, T. E., & PEARSON, P. D. (1982). *The effects of metacognitive strategy awareness training on students' question answering behavior.* Urbana: University of Illinois, Center for the Study of Reading. (Technical Report No. 238)

RAPHAEL, T. E., & WONNACOTT, C. A. (1985). Heightening fourth grade students' sensitivity to sources of information for answering comprehension questions. *Reading Research Quarterly, 16,* 301–321.

RATCLIFF, R., & MCKOON, G. (1986). More on the distinction between episodic and semantic memories. *Journal of Experimental Psychology: Learning, Memory, and Cognition, 12,* 312–313.

RAVITCH, D., & FINN, C. E., JR. (1987). *What do our 17-year-olds know?* New York: Harper & Row.

RAYNER, K., & DUFFY, S. A. (1986). Lexical complexity and fixation times in reading: Effects of word frequency, verb complexity, and lexical ambiguity. *Memory & Cognition, 14,* 191–201.

RAYNER, K., & POLLATSEK, A. (1989). *The Psychology of Reading.* Englewood Cliffs, NJ: Prentice-Hall.

RECHT, D. R., & LESLIE, L. (1988). Effect of prior knowledge on good and poor readers' memory of text. *Journal of Educational Psychology, 80,* 16–20.

REED, S. K. (1972). Pattern recognition and categorization. *Cognitive Psychology, 3,* 382–407.

REED, S. K. (1984). Estimating answers to algebra word problems. *Journal of Experimental Psychology: Learning, Memory, and Cognition, 10,* 778–790.

REED, S. K. (1987). A structure-mapping model for word problems. *Journal of Experimental Psychology: Learning, Memory, and Cognition, 13*, 124–139.

REED, S. K., DEMPSTER, A., & ETTINGER, M. (1985). Usefulness of analogous solutions for solving algebra word problems. *Journal of Experimental Psychology: Learning, Memory, and Cognition, 11*, 106–125.

REED, W. M., BURTON, J. K., & KELLY, P. P. (1985). The effects of writing quality and mode of discourse on cognitive capacity engagement. *Research in the Teaching of English, 19*, 283–297.

RESNICK, L. B. (1983). Mathematics and science learning: A new conception. *Science, 220*, 477–478.

REUTZEL, D. R. (1986). The reading basal: A sentence combining composing book. *The Reading Teacher, 40*, 194–199.

REYNOLDS, J. H., & GLASER, R. (1964). Effects of repetition and spaced review upon retention of a complex learning task. *Journal of Educational Psychology, 55*, 297–308.

REYNOLDS, R. E., & ANDERSON, J. R. (1982). Influence of questions on the allocation of attention during reading. *Journal of Educational Psychology, 74*, 623–632.

RICKARDS, J. (1979). Adjunct postquestions in text: A critical review of methods and processes. *Review of Educational Research, 49*, 181–196.

RILEY, M. S., GREENO, J. G., & HELLER, J. I. (1983). Development of children's problem-solving ability in arithmetic. In H. P. Ginsburg (Ed.), *The development of mathematical thinking* (pp. 62–71). New York: Academic Press.

ROBBINS, J. T. (1986). A study of the effect of the writing process on the development of verbal skills among elementary school children. *Dissertation Abstracts International, 47*, 08A. (University Microfilms No. 86-27, 505)

ROBINSON, F. (1972). *Effective study.* New York: Macmillan.

ROMAINE, S. (1984). *The language of children and adolescents: The acquisition of communicative competence.* Oxford: Basil Blackwell.

ROMBERG, T. A., & COLLIS, K. F. (1987). Different ways children learn to add and subtract. *Journal for Research in Mathematics Education Monograph, 2*.

ROOT, R. L. (1985). Assiduous string-savers: The idea generating strategies of professional expository writers. Paper presented at the annual meeting of the Conference of College Composition and Communication. (ERIC Document Reproduction Service No. ED 258 205)

ROSCH, E. (1978). Principles of categorization. In E. Rosch & B. B. Lloyd (Eds.), *Cognition and categorization.* Hillsdale, NJ: Erlbaum.

ROSCH, E., & MERVIS, C. B. (1975). Family resemblance: Studies in the internal structure of categories. *Cognitive Psychology, 7*, 573–605.

ROSENSHINE, B. (1984). Teaching functions in instructional programs. *Elementary School Journal, 84*, 335–351.

ROTH, I., & FRISBY, J. P. (1986). *Perception and representation.* Philadelphia: Open Press.

ROTH, K. J. (1985). Conceptual change learning and student processing of science texts. Paper presented at the annual meeting of the American Educational Research Association, Chicago.

ROTHKOPF, E. Z. (1966). Learning from written instructional materials: An exploration of the control of inspectional behaviors by test-like events. *American Educational Research Journal, 3,* 241–249.

ROWE, D. W., & RAYFORD, L. (1987). Activating background knowledge in reading comprehension. *Reading Research Quarterly, 22,* 160–176.

RUMELHART, D. E. (1975). Notes on a schema for stories. In D. C. Bobrow & A. M. Collins (Eds.), *Representation and understanding: Studies in cognitive science* (pp. 268–281). New York: Academic Press.

RUMELHART, D. E. (1977). Towards an interactive model of reading. In S. Dornic (Ed.), *Attention and performance VI* (pp. 482–509). Hillsdale, NJ: Erlbaum.

RUMELHART, D. E. (1980a). *An introduction to human information processing.* New York: Wiley.

RUMELHART, D. E. (1980b). Schemata: The building blocks of cognition. In R. J. Spiro, B. C. Bruce, & W. F. Brewer (Eds.), *Theoretical issues in reading comprehension.* Hillsdale, NJ: Erlbaum.

RUMELHART, D. E. (1981). Schemata: The building blocks of cognition. In J. T. Guthrie (Ed.), *Comprehension and teaching: Research reviews* (pp. 3–26). Newark, DE: International Reading Association.

RUMELHART, D. E. (1984). Schemata and the cognitive system. In R. S. Wyer & T. K. Srull (Eds.), *Handbook of social cognition, Vol. 1* (pp. 161–188). Hillsdale, NJ: Erlbaum.

RUMELHART, D. E., & McCLELLAND, J. L. (1981). Interactive processing through spreading activation. In A. M. Lesgold & C. A. Perfetti (Eds.), *Interactive processes in reading* (pp. 37–60). Hillsdale, NJ: Erlbaum.

RUMELHART, D. E., McCLELLAND, J. L., & PDP RESEARCH GROUP (Eds.). (1986). *Parallel distributed processing: Explorations in the microstructure of cognition. Vol. 1: Foundations.* Cambridge, MA: MIT Press.

RUMELHART, D. E., & NORMAN, D. A. (1978). Accretion, tuning, and restructuring: Three modes of learning. In J. W. Cotton & R. Klatzky (Eds.), *Semantic factors in cognition* (pp. 161–184). Hillsdale, NJ: Erlbaum.

RUMELHART, D. E., & NORMAN, D. A. (1981). Analogical processes in learning. In J. R. Anderson (Ed.), *Cognitive skills and their acquisition* (pp. 335–359). Hillsdale, NJ: Erlbaum.

RUMELHART, D. E., & NORMAN, D. A. (1982). Simulating a skilled typist: A study of skilled cognitive–motor performance. *Cognitive Science, 6,* 1–36.

RUMELHART, D. E., & ORTONY, A. (1977). The representation of knowledge in memory. In R. C. Anderson, R. J. Spiro, & W. E. Montague (Eds.), *Schooling and the acquisition of knowledge.* Hillsdale, NJ: Erlbaum.

RYAN, E. B. (1981). Identifying and remediating failures in reading comprehension: Toward an instructional approach for poor comprehenders. In T. G. Waller & G. E. Mackinnon (Eds.), *Reading research: Advances in theory and practice* (pp. 224–257). New York: Academic Press.

SAMUELS, S. J. (1988). Decoding and automaticity: Helping poor readers become automatic at word recognition. *The Reading Teacher, 41,* 756–760.

SAVALLE, J. M., TWOHIG, P. T., & RACHFORD, D. L. (1986). Empirical status of Feuerstein's "instrumental enrichments" (FIE) technique as a method of teaching thinking skills. *Review of Educational Research, 56,* 381–409.

SCARDAMALIA, M., BEREITER, C., & GOELMAN, H. (1982). The role of productive factors in writing ability. In M. Nystrand (Ed.), *What citizens know: The language, process, and structure of written discourse* (pp. 173–210). New York: Academic Press.

SCHANK, R. C., & ABELSON, R. (1977). *Scripts, plans, goals and understanding.* Hillsdale, NJ: Erlbaum.

SCHARF, B., & BUUS, S. (1986). Audition I: Stimulus, physiology, thresholds. In K. R. Boof, L. Kaufman, & J. P. Thomas (Eds.), *Handbook of perception and human performance. Vol 1: Sensory perception and human performance* (pp. 14-1 to 14-71). New York: Wiley.

SCHARF, B., & HOUTSMA, A.J.M. (1986). Audition II: Loudness, pitch, localization, aural distortion, pathology. In K. R. Boff, L. Kaufman, & J. P. Thomas (Eds.), *Handbook of perception and human performance. Vol. 2: Sensory processes and perception* (pp. 15-1 to 15-60). New York: Wiley.

SCHOENFELD, A. H. (1985). *Mathematical problem solving.* Orlando, FL: Academic Press.

SCHOENFELD, A. H. (1987). *Cognitive science and mathematics education.* Hillsdale, NJ: Erlbaum.

SCHOENFELD, A. H., & HERRMANN, D. J. (1982). Problem perception and knowledge structure in expert and novice mathematical problem solvers. *Journal of Experimental Psychology: Learning, Memory, and Cognition, 8,* 484–494.

SCHUMACHER, G. M. (1987). Executive control in studying. In B. R. Britton & S. M. Glynn (Eds.), *Executive control processes in reading* (pp. 202–244). Hillsdale, NJ: Erlbaum.

SCHWAB, E. C., & NUSBAUM, H. C. (1986). *Pattern recognition by humans and machines. Vol. 1: Speech perception.* New York: Academic Press.

SCHWANENFLUGEL, P. J., & REY, M. (1986). Interlingual semantic facilitation: Evidence for a common representational system in the bilingual lexicon. *Journal of Memory and Language, 26,* 505–518.

SCHWEIKERT, R., & BORUFF, B. (1986). Short-term memory capacity: Magic number or magic spell? *Journal of Experimental Psychology: Learning, Memory, and Cognition, 12,* 419–425.

SCRUGGS, T. E., MASTROPIERI, M. A., MCLOONE, B. B., LEVIN, J. R., & MORRISON, C. R. (1987). Mnemonic facilitation of learning disabled students' memory for expository prose. *Journal of Educational Psychology, 79,* 27–34.

SECADA, W. G. (1987). This is 1987, not 1980: A comment on a comment. *Review of Educational Research, 57,* 377–384.

SELFRIDGE, O. G. (1955). Pattern recognition in modern computers. Proceedings of the Western Joint Computer Conference.

SELFRIDGE, O. G. (1959). Pandemonium: A paradigm for learning. In *Symposium on the mechanization of thought processes* (pp. 32–88). London: H. M. Stationery Office.

SHARPLES, M. (1985). *Cognition, computers, and creative writing.* West Sussex, England: Ellis Norwood.

SHAVELSON, R. J. (1973). Learning from physics instruction. *Journal of Research in Science Teaching, 10,* 101–111.

SHELL, D., MURPHY, C., & BRUNING, R. N. (1989). Self-efficacy and outcome expectancy mechanisms in reading and writing achievement. *Journal of Educational Psychology.*

SHEPARD, R. N. (1966). Learning and recall as organization and search. *Journal of Verbal Learning and Verbal Behavior, 5,* 201–204.

SHEPARD, R. N. (1975). Form, formation, and transformation of internal representations. In R. Solso (Ed.), *Information processing and cognition: The Loyola Symposium.* Hillsdale, NJ: Erlbaum.

SHEPARD, R. N. (1978). The mental image. *American Psychologist, 33,* 125–137.

SHEPARD, R. N. (in press). Internal representation of universal regularities: A challenge for connectionism. In L. Nadel, L. A. Cooper, P. Culicover, & R. M. Harnish (Eds.), *Neural connections and mental computations.* Cambridge, MA: MIT Press/Bradboard Books.

SHEPARD, R. N., & CHIPMAN, S. (1970). Second-order isomorphism of internal representations: Shapes of states. *Cognitive Psychology, 1,* 1–17.

SHEPARD, R. N., & COOPER, L. A. (1982). *Mental images and their transformations.* Cambridge: MIT Press.

SHEPARD, R. N., & METZLER, J. (1971). Mental rotation of three-dimensional objects. *Science, 171,* 701–703.

SHIFFRIN, R. M. (1976). Capacity limitations in information processing, attention, and memory. In W. K. Estes (Ed.), *Handbook of learning and cognitive processes* (pp. 64–92). Hillsdale, NJ: Erlbaum.

SHIFFRIN, R. M., & GARDNER, G. T. (1972). Visual processing capacity and attentional control. *Journal of Experimental Psychology, 93,* 72–82.

SHIFFRIN, R. M., PISONI, D. B., & CASTANEDA-MENDEZ, K. (1974). Is attention shared between the ears? *Cognitive Psychology, 6,* 190–215.

SHIFFRIN, R. M., & SCHNEIDER, W. (1977). Controlled and automatic information processing, II: Perceptual learning, automatic attending, and a general theory. *Psychological Review, 84,* 127–190.

SHIMOJO, S., & RICHARDS, W. (1986). "Seeing" shapes that are almost totally occluded: A new look at Park's canal. *Perception & Psychophysics, 39,* 418–426.

SHORTLIFFE, E. (1976). *Computer-based medical consultations: MYCIN.* New York: Elsevier.

SIEFERT, C. M., McKOON, G., ABELSON, R. P., & RATCLIFF, R. (1986). Memory connections between thematically similar episodes. *Journal of Experimental Psychology: Learning, Memory, and Cognition, 12,* 220–231.

SILVER, E. A. (1979). Student perceptions of relatedness among mathematical verbal problems. *Journal for Research in Mathematics Education, 10,* 195–210.

SILVER, E. A. (1981). Recall of mathematical problem information: Solving related problems. *Journal for Research in Mathematics Education, 12,* 55–64.

SIMON, D. P., & SIMON, H. A. (1978). Individual differences in solving physics problems. In R. R. Siegler (Ed.), *Children's thinking: What develops?* (pp. 40–74). Hillsdale, NJ: Erlbaum.

SIMON, H. A. (1973). The structure of ill-structured problems. *Artificial Intelligence, 4,* 181–201.

SIMON, H. A. (1986). The parameters of human memory. In F. Klix & H. Hagendorf (Eds.), *Human memory and cognitive capabilities: Mechanisms and performances* (Part A, pp. 299–309). Amsterdam: North-Holland.

SKINNER, B. F. (1938). *The behavior of organisms.* New York: Appleton-Century-Crofts.

SKINNER, B. F. (1953). *Science and human behavior.* New York: Macmillan.

SKINNER, B. F. (1957). *Verbal behavior.* New York: Appleton-Century-Crofts.

SKINNER, B. F. (1968). *The technology of teaching.* New York: Appleton-Century-Crofts.

SLAMECKA, N. J., & GRAF, P. (1978). The generation effect: Delineation of a phenomenon. *Journal of Experimental Psychology: Human Learning and Memory, 4,* 592–604.

SLAMECKA, N. J., & KATSAITI, L. T. (1987). The generation effect as an artifact of selective displaced rehearsal. *Journal of Memory and Language, 26,* 589–602.

SLOMAN, S. A., HAYMAN, C.A.G., OHTA, N., LAW, J., & TULVING, E. (1988). Forgetting in primed fragment completion. *Journal of Experimental Psychology: Learning, Memory, and Cognition, 14,* 223–239.

SMITH, F. (1971). *Understanding reading.* Hillsdale, NJ: Erlbaum.

SMITH, F. (1975). *Comprehension and learning: A conceptual framework for teachers.* New York: Richard C. Owen.

SMITH, F. (1982). *Understanding reading: A psycholinguistic analysis of reading and learning to read* (3rd ed.). New York: Holt, Rinehart & Winston.

SMITH, S. M. (1979). Remembering in and out of context. *Journal of Experimental Psychology: Human Learning and Memory, 5,* 460–471.

SMITH, S. M. (1985). Environmental context and recognition memory reconsidered. *Bulletin of the Psychonomic Society, 23,* 173–176.

SMITH, S. M. (1986). Environmental context-dependent recognition memory using a short-term memory task for input. *Memory & Cognition, 14,* 347–354.

SMITH, S. M., VELA, E., & WILLIAMSON, S. E. (1988). Shallow input processing does not induce environmental context dependent recognition. *Bulletin of the Psychonomic Society, 26,* 537–540.

SNODDY, G. S. (1926). Learning and stability. *Journal of Applied Psychology, 10,* 1–36.

SOLSO, R. L. (1988). *Cognitive psychology* (2nd ed.). Boston: Allyn and Bacon.

SORKIN, R. D., & POHLMAN, L. D. (1973). Some models of observer behavior in two channel auditory signal detection. *Perception & Psychophysics, 14,* 101–109.

SPEER, J. R., & FLAVELL, J. H. (1979). Young children's knowledge of the relative difficulty of recognition and recall memory tasks. *Developmental Psychology, 15,* 214–217.

SPENCE, K. W. (1936). The nature of discrimination learning in animals. *Psychological Review, 43,* 427–449.

SPENCE, K. W. (1956). *Behavior theory and conditioning.* New Haven, CT: Yale University Press.

SPERLING, G. (1960). The information available in brief visual presentations. *Psychological Monographs, 74* (Whole No. 498).

SPERLING, G. (1983). *Unified theory of attention and signal detection.* Mathematical studies in perception and cognition (83-3). New York: New York University, Department of Psychology.

SPERLING, G., & DOSHER, B. A. (1986). Strategy and optimization in human information processing. In K. R. Boff, L. Kaufman, & J. P. Thomas (Eds.),

Handbook of perception and human performance. Vol. 1: Sensory processes and perception (pp. 2-1 to 2-65). New York: Wiley.

SPIRO, R. J. (1977). Remembering information from text: The "State of Schema" approach. In R. C. Anderson, R. J. Spiro, & W. E. Montague (Eds.), *Schooling and the acquisition of knowledge* (pp. 336–351). Hillsdale, NJ: Erlbaum.

SPIRO, R. J. (1980). Constructive processes in prose comprehension and recall. In R. J. Spiro, B. C. Bruce, & W. F. Brewer (Eds.), *Theoretical issues in reading comprehension* (pp. 245–278). Hillsdale, NJ: Erlbaum.

SPIRO, R. J., BRUCE, B. C., & BREWER, W. F. (EDS.). (1980). *Theoretical issues in reading comprehension.* Hillsdale, NJ: Erlbaum.

STADDON, J. E. (1984). Time and memory. *Annals of the New York Academy of Sciences, 423,* 322–334.

STAHL, S. A., & FAIRBANKS, M. M. (1986). The effects of vocabulary instruction: A model-based meta-analysis. *Review of Reading Research, 56,* 72–110.

STANDING, L. (1973). Learning 10,000 pictures. *Quarterly Journal of Experimental Psychology, 25,* 207–222.

STANDING, L., CONEZIO, J., & HABER, R. N. (1970). Perception and memory for pictures: Single trial learning of 2500 visual stimuli. *Psychonomic Science, 19,* 73–74.

STEIN, B. S., WAY, K. R., BENNINGFIELD, S. E., & HEDGECOUGH, C. A. (1986). Constraints on spontaneous transfer in problem solving tasks. *Memory & Cognition, 14,* 432–441.

STERNBERG, R. J. (1984). A theory of knowledge acquisition in the development of verbal concepts. *Developmental Review, 4,* 113–138.

STERNBERG, R. J. (1987). Most vocabulary is learned from context. In M. G. McKeown & M. E. Curtis (Eds.), *The nature of vocabulary acquisition* (pp. 89–105). Hillsdale, NJ: Erlbaum.

STERNBERG, R. J., & DETTERMAN, D. K. (1986). *What is intelligence?* Norwood, NJ: Ablex.

STERNBERG, R. J., & POWELL, J. S. (1983). Comprehending verbal comprehension. *American Psychologist, 38,* 878–893.

STERNBERG, R. J., POWELL, J. S., & KAYE, D. B. (1983). Teaching vocabulary-building skills: A contextual approach. In *Classroom computers and cognitive science* (pp. 121–143). Madison: University of Wisconsin.

STEVENS, R. J. (1988). Effects of strategy training on the identification of the main idea of expository passages. *Journal of Educational Psychology, 80,* 21–26.

STEWART, M. F., & LEAMAN, H. L. (1983). Teachers' writing assessments across the high school curriculum. *Research in the Teaching of English, 17,* 113–125.

STUBBS, M. (1983). *Discourse analysis: The sociolinguistic analysis of natural language.* Chicago: University of Chicago Press.

SULZBY, E. (1986). Young children's concepts for oral and written text. In K. Durkin (Ed.), *Language development in the school years* (pp. 95–116). Cambridge, MA: Brookline Books.

SULZER-AZAROFF, B., & MAYER, G. R. (1977). *Applying behavior analysis procedures with children and youth.* New York: Holt, Rinehart & Winston.

SVENGAS, A. G., & JOHNSON, M. K. (1988). Qualitative effects of rehearsal on memories for perceived and imagined complex events. *Journal of Experimental Psychology: General, 117,* 377–389.

TAFT, M. L., & LESLIE, L. (1985). The effects of prior knowledge and oral reading accuracy on miscues and comprehension. *Journal of Reading Behavior, 17,* 163–179.

TAYLOR, B. M. (1982). Text structure and children's comprehension and memory for expository material. *Journal of Educational Psychology, 74,* 323–340.

TAYLOR, B. M., & BEACH, R. W. (1984). The effects of text structure instruction on middle-grade students' comprehension and production of expository text. *Reading Research Quarterly, 14,* 134–146.

TEALE, W. H., & SULZBY, E. (1986a). *Emergent literacy.* Norwood, NJ: Ablex.

TEALE, W. H., & SULZBY, E. (1986b). Introduction: Emergent literacy as a perspective for examining how young children become writers and readers. In W. H. Teale & E. Sulzby (Eds.), *Emergent literacy.* Norwood, NJ: Ablex.

THORNDIKE, E. L. (1932). *The fundamentals of learning.* New York: Teachers College, Columbia University.

TIERNEY, R. J., & PEARSON, P. D. (1983). Toward a composing model of reading. *Language Arts, 60*(5), 33–45.

TREIMAN, R., & DANIS, C. (1988). Short-term memory errors for spoken syllables are affected by the linguistic structure of the syllables. *Journal of Experimental Psychology: Learning, Memory, and Cognition, 14,* 145–152.

TRIESMAN, A. M. (1964). Selective attention in man. *British Medical Journal, 20,* 12–16.

TRIESMAN, A. M. (1969). Strategies and models of selective attention. *Psychological Review, 76,* 282–299.

TRIESMAN, A. M. (1987). *Properties, parts and objects, Vol. 2* (pp. 35-1 to 35-64). New York: Springer-Verlag.

TRIESMAN, A. M., & GEFFEN, G. (1967). Selective attention: Perception or response? *Quarterly Journal of Experimental Psychology, 19,* 1–17.

TRIESMAN, A. M., & GELADE, G. (1980). A feature integration theory of attention. *Cognitive Psychology, 12,* 97–136.

TRIESMAN, A. M., & RILEY, J.G.A. (1969). Is selective attention selective perception or selective response? A further test. *Journal of Experimental Psychology, 79,* 27–34.

TRIESMAN, A. M., & SCHMIDT, H. (1982). Illusory conjunctions in the perception of objects. *Cognitive Psychology, 14,* 107–141.

TRIESMAN, A. M., SQUIRE, R., & GREEN, J. (1974). Semantic processing in dichotic listening? A replication. *Memory & Cognition, 2,* 641–646.

TULVING, E. (1962). Subjective organization in free recall of "unrelated" words. *Psychology Review, 69,* 344–354.

TULVING, E. (1972). Episodic and semantic memory. In E. Tulving and W. Donaldson (Eds.), *Organization of memory* (pp. 381–403). New York: Academic Press.

TULVING, E. (1983). *Elements of episodic memory.* Oxford: Oxford University Press.

TULVING, E. (1985). On the classification problem in learning and memory. In L. Nilsson & T. Archer (Eds.), *Perspectives on learning and memory* (pp. 73–101). Hillsdale, NJ: Erlbaum.

TULVING, E. (1986). What kind of hypothesis is the distinction between episodic and semantic memory? *Journal of Experimental Psychology: Learning, Memory, and Cognition, 12*, 307–311.

TULVING, E., & OSLER, S. (1968). Effectiveness of retrieval cues in memory for words. *Journal of Experimental Psychology, 77*, 593–601.

TULVING, E., & THOMPSON, D. M. (1973). Encoding specificity and retrieval processes in episodic memory. *Psychological Review, 80*, 352–373.

TUNMER, W. E., HERRIMAN, M. L., & NESDALE, A. R. (1988). Metalinguistic abilities and beginning reading. *Reading Research Quarterly, 23*, 134–158.

UNDERWOOD, B. J. (1957). Interference and forgetting. *Psychological Review, 64*, 49–60.

UNDERWOOD, B. J., & SCHULZ, R. W. (1960). *Meaningfulness and verbal learning.* New York: Lippincott.

VAN DIJK, T. A., & KINTSCH, W. (1983). *Strategies of discourse comprehension.* New York: Academic Press.

VON WRIGHT, J. M. (1972). On the problem of selection in iconic memory. *Scandinavian Journal of Psychology, 13*, 159–171.

VOSNIADOU, S., PEARSON, P. D., & ROGERS, T. (1988). What causes children's failures to detect inconsistencies in text? Representation versus comparison difficulties. *Journal of Educational Psychology, 80*, 27–39.

VOSS, J. F. (in press). Informal reasoning and international relations. In J. F. Voss, D. N. Perkins, & J. Segal (Eds.), *Informal reasoning and instruction.* Hillsdale, NJ: Erlbaum.

VOSS, J. F., BLAIS, J., MEANS, M. L., GREENE, T. R., & AHWESH, E. (1986). Informal reasoning and subject matter knowledge in the solving of economics problems by naive and novice individuals. *Cognition and Instruction, 4*, 269–302.

VOSS, J. F., GREENE, T. R., POST, T. A., & PENNER, P. C. (1983a). Problem solving skill in the social sciences. In G. H. Bower (Ed.), *The psychology of learning and motivation: Advances in research and theory, Vol. 17* (pp. 165–213). New York: Academic Press.

VOSS, J. F., & POST, T. A. (in press). On the solving of ill-structured problems. In M.T.H. Chi, R. Glaser, & M. Farr (Eds.), *The nature of expertise.* Hillsdale, NJ: Erlbaum.

VOSS, J. F., TYLER, S. W., & YENGO, L. A. (1983b). Individual differences in the solving of social science problems. In R. F. Dillon & R. R. Schmeck (Eds.), *Individual differences in cognition* (pp. 205–232). New York: Academic Press.

WAGNER, K. (1971). Tony and his friends. In L. B. Jacobs (Ed.), *The read-it-yourself storybook.* New York: Western Publishing.

WALBERG, H. J., & FOWLER, W. J. (1987). Expenditure and size efficiencies of public school districts. *Educational Research, 16*, 5–15.

WALKER, N. (1986). Direct retrieval from elaborated memory traces. *Memory & Cognition, 74*, 321–328.

WALLER, T. G. (1987). *Reading research: Advances in theory and practice, Vol. 5.* New York: Academic Press.

WALSH, D. J., PRICE, G. G., & GILLINGHAM, M. G. (1988). The critical but transitory importance of letter naming. *Reading Research Quarterly, 23*, 108–122.

WATSON, J. B. (1924). *Behaviorism.* New York: Norton.

WATT, E. (1988). *Visual processing research.* Hillsdale, NJ: Erlbaum.

WATTENMAKER, W. D., DEWEY, G. I., MURPHY, T. D., & MEDIN, D. L. (1986). Linear separability and concept learning: Context, relational properties, and concept naturalness. *Cognitive Psychology, 18,* 158–194.

WAUGH, N. C., & NORMAN, D. A. (1965). Primary memory. *Psychological Review, 72,* 89–104.

WEAVER, C. (1988). *Reading process and practice.* Portsmouth, NH: Heinemann.

WEINERT, F. E., & KLUWE, R. H. (EDS.). (1987). *Metacognition, motivation, and understanding.* Hillsdale, NJ: Erlbaum.

WELLS, G. (1985). *Language, learning, and education.* Philadelphia: NFER–Nelson.

WENGER, E. (1987). *Artificial intelligence and tutoring systems.* Los Altos, CA: Kaufmann.

WHITE, T. G. (1985). Background knowledge vs. individual words. *Educational Perspectives, 23,* 22–27.

WICKENS, D. D. (1980). The structure of attentional resources. In R. S. Nickerson (Ed.), *Attention and performance VIII* (pp. 260–304). Hillsdale, NJ: Erlbaum.

WILHITE, S. C. (1986, April). Multiple-choice test performance: Effects of headings, questions, motivation, and type of retention test question. Paper presented at the annual meeting of the American Educational Research Association, San Francisco.

WILLIAMS, R. L. Classroom management. In J. A. Glover & R. R. Ronning (Eds.), *Historical foundations of educational psychology* (pp. 297–326). New York: Plenum.

WILLIG, A. C. (1985). A meta-analysis of selected studies on the effectiveness of bilingual education. *Review of Educational Research, 55,* 269–317.

WILLIG, A. C. (1987). Examining bilingual education research through meta-analysis and narrative review: A response to Baker. *Review of Educational Research, 57,* 363–376.

WINOGRAD, P. N. (1984). Strategic difficulties in summarizing texts. *Reading Research Quarterly, 14,* 404–424.

WINOGRAD, T. (1975). Frame representations and the declarative–procedural controversy. In D. G. Bobrow & A. M. Collins (Eds.), *Representation and understanding: Studies in cognitive science.* New York: Academic Press.

WITTE, S. P. (1988). The real issues in writing assessment. Paper presented to the annual meeting of the American Educational Research Association, New Orleans.

WIXSON, K. K. (1986). Vocabulary instruction and children's comprehension of basal stories. *Reading Research Quarterly, 21,* 317–329.

WOLLEN, K. A., & COS, S. (1981). Sentence cueing and the effectiveness of bizarre imagery. *Journal of Experimental Psychology: Human Learning and Cognition, 7,* 386–392.

WOLLEN, K. A., WEBER, A., & LOWRY, D. H. (1972). Bizarreness versus interaction of mental images as determinants of learning. *Cognitive Psychology, 3,* 518–523.

WOLTZ, D. J. (1988). An investigation of the role of working memory in procedural skill acquisition. *Journal of Experimental Psychology: General, 117,* 319–331.

WYSOCKI, K., & JENKINS, J. (1987). Deriving word meanings through morphological generalization. *Reading Research Quarterly, 22,* 66–81.

YATES, F. A. (1966). *The art of memory.* Chicago: University of Chicago Press.

YU, V. L., BUCHANAN, B. G., SHORTLIFFE, E. H., WRAITH, S. M., DAVIS, R., SCOTT, A. C., & COHEN, F. M. (1979). Multiple model contrasts. *Computer Programs in Biomedicine, 9,* 95.

YUILL, N., & JOSCELYNE, T. (1988). Effect of organizational cues and strategies on good and poor comprehenders' story understanding. *Journal of Educational Psychology, 80,* 152–158.

YUSSEN, S. R., & LEVY, V. M., JR. (1975). Developmental changes in predicting one's own span of short-term memory. *Journal of Experimental Child Psychology, 19,* 502–508.

ZIMMER, J. W., PETERSEN, C. H., RONNING, R. R., & GLOVER, J. A. (1978). The effect of adjunct aids on prose processing. *The Journal of Instructional Psychology, 5,* 27–34.

ZWICKY, A. M., & KANTOR, R. H. (1980). A survey of syntax. In *Language development, grammar, and semantics: The contribution of linguistics to bilingual education.* (Bilingual Education Series No. 7). Arlington, VA: Center for Applied Linguistics.

Index